PARENTS LEARN
THROUGH DISCUSSION

PARENTS LEARN THROUGH DISCUSSION:
Principles and Practices of Parent Group Education

ALINE B. AUERBACH

in cooperation with
CHILD STUDY ASSOCIATION OF AMERICA

JOHN WILEY & SONS, INC., New York | London | Sydney

Foreword

There is an ever-increasing interest in setting up more adequate and more specialized programs for children: better schools, a steadily growing number of nurseries, the Head-Start Program, and in the mental health field, an added variety of facilities to serve the various needs of the child. As we create the community mental health center, an integration and coordination of services is required, encompassing a regional community. I think we would all agree that the primary approach to the healthy development of children and the prevention of deviant development is best accomplished in assisting the parents. This has been a long-standing focus of the Child Study Association of America.

This then is a book which addresses itself to this very important task: to aid in the education of parents. A new technique is presented here. Having been privileged by the author with the opportunity to be in contact with this over the years, I was first impressed by the thoughtful experimental evolvement of the work, and, later, by the sureness with which this new method could be used. It is an original contribution, well tested and ready for wide application.

December, 1967   *Peter B. Neubauer, M.D.*

Acknowledgments

Many people have contributed to the contents of this book, often without having been aware of it.

The principles of parent group education described here were developed cooperatively by a creative and devoted staff of social workers interested in the potential of educational intervention through group discussion as a method of strengthening family life and preventing emotional difficulties. Among these, I should like to make special acknowledgement of the sound and imaginative contribution of Gertrude Goller Benton, my associate in the early years of the Child Study Association's programs of training for group leadership; but each staff member also contributed his or her share in deepening the concepts and improving the practice. These were further enriched by the informed ideas and vivid practical experiences of the many interested professional workers who took part in the training programs.

Those who probably contributed the most, however, were the parents and expectant parents from all socioeconomic and educational backgrounds who met in groups throughout the country. Their honest self-searching, in the interest of bettering the lives of their children, has given parent group education its unique flavor. This quality is difficult to reproduce in words, but I hope that to some extent it is reflected in the pages that follow.

For their share in the preparation of this book, I am most grateful to Mildred Rabinow, who read critically a large portion of its contents, and to Orville G. Brim, Jr., Ada M. Daniels, and Oscar Rabinowitz, who advised on special chapters. All made significant comments and suggestions. Mildred Rabinow also contributed the list of recommended readings. To A. D. Buchmueller, Executive Director of the Child Study Association of America, I am greatly indebted for his encouragement of this work as well as for his personal and administrative support.

Finally, my deep appreciation goes to my long-time colleague and friend Josette Frank, who painstakingly read and checked every page of the book with an active red pencil, to insure the clarity and relevance of its contents. Her help was invaluable.

December, 1967   *Aline B. Auerbach*

Contents

Appendices:

Introduction

Parents have been concerned in one way or another about the responsibilities of rearing their children since the beginning of human society. When one considers parent education in its broadest sense, it is also true that parents have been helped, and have helped each other, to fulfill these responsibilities for an equally lengthy period of time. Tasks related to providing for the physical needs of children as well as the dissemination of moral and ethical values have been described and discussed in literature for centuries. In a given culture, certain practices of child-rearing have been handed down from generation to generation. In a more specific sense, that is, in planned, organized efforts to assist parents in their tasks, parent education had its beginnings in the United States in the nineteenth century.

The Child Study Association of America had its origin in 1888, when a small group of mothers in New York City joined together for the purpose of determining how they could become better parents. In succeeding decades, the Association has continued in its attempts to further these aims: to help parents in their tasks of fostering their children's optimum physical, mental, emotional, and social development. As new knowledge was gained from research and experience in the fields of child development, dynamic psychiatry, education, sociology, social work, and, broadly, the behavioral sciences, such knowledge has been correlated and utilized in the development and implementation of the Association's programs.

Basic to the Association's programs is the concept that increasing parents' competence will help them help themselves to understand and deal with their and their children's day-to-day problems; to understand more fully the impact of parent-child relationships on the total development of the child; to understand and cope with the forces in the community which interplay with those within the family. Concurrently, as new knowledge and experience has been gained from small-group research and practice, the use of continuous small-group discussions under professional skilled leadership has become the major method utilized by the Association in its educational programs.

For many years Mrs. Auerbach was a member of the staff of the

Child Study Association of America. During these years she was a participant and a leader in the development of its programs. From 1950 to 1965 she was the major guiding force in leadership with the professional staff in the development of training programs in which others in various parts of the country have been trained in the concepts, theory, and skill of parent group education as developed by the Association. Social workers, nurses, clergy, religious educators, and others, have been trained to implement and conduct educational programs in their own settings, geared to parents' and children's needs. As staff member, Director of Training, Program Director, and Assistant Director, Mrs. Auerbach has made an outstanding contribution to the agency and the field of parent education.

In this book, Mrs. Auerbach has clearly and thoroughly articulated these basic concepts, theories, and practices, and has placed them in historical perspective. It is my conviction that it will be of major value to all who have the difficult but rewarding challenge and task of helping parents improve their role functions, and it will eventually help healthier children to live in healthier families in better communities in our society.

A. D. Buchmueller,
Executive Director,
Child Study Association of America

PARENTS LEARN
THROUGH DISCUSSION

I

Parent Group Education: Philosophy and Goals

WHAT THIS BOOK IS ABOUT

This book was written in response to many requests for a book about parent group education. They have come from people in various professions—social workers, nurses, guidance counselors, psychologists, teachers, religious educators, and others—who knew of the programs of parent groups carried on by the Child Study Association of America, who wanted help in establishing similar groups in their own settings and in preparing themselves to become group leaders. They seemed to be looking for a manual or handbook of the techniques of parent group discussion.

Some had never led groups but were eager to try. Others, wishing to extend their traditional teaching methods in new directions, were already experimenting with new methods but were dissatisfied with the results. Still others were thoughtfully seeking a conceptualized base for what they were doing, either to confirm or improve their leadership skills.

Many handbooks have already been written about discussion techniques. Here, however, we are outlining the methods that have been specifically developed to meet the needs of parents in educational discussion groups. The aim of the Child Study Association of America has always been to develop programs and procedures within a sound, ideological framework of parent education as a whole. The techniques, we believe, are meaningless unless they are related to a philosophy that has specific educational goals and that serves as the matrix within which discussion group procedures are developed to further these goals.

This book, then, is not a handbook as the term is generally understood. It is offered rather as a guide presenting a philosophy based on experience and practices that have been found useful in giving meaning to certain philosophical concepts. These practices are for leaders to use consciously and creatively in their own way. Used mechanically, procedures can become rigid, static—and defeat their main purpose, which is to provide a fluid group experience of learning and growth for parents.

1

So, in this book, the philosophy, purposes, and procedures of parent group education will be interrelated. This, we believe, is an educational approach that many parents and expectant parents have found useful and enriching.

Leadership in parent group education calls for the use of group techniques and skills in connection with a specific body of information. This is in keeping with the concept that "in true education content and process must be interwoven." [1] Thus the leader in parent group education must have a thorough knowledge of child development and normal family relationships. He must also be thoroughly aware of the variety of social and cultural backgrounds of the groups' members and the implications of any special circumstance which may bring parents together, such as having a retarded or handicapped child, being a one-parent family, or whatever. This background of knowledge will provide the *content* of parent group education as contrasted with *techniques*. The nature of this content can be presented only in general terms in this book and is suggested in its illustrative examples.

The group work described in the following pages has grown out of the experiences of the Child Study Association over many years in developing principles and practices of group education to meet the educational needs of parents. As the concepts of parent group education were more clearly formulated by a creative staff, they became the focus of a series of training programs in parent group leadership given under the direction of the author for workers from different professional backgrounds (See Chapter XIV). The principles and procedures of parent group education were found to be applicable and useful not only to parents of children of different ages, but also to expectant parents, to parents of children with handicapping conditions, and to parents living in widely divergent social, economic, and cultural circumstances. Accordingly, training programs were also given for leadership of groups of parents in these special situations. Parent group education has also been adapted to in-service group teaching and group consultation for workers in the health care, guidance, and/or teaching of children under various auspices, including nursery schools, day care centers, high schools, and church schools. (For the special implications of group education as it has been used for these different purposes, see Chapter XIII).

In this book group education is discussed in relation to the fields in which it has been put into practice in the work of this Association. It describes a method of learning that has value and potential for other

[1] Gordon Hamilton, "A Theory of Personality: Freud's Contribution to Social Work," in J. Howard Parad (Editor), *Ego Psychology and Dynamic Casework*, Family Service Association of America, New York, 1958, p. 31.

aspects of human relations, which, by their very nature, have strong emotional overtones, and in which individuals can achieve greater maturity and satisfaction.

PARENT GROUP EDUCATION: ITS PLACE IN THE FIELD OF PARENT EDUCATION

Parent group education is only one form of parent education, a term used to cover a wide range of educational programs to help parents increase their competence as parents and develop effective methods of child care. Based on the belief that parents are the key figures in developing their children's healthy personalities, parent education is offered as "primary prevention" in the hope of avoiding emotional and social maladjustment in children.

"In dealing with those who are not sick, primary prevention includes efforts to improve their mental health as a means of increasing their resistance to mental disorder and as a desirable goal in its own right." [2] In this sense, all parent education may be seen as mental health education for families.

Since *prevention* carries with it a connotation of action, parent education is actually *intervention* to help parents function more effectively in their parental role. It introduces new educational experiences that will give parents added knowledge and understanding, cause them to question their habitual ways of thinking, feeling, and acting, and help them develop new methods (where new methods are indicated) of dealing with their children, with themselves, and with their social environment. Thus educational intervention can often be a step toward a more effective way of life.

Parent education has many faces. Orville G. Brim, Jr., in his important study of parent education, points out that:

"At present many organizations, both public and private, commercial and non-profit, at the national, state and local level are engaged in educating parents about child rearing. Parents are counselled by physicians, clergymen, teachers and nurses. They participate in groups discussing child rearing which meet under the auspices of mental health, parent-teacher and other associations; read books, pamphlets, magazines or newspaper columns; view films, plays and television programs; and listen to lectures and radio programs, all concerned with educating them in child care." [3]

[2] Gerald Caplan, *Principles of Preventive Psychiatry*, Basic Books, New York, 1964.
[3] Orville G. Brim, Jr., *Education for Child Rearing*, Russell Sage Foundation, New York, 1959, p. 17; also available in paperback with new introduction, The Free Press, New York, 1965.

These programs cover a wide spectrum of services for parents and families. At one end are the information-giving projects of printed materials and other mass media. Toward the other end of the scale are programs of individual, educationally oriented counseling in those situations which seem to require and lend themselves to a one-to-one approach. And beyond the educational spectrum are those services that offer intensive counseling, casework treatment, or therapy either on an individual or group basis. Group educational activities fall somewhere in the middle of this spectrum.

The term *parent education* often is used interchangeably with *family life education.* The latter, however, includes the many different educational activities and programs which serve to enrich understanding of the complex interplay of family relations, whether for parents, for young married couples, for those contemplating marriage, or for children in high school or college. Parent education thus also falls into place as one aspect of family life education. (However, "family life education" is also applied specifically to courses on human behavior and human relationships given to children and young people.)

Parent education is also certainly a part of the *adult education movement,* although its chief focus is on the parent's role in bringing up his children, whereas adult education is concerned with this as well as many other aspects of adult life.

The parent education movement also has many of the same goals as the *mental health movement* and they overlap at many points. They differ, however, in that the mental health movement is primarily concerned with mental illness, its causes, care, and cure, in all segments of the community, whereas the parent education movement directs its attention primarily to promoting family mental health. Both work toward the prevention of emotional difficulty and mental illness, but parent education concentrates on the mental health of the child—and the parent—and on the relationship between them, always within the context of the community. Thus parent education may be thought of as an important part of the mental health movement as a whole.[4]

Parent group education—group education for parents through the use of guided group discussion—is only one of many kinds of group educational services for family living, all of which have a common basic purpose. They all aim to help parents become more familiar with basic concepts of child growth and development and parent-child family interaction from a dynamic point of view; to recognize some of the crisis points

---

[4] These differentiations are taken from Aline B. Auerbach, *Trends and Techniques in Parent Education: A Critical Review,* prepared for the 1960 White House Conference on Children and Youth. Child Study Association of America, New York, pp. 3–4.

in different stages of the normal family cycle; to clarify the parents' own role and those of their children, within the family and the community; and to enlarge their understanding of the complexities of their everyday situations so that they will have a wider background against which to make choices.

In the experience of the Child Study Association, the type of group education that comes closest to achieving these goals is the small continuous discussion group made up of approximately fifteen members who meet together for a series of eight to twelve weekly sessions under skilled leadership. It is this type of program that has been identified as parent group education and will be the focus of this book. Even in the initial definition, however, the term "parent group education" is inadequate and at times misleading. Thus far, it has not been possible to devise a better one. We hope its meaning will become more clear as this group method is described in terms of its philosophy, goals, procedures, and organizational structure.

For many adults, the term "education" has a connotation of the formal, academic teaching they experienced in their school or college days. This idea of "an authoritarian form of instruction and passive receptivity by the pupil," [5] as H. H. Stern has pointed out in his international survey of parent education, "is too restricted an interpretation of the concept of education." The principles and practices of parent group education, in marked contrast, offer a dynamic learning experience, which grows out of the parents' interests and needs and in which they participate in their own individual ways. Furthermore, the educational process does not apply "only to the intellectual capacity of the group members. Here the educational experience takes on a broader meaning. It recognizes the importance of the feelings and attitudes and uses emotional mobilization as well as intellectual stimulation." [6]

This philosophy and approach is in keeping with new formulations of general educational theory, such as those outlined in the book, *Perceiving, Behaving, Becoming: A New Focus for Education*,[7] which pictures education as a dynamic process of learning in which the learner is helped to relate new information and ideas to his own life and thinking. The goal of this educational process is "the truly adequate person, fully-functioning and self-actualizing" both for himself and in cooperation with others.

[5] H. H. Stern, *Parent Education: An International Survey*, University of Hull and the UNESCO Institute for Education, Hamburg, 1960, p. 117.
[6] Peter B. Neubauer, "The Technique of Parent Group Education: Some Basic Concepts," in *Parent Group Education and Leadership Training*, Child Study Association of America, New York, 1953, p. 11. (O.P.)
[7] Yearbook 1962, Association for Supervision and Curriculum Development, National Education Association, Washington, D. C., 1962.

Parents don't talk about the groups in these terms, of course, but they do make spontaneous comments that give us clues to some of the changes that are taking place. In the fifth session of a group in a low-income housing project, for example, one mother reported that things were going better at home and added, "Now I think before I jump." Another mother in the same group, who, the leader said, "has suddenly begun to smile," said, "Now I am willing to glide over things that made me pretty mad before."

A mother in a so-called "disadvantaged" section of a southern city volunteered, "Every week I get at least one idea and try out different ways of handling things at home." And another mother in the same group said she had been thinking things over after the last meeting and agreed with the mother who had said we expect much too much of our second children. "It was," she said, "as if we thought they were just as far along as the first one and that wasn't fair." She said she had begun to ease up on the younger one, and was trying to give the older one not just the jobs but some of the privileges of being older. But, she concluded, it wasn't always easy to remember all that!

WHY PARENT EDUCATION?

What is there about parenthood today that has created the need for educational programs? Why in this particular period of world history do parents want to become more knowledgeable? In other words, what has happened to break down the myth that "mother (or father) knows best"?

Many volumes have been written to explain parent education in its psychological, sociological, and cultural implications. It has been ascribed, for example, to the increasing instability of family life and the many forces in the modern world that are bringing this about. The geographic and social mobility so characteristic of our times tends to cut off many young families from their traditional moorings and leaves them vulnerable to a wider range of conflicting pressures and uncertainties.

Surely the breakdown of tradition in all phases of life is important here too. Brim [8] describes the change in the status of women in our society, with their increased independence in the family and the outside world; the isolation today of many young families, often far removed from their parents and other family members and less exposed to cultural traditions of child care; their greater mobility and resulting exposure to families from different ethnic backgrounds and social classes who have different ways of child rearing. All these influences, he says, force the modern parent to become more conscious of his child-rearing practices and to work out his own way of being a parent, drawing on his own resources or with help from persons outside the family group.

[8] Brim, *op. cit.*, p. 17.

To help parents in this task, a large body of new knowledge is available—knowledge of child development, family relations, and the psychodynamics of behavior—and has been increasing in quantity, depth, and intensity during the past fifty years or more. This knowledge appears in many shapes and places, from professional journals to the many forms of the mass media. It is to be found on the airwaves, in popular magazines, and in hard cover and paperback books, as straight factual material or as the basis for fictional versions of family life drama.

The flood of sometimes ill-digested and unsorted information, however, has not been an unmixed blessing, since parents—and educators, too—have been confused in their application of this knowledge. One example of this confusion is seen in parental attitudes toward discipline. As parents revolted against the more Victorian, authoritarian attitudes of parental dominance in the family, and as clinical evidence of the results of repression on children reinforced their concern, many parents became more aware of a child's need for freedom and experimentation and took on a new "permissive" role. They found, however, that this attitude created new problems in many homes. The children often seemed to get out of bounds and did not seem always to be as happy with their freedom as their parents had expected. It took some time for these parents to catch up with the fact that in their overpermissive behavior, they had acted on only a partial understanding of their children's needs. Today it is being recognized that children need guidance and control as well as appropriate freedom and independence. Without some help from their parents in setting up limits for behavior which they can gradually take over as part of themselves, children, by and large, do not develop most healthfully.

In the face of new and sometimes apparently conflicting scientific findings such as these, it is understandable that parents have been confused. Yet despite some confusion, parents do recognize that their role in their children's development is an essential one. At the same time, the influence of parents has to be seen in its proper relation: it is only one of many influences that have their impact on the very special constitutional makeup, characteristics, and potentialities of each individual child. Parents have come to recognize, too, that it is their long-term relationship with their children that matters, rather than each detail of daily family living. Nevertheless, within this balanced concept, emphasis on the importance of the parental role has moved many parents to examine critically the way they carry out their parenthood, in order to function to the best of their ability.

This desire may have many motivations, such as a parent's need for self-esteem and for a sense of success as a parent. But without looking for deeper meanings, it is evident—as one listens to them—that, by and large, parents want to do well by their children for *their children's* sake. Whether they live in a cabin in the Tennessee mountains or in a crowded city slum or in a more affluent suburb, most parents want a good life for their children—a fulfilled, productive one. Unless parents are emotionally disturbed or completely overwhelmed by life's difficulties, with few exceptions they want their children to do better than they have done themselves. As Margaret Mead has pointed out, this attitude and this hope are in keeping with the pioneer spirit so characteristic of our Western culture. It is even possible that parents' deep concern for their children is a positive force in all mankind, bringing with it the courage to go on in the face of worldwide discouragement and foreboding. Perhaps, somehow, where there are children there is hope. And hope often is the mainspring for action.

For parents, action means helping children grow to their best capacity. This, in turn, means reaching out for knowledge that will not only facilitate this but will also help them to become more aware of themselves and how they function as parents. Further, parents must take increasing responsibility in relation to those forces outside the home that affect their children's happiness and well-being. They must be concerned about the schools, the economic and social aspects of their communities: poor housing, limited job opportunities, inadequate recreational facilities, discrimination and intergroup tensions, and all the crippling conditions that are so much a part of modern life. Parents need to understand the true nature of these conditions without exaggeration or denial. They need to understand the impact of these conditions on their children in order to help them meet and cope with them. At the same time, they themselves need to be strengthened so they can use their weight, individually and in groups, to improve conditions wherever this is realistically possible. Here, too, education under thoughtful, balanced auspices is vital.

WHY DO PARENTS COME?

What is it that parents are looking for when they come to a parent group program? They seem to be seeking a variety of things, some separate, some overlapping, some conscious, some reflecting wishes or needs or insecurities of which they themselves are often unaware.

Most often they say, "I want to do a good job with my children." Or even better, "*We* want to. . . ." Sometimes they say, "I want to do a better job than my parents did with me." Sometimes young parents, aware of their inexperience—and possible ignorance—reach out for educational help early in their parenthood, some even before their babies are born. They may say, "I don't know much about kids; I haven't been around them much since I moved away from my family," or "I was an only child and I didn't grow up with a lot of children around." These comments suggest not only their ignorance about children and how they grow but some doubts about their competence to cope with the daily demands of child-rearing.

More generally, though, it takes some special situation to bring them face to face with the meaning of their parenthood and to mobilize them to prepare for their responsibilities. A seven-month-old baby's sudden fear of strangers, a two-year-old's "stubbornness," a four-year-old's resistance to staying at a day-care center, the constant bickering between school-age brothers and sisters, an eight-year-old's aloofness and apparent inability to hear (except when he wants to), a sudden change in a child's school performance, the constant sloppiness of an eleven-year-old, the many whims and unpredictable actions of teen-agers at various stages—these kinds of difficult behavior are reported again and again. The mere listing of these areas of difficulty serves to point up many of the crisis phases in child development, points for which parents are unprepared and which often seem perverse and hard to understand.

Then, too, parents sometimes come to groups pressed by more unusual situations that stem from some special, often emergency occurrence. The death of a family member, the birth of a new baby, the father's loss of a job, the parents' divorce—these frequently arouse responses in children that baffle parents and that they feel they cannot handle alone.

Both kinds of "acute crisis" have been identified by Gerald Caplan et al,[9] who noted that they represent "relatively short periods of psychological disequilibrium, which occur in everyone's life in response to developmental transition or to situational hazards and challenges." Caplan has voiced the conviction that during the upset of a crisis, a person usually has an increased desire to be helped, and is more susceptible to influence than during periods of relatively stable functioning.[10]

Others have pointed to the value of discussion groups for parents at critical points in the child's maturing. In a study of the impact of school entry on the family and of the "characteristic ways families have of meeting and adapting to the new status and life situation of the kindergartner," Klein and Ross reported:

Parents themselves universally report that the discussions have helped them understand and accept their own feelings and concerns and have provided a sense of fellowship with others going through the same experience. At points of rapid transition, there is reason to believe, a relatively few hours of group

[9] Gerald Caplan et al., "Four Studies of Crisis of Parents of Prematures," *Community Mental Health Journal,* 1, No. 2 (Summer 1965).

[10] Gerald Caplan, *Principles of Preventive Psychiatry*, New York, Basic Books, 1964.

meetings may help participants identify and cope with deep areas of feelings and important points of personal and family conflict and concern.[11]

At any critical stage, or even without the stress of a particular phase or situation, a parent may be troubled by his or her own response to a child. A working mother who is deluged by her children's demands when she gets home says she is so dead tired that she can only meet them by being cross and pushing the children away. An urban mother of a six-month-old reports her feeling that she will never again be free to do something for herself; is she *always* going to have to sit with a baby carriage in the playground? Her frustration about being tied down so completely keeps her from enjoying her baby and makes her uneasy. A father of a (to him) difficult seven-year-old suddenly comes up against the realization that he "doesn't like the kid at all—*my* kid," and is aghast at the implications of his feeling. In all these instances the parents are concerned not about their children but about themselves. And obviously they want to do something about their "disequilibrium."

Parents bring up many problems that call for resolutions where resolutions seem impossible. One mother is at her wits' end because her five-year-old has a persistent sleeping problem and keeps disturbing the baby and the eight-year-old with whom she shares the bedroom. Another mother feels that her twelve-year-old needs help with his homework, but says, "How can I help him, when I only went through elementary school myself?"

There are also many situations which alarm parents not only because of their immediate meaning but because of what may develop from them in the future. If a child pilfers small items from the 5-and-10-cent store when he is eight, does this mean he will be a thief when he grows up? What can a mother do to raise her boy when there's no father in the home? How can she help him grow up to be the right kind of man, especially, as one mother said, "When you hear so much about queer behavior these days?" What about the influence of so-called "bad companions" on vulnerable twelve- or thirteen-year-old boys and girls? Is their association with these children the beginning of gang behavior that may end in their becoming real "delinquents"? What about the teen-agers—both boys and girls— who won't come home at a reasonable hour and who live in neighborhoods "where anything can happen"? How can they as parents deal with these problems and protect their children as they feel they should?

Not all of the different, intertwined levels of concern become clear at

[11] Donald C. Klein and Anne Ross, "Kindergarten Entry: A Study of Role Transition," in J. Howard Parad (Editor), *Crisis Intervention: Selected Readings,* Family Service Association of America, New York, 1965, p. 148.

once in parent group discussions. Moreover, parents' concerns are never static. One of the challenges of parent group education is the fluidity and shifting nature of parents' needs as they participate during a series of sessions or even during a single meeting of a series.

We cannot expect that parent group education will meet and resolve all of their concerns. Nor can we predict just when or how any given group of parent-members will move into different levels of functioning. Experienced leaders who have met with many different groups, however, are often astounded at how much the parents find they *do* know, much to their own surprise. The leaders are also frequently amazed at the wide coverage of interests, the rich sharing of experiences, and the apparent changes in feelings, attitudes, and coping behavior that seem to occur, sometimes even within a comparatively short time.

II

Why Group Education for Parents

With all the channels of communication pouring out information to parents, why is there need for parents' groups? What can group programs accomplish that cannot be gained in other ways?

The results of various forms of parent education are difficult to measure and so far have not leant themselves to productive evaluative research. The factors involved are complex and difficult to separate and define. People participating in any one type of program are also being exposed to many other influences that have bearing on their relationships with their children. A number of studies are now in progress that may provide some answers regarding the effectiveness of different approaches. Until such answers are available, we must rely on the judgment of responsible workers and agency administrators, based on empirical evidence.[1]

The nature and quality of parent group education and what it can give to parents will be discussed more fully in later chapters. It can be said here briefly, however, that:

1. Education through the various forms of the mass media is a broadside approach, offered on as wide a basis as possible *in the hope that* it will meet the needs of those who hear or read it. There is no feedback to show what the "consumer" takes from it, or what use he makes of it, and he cannot ask questions to clarify what he does not understand. By contrast, what is provided in parent groups is closely related to the needs of those who attend, since they themselves determine the content and provide the material that is discussed: the life experiences, ideas, hopes, and fears which permeate their parenthood. They also have an opportunity to respond and digest the matters discussed and, in successive meetings, to report their continuing reactions, the effects on their ideas and behavior,

[1] For detailed discussion of the findings and problems of evaluative research in parent education, see Orville G. Brim, Jr., *Education for Child Rearing*, Russell Sage Foundation, New York, 1959; also paperback edition, The Free Press, New York, 1965, Chapter 9.

over a period of time. Thus the content of the discussions closely meets their developing interests and concerns, and their responses to it are open, articulated, and shared with the group. Because of the parents' own active role in the group educational process, they have the opportunity and responsibility to see that the learning is directed toward the realities of their daily lives and therefore has meaning for them *as they need it*.

2. Taking part in an educationally oriented discussion group adds a special dimension to learning. Because of the stimulation of different personalities, with a variety of experiences and ideas about many forms of children's behavior and their own responses to them, the substance from which these parents can draw for their learning is rich and varied, dynamic and real. In the group, they learn from one another, evaluating, selecting, rejecting, building on the contributions of others, extending their ideas and concepts to new dimensions. The group also offers parents the chance to grow through the group interplay: they find their own place as persons, develop their own ideas, choose ways of acting toward their children, family, and community that are right for them.

THE EVOLUTION OF PARENT GROUP EDUCATION

Parent group education as carried on at the Child Study Association of America did not appear suddenly, full blown, in its present form. It evolved slowly over a period of years as an essential part of the Association's varied services to parents. These have fallen into three main categories: (1) a program of public education by means of large meetings and conferences and a wide list of books and pamphlets, making available to the public at large the newer findings of the social sciences, education, and psychology relating to child rearing and family life; (2) parent groups meeting in and around the Association's headquarters in New York; and (3) again at its headquarters, a program of family counseling offered in individual or family interviews directed toward educational rather than therapeutic goals.

The last two parts of the program have been conducted on an experimental and demonstration basis, in an effort, first, to find increasingly effective methods to meet the needs of parents through varied approaches and second, to develop methods of parent education that can be conceptualized and made available to other workers in parent education. From this source stemmed papers, reports, consultation, and a growing series of training programs conducted either at the Association or in conjunction with academic centers devoted to the training of different professional groups.

Parent groups have been a mainstay of the Association's program since its inception in 1888. At that time a small group of mothers came together to get the best information they could find to help them understand and deal with their children. There were no books on child care available for them then, so they turned to philosophers—Locke, Rousseau, Felix Adler —and to educators—Pestalozzi, later Montessori, Dewey, and many others. These parents and their successors reached out eagerly for the new knowledge that soon poured out from academic psychology, child development, and psychoanalysis. The Association played a pioneer role in making known to parents the ideas of Freud and his followers and in relating them to the development of children and the functioning of parents in normal families. It has continued to make use of relevant new knowledge from psychology, psychiatry, psychoanalysis, social work, and education—from all the behavioral sciences—and from research. This expanding background of knowledge then became part of the leaders' equipment. They, in turn, used it to enrich the knowledge of the parents who came to groups.

Soon it became apparent that to become more effective, parents need to understand not only their children, their needs and motivations at each stage of development, but also themselves as parents, their own attitudes, feelings, and expectations, and the role they play in the parent-child relationship. Recognizing that some parents need to work toward this understanding in an individual, personal way, the Association soon set up a counseling service under psychiatric supervision. The program of parent groups, however, was continued as an essential part of the agency's services for those parents who, it was felt, could gain from an educationally oriented group experience under skilled leadership. The methods shifted, however. At first, groups were conducted didactically, with the leader acting as the teacher in the traditional, academic sense. They then became lecture-discussions, with the leader acting as a speaker and answering questions in a discussion period. Subsequently, they took the form of discussion groups, in which parents learn through participation in the group process. Here the leader uses his knowledge of the dynamics of individual behavior and of the interrelationships of people in groups to help the parents share their thinking and feelings about common problems, examine the meaning of their daily experiences, and build on their inner strengths as they take on a more integrated parental role.

In its evolution, parent group education has drawn from many disciplines. Although the content of the sessions is initiated by the parent-members and stems from their everyday living with their children, the leader guides the discussion so that it explores many aspects of child development and family relations. The leader reinforces those concepts that are significant and sound and adds information and interpretation when they seem needed. (See Chapter XI on the Role of the Leader.)

In its methodology, parent group education has adapted knowledge from many sources about the ways in which growth and learning can be facilitated in groups. It has taken from the "progressive education" movement its emphasis on the value of the group in the development of a well-integrated human being. It makes use of newer theories of learning, especially those that throw light on the role of motivation and emotional involvement in the learning process. It has taken from sociology, social psychology, and cultural anthropology an understanding of how people interact in their groupings, with similarities and differences. From the field of group dynamics, initiated by Kurt Lewin and developed by his colleagues, it has drawn concepts of the dynamics of group processes and has consciously chosen to utilize those findings that are relevant to the specific purposes of group education. From the field of small group research, it has added a sensitivity to aspects of group interaction and member interplay that tend to occur in small, "leaderless" groups and that may operate to enhance or to block the goals of parent group education. The field of social casework has contributed much, both in the philosophy of its approach to people and its awareness of the dynamics of individual behavior and of the individual's potential for change; here, of course, these concepts are applied to a number of individuals at one time in the group setting. Social group work has also supplied special insights, which, in parent group education, are used toward educational goals in the areas of child-rearing and family relations. And, finally, much has been learned from the growing field of group therapy, which, in developing therapeutic methods for working with individuals in groups around symptoms of pathology, has also made an important contribution to an understanding of how so-called "normal" people function together in groups that have broadly educational goals.

Group techniques have developed so quickly and have drawn from so many divergent fields and methodologies that inevitably this growth has brought with it some confusion and overlapping in the goals, the methods that are appropriate to specific purposes, and the needs these methods can serve. The elaboration of the goals and methods of parent group education in later chapters will, it is hoped, make more vivid the distinctions between this group approach and the other significant group programs from which it has selectively drawn.

THE OUTREACH OF PARENT EDUCATION

The general field of parent education has sometimes been described as a middle-class movement. Yet, by definition, parent group education offers a methodology which, when properly carried out, is applied flexibly to further the growth and learning of the particular parents who choose to attend. In practice, it has been found that this approach meets the needs of parents from all socioeconomic levels and educational backgrounds. Since its inception, the Child Study Association of America has conducted group programs in all kinds of settings—schools, churches, public housing projects, women's clubs, neighborhood centers, settlement houses —wherever parents naturally congregated. In the past fifteen years, in connection with a series of programs of training for leadership, as well as in demonstration projects carried on by members of its staff, the Association has conducted, observed, and supervised the leadership of hundreds of groups of parents and expectant parents. These have been offered under the auspices of public health and medical agencies, welfare departments, community centers, family and children's agencies, and religious and educational organizations, including schools.

Whether it was a group of mothers of ADC (Aid to Dependent Children) families in a city in the midwest, a group of Negro mothers in a public housing project in a southern state, a group of parents from varied racial and religious backgrounds whose children had muscular dystrophy and who met in a rehabilitation center, a group of unmarried mothers in a Florence Crittendon home, or a group of parents of teen-agers meeting in a parish house in a comfortable eastern suburb, the parent-members all took part in a directed group educational experience. In varying degrees, this experience seemed to help them unloose the ties of old ideas and feelings and examine them, which led to new development and effectiveness as parents and as people in the community.

WHAT CAN THE GROUP ACCOMPLISH?: A SUMMARY

Learning about the experience of many parents with many children in a variety of families gives the group members a wider knowledge, which serves as a backdrop against which they can look at their own children and themselves.

They begin to understand children's needs at different stages of their growth, recognizing their basic similarities, yet appreciating the individual differences that make each child a unique person with his own constitutional make-up, his own rate of growth, his own wishes, and his own drives. This understanding seems to enable the parents to adapt their expectations for the child's achievement to what he is able to do. It also helps them respond to the child in ways that are more appropriate to the realities of the child's feelings and needs. For example, a better understanding of a child's readiness for, and response to, parents' demands for toilet training helps this part of a child's learning go forward more smoothly and eliminates this as a battleground between parent and child.

They begin to examine what they expect of themselves as parents and how their goals have been influenced by their earlier experiences, social and economic environment, and previous knowledge about children and family life. This understanding can help parents not to project onto their children wishes they had or still have for themselves. They are better able to evaluate the appropriateness of their expectations and goals for their children. When a parent's expectations of himself are attuned to the reality of his situation rather than to some fantasy picture of what the situation should be, he is more likely to find satisfaction in his relationship with his child.

A parent expects too much of himself if he feels he must never be irritable, or must always be able to respond to his child in order to make him happy. Implied in this attitude is the belief that everything the child is and does depends entirely on what his parent does and feels about him. At the opposite extreme, a parent who has too little expectation of himself may fail to recognize his responsibility to stimulate and guide his children, even from the earliest years, feeling that no matter what he does the child will still develop in his own way. This often results in his failing to provide a general atmosphere in which the child can grow and learn to get along with others and to move out toward new ideas and experiences.

They gain some knowledge of the interaction that takes place between parent and child, sibling and child, child and the total family. This helps parents assess their attitudes and practices, not as "good" or "bad" but dynamically in terms of what is really happening. A new awareness helps them recognize the nature of the child's response to some attitude or behavior on their part and how the interplay between the two affects their respective behavior. Sensitivity to this interplay increases the parents' perception of the uniqueness of their particular family situation.

They begin to appreciate the many influences on the child and on the parent of situations outside the immediate family, such as school, friends, religious influences, economic status, the presence or absence of other family members, illnesses, and pervasive tensions in the community and the world. Both parent and child are helped by new insights to sort out the particular influences to which they are responding, and thus to understand their significance and learn to deal with them.

These four areas of increased understanding seem to open the way for modifications of attitudes and behavior, for greater flexibility in reactions to the child and more appropriate choices of action.

In all of this they also learn—often indirectly—that problems and situations need to be looked at in their many aspects before one can meet them with full understanding. Thus they learn an approach to human behavior and problem solving that can be applied to other situations.

Indirectly, parents also gain many intangibles that are often never articulated. They seem to lose their sense of isolation, their feeling that each one is coping with his or her problems alone. They acquire a new respect for themselves because they are treated with respect, and because they begin to see that they are capable of responding in ways they had not anticipated. This, in turn, gives them new confidence.

Later chapters will attempt to describe some of the ways in which these results can be brought about. It may be of interest here, however, to see something of what goes on specifically in such groups, if only to suggest the quality of the experience.

From the record of a group of mothers and fathers meeting in a low-income housing project in a midwestern city:

In this group from the outset there was a tendency for the parents to express frustration, anger, and hostility toward their children, with frequent allusions to original sin and the concept that children needed to be beaten into submission so that they would not end up as delinquents or adult criminals. Mr. R., who was a lay preacher, had provided a steady theme of hell-fire and brimstone as futures for children unless they were "broken." As the sessions went on, however, the group disagreed with him and with each other as to the best method to help children and began to test new ways of coping with their large family interaction, drawing on what they had learned in the group.

Mr. R. said that he had been thinking a lot about his family situation since the last meeting. He wanted to talk about laziness. He described with some feeling the behavior of his second eldest son, who pokes along with the dishes, taking as long as three hours so that he cannot go out to play or do homework because he takes so long. Even then he doesn't do a very good job. Mr. R. said he either could tear his hair out or just accept the situation as it was. The leader commented on how frustrated Mr. R. must be and he responded that he could see his son twenty years from now, down at the Mission, with a beard, like so many others.

Mrs. C. agreed that it was all pretty frustrating. One of her children stalls; all the others work around him and he is the lazy one. There seems to be no way she can win. Mrs. A. said, "Maybe it's lazy and maybe it isn't," but her oldest boy just refuses to do jobs like carrying out the trash. She handles it by giving him another job which she considers worse, like doing the dishes—he goes ahead and does them without complaining. . . . (She has ten children.)

Mrs. C. said she thought things were different when she was a child. She could read a book or just do nothing and it didn't seem to make any difference. Now she doesn't seem to give her children the chance to do this. She appears to want them to keep the same pace she has to keep. Just because she is under pressure is no real reason why she should feel her children should be under the same pressure or go along with it. The group then talked for a bit about how complicated the modern world is with so much homework, the arithmetic, and all that.

Mrs. A. said that when you had a big family you kind of lumped them all together. Since she has been coming to the group she has realized that when her children were younger she always helped them with the dishes. She would clear the table, set them up at the sink with the rinse water and she would do the pots and pans. She thought it might be too much if they were just left to do things on their own. "It's too much for me when I see all the dishes for a big dinner for twelve people with all the pots and pans." She had begun to do this now with the smaller girls so that the work was shared and the little ones had a feeling that their mother was involved instead of having the older sisters boss them around. She said that she wanted her girls to grow up and enjoy their families and if they had to be Mammas now maybe this wouldn't happen. Another mother added that she knew her children took much less time and did a better job if she helped them. Sometimes she didn't do it because she just didn't feel like doing the dishes, but she thought it was much less painful for everybody if she did. . . .

Mr. R. gave an example of how he is handling his son a little differently since he came to the group. His son had come home later than he had said and he had suggested that he watch this, since he expects him to get in on time. His son said, "Or else what? What will happen?" This brought laughter from the group and Mr. R. said, "Isn't that plain impertinent?" Mrs. A. said, "Maybe he just wants to know what the 'or else' is." Mrs. C. thought the boy was not as afraid of his father as he used to be. She went on to say that when she was a teen-ager she was so frightened of her father that she could not remember ever really having had a conversation with him. She had practically no social life because she was so afraid to approach him to ask whether she could go to a party. Since she has been coming to the group she realizes that she has been doing some of the same things with her children. Now that she is able to talk, she finds out what the situation is first and then she and her husband decide whether it is possible for the child to attend a school dance or a church party. "I don't want them to grow up afraid of us."

From the record of an expectant parents group in a small eastern city:

In the second session, the mothers and fathers talked about how they had felt when the mothers first knew that they were pregnant. Several mothers said that even though they had planned to have the baby and wanted it very much, they found themselves feeling quite differently when the doctor told them "the good news." Had they been right in wanting a baby now? Did they really want the baby so much after all? And wouldn't the baby's coming interfere with their lives as they were living them now? At this point, one of the fathers broke in, saying that he too had had some of the same ideas when his wife told him she was definitely expecting. Suddenly, he said, he had felt trapped, caught in something that he could not stop. How would they manage? Would there be enough room in their apartment? Would he be able to earn enough money to support a whole family? And would they be able to be "good" parents? Other fathers joined in, sharing some of the same ideas. After a few moments, however, the conversation took a new turn, when the first father said, "But I am talking about the way we felt in the beginning; by now we have settled down and are looking forward to having the baby. Somehow, now we feel that we will be able to work it out." The rest of the group seemed to relax as they began to talk about specific ways in which they would begin "to work it out."

From the record of a group of parents of young children with cerebral palsy, meeting in a suburban community:

The group discussed their problems with some of their young children, who at three and four were not yet walking or talking. One of the mothers said that her four-year-old, who as yet was not talking clearly or able to navigate on her own, whined and cried for hours, and the endless crying was almost more than she could bear. A father of a three-year-old who also had not developed these skills began to talk about the things he had invented for his child to do. (He had to make them up, he said, as he had found no place that could give him any guidelines.) He found a carton in which he put crumpled pieces of paper, which entertained his little boy for hours on end; he tried to encourage him to use a walker, although at the first attempt this was unsuccessful. Gradually, he found other activities which the child could do and which he enjoyed. The mother of the four-year-old listened but made no comment. In later meetings, however, she reported that she too had tried new ways of giving her girl a chance to be active, experimenting with large blocks, putting things in and out of boxes, and so on. She was surprised to find that the child cried considerably less and even seemed in those few weeks to be able to do a little more by herself. As she talked, she showed that she was thinking of her little girl as a person and not just as a heavy lump. Out of the practical suggestions which she had picked up, she had come to look at her in a new way.

III

Parent Group Education: Basic Principles

Building on the parents' strength and helping them change through an experience of guided group discussion: these are the goals of parent group education. This approach is founded on the belief that people can learn and grow, and on respect for their ability to do so, each in his or her own way. It recognizes that many parents have not had the opportunity, or perhaps have not been challenged, to explore the needs of their children and to examine their own ways of meeting these needs. Some have been preoccupied in making adjustments to other aspects of their lives and have only recently come to recognize the responsibilities of their parenthood. Parent group education "is predicated on the belief that parents are mature enough to be able to work with others toward an acceptable and constructive group goal and have available psychic forces to use toward this end, in spite of the fact that they may have problems about their children and their relationship to them." [1]

It has been shown that regardless of their educational background, parents can utilize the group experience to gain additional understanding of their children, their family relationships, and the circumstances under which they are living; and that they can come to constructive conclusions about the nature of their relationships with their children and gain confidence and courage to take more positive action in handling the details of their lives. These goals are achieved in parent group education by giving parents an opportunity to share their common experiences as parents, their concerns and ideas, their frustrations and hopes for their children.

Yet in our American culture many parents have had little or no experience in talking directly about their everyday problems in groups, where they can voice their gripes and puzzlements as well as their pleasures and satisfactions. Historically, casual conversations with other adults about

[1] Peter B. Neubauer, "The Technique of Parent Group Education: Some Basic Concepts," in *Parent Group Education and Leadership Training*, Child Study Association of America, New York, 1953, p. 10. (O.P.)

matters of immediate concern were very much a part of daily living. They took place over the back fence, at the neighborhood store, around school and church meetings. But social changes and urban living have made such casual contacts less possible and less frequent. The meetings people do attend are likely to be set up to discuss a common community problem or local issue. They usually take the form of town meetings, political caucuses, union policy meetings, and the like. These are meetings specifically for social action. Group discussions about people's own lives are relatively unknown even today. As Dr. Neubauer has pointed out, people are still essentially alone in their efforts to solve their individual problems.

Because of this unfamiliarity, group meetings on problems of child-rearing sometimes run into obstacles. Some parents are reluctant to participate in the discussion, out of a possible fear of seeming "gossipy" or of talking about private affairs that are not usually shared with others. For some this feeling amounts almost to a sense of guilt and hinders their ability to discuss their problems easily and especially to admit their failures. Often parents are suspicious, afraid of becoming involved, while at the same time their very presence at group meetings shows that they are eager to learn and to improve the part of their lives that has to do with their parenthood.

These mixed reactions are often seen in the opening sessions of a group. Parents, like all people in a new educational experience, have to learn how to use the experience, and it is the responsibility of those who provide the programs to give leadership that will make it possible for them to do so. This is not as difficult as it may seem. Just by their coming, parents have already begun to take up one side of a contract which should be made explicit, in terms of the purposes of the group and the parents' obligations as well as those of the leader. (See Chapter VI: How A Group Begins.) It is up to them to go ahead with the deal or not, as they choose. And in most cases, they stay with the group, if it seems to offer them something real.

Fortunately, getting together for a common purpose often carries with it a sense of excitement and exhilaration which helps overcome some of the negative feelings. Although learning is sometimes painful, since it causes the learner to question many ideas that he has long accepted, at the same time it carries a challenge. And the rewards come when the parents find themselves thinking and acting differently and experiencing a new feeling of power.

ASSUMPTIONS

In working toward its stated goals, parent group education bases its program and techniques on a number of important assumptions, all of which have implications for practice. It is important that these assumptions be conceptualized clearly—not taken for granted. They need to be examined and challenged, studied and restudied, as group programs become more numerous and are thoughtfully carried out.

The assumptions underlying parent group education parallel many of the basic principles of learning outlined by Nathaniel Cantor in his book, *The Teaching-Learning Process*. In a chapter titled, "The Propositions of Modern Learning," Cantor points out that these propositions are derived from clinical studies of personality development, with "a great deal of support from inquiry that is psychologically, sociologically and psychiatrically oriented." [2]

Cantor's propositions relate to general learning, but here the assumptions are related specifically to parents, since this is our focus. The formulations which follow are based on experience with parents in many different settings over many years.

Assumption 1. Parents can learn. Learning can take place at any period of one's life, regardless of one's age. Parents are not equipped, merely by virtue of their parenthood, to understand all aspects of their parental role. Barbara Biber, speaking at a parent-education conference of the Child Study Association of America in 1953, said, "Being a parent does not of itself carry with it the natural capacity to function successfully and satisfyingly as a parent." She added, "With thought and the wish to do so, parents can learn and change."

The rationale for education for parenthood and child-rearing is based on the belief that the more parents know about child development, about the effects of the interaction between parent and child, about their own goals and desires, their own emotional responses and the influence on the family of the environment in which they live, the more adequately will they be prepared to handle their family situations. This assumption provides the impetus for offering educational opportunities to parents on a wide basis.

IMPLICATIONS FOR PRACTICE: *It is essential that educational group programs for parents provide an exchange of information by group members and/or the contribution of additional information by the leader or from outside sources to supplement what the group knows. The group is then helped to relate this material—these experiences and ideas—to what they already know from many facets of their lives, reviewing its meaning, analyzing separate aspects of it that are significant, and putting the pieces into a new perspective that serves as a basis for new feelings and performance.*

[2] Nathaniel Cantor, *The Teaching-Learning Process*, Holt, Rinehart and Winston, New York, 1953, pp. 286–314.

Assumption 2.   Parents want to learn, particularly about those issues
and relationships which affect the growth and development of their children. In most parents this wish to learn seems to be part of some dynamic
force that accounts for their activity,[3] a force that is strong and clear
when they can participate in an activity that has meaning for them.

IMPLICATIONS FOR PRACTICE: *It is because of the conviction that parents
want to learn that programs are offered, particularly those of parent group
education. Here, parents are given an opportunity to join a group on their
own initiative, usually on the basis of a general invitation or a public
announcement, and to participate as they are ready to do so.* (For other
situations in which parents are selected and referred to group programs,
see Chapter V: Planning and Organizing Parent Group Programs.) The
response to this open-end invitation indicates that for certain parents the
drive to learn to improve their functioning in the family is strong. However, the response of parents to such group programs differs widely in
different communities, as will be described in a subsequent chapter. Yet
the continuation of these programs stands on its own merits, as evidence
that those parents who come to the group do so usually of their own
volition. Many professional persons believe that more parents would avail
themselves of group educational opportunities if they understood them
more completely, for then the idea of participation in an unknown experience might be less threatening.

Assumption 3.   Parents (like all those who wish to extend their knowledge through education) *learn best what they are interested in learning.*
In fact, some educators go so far as to say that they learn *only* what they
are interested in learning. This assumption has been part of modern
educational theory since it was first formulated by John Dewey and
William Heard Kilpatrick, who stressed that education is most successful
when the material to be learned is related directly to the specific interest
and experience of the learner. As a corollary to this assumption, it can be
stated that parents learn best when they share in the development of the
content of the discussion and take an active part in shaping the educational experience to their own wishes and ends.

IMPLICATIONS FOR PRACTICE: *This assumption is the basis for the procedures in parent group education whereby the group is presented with
no set curriculum but develops its own "agenda" in the first meeting and
as the sessions go on.*

The development of the content of group sessions in keeping with the
needs of the whole group is one of the most strategic and delicate aspects

---

[3] Adapted from Helen Durken, *The Group In Depth,* International Universities
Press, New York, 1964, p. 62.

of parent group education leadership, and it will be discussed in detail. Important to stress here is the responsibility of the leader to see that the group sessions are meaningful to the group as a whole, as well as to the individual members who participate. He must also see that the discussion fulfills the nature of the contract between the participants and those who set up the program: the material discussed must be related to aspects of child-rearing and family life that have significance for the parent-members. Yet even here there is a need for flexibility, so that the material brought in by the group is as rich and varied as possible. If the discussion is focused on general "subject" areas or held rigidly to "topics" the group has suggested, it tends to become stilted and lose new insights that may come even peripherally from its very variety.

Assumption 4.   Learning is most significant when the subject matter is closely related to the parents' own immediate experiences with their children and with one another in relation to their children. The everyday happenings of life at home and in the community are those explored and evaluated in the group. These day-by-day happenings bring life into the group meetings and furnish the raw materials from which broader interpretations can be drawn, interpretations that open the way for action.

IMPLICATIONS FOR PRACTICE: *Parent-members are encouraged to be specific when they pose their questions or concerns and to describe in some detail the immediate occurrences which brought the issues to the fore.*

It is important that the specific nature of each family's experience be given its full weight. This has much more meaning than generalized intellectualizations about behavior. Parents—like other people—can philosophize endlessly about such matters without coming to grips with the problems they are facing.

Assumption 5.   Parents can learn best when they are free to create their own response to a situation. In reacting to ideas of other members of the group, parents have an opportunity to formulate their own ideas, as they may never have done before, and to look at them more thoughtfully. They feel free to maintain the positions they think are appropriate, or to change them if they see the need to do so.

IMPLICATIONS FOR PRACTICE: *To provide for the free responses of the group members to the material under discussion and to ideas presented by other group members, the leader encourages an open exchange of experiences and opinions and listens carefully to the comments of each group member. At no time is there any pressure toward group consensus or conformity; on the contrary, each member is encouraged—by implication rather than overtly—to come to his or her own decisions.*

Assumption 6. Parent group education is as much an emotional experience as it is an intellectual one. Throughout the discussion, it is recognized that the facts of human behavior are important, as is an understanding of the dynamics behind the facts. Inevitably intertwined with these are the feelings that accompany them in both parents and children. As stated by Barbara Biber,[4] "Learning for parents includes not only the acquiring of management techniques and skills but an understanding of the meaning and importance of relationships. Individuals vary in their ability to learn and change, depending on: (1) their personality makeups and needs, (2) their intellectual understanding, and (3) the extent to which knowledge and feelings can fuse."

IMPLICATIONS FOR PRACTICE: *Parent group education therefore encourages the expression of feelings, not for their own sake in a vacuum, but in relation to the substance of parent-child relationships and family living. The leaders are always alert to the need for maintaining some kind of balance between fact and feeling, between the outer reality and the emotional responses of parents to their real-life situations.*

This encouragement of the expression of feelings is sometimes taken to mean that parent group education, by virtue of this fact, is directed toward therapeutic goals. This is a fallacious conclusion based on the assumption that all intense feelings are pathological. Within the concept of parent group education, feelings are a natural, normal part of human life. Those feelings which are close to the surface of consciousness and easily expressed by the parent represent an essential part of human existence, even though they may not always be recognized as such.

Nevertheless, the expression of feelings, since it is not usually a part of social communication, often causes some anxiety in the group members. This is especially so if some of the feelings expressed are negative ones, colored with hostility or tinged with guilt. Such feelings can and should be explored along with the "safer," more positive ones. They are all appropriate within the educational goals of such a program. So also is the recognition of conflict, uncertainty, ambivalence—all parts of normal human living.

Assumption 7. Parents can learn from one another. In parent group education, the very exchange of experiences, ideas, expectations, hopes, and fears offers a wide and rich palette to which various members can react and contribute, selecting those parts which have meaning for them. Within this interchange, parents learn much from one another, sometimes sensing that others are reporting misinterpretations and false ideas, some-

[4] Speaking at a parent-education conference of the Child Study Association of America, 1953.

times recognizing—almost with a start—that another group member has insight into something which they have approximated but not yet quite reached. The very mass of factual information about how children respond at different ages, how they move from one characteristic phase into another as they grow, how they react similarly and differently from other children, how they are affected by the positive and negative complex social situations in their communities and neighborhoods: all this adds to the body of knowledge which any single parent may have from his own limited experience with the children he knows. As they talk, parents learn a great deal about the range of parental responses, the different feelings any one situation may provoke, the many ways in which parents judge their own performance and reactions, and their various methods of dealing with their family's problems.

IMPLICATIONS FOR PRACTICE: *As already implied, parent group discussion encourages a wealth of material "on the table," based on living experiences with living children; it encourages parents to respond freely to one another, questioning, challenging, agreeing, adding, commenting, disagreeing, as they test their own ideas and convictions and gradually take a position for themselves. The leader facilitates this process by encouraging more comments, by giving due respect to those made by any one member of the group, and by giving particular encouragement to those who may not participate as freely at first. The leader is careful to underscore what the parents already do know and to add information they obviously do not have.*

It is interesting to note that with freedom to respond to one another, differences in social status or educational background soon disappear as the parents learn to really listen, to respect the contributions of their group associates and react to them directly.

Assumption 8.   Parent group education provides the basis for a remaking of experience. This takes place through the process already described of group interchange, of gleaning general principles from specific illustrations, making and accepting interpretations that seem appropriate for an individual parent, and gradually sensing and conceptualizing some of the basic meaning of human relations that are essential to an understanding of family life. This remaking of experience comes about through exposure to a larger mass of material about behavior, and the attempt to see general patterns that may be present throughout—patterns that are then redefined and applied to one's own life.

IMPLICATIONS FOR PRACTICE: *This slow process of learning necessitates groups meeting over a period of some time, usually for from eight to twelve weekly sessions, with a continuity of parents who get to know one another. The leader creates a climate of trust and safety in which parents can participate freely and honestly without fear of being judged. To facilitate the complex learning process, he helps the group find a way to examine a situation and learn from it concepts that are applicable not only to this set of circumstances but to many others they will meet with their families—situations that have not been discussed within the sessions of the group.*

It is the exploration, analysis, and application learned from any one situation that is the most important aspect of parent group education, since it carries over into other specific episodes in the members daily lives and can bring about new insights and behavior as time goes on.

Assumption 9.   Each parent learns in his own way. Everyone who has observed students in classes of any kind is aware of the way in which individuals learn at different paces, in different patterns, and with different degrees of clarity. This is, of course, true of parents who bring to their parenthood their individual differences of temperament, personality, and intellectual capacity and also their own previous experiences with their individual families. Probably the most important determinant of a person's attitude toward his own parenthood stems from experiences as a child with his own mother and father. The carry-over of these early childhood experiences colors not only the ability to look at one's own children realistically, but also one's willingness to do so. In addition, parents' own individual sets of values influence their goals for their children and themselves, values of which they themselves often are unaware. Small wonder then that a parent in a group reacts to the group educational experience in his own way, often having to free himself from many layers of his past almost as one peels the various layers of an onion. As he sheds limiting and confusing relics of his earlier life he becomes more free to examine his present situation honestly and to learn from it.

IMPLICATIONS FOR PRACTICE: *Because of these wide differences in individual learning, the group discussion approach at no time puts pressure on an individual member to move into the discussion faster than he is prepared to or to come to any set conclusions. Rather, he is encouraged to expand his horizons at his own rate of speed, free to pick up what he feels is meaningful from the content of the discussion, and to come to his own decisions.*

❋   ❋   ❋   ❋   ❋

These then are some of the assumptions on which parent group education is based. It is obvious that they need to be clear in the mind of the leader so that he may constantly try to develop specific practices that are consistent with the philosophy and goals of the program.

IV

How Does Parent Group Education Differ from Other Group Approaches?

The procedures and practices of parent group education are sharpened when they are consciously selected as appropriate for its particular ends and contrasted with different procedures used in certain other types of group experience. Some of these differentiations are obvious; others are more subtle and overlapping and are still in need of additional formulation and sensitive test performance. The similarities and differences are often hard to define, since many of the terms used to describe various group approaches have no generally accepted meaning and can only be evaluated in terms of their stated goals. They are introduced here, however, to clarify—by contrast—the conceptual background for the techniques described in the sections that follow.

HOW DOES PARENT GROUP EDUCATION DIFFER FROM FORMAL ACADEMIC TEACHING ABOUT CHILD DEVELOPMENT AND FAMILY RELATIONS?

Both parent group education and formal academic teaching about child development and family relations have as their purpose to enlarge the intellectual understanding of those they reach. Although formal academic teaching has been and is constantly being modified in its procedures, it is usually based on a curriculum determined in advance by the instructor, covering material and issues he thinks are important. Parent group education follows no set curriculum but proceeds from the interests and concerns of the parent members as they emerge in their daily lives with their children.

Academic teaching is made dynamic and meaningful by a gifted teacher who presents knowledge and interpretations that are clearly related to the participants' thinking and living. Yet, if even a gifted teacher follows a formal teaching structure and plan too rigidly, the learning often becomes too general and intellectual. The parent is thus left to make the application to his own experiences—or not. Where lectures are followed by a discussion or question period, parents have some chance to test the meaning of the presentation for their own situations. Usually, however, this part of the session is short, so that only a few parents can be heard. In contrast, group education for parents starts on a different plane—the living, feeling happenings in families—and thus introduces the immediate essence of parent-child behavior and interplay. It allows also for all the parents to share both the real circumstances and the emotional concomitants for themselves and their children.

There is an intangible but essential difference in atmosphere between parent group education and formal academic teaching. The more formal program often tends to perpetuate the teacher-pupil relationship parents experienced in the classroom when they were children. The teacher is the authority; they are the recipients of wisdom. In group education, parents are deliberately encouraged to develop independent thinking; the leader is an enabler, who uses his knowledge to help them function as individuals, evolving their own answers in feeling-responses and behavior. Both situations call for a wide background of understanding in the leader or teacher, but this knowledge is utilized in vastly different ways.

In another type of program, the Parent Education Project of the University of Chicago, parent "study-discussion" groups follow a basic course of printed materials known as *Parenthood in a Free Nation*.[1] The focus is on didactic content. The parent-members report on assigned readings which are then discussed in the group at an intellectual level, with a leader trained in this approach. The parents share their general ideas about child development and parenthood, but are not encouraged to bring in live, personal material. Here, too, the application of the content to the everyday happenings in the family is left for the parents to work out by themselves. In parent group education, the parent members are helped by the leader to take the initiative in determining a flexible "agenda" or plan to meet their needs and in supplying specific happenings and ideas that are the substance of the sessions.

HOW DOES GROUP EDUCATION DIFFER
FROM GROUP DYNAMICS?

Both group education and group dynamics make use of the dynamics of group processes, but toward different goals.

Group dynamics has been one of the major influences in the develop-

---

[1] Ethel Kawin, *Parenthood in a Free Nation* (3 vols.), Macmillan, New York, 1963.

ment of small group research. It has "emphasized the need for obtaining an objective understanding of the functioning of small groups" and has "attempted to utilize this understanding to facilitate individual and group change." It also "exemplifies one of the few attempts to create procedures designed to enhance the function of normal persons rather than of those who are physically or emotionally crippled." [2] Although "the major fruit of research into group dynamics . . . was the evolution of the laboratory method of human relations training . . . as a vehicle for the production of insight and behavior change," [3] it has been pointed out that even group dynamics scientists have had some difficulty in bridging the gap between research and practice. As in any developing field of inquiry, there have been certain shifts of emphasis. Take, for example, the matter of unanimity of thinking or consensus.

Since many groups conducted according to the practice of group dynamics were directed toward some kind of action, it is understandable that consensus was considered necessary if the group were to achieve its goal. Many group dynamics groups came to be conducted according to this concept, with consensus becoming almost an end in itself. More recently, however, as groups have been studied intensively, it has been recognized that although group pressures toward uniformity (and unanimity) are ever present, they function in various ways in different settings for many different reasons. As described by Cartwright and Zander, "pressures toward uniformity can serve at least three functions: (a) to help the group accomplish its goals, (b) to help the group maintain itself as a group, and (c) to help the members develop validity or 'reality' for their opinions." [4] And again, "The established orderliness stemming from pressures toward uniformity helps the group in its work. The (group) standards reduce confusion and wasted effort, but at the same time they often cause uneasiness, inflexibility, and a reduction of creativeness among members. Pressures toward conformity, then, can be both beneficial and harmful to members." [5] Moreover, their appropriateness depends on the purposes for which the group meets.

Parent group education, as we have seen, is primarily directed toward the third of the functions just mentioned: to help the members develop validity for their opinions. In other words, it aims to promote independent thinking, individual decision-making. Yet, as a result of the educational experience, a certain kind of consensus is often achieved. What frequently

[2] John Mann, *Changing Human Behavior*, Scribners, New York, 1965, p. 94.
[3] *Ibid.*, p. 95.
[4] Dorwin Cartwright and Alvin Zander, *Group Dynamics: Research and Theory*, Second Edition, Row Peterson and Company, Evanston, Ill., 1960, p. 169.
[5] *Ibid.*, p. 179.

emerges is agreement on a principle of human behavior that is sound and relevant. It may be a new appreciation of the meaning of a particular kind of behavior which influences the parents' handling of the matter. The group may agree, for example, on a principle of family interaction, such as the concept that a child is quick to sense and be upset when his parent overreacts to him in any exaggerated way. Whatever form one parent's behavior takes, the group's agreement on the principle prods him to think about the effect on his child of what he is doing and to consider whether to modify his behavior if he can. The group may also reach a kind of consensus when the parents share a common feeling, such as utter bafflement and helplessness in the face of the unpredictable behavior of many adolescents. Such agreement often gives parents a sense of relief—and a better perspective on their own emotional reactions.

Regardless of the extent to which consensus is or is not a primary goal, group dynamics has made an invaluable contribution to group activities of all kinds by pointing out the pervasiveness of group pressures toward uniformity and some of the reasons for the influence of the group on its members.[6] The goal of parent group education, as we have seen, is clear in its stress on helping the parents find their own place in their individual thinking and come to their own individual conclusions. With the recognition of the forces in groups that tend to work against this goal, the challenge of parent education becomes greater. There is need to develop skills to counteract this effect of group interplay and utilize other aspects of the group process which contribute to the parents' strength and individuality.

Group dynamics places emphasis on wider self-understanding, learned through awareness of one's performance in the group in relation to other group members, the leader, and the task in hand. Such behavior is thought to be an index of a person's behavior in other situations as well. Parent group education also has as its goal the acquisition of greater self-awareness for the parents, but this is brought about through their evaluation of themselves primarily in relation to their children and families, as they report and think about their role in everyday situations in the home and as they look at themselves in the light of the reports and thinking of other parents in similar situations.

Group dynamics is concerned primarily that participants should learn to become "good" group members and assumes that this will affect their ability to function better with people outside the group, including their children and other family members. Parent group education also sees parents becoming "good" group members during a series of discussion meetings, as they learn to contribute more easily, to listen more thoughtfully to others, and to relate what they say and hear to their own thinking

[6] *Ibid.*, Part III: Group Pressures and Group Standards.

and home situations. These gains are considered to be valuable; but they are seen as secondary achievements that occur while the parents are focusing on the primary purpose of the group, which is to get a better understanding and a larger perspective on their lives in the family.

In practice, parent group education does not encourage comments from the participants about the nature of any one member's participation in the group and its effect on the others, as is often done in group dynamics sessions. Occasionally the leader may comment not on the role a parent is playing as a group member but on his reaction to the content of the discussion, in order to get additional material to be considered by the individual parent and by the group as a whole. Such comments are injected only when the leader feels that this additional material is needed to clarify the situation and sharpen its implications. The leader may prefer, however, to bring into the open the behavior or tone of the group as a whole. Without pointing at any one individual, such comments bring the *general atmosphere* of the group to the attention of all group members and often free them to move ahead with the group task.

In parent group education the leader does not take a poll of the members' decisions on a particular issue, such as whether all the members of an expectant mothers' group plan to breast-feed their babies. The important thing is that the group has looked at all sides of the issue—practical and personal—as it affects both parent and child, many parents and many children. This gives each parent a better basis on which to make an individual judgment. Nor is there any attempt to "check up" on parents' actions, even when they have committed themselves in words. It is understood that they must also feel free to change their minds if they wish to do so.

As we have seen, group dynamics is often directed to bring its members toward specific action as a group, often social action. Group education may also arouse its group members to social action but they are left free to join in or not. Here group action is seen as a possible by-product of greater understanding.

The implications of social conditions and social practices have always been part and parcel of parent group education sessions, insofar as they affect the well-being and functioning of the children and the family as a whole. Discussions often center on such matters as when to go to a school principal if a teacher and a child seem to be at loggerheads; when and how a parent might ask for a change of teacher or of a class assignment or even of a school; on what basis a group of parents might ask for the elimination of social dancing in the sixth grade; whether a child should stay out of school during a teachers' strike; what attitude one should take about bussing arrangements established to create a racially integrated school population, for what age children and in relation to what distance from home. Such issues have been part of innumerable group sessions and have been discussed in keeping with the principles of parent group education, which stress that greater understanding of all aspects of the issue—individual, personal, and community—will equip parents to deal with them more effectively. Sometimes a few members have constituted themselves a committee and have followed through on some plan for social action. Sometimes individual members, stimulated and encouraged by the group discussion, have initiated an activity in a neighborhood or Parents' Association to improve a social situation that was felt to be undesirable. In its purer sense, however, parent group education has considered such plans for action as secondary rather than primary goals for the group as a whole.

As new programs are developing, their scope is being extended to meet pressing social needs and is being directed toward initiating and carrying out appropriate steps to meet social problems that impinge on the family. This kind of activity may take place at several sessions in which the whole group is involved, as the issues become clear. Or it may be undertaken by a few of the members who choose to take responsibility in these areas, either within or outside the group or both. In whatever form this action occurs, the leader plays an active part in its development. This extension is being tried in order to add a new dimension to the parents' self-concept, which is often threatened when they live under adverse social and economic conditions. It is felt that sharing in projects of social action, which are determined in the group through educational processes, may give parents a new sense of solidarity and personal worth and a feeling of mastery over at least some parts of their life situations about which they feel victimized and powerless.

It may be that these goals can be accomplished in keeping with the basic principles of parent group education previously outlined. It is important, however, that the interpersonal and intrafamilial problems that bring the parents together remain the primary focus of the group and that the social issues be examined and acted upon in relation to their impact on the children and their families. The extension of parent group education into this area is still in an exploratory phase. It is being studied to determine whether, and in what ways, this emphasis on social issues may strengthen the learning experience for parents and increase their initiative and personal growth. In becoming a social action group, even in the limited area of family concerns, the dynamics of the group may be found to take on a different quality, a different kind of group response and group interrelationships, which may call for different leadership techniques—and a descriptive label other than parent group education.

HOW DOES PARENT GROUP EDUCATION DIFFER
FROM PARENT GROUP COUNSELING?

The distinctions between parent group education and parent group counseling are not clear, since the latter term is used to cover many shadings of group learning. Here the goals are sometimes closely allied to the goals of parent group education, sometimes more closely allied to the goals of group therapy. The fact that there seems to be great variation in the practice of group counseling from one individual worker to another and from agency to agency makes it difficult to define the differences in practice between parent group counseling and parent group education. Other terms have been introduced that complicate these distinctions. For example, the group approach developed by S. R. Slavson, which he calls "Child-Centered Group Guidance of Parents," [7] is similar in its goals to parent group education. It seems to fall more into the category of group counseling, however, because it is offered to parents who come together usually under clinic-agency auspices and already are clearly conscious of the existence of their problems. Understandably, then, these groups tend to focus on the use of the group to help an individual parent understand and resolve his particular problem.

In general, it is this direction toward individual problem-solving that is one of the main characteristics of group counseling, as we understand it. The parents who come consider that they have a problem, have identified it in their own minds, and are asking specifically for help with it. They already see themselves as clients of a social agency or as patients in a therapeutic service, rather than as applicants for a broad educational experience. They have put themselves into the agency's hands, often with the understanding that the counseling process may take place over a considerable period of time.[8] Parent group education, on the other hand, stresses primarily the need to understand the meaning of behavior within a family (and of similar behavior in other families) so that parents may respond more effectively. The group experience is also time-limited.

In other descriptions, group counseling—treating clients in small groups with casework goals—aligns itself with group treatment. In a recent report on "Group Treatment in Family Service Agencies," [9] the words "group

[7] S. R. Slavson, *Child-Centered Group Guidance of Parents,* International Universities Press, New York, 1958.

[8] Hannah Grunwald, "Group Counseling of the Multiproblem Family," in *The Use of Group Techniques in Family Agencies,* Family Service Association of America, New York, 1959.

[9] *Report of a Committee on Group Treatment in Family Service Agencies,* Family Service Association of America, New York, 1964.

counseling" are not used at all. In this report, group treatment is defined as being based on the same psychosocial framework as casework treatment, which is given in individual interviews, multiple-client interviews, and family sessions. The group treatment method, however, requires additional learning on the part of caseworkers. Besides their casework skills, they must have knowledge of group process and skill in using group techniques.

"In general," says this report, "the groups in family agencies are composed of clients who have considerable motivation for seeking help and are willing to involve themselves in the experience." [10] Group treatment as defined here has the same overall goal as parent group education: to enhance the parent-client's effectiveness in his daily functioning. Both casework treatment and group treatment, however, aim primarily "to correct social disfunctioning and change adaptive patterns." [11] The report recognizes that the constellation of techniques of group treatment is "designed largely to strengthen and repair a weak or damaged ego," whereas that of casework treatment is "designed to foster ego integration and self-awareness." [12] In these respects, the goals of parent group education are more in keeping with those of casework treatment, and those of group treatment are more in keeping with those of group therapy.

These distinctions may appear overrefined. They are made here, however, particularly for those leaders who are immersed in one type of group and who may want to try other approaches.

HOW DOES PARENT GROUP EDUCATION DIFFER FROM PARENT GROUP THERAPY?

Here the differences are more clear-cut both in goals and procedures, even though it is generally recognized that effective group education—like all education—has its therapeutic aspects, just as effective group therapy—like all therapy—has educational values and gains. The important point of comparison here is the nature of the primary objective, not its secondary by-products.

Group education addresses itself to the ego-function of individuals. In its use of ego psychology, group education addresses itself to strengthening the ways in which the human personality "deals with the complicated network of forces and counter forces from instinct, conscience and the larger social environment. . . ." It recognizes "the ego's patterns of adaptation and its way of coping with and mastering ordinary demands and extraordinary stresses, both internal and external, the ego defenses against various kinds of anxiety and the part they play in everyday social func-

[10] *Ibid.*, p. 12.
[11] *Ibid.*, p. 18.
[12] *Ibid.*, p. 19.

tioning." [13] It concentrates on building ego strength, which, as Annette Garett points out, represents "the ability and the freedom to do various things, without one's being irrationally coerced to do them. . . . Real ego strength involves an active acceptance that marshalls new strength with which to confront a difficult situation." [14] Thus the emphasis is on the total functioning of the individual (the parent) in the real, present world.

In contrast, group psychotherapy is seen as a process of emotional re-education designed to remove what are already pathological blocks that stand in the way of the continuing acquisition of knowledge and understanding needed to enable the growth process to continue. There are many forms of group therapy, of course, but all have this common goal.

To state the distinction more simply, "The educator deals with that capacity available to learn by experience, and helps the individual grow in society towards social goals, while the therapist attempts to free those forces still bound in pathological conflict." [15]

These differences in goals are sharply reflected in practice: in the selection and composition of the groups, the focus of the discussions, the nature of the material introduced, and the use that is made of it.

Parent group education is usually offered on a nonselective basis to all who choose to attend. In most cases there is no personal contact between the leader and the members until they sit down at the meeting table together. Sometimes, as with groups offered in the programs of the Child Study Association of America at its headquarters, prospective parent-members discuss the group briefly with a staff member (not necessarily the leader), usually over the telephone. The purpose of this preliminary contact is to interpret the program in broad terms and to indicate its purposes and general procedures so that the parents will understand what to expect. Occasionally staff members discourage a parent from enrolling when it seems reasonably clear that the program is not what he or she wants. For example, a parent may say he wants a lecture-series given by experts rather than group discussion. The interviews also discourage a parent from registering when it is apparent that he expects specific help in solving an individual problem. Such an expectation is unrealistic in view of the purpose of an educationally oriented discussion group, and his entering the group would probably only lead to the parent's ultimate disappointment. In such circumstances, alternate programs or services are suggested, if they are available. But the final decision is left to the applicant.

[13] Howard J. Parad, Introduction to Parad (Editor), *Ego Psychology and Dynamic Casework*, Family Service Association of America, New York, 1958, pp. 2–4.

[14] Annette Garett, "Modern Casework: The Contribution of Ego Psychology," in Parad, *op. cit.*, p. 44.

[15] Peter B. Neubauer, "The Place of Education and Psychotherapy in Mental Health," *American Journal of Orthopsychiatry*, XXIII, No. 2 (April 1953).

In general, parent group education programs proceed on the conviction that people who enroll can make use of the experience, though in varying degrees. While group education cannot be expected to help a parent whose problems lie close to the core of a deep-rooted, emotional disturbance, it has been found that many persons who have some degree of neurotic conflict can gain from group education, developing ego strengths which enable them to function despite or around the areas of conflict. Where the leader finds that a parent is clearly not able to gain from the experience because of acute emotional difficulties, he refers the parent to casework or treatment services, if he thinks this advisable, doing so sometimes during the series of meetings, sometimes after the series is ended. In only very rare instances have parents been asked to leave a group because they were so disturbed that their behavior interfered with the group's functioning or because it was apparent that their inner turmoil prevented them from assimilating anything from the group interchange.

Group therapy, in contrast, approaches the problem of group composition quite differently. Parents are *selected* to attend the particular therapy group on the basis of varied criteria: the nature of their problem, its likeness to or difference from that of others (depending on the purposes or goals of the leader or the agency sponsoring the program), and the severity of the problem, again either because of similarity or difference. These factors are evaluated in terms of setting up a particular atmosphere which will further the therapeutic purpose of the group. Here it is not left to the initiative and decision of the parents themselves.

An interesting procedure is followed at the Child Development Center in New York City, a diagnostic and treatment center for preschool children: parents are assigned to a parent education group, a therapy group, or a parent therapy group according to the agency's judgment of his particular need, his interest, and his readiness to participate.

(A distinction must be made here between parent group therapy and group therapy. As Dr. Peter B. Neubauer pointed out in an unpublished paper presented at a meeting of the American Orthopsychiatric Association in 1954, individuals come to therapy groups for help with emotional difficulties in any aspect of their functioning; parents come to parent therapy groups because of emotional disturbances in the special area of their parent-child relationships. Thus the material brought out in a parent therapy session deals only with this particular aspect of their life problems. Although parent therapy groups have this special, limited focus, they follow the procedures of group therapy in other respects.)

Once assembled, the two types of groups focus on different aspects of the parents' concerns. Parent group education, as we have said, brings out material from their everyday experience with their families, looking at the reality factors they represent and the problems they pose. An attempt is made to examine some of the causes of the behavior they are reporting, the situations that preceded it, the episodes that may have precipitated it, and the attitudes that accompany it, both in the children and the parents themselves. Where the parents of their own accord (or sparked by comments of other parents) reveal significant experiences in their past, these are accepted as illuminating the sources of their own ideas and attitudes. But no attempt is made to explore the forgotten or unconscious material, which is an important aspect of therapeutic sessions.

There is another subtle difference. In parent group education, the "history" of the behavior reported by one parent is explored only sufficiently to get a picture of what it may mean; this information is then used as a frame of reference for similar or different reports and reactions from other parents. The picture thus becomes a broader one, against which all parents can begin to see themselves and their children and learn from the comparison. In parent group therapy the focus is on a more thorough working through of one person's problems, in relation to factors in his earlier experience of which he may not now be aware, but which are revealed in his present conflicts or in his relation to the leader and the other group members. The exploration and solution of his problem are also expected to throw light on the problems of other group members, and stimulate in them other ideas, reactions, identifications, by association. When these are brought out they, too, are worked through in ways that are not possible or appropriate in parent group education.

*   *   *   *   *

These then are some important types of group programs in which parents take part. They are being carried on with increasing self-scrutiny and attempts at evaluation. They are being reported and discussed at professional meetings and in journals with an awareness of fine points of purpose and procedure that can only be suggested here. Where concepts and experiences have been shared with others whose programs had different goals and practices, the discussions have been challenging and productive. Out of this exchange, as in parent groups, leaders and the agencies they represent have found their thinking sharpened. Sometimes they have found that in describing their work it became more clear even to themselves and took on new stature and validity. Sometimes they have been challenged to try new, more flexible procedures. In any case, they have come away with a better picture of the relation of their program to those of others and a greater appreciation of the many ways in which professional persons are experimenting to make the group process an effective instrument of learning for parents.

V

Planning and Organizing
Parent Group Programs

Experience has shown that group educational programs for parents, like other thoughtful and sound service programs, require careful planning if they are to be successful. It is not enough for a few people to decide that it would be a good idea to offer programs for parent groups and then expect to have parents appear in answer to a public announcement. Even though many parents are interested in finding out more about themselves and their children, there are potential blocks that stand between this interest and their actual enrollment in a group. First, there are the many conflicting interests and demands of their everyday lives, even for those mothers who are not working. Can they be expected suddenly to find a period of an hour and a half or so a week to devote to this project? Do they not need some advance notice so that they can plan their days accordingly? Second, parents are skeptical of a new service and need to know just what it can offer them before they are willing to commit themselves. For those mothers who are carrying a heavy work load, these issues become even more real.

Much work has to be done in any community to lay the groundwork for such a program. It takes thorough and intensive planning, over a considerable period of time, with key people in the community—PTA officers, church leaders, committees of many sorts—and other professional persons in different agencies and organizations. For the encouragement of the practitioner, however, it can be said that once a program is initiated and has had some measure of success, the word spreads through the community. Planning and organization of groups become easier as parents begin to know about them and recognize what they can accomplish.

PLANNING FOR THE GROUPS

Assessing the Need

Since parent group education is predicated on meeting the particular needs of the parents who attend, it is important that there are parents in the community who actively want such a program so that, by bringing the parents and the program together, the interaction can begin. As a first step, one must judge as best one can just which parents in the community can be expected to respond to the idea of a parent group program. If such a project is just being initiated it is important to determine the following:

1. Have there been any requests for parent groups or parent meetings? This may mean contacting a large number of groups or at least the ones that seem most logical and strategic. Requests may have come in to schools, and especially to the PTAs, day-care centers, churches, neighborhood centers, family or social agencies, health centers, hospital services, welfare departments, housing projects, parent organizations concerned with special disabilities, and other community groups.

If there has been some interest, it should be explored further and capitalized on. On the other hand, if parents have shown no interest, this does not necessarily mean that the parents do not want educational activities. They may not have thought of such a possibility or they may not have known how to go about asking for them. They may be glad to join if they learn about a program and if it seems to meet their needs.

2. What other programs are currently being offered in the community? One needs to know about them in some detail—their auspices, purposes, the approach they will use (such as lecture or discussion), the qualifications and experience of the leaders, and the particular part of the parent population from which they will draw.

It is also important to know something about the response that is being shown to these programs. If the programs already in operation are similar to those being planned, the sponsoring group will have to decide whether the community can absorb additional educational services. If the programs are different, consideration will have to be given to whether they are drawing from other sources in the community and whether there are likely to be enough parents available who may be expected to respond to the *new* program. In this rather complicated situation, all those who are involved in these services must, of course, know clearly the differences in the various approaches.

Expectant parent groups, for example, have been well received even in communities that have already had more formal classes for expectant

mothers and fathers. Both approaches have very much the same end goals in mind: to prepare young people for their coming parenthood and to help them understand and cope with the physical, emotional and personal-social changes that accompany it. But their emphases are different, as are their methods. The more formal classes, which are usually in the form of lectures with question and answer periods, tend to stress the facts of pregnancy, labor and delivery, and the care of the new baby. Parent group education, through the use of guided discussion, gives these young people factual information, as they need it, and stresses its personal meaning for them, as it applies to their current situations and their thinking ahead for the future. In most communities, there is room enough for both kinds of learning opportunities.

3. What has been the history of parent group programs in the past? What kinds have been tried and with what success? Success is difficult to evaluate, of course, because of the many intangible variables that enter into the experience, such as the public impression of the sponsoring agency —its "public image," in other words; the effect on the group of the particular leaders; and the ever-unpredictable chance make-up of the group itself. If past experience has been favorable, there is more encouragement to begin. If the experience has not been successful, one must remember that parents present a constantly fluctuating source of recruitment, and that there is always a new group which might be exposed to the educational experience. Moreover, a new program, when it is well planned and carefully interpreted, may have great appeal. Skillfully carried out, it can be meaningful not only to those who come to parent education fresh, but also to those who may not have been satisfied with an earlier program. The important thing is that they come to recognize that this program will give them something they will find helpful.

Working Cooperatively with Other Organizations and Agencies

No matter under what auspices the parent program will be held, it is best to work with other groups that have direct contact with families, contacts that may be different and that may reach into other segments of the neighborhood. Contacts with community groups such as those already mentioned are essential in order to assess the need of the community properly and to judge something of its climate. In the original contacts with these organizations, one has an opportunity to build up a cooperative relationship that can benefit both sides. At the outset it is particularly important to interpret the program clearly to other organizations. The agencies or organizations considered most strategic in the area must know what kind of program is being planned, for they are actually being asked for their endorsement. They must have some appreciation of the potential

values of such a project. They must feel that in helping to make such a program available to the families they serve and in reaching out to families they may not have served before, they are contributing to the mental health of the community in a way that will bring credit to their agencies as well as to the one responsible for the project.

The understanding and support of key agencies or individuals are particularly important in work with expectant parents which is usually, though not always, given under medical auspices and therefore needs the endorsement and cooperation of local medical societies or representative obstetricians or general practitioners in the community. In a number of instances, nurses who were initiating these new programs have had to overcome considerable resistance from medical people who were not at first convinced of the value of this approach. They were hesitant about endorsing new programs until they understood their nature, purposes, and methods and were assured of the professional competence of the leaders. In most cases, the nurses were able to interpret their project satisfactorily and sometimes gained not only the necessary medical support but also active encouragement and help in recruiting patients for the new groups.

Agencies can be asked to cooperate in many different ways and usually respond. Even if they seem to be skeptical, they are usually prepared to listen and to find out more about what you are offering. Not only can they be helpful in evaluating the needs of the community, but they can also help in the organization of parent groups, if this seems advisable. Sometimes it may be appropriate to have them take greater responsibility and actively sponsor a new program or share the sponsorship. In any cooperative effort, the respective roles of the cooperating groups or individuals must be defined so that each takes on the responsibility appropriate to his role without duplication.

Involving the Parents

Even in the preplanning stage, it has been found effective to involve the parents themselves either informally or in a somewhat more organized way. For many years the Child Study Association of America has recommended that committees of parents be set up to help in the planning and to cooperate at every stage of the project.[1] Throughout the country and especially in the new antipoverty programs, increasing emphasis is currently being placed on using participants of programs to help in their organization. Parents who help to interpret the program and bring word of it to their neighbors serve as a kind of intermediary between the profes-

[1] For this and other suggestions, see Gertrude Goller, *When Parents Get Together: How to Organize a Parent Education Program,* Child Study Association of America, New York, 1955; revised edition, 1964.

sional workers, who plan and administer the project and lead the groups, and the lay public, who are to be group members. The presence of these parents as program aides or neighborhood representatives helps to break down the natural feeling of social distance that often exists on both sides. They are a connecting bridge, as it were, which also helps to dispel the parents' distrust of something new and therefore unknown. They bring the program closer to home, and, in a sense, give real substance to the idea that the program is to be *theirs* (the parents'), set up to serve *them* as they see the need.

Small committees selected from parents who are to be reached seem to be most effective when they include one or two key people who are recognized for their leadership qualities in the groups in which they live. It is essential, however, to balance their contribution with those of other parents who may not have stood out in their neighborhoods but who represent a large segment of the community. Mobilizing the interest and developing the involvement of parents from the beginning can be helpful not only in establishing general procedures but in testing some of the details of the plan as it develops. For example, what are the most favorable hours for holding the meetings, the type of meeting place that seems most acceptable, and the age interest which seems to have the greatest appeal for these parents: preschool? school-age? adolescents?

Coming to a Decision

It may seem odd to ask at this point if the agency is sure that what it wants to offer is a program of parent group education. And yet, it is important that the decision to set up such a project be made carefully, that the climate of the community be at least hopeful, and that the leader and the agency be clear that they wish to put their energies into this channel. Programs of this kind usually take more time and energy in the planning and organization stages than one would expect, and still more time in conducting the groups themselves. The hours spent in the meetings are only the beginning. Leaders must also have a chance to prepare thoughtfully for each session by reviewing what the group has discussed up to that point; they need time afterwards to make some records of what transpired, evaluating for themselves what was accomplished and what remained to be picked up and developed. These factors must be taken into account before a program can be entered on with confidence that it will succeed.

After the community has been evaluated and the decision reached to offer a program of parent discussion groups, those who set up the project must have conviction as to its value for those who come. It is not likely to succeed if it is offered as a "second best" project, set up in order to save time by reaching a large group all at once.

The leader should also feel reasonably competent to conduct a discussion group. If he does not, he should try to supplement his knowledge of subject areas and of the skills of group discussion for parents, so that he will become more effective. Above all, he should be willing to experiment thoughtfully, to learn from his mistakes, or (since there really are no black and white "mistakes") to find better ways of accomplishing the purposes he has in mind.

He must recognize that to take on a program of this kind will call on all his resources. He will find it demanding, but he will also find it rewarding and worth all the effort he has put into it.

In coming to a decision, the following points must be considered:

WHAT IS THE REAL PURPOSE FOR THE GROUP? Is it to provide an educational experience on a broad basis for parents or expectant parents, with the ultimate goal of prevention of future difficulties? Or will the group be used for early case-finding of the beginnings of problem behavior, again on a broad community basis? Or will it have both goals? In either case, the educational procedures for the group would be the same. Or will the group be set up as an educational service for clients of the agency—possibly a family agency or a mental health clinic—who are waiting to be seen? If so, the organization must expect that parents will come with problems of which they are probably quite aware. Even this group can be carried on toward educational goals provided the leader is prepared for the material that may be presented and chooses to help these parents through a group educational approach.

In one experience of this kind, a public health nurse offered a parent discussion group with educational goals to parents on the waiting list of a mental health clinic for children. Although, as she had anticipated, the problems the parents presented were rather acute, many other concerns they brought up seemed to parallel those of parents whose children had not presented severe problems. She was able to direct the discussion in such a way that both types of concerns were explored in appropriate ways. In a few instances, it became clear that the problems were beyond the usual scope of a group of this kind; these parents, however, realized that their problems were more specialized and more intense and were prepared to turn to the therapeutic services of the clinic for further exploration of them. In the meantime, however, they gained a great deal of general understanding of their children, of the interplay between the various members of the family, and what they could do to facilitate their children's growth.

Caseworkers from family and/or children's agencies who have also offered groups to parents of families on their waiting lists have had similar experiences. In both situations, the leaders—and the parents—knew that additional services would subsequently be available to help them with their more severe and persistent problems.

TO WHAT SEGMENT OF THE POPULATION IS THE GROUP TO BE OFFERED? Is the program to be open to whoever applies in response to a general announcement? Or is it to be limited to people who are served in a specialized program, such as the parents of children in a neighborhood house, expectant parents who are enrolled in a health clinic for prenatal care, parents of children in a day-care center or in certain grades of a public school, parents from a particular religious affiliation, parents of a children's health or rehabilitation agency, or others?

There are no fixed rules by which to make these decisions. They must be made on the basis of agency policy and what seems to be most helpful for the community. At the Child Study Association of America we have seen a variety of patterns developing. For example, some groups for expectant parents in health centers of public health agencies have drawn primarily from the group registered there for prenatal care; members have also been accepted from the larger community who heard about the group in one way or another. Similarly, parents of retarded children, who were members of a local Association for the Help of Retarded Children that sponsored a group, have met with parents who were not affiliated with the organization but also had retarded children. (Sometimes agencies in this field are glad to open their groups to nonmembers, hoping to find more parents in similar situations who will later join the sponsoring group.)

A question that comes up occasionally is that of voluntary versus compulsory attendance. This is particularly important where the group is seen as an essential part of a total plan of care for the family of the children involved. This might be in a day-care center or a nursery school or in connection with a rehabilitation clinic offering health care and supervision to children with a special disability, such as muscular dystrophy or cerebral palsy. Sometimes the children are not accepted for the service unless the parents understand that they are expected to attend parent meetings. We have known of only a few cases, however, in which such parent meetings took the form of a series of discussion sessions as these are discussed in this book. Usually the meetings are large, informational sessions held at fairly long intervals. Where parents accept the parent education aspects of the total service as routine, there is usually no problem about their attending. Where, however, they feel they are put under pressure to attend and resent this, their resentment may block the freedom of their participation. If this occurs, the situation will need to be faced either in the group or individually with a parent, so that the feelings can be brought out and worked through.

Occasionally there are programs in which parents are forced to come because of ominous situations. For example, a group was provided, without choice, for parents of boys and girls who had appeared in children's court for a variety of offenses. The project was reported to be educational in its goals, to help the parents gain a better understanding of some of the forces that lead children into troublesome and even delinquent behavior. It was distinctly not directed toward individual problem-solving or therapy. The feature of compulsory attendance raised considerable question among those who first heard about this project, but the report indicated that the parents were helped to express their feelings about being forced to come (under penalty of further action by the judge and/or the probation officer) and, once past this hurdle, seemed to be able to use the group quite effectively.

Such experiences raise a new question. Are we too concerned about the compulsory nature of attendance in some settings at the present stage of parent group education? Is it not possible that in time group educational programs for parents will be built into many services as part of a program of total care? It is conceivable that all expectant mothers who register at a public health center for prenatal care might be told that they are to come to expectant parent groups, either for mothers in the afternoon or couples in the evening, and that they will accept this procedure quite easily. They may even be pleased that it is being offered to them. Similarly, parents of children attending a day-care center may well accept the fact that they are to come to parent meetings, if it is expected of them—even though it may be something of a burden.

THE SPECIFIC PLAN AND STRUCTURE

The Meetings

It is best to approach the community or a specific parent group with a definite plan, including the number of meetings, the spacing, the time at which they will be held, and the place. If the original notice or invitation is too vague, much time is lost and the parents may feel lukewarm about a plan whose details they do not yet know. How can they decide whether they will come unless they know where the meetings will be held, how often, at what time, and so on? Accordingly, then, in arranging these details it is well to involve the parents' committee, if there is one, and others who know the realities of the lives of the people who are to be reached. There can, however, be some flexibility in changing some details of the arrangements if the group wants to, and if they agree to the new plan after they meet.

Experience has shown that a successful program of parent group education usually requires a series of somewhere between eight and twelve meetings, preferably at weekly intervals. For some parents this may appear to be a heavy commitment. This is so particularly in lower-income groups where many parents are primarily "present-oriented," as the sociologists say. Because they are preoccupied with their urgent and immediate problems and heavily caught up in the daily struggle for economic survival, they find it difficult to think ahead or commit themselves for the future.

Even for parents with wider educational experience, who are used to programs that run for fifteen sessions in academic institutions, eight to twelve sessions sometimes seems a long span of time for which to commit themselves. Many communities report they find it hard to get parents to attend even six sessions. On the other hand, there is growing evidence that parents accept the idea of a long series with little difficulty when they understand the reasons for meeting over a period of time, and begin to appreciate the special quality of continuous discussion that builds up from week to week. (Sometimes they even want a group to continue beyond the period that was originally planned.) If a longer period of time is considered essential by those who plan the program and is offered without apology, parents are apt to accept it, if they are interested in coming in the first place.

Sometimes parents say it is difficult for them to arrange to come every week, but this has often been found to be a preconceived notion that is not necessarily valid. Granted there are periods in the lives of parents of very young children when their frequent colds and other diseases keep them—and their parents—at home. In times of epidemics of measles, flu, and the like, parents will be absent, of course. But barring such difficulties, parents do learn to accommodate themselves to a weekly plan and leaders are often surprised at the lengths to which they will go to be sure that they can attend.

If programs are held only every other week, both the leaders and the parents find that the development of the group discussion moves more slowly. The beginning of each session tends to lag, as parents try to get themselves back into the mood of two weeks ago; so much has happened since then that the train of thought is often broken, even for those who have been able to attend regularly. For those who, for any reason, have to be absent from one meeting, the interval becomes a month, and the distance from the earlier discussions is even more marked. Groups that meet weekly seem to move ahead at a good pace from week to week. The days in between give parents time to think over what has been discussed and try out different ways of handling situations at home. They report these developments with a freshness that adds momentum to the weekly sessions.

To meet the needs of expectant parents who register for groups in late pregnancy, some programs, particularly those carried on by the American

Red Cross, are offered on a twice-a-week basis. This adds to the intensity of the experience, sometimes providing a quality almost of breathlessness, as the expectant parents try earnestly to cover all the questions and issues they have in their minds before they go to the hospital. Some leaders prefer this scheduling, saying that the intensity spurs the group's learning. Others, however, feel that there is an advantage in spreading the learning process over a longer period of time, so that the participants get a better understanding of themselves at various points in the pregnancy, and of the different ways they may react as they move through the three trimesters. Obviously, though, when faced with an impending "due date," there is little choice except to offer a speeded-up program.

The length of meetings is usually one and one-half hours, although in some instances, such as in groups for expectant parents, sessions are scheduled for two hours. The period of ninety minutes has been arrived at on the basis of considerable experience. Although no sessions ever seem long enough, the ninety-minute period seems to be short enough for parents to participate without getting tired or restless, and long enough to develop the material to a considerable extent. Leaders who have experimented with shorter sessions, as is done occasionally in public schools when parents come during their children's school hours, find that an hour is sometimes frustrating. It takes a short while for the group to "warm up" and to clarify what they want to talk about; minutes fly by so quickly that at the end of an hour not much has been accomplished. There has been little opportunity for the parents to develop the discussion to the point where they have something to take home with them, think about, and experiment with.

The pattern of time scheduling for group programs varies according to the other demands on the lives of the parents who come. For mothers who are at home, either because they do not need or choose to work or because they are on public assistance, it is quite reasonable to hold mothers' meetings during the school hours of their children. For those who are working a full day, meetings will naturally have to be held in the evening. In some instances this presents an acute problem, since many parents are tired at the end of the day and do not find it easy to leave their homes with unfinished chores to come to a parent meeting. Groups have been held at different times to try to solve these problems. For example, in day-care centers groups have been held at the end of the afternoon, sometimes with an inexpensive supper and a supervised playroom for the children. Thus the parents who come to the center anyway to pick up their children can stay for the meeting and still get home early. Other programs are offered in the evening, in the expectation that they will be meaningful enough to stir the parents to come, in spite of their fatigue.

The scheduling of the meetings affects one very significant aspect of the parent education movement: that of offering programs that fathers as well as mothers will attend. We recognize that the pattern throughout the United States today is largely that of expecting mothers to attend discussion groups, since they are primarily responsible for the care of the children. In recent years, however, this pattern has been changing. Many fathers are taking a more active part in PTA organizations as well as in parent groups that have been formed around special disabilities of children. These fathers are actively involved in the care of their children and the services that are available for their education. A marked shift in the response of fathers has also been seen in the expectant parent field. Spurred on partly by the stress on the fathers' presence and support during their wives' labor, which has been emphasized by the natural childbirth movement and similar philosophies, the old attitude that "it's the mother's job" seems to be breaking down.

So we see young fathers not only participating in the care of their new babies but also becoming vitally involved in discussions in couples' classes in hospitals and health centers throughout the country. This trend must, of course, be taken into account in setting the time for the group sessions. More groups will have to be set up in the evenings, when leaders are already tired, especially if they are adding group leadership to a full professional commitment. This means that such leaders must be relieved of time during the day so they can be fresh to do a good job in parent group education. The advantages of a shift of this kind are enormous. Evening programs show fathers that they are not only accepted but wanted. This attitude increases their recognition of their own role in the family and adds an important dimension to the group discussions they attend.

The choice of a place for the meeting is also extremely important. The building and the room should represent to parents an atmosphere of friendly acceptance, of a place committed to service. Whether the meeting is in a school, a neighborhood center, a health center, a church, or a housing project, it is important that those responsible for the building and the services it provides contribute to the feeling that the public (in this case the parents) are wanted. If there is a comfortable meeting room in the building, it is to be hoped that this will be made available. On the other hand, groups that have met practically in the boiler rooms of health centers, in most uncomfortable physical surroundings, have still been productive and educationally valuable because of the atmosphere provided by the agency that sponsored the group and by the leader. It is surely better, however, not to have to work against the physical odds of unsatisfactory chairs, crowded rooms, lack of privacy, competing noise (as in one group which met in a school anteroom adjacent to a gymnasium where basketball practice was held every evening), and all of the other environmental factors that can create discomfort.

Ideally, then, the group should be held in a building whose sponsorship presents no threat to the community but rather is identified with a general service of some kind. Wherever possible, the meeting should be held in a room where there will be no interruptions; the chairs that are provided should be movable rather than stationary and placed comfortably in a circle or a square, preferably around a table. The room should be adequately heated and ventilated and have toilet facilities nearby. All these arrangements are actually minimal for the group's comfort.

The Size of the Group

For a rich sharing of experience, the group should be neither too large nor too small. It should be small enough to permit each parent to have his say when he wants to, and yet large enough to provide a variety of experience from many homes. Some leaders prefer a group of from ten to fifteen members; others feel more comfortable with a slightly larger group, although they recognize that it imposes greater problems for the leader and the group if all members are to share in the discussion.

Usually some parents drop out between registration and the first meeting, so it is best to enroll a larger number to make reasonably certain that there will be a group of the desired size. In practice, leaders often enroll as many as twenty or twenty-two in a group, and even more if the program is new to the community. Where the group is for couples, registration can well be larger, since the total represents only half as many families. Couples tend to function as pairs, with one member taking the initiative for the family, particularly in the opening sessions. In addition, the absence of one couple makes a larger gap in the group membership than when only one parent stays away. The size of a particular group, however, should be determined not only by the composition of the parent-members but by the purposes for which it meets, modified to suit the leader's preference for the group size with which he feels most comfortable.

Subject Area

Parent groups are usually set up for parents of children of specific age periods, such as infancy through two, preschool years, school years, early adolescence, later adolescence, or college age. The choice of age area depends on the agency's estimate of the period of development that will be of special interest in the community. This focus is generally advisable because parents seem to identify with one another more readily and share their experiences more freely when their children are of the same age and present similar problems as they meet the developmental phases of growth. This is as true in an overcrowded low-income section of a big city as in a suburban area with a middle-class population.

And yet even this prescription need not be followed, if, in the judgment of those planning the groups, it seems best to do otherwise. Groups have been held for parents of children of a wide age range. One such group, meeting in the parish house of the church in a small eastern city and led by a caseworker, was offered to parents of children from infancy through adolescence—any parents who were generally concerned about how best to help their children. This group was not easy for the leader, for he had to help the group come to universal problems of child development and the parent-child relationships that underlie all age periods. As it developed, the emphasis was largely on parental expectations and attitudes rather than the specific problems of children in their homes, although these too had to be included to make the issues vivid and real. There was almost a dividing line between the parents who had very young children and those parents who had adolescent boys and girls nearly as old as the young parents, many of whom looked like adolescents themselves. At first, the older parents took over and the younger ones listened, but as the sessions progressed, the older parents began to listen and respect the contributions of the younger group members, who then became more confident in speaking out. Because the process in such groups is slower and calls for greater skill on the part of the leader, these plans are not usually attempted except under very special circumstances.

One such circumstance is that involving parents of children with special disabilities. Here again it takes the group a little time to get to know one another and to work well together but, in general, parents of children with handicapping conditions identify with one another from the start. As a result, they tend to get into deeper areas of personal concern more quickly than other groups, no matter what the differences in the ages of the parents and of their children. Furthermore, the interchange is extremely valuable. For example, parents who have lived for sixteen or eighteen years with children with muscular dystrophy have much to offer younger parents in experience and an attitude toward these children which they have evolved over a period of years. Although younger parents do not have as much to contribute to the older ones, their attitudes and questions are sometimes extremely meaningful, and often challenge the older ones to a new way of looking at themselves. There is no doubt that the wide sweep of reported happenings adds a perspective to the group discussion and gives the basis for general concepts that can make the group experience significant for all.

Facilitating Continuous Attendance

Many of the methods that make it possible for parents to come to a first meeting have to be carried on throughout the series of meetings as well. They, too, take preplanning and a thoughtful staffing of services, if they are to be effective. This is particularly true in relation to providing facilities or supervised playrooms for the children of the parents who come. This is a service that seems to be most needed, since without it parents are often unable to leave their homes.

Setting up playrooms for temporary baby and child care, however, presents some realistic problems. First, there is the question of staffing. Often agencies draw on volunteers for activities of this kind, but taking care of small children, especially if they are not walking yet, takes strong arms and a good back. In adjusting to being separated from their parents in this way, small children often need a great deal of individual attention and comforting. The setting should also allow for their being able to go to their mothers in the meeting, if they need to. Often they only want to see where their mothers are, and soon are able to go back to the playroom. Volunteers are usually not prepared to take care of young children under these circumstances and need the supervision and help of a trained person. Sometimes a volunteer is available who has had special training in early childhood education, nursing, or some other aspect of child care and who can take over the responsibility of the playroom service. In any case, it is advisable to have an experienced person in charge, not only to safeguard the well-being of the babies and children, but also to protect the agency from any criticism should some untoward situation develop. Obviously, these problems do not come up in the same way in connection with parent education programs in cooperative nursery schools. There the meetings are often held while the children's program is in operation.

Besides having a suitable room with accessible toilets, play and child care services call for well selected play materials at various age levels, story books with many pictures, and some provision for the inevitable nourishment that quiets children while it gives them additional food intake. As in day-care centers or nursery schools, playrooms frequently provide juice served in paper cups. For this, of course, one should have the approval of the parents to avoid offering a child something to which he may be allergic.

The running of such playrooms poses a further problem in relation to the mothers and fathers. Are the people running this service able to interpret to parents the behavior of their children, without either threatening them or antagonizing them? To what extent should playroom personnel share with the parents and the leader the experiences they are having with the children during the meetings? And what use should the leader make of the information that is given him?

In general, experience has shown that it is artificial to prohibit communication between playroom staff and parents. There is and should be a friendly, limited flow of relevant information about the child's behavior in the immediate situation or just before it, as there is in a nursery school or day-care center. This takes place naturally when the children come and when they leave. But these children come to the playroom for a short period of time, usually only once a week, and their relation to the project is as an accommodation, to make it possible for the parents to attend. While the children may gain from being with other children and a new friendly adult, this is not the main purpose of their coming. If it were, this service would have to be set up on a different basis. Wherever possible, exchange of important information should be made by and to a trained person who is competent to interpret to parents the meaning of their children's behavior and what this may require of them in handling it. Similarly, any acute episode should be shared with the leader. However, he does not bring into the group information given him by the playroom staff. If the parent chooses to make a situation known to the group, the leader can feel comfortable about having the group respond to it. For the leader to introduce it would be a violation of confidence from one professional person to another. To expose a child, or his parent, without the parent's consent might well make him uneasy. It could be taken by the parent as an invasion of his privacy, and might create tensions in the other members as well.

In some communities, attempts have been made to send baby-sitters into the homes of children who may be either too young or unable to come to a playroom for other reasons. This plan is helpful during evening meetings when it is usually not advisable to take small children out of their homes. But it also needs careful safeguarding in the choice of the baby-sitters, their maturity and experience, and the neighborhoods into which they are asked to go. Where college students have taken part in such programs as volunteers, they have needed some preparation for unexpected emergencies, both in the behavior of the children they will be caring for and in possible episodes that might threaten their own well-being. Agencies have understandably been reluctant to enter into programs of this kind since these services are most needed in areas where there may be some danger to the volunteers. As an alternate plan, in some groups parents are encouraged to band together for community or neighborhood baby-sitting, possibly on a rotating basis, in which the parents who live in the same house or nearby bring a few children together for one parent to supervise while the others attend the meeting.

ORGANIZING THE GROUPS

Interpreting the Program

Interpreting a new program is a continuous process. It starts at the moment of assessing the need, continues through the period of planning, and becomes even more vital when an attempt is made to explain to the community at large and to the particular target parent group just what they may expect. The essential facts to be presented are the same, whether to the parents themselves or to colleagues who may help in recruiting the groups or to the board and staff members of a cooperating agency. They may, however, be given in more or less detail and in somewhat different language. In any case, it is important to have a simple, direct formulation which stresses the essential nature of the group experience.

Each leader will formulate his interpretation in his own way. But a statement along the following lines may be helpful as a start. "In these groups, parents share with one another their everyday experiences in raising their children and discuss their questions, their concerns, and the problems that confront them. In the group, they gain further knowledge and understanding of their relationships with their children and work out ways of meeting their family situations to their better satisfaction."

Statements such as this can be adapted to the purposes of groups of expectant parents or parents of children with handicapping conditions or of children in other specific circumstances. It must be made clear by implication, if not directly, that this is not the usual kind of classroom experience in which an authority or teacher-expert brings them words of wisdom and tells them what to do. Suggesting that the group will take up the everyday situations parents are dealing with takes the project away from the idea of a classroom and indicates at the same time that the discussion will be closely related to the parents' current thinking and needs. It also assures them that the discussion will have meaning for all the parents who come, and that it will not be oriented to severe or special problems, though these will not be excluded. The statement also makes it clear that the subject matter to be discussed will not be in categories or generalizations but in terms of the live experiences of the parents participating, and will include many aspects of parenthood, child development, and parent-child relations. It suggests also that there will be participation among the group members, not as a required part of the experience, but so that the members and the leader may understand the problems on which they need help, and also so that the members may contribute to each other's learning, under the leader's guidance. Obviously, an interpretation can only give a general picture of what is going to happen. The words may not have much meaning. They come to life with the experience itself.

Along with the general introductory statement, the interpretation must, of course, include specific information regarding the content area which will be the focus of the group (preparation for parenthood, or the particular age period that is decided upon, for example), sponsorship, leader, and details of time, place, and so on. Here again the details will show that the organizing group is aware of the real situations of the prospective group members. Setting the meetings during school hours recognizes that these parents may be more free at that time than at others. Evening sessions, as we have already suggested, open the way for mothers and fathers to come, if it is intended that fathers are to be an important part of the enrolling group.

Avenues of Publicity for Recruitment

The methods you will use to tell your potential "consumer" of the plans for the group will vary according to the nature of your community and the avenues of communication that seem to be effective there. We can only suggest here some of the more usual channels that have been found to be useful.

GENERAL ANNOUNCEMENTS. To reach the general public on an unselected basis, it is well to use all the usual channels of public information—newspaper publicity, spot announcements on local radio or television stations, and general announcements or releases to community agencies and institutions that reach into all levels of the population. Churches and synagogues can be very helpful in spreading general information about educational projects.

LETTERS OF INVITATION. To supplement the general announcements, many organizations or groups sponsoring parent programs send letters of invitation to possible applicants, concentrating on those for whom the programs are felt to be particularly appropriate. Parents of children in certain grades of elementary, junior high, or high school, for example, are often invited in a special letter. Here, guidance counselors and other school personnel are particularly helpful. They should be involved in the project long before the letters are sent out so they can help draw up the plans, determine which parents are to receive the invitations, the age content, the timing of the meetings, and the particular problems of the parents and the neighborhood which should be taken into account. The school personnel can be extremely helpful in maintaining a continuing attendance; their follow-up "reminder" notices, and even sometimes personal contacts, are most effective.

In sending out invitations, an interesting question arises: how are they best delivered? Few school organizations have money to spend on postage, so they are inclined to distribute the letters to the classrooms for the children to take home to their parents. The results in certain communities, however, have been disappointing. Often the letters never get to the parents. Children lose them on the way or leave them in their desks. Letters are often mislaid even in their homes and parents frequently say they never received any announcements. Where possible, therefore, it is better to use the mails, if the agency can afford the postage.

Invitations have proven to be more effective in settings where the feeling of urgency may be somewhat more acute. In planning for expectant parent classes, for example, parents registered for prenatal care in a hospital or public health clinic are more apt to respond to an invitation sent through the mail, though this often needs to be reinforced by some personal discussion of the plan. Parents of children with special disabilities, such as mental retardation or cerebral palsy, respond in varying degrees to invitations, depending on what other programs have been offered them and their readiness to participate in a group educational experience. In general, it seems that educational programs identified with a specific service to the parent or to the children have a better chance of success. Parents who feel close to or dependent on such services generally respond to an announcement or invitation if it reaches them.

Many questions have been raised as to the number of invitations that should be sent out in order to achieve an enrollment of from fifteen to twenty. One can give no specific figure, but it is safe to say that when a program is beginning fresh in the community, one must contact many times more parents than one would anticipate, in order to have sufficient enrollment for a first group. The exact ratio of invitations to registrants is a matter that needs much further experimentation.

DIRECT INTERPRETATION. Direct interpretation of the program to parents can be carried on at many different levels and in many settings. Plans for a parent discussion group can be introduced at a formal meeting of parents in a school or day-care center, in a rehabilitation agency, or wherever. It is worth the time for the leader or one of his colleagues to interpret the program at any gathering to which parents may come, knowing, of course, that in a large group only relatively few may be interested. Nevertheless, having the project described to them briefly, with some feeling of warmth and conviction, brings it to their attention in a personal way and accomplishes what the printed word cannot do.

In addition, special "one-shot" meetings are often set up especially to interest parents and pave the way for group programs that will meet for a series of sessions. In one low-income housing project in a midwestern city, plans for a large introductory meeting were worked on for months by the staff of the agency offering the program, together with the staff of the housing project. All the usual avenues of communication were used to reach the parents—notices in the mail-boxes, posters, and so forth—plus a dramatic parade on the evening of the meeting, in which the local parents' committee and their children marched through the project with drums, literally "drumming up business." Six hundred people came to the meeting, and out of it an active group program developed in which four groups are being held almost continuously.

INFORMAL CONTACTS. An even more productive method may be informal contacts. A personal conversation with an expectant parent, or parent of a four-year-old in a day-care center, or parents of a child coming to an orthopedic clinic, can point out the values of meeting with other parents. Usually these contacts can take place in the course of a parent's visit to the institution or agency, such as when the parent picks up a child at the end of a long day in a day-care center, or when a parent brings his boy or girl to a clinic for treatment.

Increasingly, however, those who are interested in developing new programs are seeing the need for a more active kind of parent contact, not waiting for them to come but going into their homes or communities on an organized basis, to reach them where they are and show them that the program can be of help to them in their immediate lives, if they care to make use of it. This can be done by those who are organizing the program or, as we have seen, by involving other people or agencies in close contact with parents for interpretation or recruitment.[2] Particularly in areas where parents are not accustomed to educational programs—in low-income neighborhoods, public housing projects, and crowded slum areas—it has been found effective to tell them about the program in personal conversations in their homes. Sometimes this can be done on a casual basis, in connection with professional visits for other purposes. A public health nurse on a home visit for any reason will often find expectant mothers or mothers of young children who have never heard of groups in which they might take part. They can talk together about the program to see if it is something they might be interested in and whether they have concerns that might be met and eased off in the group. But it takes more than these chance contacts for recruitment to be effective. In the more depressed areas of cities or in rural sections, workers must knock on doors, many doors, aggressively seeking parents who need to be encouraged to come. Here recruitment is not easy, and agencies are creatively trying out many new ways of reaching parents they have not succeeded in reaching before.

A visit to interpret the program has to be handled without pressure so that the parents are left feeling free to come or not. The atmosphere must be friendly without being overly so. While the person who makes the home visit must be enthusiastic and convinced that the project has merit, he must be careful not to have his sense of urgency show. Some workers have found they are more effective if they use the visit not to "sell" themselves or their program, but rather to introduce the parents to something they honestly believe will be of value to them. In the process, they get to know the parents, have a chance to answer some of their questions about

[2] See Carl A. Scott, Report I in *Recruiting Low-Income Families for Family Life Education Programs*, Child Study Association of America, New York, 1965.

the project and, in some instances, help them overcome some of their hesitation about joining. The establishment of even a brief relationship of this kind often makes it easier for parents to take what is for them an unprecedented step.

It must be remembered, however, that parents who say they will join a new project in a personal contact either at home or within the walls of an agency, may not actually do so. There are a variety of reasons why they may say they are planning to come. Sometimes they do so to please the visitor and make up to him for his time and effort. Sometimes they really mean to come but do not anticipate some of the real circumstances which may keep them from doing so. They may even say they are coming in order to get rid of their visitor! In any case, the strength of their commitment is often uncertain—even to themselves—and neither they nor the leader can be sure until they actually appear at the first meeting. For this reason, leaders and those who helped with the planning always have some anxiety before the beginning of a program. How many people will come? Will there be anyone to take part in the project? How can we know?

Out of experience, one can only say that there are many surprises. Occasionally leaders who expect a very small group find themselves swamped with a large attendance, larger than they can handle, sometimes necessitating that they divide the group into two. On the other hand, there may be some disappointing times when only a few people come to a first meeting. This may mean extending the period of registration and recruitment and perhaps suggesting that those who have come ask friends and neighbors to join the group, too. Other attempts should then be made to reach many more parents, for a larger enrollment.

It is often necessary to have personal conversations with other strategic persons in the community. A conversation with the receptionists or nurses in doctors' offices, for example, may be extremely helpful in organizing an expectant parent group. Even sales people in stores that sell maternity clothes can be helpful. There may be people in the community who have contacts with other parents, too—club leaders of boys and girls or scout troop leaders, for example—who might be glad to tell parents of the children they are working with about the program.

All of these contacts, whether through the mass media, announcements, releases, personal invitations, or personal interviews should include the following information:

Name and Address of sponsoring agency.
Kind of group (a brief description of the objectives of the program and the subject area: age range of the children, period of pregnancy, living with children with handicaps of one sort or another).

Time and place the group will meet.

Length and frequency of each session (usually weekly for one and one-half hours).

Starting date.

Number of sessions (usually eight to twelve but the exact number to be decided in advance).

The fact that *the size of the group will be limited* and that applications will be considered in the order of their receipt.

Method of registration: place and time to register in person, or by phone or registration application to be forwarded by mail.

Registration

The particular method you may choose for registration will be determined by the procedures you and your agency decide will be most appropriate. There are several alternatives, to be used separately or together.

1. A written statement of the parent's intent to join, accompanied by a registration fee if this is part of the plan. This procedure requires a return communication, accepting the registration, usually with a friendly word of pleasure that they are coming and reminding them of the time and place of the first meeting.

2. A brief registration interview with the leader or another person in the agency who is thoroughly familiar with the program. This procedure is not always possible but is recommended. The interview can be carried on in person or over the telephone and provides an opportunity for the interested parent to learn something about the program, to judge whether this is something he is looking for. It also gives the person who is taking the registration an opportunity to evaluate, even if only tentatively, whether the person is making an appropriate application and may be expected to gain from the group. (For a statement of the content of the registration interview for enrollment in parent groups formulated by the Child Study Association of America for participation in its program, see Appendix I.)

The question has often been raised whether applicants who are not parents but who are involved in some other relationship with children should be accepted in parent or expectant parent groups. Occasionally a grandmother (usually the mother of the young mother) may apply in order to gain up-to-date knowledge about child care, especially if she is to be heavily involved in the care of the new baby or the small child. Sometimes the mother's sister may attend, especially if the mother has died and the sister is in charge of the household. Such special circumstances raise the questions of whether persons not in parental roles can gain from a group experience with others who are directly involved as parents, and whether their participation will help or block the progress in the group.

There is no categorical answer to this problem. In general, it is felt that auxiliary persons, not parents, cannot be participating group members in the same way that parents can, since they function in a different role in the family and bring to it different degrees of involvement and a variety of emotional responses. On the other hand, groups have been able to absorb such people as group members, provided they are in some kind of close relationship to the children and provided they and the others in the group understand their role. Their presence does present additional problems for leaders, who want to draw out their contributions and ideas where they are appropriate, but who recognize that their inner feelings about themselves in relation to the children are of necessity very different from those of the parents in the group. Sometimes they maintain an attitude of apparent or real aloofness or objectivity. Sometimes being a parent substitute in a group of true parents may stir up feelings that are more than they can face.

The decision whether or not to include such peripheral people should be made by the leader together with those, in or outside of the agency, who have been helping in the planning and who understand the special problems that their presence may create.

Fees

There is a wide variation in practice about charging a fee for these group educational experiences. Some groups offered by voluntary agencies charge a fee similar to that of an academic institution. Others, feeling committed to a public service, moderate this fee in accordance with what they judge to be the "ability to pay" of their potential group members, sometimes charge no fee or ask only a minimal registration fee. Public agencies usually do not charge any fee at all.

The field of social work has discussed for many years what fee-charging means for the client, and how it should be handled. It has recognized, of course, that beyond the support it gives to the agency's program, it has significant personal meaning. One often hears expressed in any circle the idea that "if you pay for something, you value it more highly." Those who follow this philosophy feel that even a token payment is important, as a sign of commitment from those who attend. They believe it is evidence of their interest, and may be a means of tieing them to the program because they are more likely to stay with something for which they have paid.

Inevitably, the decision whether to charge a fee will be influenced by the usual pattern in the community and the economic status of the parents we want to reach, as well as by the other considerations we have raised.

VI

The Practice of Parent Group Education:
How a Group Begins

ESTABLISHING THE GROUP ATMOSPHERE

When a parent steps through the door for the first meeting, he already has some impression of the program in which he plans to take part. Each parent, however, may have a different impression, depending on how much he absorbed of the description and what aspect of the program appealed to him in the light of his individual experience and personal needs. The impression must have been favorable or he would not have come at all. Nevertheless, parents sometimes only half-understand or even misunderstand what is really being offered, and even those who do have a good picture of what the group will be like may have some reservations about the extent to which it will be helpful to them and about their ability to take part in it.

So, in establishing a climate favorable for learning, the leader has not only to interpret the project again but has to make the interpretation become real. He does this in many ways at once: in words—and they are important; in his manner and the attitudes his manner reveals; and even in the physical arrangements of the meeting place, planned for the parents' comfort and ease in talking with one another and with him. His job is to set up a friendly, positive approach which will enable the parents to comment, to react to one another, to ask questions, and to clarify their thinking as the group progresses. He must establish an environment in which interaction can take place for learning. He must help them understand what they are doing. And he must help them learn how to use the experience. Throughout, he must see that the members feel the group is theirs, no matter what their background and previous experience, and that it is being offered in a spirit of helpfulness, to meet their needs.

THE FIRST MEETING

The Setting

The parents come into a room clearly arranged for a group meeting rather than a lecture, with the chairs placed around a table or in a circle. If there is no large table available it is helpful to have a small one for the leader's notes and records; but there is no question that a table around which the group can sit comfortably becomes more than a place on which to put their ash trays or handbags. It is a symbol of the group process itself.

Enrollment

If the members have already been enrolled, no further mechanics are needed except to check their names against the records. If they are not enrolled they have to fill out whatever registration form is being used.

The degree of detailed information required for registration varies according to the policy and purposes of the sponsoring group. Usually parents are asked to give simple identifying information, such as name, address, telephone number, if they have one, and the number and ages of their children, or the stage of their pregnancy, if it is an expectant parent group. Sometimes, to help in planning for other groups, they are asked to say how they heard about the group.

The information asked for in enrolling—and that not asked for—also contributes to the atmosphere of the group. Parents naturally wonder "Why do they want to know this about me?" They may also wonder who is to use the information they give and how widely it will be known. A request for certain simple and seemingly obvious facts sometimes misfires. Asked to indicate the last year of their own schooling, for example, parents may wonder whether this experience will turn out to be like that of a schoolroom about which they may have unpleasant memories. Besides, parents whose early schooling was curtailed often hesitate to take part with others who they think may be "better educated." Similar questions of relative competence and status may be raised by asking for the husband's occupation, the family income or religious affiliation. Although these facts may be important for sociological research or agency policy-making, parents may interpret them an invasion of their privacy. Actually, they are unnecessary and irrelevant to the main purpose of the group, which is to offer an educational opportunity to all parents or expectant parents who want to come.

Some organizations even omit asking the names of members' husbands, because they do not want to embarass any who may be in special circumstances they do not want to have known. Members are free to tell the group anything they care to and often say that their husbands are dead or that they are separated or divorced. Only rarely do they say that they have been deserted or that they were not married. This is a particularly sensitive point in expectant parent groups, where young mothers often do not want it known that they are not married and go to great lengths in the group to keep up the pretense that they have a husband. Under all circumstances, it is important that parents be left free to divulge what they want the group to know. Then what they choose to say becomes common knowledge and can be handled within the group for whatever its meaning.

It is interesting that the choice of questions to ask on a registration card can have such significance. Even the act of filling out the card can be complicated, although it takes only a few moments. Occasionally a parent may have difficulty in writing, or may panic because he is intimidated by any form to be filled out. If a leader sees any sign of this, he can quite simply step in to help. Or, even better, a secretary or volunteer aide might be available to handle whatever mechanics are involved. This is especially desirable if there is an enrollment or registration fee which involves the handling of money, making change and additional record-keeping. Wherever possible, the leader should be free to greet the members as they come in, to make them feel at home, and to bridge the gap of time until the meeting actually starts.

Identification of Members

Some leaders find it useful to provide large cards or stiff paper that can be folded and placed on the table, in front of each member. These are then filled out by the group members with their name and possibly the names and ages of their children.

This device serves many purposes. It gives the leader an opportunity to connect the names with the faces of members around the table; it gives the members a chance to know how to address their neighbors; and in a subtle way, by identifying each person as an individual, it sets the tone for his being an important part of the group. Then, too, having them give the names and ages of their children serves to bring the children right into the group, as it were, and, by implication, reinforces the fact that they are having real experiences with real children to draw on. It also helps stimulate points of identification among the members. It is not uncommon to hear them comment "We both have boys," or "You and I have large families," or "Several of us have only children."

Filling out these cards gives the members something to do when they come in, and often relieves a little of the initial tension. Where there are no tables on which to put identification cards, leaders sometimes suggest pinning on large name tags with the same information. It is interesting to note how long these identifications are used as groups progress. In some cases, they are automatically discarded after the second or third meeting. In others, especially where the leader has difficulty in remembering names, they may be used throughout the meetings.

Premeeting Activity

Some leaders find the premeeting time difficult, but it need not be so. Of course, there may be some awkwardness before the parents get to know one another. There are a number of ways in which one can ease the situation. Some agencies serve coffee before the meeting starts, to break the ice; others distribute material describing the general program of the agency. The leader will not want to start the discussion until most of the members are there, nor will he want to become involved in one or two individual situations before the meeting really begins. But "small talk" is usually not too difficult—and there is always the weather!

Sometimes a mother comes full of something that has just happened either in the community or at home or at her child's school, and she feels she *must* talk about it with the others who have come early. An expectant mother may mention something about how she feels "today," which she must share and compare with the others. It would be artificial for the leader to stop such comments and equally so to pretend not to hear them. He can listen politely without commenting or becoming involved in the situation and at some strategic point may say something like, "You may want to bring this up with the others when the meeting gets under way so we can see a little better what it means."

Such a comment enriches the general atmosphere. It suggests that anything is important if it seems so to the parent; that anything—if it is in some way related to the subject area which brings them there—is appropriate for discussion if the parent chooses to bring it up; and that whatever is introduced needs proper and thorough discussion. Already, by his words, facial expression, and attitude, the leader conveys an atmosphere of friendliness, interest, and respect. Already he has confirmed that he knows that the parents come for a purpose, and he shows that he is there to make it meaningful to them all.

Procedures that have been found useful in first meetings are exemplified in the group records included in Appendix II. These groups were conducted by leaders who had had varying degrees of experience with this type of group. The reports illustrate the steps by which these first meetings proceeded and the variety of parental concerns that still seem to fall into almost universal patterns, if one looks beneath the surface.

Those who gain from specific live material may want to read from Records 1 through 6 at this point, and then come back to the formulations that follow here. Others may wish to become generally familiar with the procedures first, and then turn to the group examples. These can help readers evaluate the extent to which they believe the leaders of the groups used these approaches effectively and also think about what else they might have done to further the parents' learning.

When the Meeting Begins

The time comes, however, when the leader must step in to start the meeting. At just what magic point should this be? This he must judge for himself, in relation to the number of people who are there, the hour and the state of restlessness of those who have already come. Usually one waits ten minutes or so past the specified time. If there is a very small attendance, one is tempted to delay further. It is best, however, not to wait too long; those who have come deserve the courtesy of having the meeting go on for them. The leader may begin by commenting on the small attendance and saying that even though there are only a few as yet, it is best to start. Before the end of the session, he may want to discuss the small attendance with the rest of the group, if it has not changed, and even possibly get their thinking on what may have caused this, what it means in the community, and what might be done about it.

For the encouragement of those new to this kind of work, it should be reported that some groups where only three or four parents or expectant parents came to a first session built up to ten or so within a week or two and functioned quite successfully. On the other hand, small attendance may put something of a damper on the enterprise and on the leader, who naturally feels discouraged at the lack of response. There is no question that an adequate attendance of twelve to eighteen people at a first meeting generates an atmosphere of excitement and stimulation that is a valuable booster in getting the program off the ground.

The leader now opens the meeting, saying, perhaps, "Let us begin," and thus he formally separates the guided discussion of the session itself from the casual chit-chat (or, in some cases, rather uneasy silence) that preceded it. Everything the leader does from here on focuses on helping people use the group through procedures that have been found useful and which the parents enter into almost without being conscious of doing so.

AN OPENING STATEMENT. The leader begins with an opening statement, a reorientation of a sort, to confirm the general plan and establish a contract between himself and the group by implication. Whatever he chooses to say should be very specific and it should include some introduction of himself. He may want to identify his professional background and/or his leadership experience or agency identification if he has one. In some cases, a leader merely says, "I am Mr. or Miss or Mrs. ——, your leader."

He can then go on to interpret the purpose of the group, why they are there, and what subject area they will discuss. This establishes the focus for the group sessions and reaffirms what will be the center of discussion, whether it is the pregnancy period and preparing for a new baby, living with preschoolers, school-agers, or adolescents, the special concerns of parents whose children have a particular disability, or whatever. It is also helpful to suggest briefly what the members may hope to get from the group, emphasizing the goal of broad understanding of their life situations rather than any specific formulas or answers.

Again, it is wise to repeat the details of the plan—the number of meetings, the dates, the time, and so forth. Here there may be need for flexibility to adjust to some of the particular wishes of the parent-members, especially as to dates during holiday periods or the scheduled time of the meetings, which can usually be adjusted by half an hour or so, if this will make it more convenient for the members.

Without making a big story of this or labeling it as different from other experiences, one can also suggest quite simply that the group will be conducted without an outline planned ahead, but rather that the members themselves will build the plan, based on their day-by-day concerns regarding their children and/or (especially in the case of expectant parents) themselves, and that this plan will be added to as the sessions progress and as they have new ideas. One can suggest that in the discussion they will share their ideas and experiences, and also point up, though indirectly, the value of their learning from one another about many children and many parents' ways of coping with them. This confirms, of course, that the group will concern itself with its members' needs and indicates from the very beginning that there is "no one way."

The parents are also entitled to know from the outset that the leader will play a definite part in keeping the discussion focused and meaningful to everyone, that he will help them consider many sides of a question, see that they share with the group what they know about children and families, and he will add what they may not know, in keeping with sound thinking today, drawing on his own experience with parents and children and his knowledge of other projects, studies, and research. This confirms that it is to be a focused, directed experience and not a "free for all."

One should also bring in, in some way, the importance of steady attendance on a continuing basis. This can be suggested by asking the members to let the leader know by phone or a message of some kind if they cannot come to a session. This emphasizes that the continuity of the discussion from week to week is important and also shows the leader's concern for them and interest in their participation.

It is helpful for the leader to say he is going to take notes and explain what he has in mind in doing so. The group will usually accept this without question when they understand that his purpose is to keep track of their interests and not to lose any points they want to have brought up. Without this explanation they might feel that he was taking notes "about them," possibly to use against them later.

If the leader expects visitors during any of the sessions, either from the community or the sponsoring agency, he should inform the group in advance so they will be prepared for the presence of a visitor and understand the purpose of the visit. It is important to make clear that observers come either out of a professional interest in parent education in general or out of a wish to know more about how parent groups function, rather than as observers of individual parents. Every effort must be made to keep the experience on an objective group level and to forestall any possibility that group members may feel they are being spied upon or their comments used in any way, outside of the group.

Although it takes some pages to describe them here, these points can be introduced very concisely. They can be made at any language level, in terms that are understandable by any group. One need not be discouraged if all of the facts are not absorbed at once. The details mentioned in an opening statement need to be reinforced at every step of the way by the leader's actions and attitudes and by the way in which he helps the parents take part in the group. The importance of an opening statement is that it sets up the leader's side of the contract, making clear what he expects and what he will do. At the same time it shows them what is expected of them on their side: that it is hoped they will come regularly, that they will work together for their own individual gain and for that of the group. By coming to subsequent meetings, they take up their side of the contract as it has been laid down for them.

HELPING THE PARENTS BECOME ACQUAINTED. Members are asked to identify themselves, not only through namecards, if these are used, but also verbally. It is suggested that they begin by introducing themselves and telling the ages and sex of their children. They usually add their children's names even if they are not asked to do so, and Molly and Jack soon become well known to the group as a whole. In expectant parent groups, the members usually are asked to give their "due dates."

In identifying themselves even on the cards, parents usually give their first and last names. Some leaders like to call parents by their first names, feeling that this adds to the informality of the meetings. Others find that this may have a boomerang effect and that the informality takes away from the dignity and serious purpose of the group. Besides, it may seem patronizing, since only rarely do the parents call a leader by his or her first name and it may take away from his recognized position in the group if they do. As a rule, leaders prefer to address group members as Mr. or Mrs., leaving the group members free to follow or not as they wish.

This is a particularly important question in expectant parent groups, where there is a great temptation for nurse-leaders to call the young women by their first names, partly because they feel quite motherly toward them and partly because they feel that this enhances the group feeling of friendliness. Particularly at a period in life when young people are struggling to establish their identity in their new roles as married adults and as prospective parents, it seems especially desirable for leaders or other helping persons to show their recognition of the new position by addressing them with appropriate dignity. Some nurses have found this difficult, especially where they have had fifteen-year-old expectant mothers along with older women in the group. In such cases, however, it is rewarding to see how the young person responds to being called "Mrs." with a justifiable feeling of pride.

BUILDING AN AGENDA. A next step in helping the group members get acquainted is to ask them to say what they would like to have discussed in the group: their interests, questions, and concerns. This process of "making an agenda" usually takes place at the same time as the group members identify themselves. Some leaders prefer to separate the two procedures: they first ask the parents to say who they are and then go around again to ask what they would like the group to discuss. This "twice-around" process can get cumbersome.

The words the leader uses to elicit this material are quite important. Any words given as directives take on meaning only when the group begins to give them substance. Still, it helps for the leader to know in advance what the effects of certain words may be. For example, if the group is asked to raise their "questions," they will probably expect categorical and specific "answers." On the other hand, asking for their "problems" may imply that the discussion will be problem-oriented, as in therapy, and may imply that problems can be resolved more fully than is possible within an educational group experience. Whatever words are used, it is their context that usually conveys the intent of the procedure, which is to have the parents begin to talk, to "lay on the table" some of the things they are thinking about and which they hope they can come to understand better through the discussion.

And so there is established a general "go-around" in which, as the parents identify themselves and their interests, they begin to set out a plan for the sessions to follow. This process serves as a bridge to help them move into the group experience. *They* are doing something, and the very doing seems to ease their anxiety about what they are expected to do. They accept a task, which shows that they are ready to take some part in the proceedings and, in a way, binds their side of the contract. Their thinking is directed to the realities they face. At the same time, the leader learns from the agenda something of why the parents have come, gets some picture of the nature of their concerns, and begins to sense whether their being in the group is appropriate or not.

Even in the first interchange, the leader—and the group members— also begin to see how the others will behave individually and as a group. Some parents will respond shyly, some more aggressively, some will tend to dominate the group, others will have difficulty talking at all. Such varied reactions are to be expected, of course. Some will be more spontaneous and freer not only to talk in general terms but to give specific instances. Some will retreat behind generalities, saying that they would like to talk about "everything" or "I haven't any specific questions. I'm here to learn." Often after everyone has spoken in an easily accepted progression around the table, someone will add a new idea, stimulated by a remark from one of the other parents, and a new burst of comments will pour out to which others, in turn, respond. This simple procedure has been found extremely useful in getting a group off the ground. Already group members are participating; their interaction with one another is already under way.

ROLE OF THE LEADER. And what about the leader during this process? How does he respond to their listing of their concerns or their interests? There is no universal rule for the behavior of leaders in this situation or in any other. Leaders will always have their own individual styles, colored by their own particular personalities. But, to be effective in carrying out their programs, it is important that there be some commonly accepted goals and some commonly accepted general procedures.

Depending on the leader's judgment, he will occasionally ask a parent for clarification during the "go-around," especially if the parent mentions a general topic such as "discipline" as an area for discussion. Without going into the matter too deeply, the leader may ask what kind of situation this parent had in mind. Such a question does not mean that he will expect a long and detailed description. (If this is what is forthcoming, the leader must find a way to turn it off without cutting it off. He can say that now they have some idea of the parent's concern; the parent will surely have a chance to say more about it later.) At this point, the leader is asking only for information that pictures the live situation which presented the discipline issue. His question also shows the group that they will be talking about concrete experiences rather than abstract subject areas.

The leader accepts each comment, of course, and listens carefully so that each parent feels he is being given his proper due. Thus the leader again sets a tone by behaving in such a way that he serves as a model with which members begin to identify. If he listens and accepts different kinds of comments with equanimity and a sympathetic, yet reflective attitude, they usually begin to follow this pattern too.

After the "go-around" has been completed, or sometimes even while the parents are still building up the agenda, the leader may decide to group their points or questions into categories, pulling together or restating them. He may generalize from specific situations, drawing from them the common areas of concern they seem to represent. Or he may comment on the variety of their interests, pointing out that they all fall within what one expects of families today and are important to discuss. Such a comment tends to relieve parents of possible anxiety that their situations may be extremely unusual or different. By stressing the common points, he strengthens their feelings for one another and puts them all on an even basis to start. Yet, even in the way he listens and interprets, he accepts the fact that in each family, the situation has its own special meaning.

A summary interpretation is most effective if it is brief and concise, so that the parents are not overwhelmed. The fact that the leader does comment, however, is important, since in doing so he already uses the material from the parents themselves, and gives it a new perspective. The "go-around" has provided a flexible framework for future discussions; his statement about it—in whatever form—gives it weight and substance. There is something out on the table from which to start the real work of the group.

And what about the parents during all this? Sometimes they sit quietly, waiting for each to have his turn. More often, however, as the comments come from more and more people around the circle, they are likely to be brought out of their passivity and begin to relate to one another. Sometimes they ask other members questions for clarification, as they have seen the leader do. Sometimes they say, "Oh, that is just the way it is with us." Sometimes they move in very quickly to give advice, and in doing so focus the interest of the group on the person to whose comments they are responding.

There is a danger in letting the group become absorbed too quickly in one person's concern. This may give the impression that this is the way things are to go: quickly, by superficial comment, or advice-giving. When this occurs, the leader needs to step in and perhaps suggest that the group can come back to this later, thus continuing with the process of giving each one his say. Again, from the leader's example, the parents learn how to work on a situation (and how not to) and the group is kept from being caught in something that may not be to their best advantage.

Even these suggestions have to be tempered, however, to the particular group situation. Group members need to feel that they can talk freely, even if in the beginning they do so rather inappropriately. Sometimes the group may need to be given some latitude, until the leader is clear as to what direction the discussion is taking. There is ample time for him to redirect the discussion, if he thinks this is necessary.

Beginning the Discussion as a Group

The next step is to help the group begin the discussion on a group basis. After he has made his interpretative comments, the leader can ask, "Where should we begin?" or "Where do you want to begin?" The group may meet such an opening with a deep silence, while the members take time to consider how they want to respond. Naturally, each parent wants to start with the "topic" or situation he himself may have brought out in the "go-around" but he is hesitant to impose this on the group. There usually is someone, however, who comes out with a suggestion, based either on a strong feeling of personal urgency, or the wish to please the leader, or to break through a silence that may be somewhat uncomfortable for all of them. Leaders are grateful for a first suggestion and sometimes accept it without any further exploration. It is better to get more than one suggestion, if possible, so the group can have several to consider. Each suggestion has to be expanded—a little—so the group will know what the parent is really concerned about, in terms of the experiences that cause him to bring it up. They need also to have some idea of what aspect of the situation he is truly concerned with. This has been called "getting at the question behind the question." Again, in this process, the leader can sometimes tie together several different suggestions under the "umbrella" of a larger idea, such as how two-year-olds behave or how parents react when their children—of any age—do not listen, or how do we guide our children anyway.

Then, whether in terms of specific situations or of more general issues that arise from specific situations, the selection of where to begin must be brought to the group. Are these the matters that are of interest to the other parents? Or do they have still other ideas or situations they would like to have the group consider? In this preliminary exploration there usually emerges some area that is important for most of the parents in the group, and to which the leader responds, because of their concern and often because his previous experience with other families has shown him that this is an important issue for parents. The decision about where to start, however, should be made by the group, not by a show of hands, which makes for an artificial performance, but by the general atmosphere created by the parents' verbal comments, supplemented by nodding heads, smiles of acceptance, frowns, bored expressions, or whatever the leader sees around the table. He then, in his own fashion, puts this feeling-tone into words, to test whether he has interpreted the parents' reactions correctly. If the members agree, he presents a simple formulation of the area which the parents and the leader have evolved together, as a common starting point which they all share, at least in words. This procedure has come to be called "checking with the group." It makes extra clear that the decision has been made in the interest of the group as a whole and that the parents have a determining role in directing the content of the discussion. In addition, it gives the parents a sense of direction and involvement without which discussions often become desultory and inconclusive.

Sometimes this process occurs spontaneously, as when a member comments that "We all seem most worried about these school situations." The leader can then "check" informally. He may say something like "Do you all see it that way, too?" and then watch for their response in facial expression as well as in words. This may also be a strategic time to add—as one should at some point—that the group will be meeting for many weeks and that eventually "We hope to get to what is important for all of you."

Once an area or situation has been chosen for discussion, the leader then helps the group to sharpen the issue by getting more information, both from those who have brought it up and from the group as a whole. This process, sometimes described as "establishing the focus," is described more fully in Chapter VII. Its purpose is not to choose a general "topic" for discussion, but rather to select and pinpoint an aspect of these parents' experience that is of concern to them and to see it as it takes place within the family interplay. And so the discussion starts, with more and more vivid, live talk bringing into the room those troubling or gratifying real experiences that are part of every family's daily living.

In a first meeting, a great deal of time may be taken up in gathering the agenda; there is usually little opportunity to begin to develop any one area. The point at which a particular group moves beyond gathering the agenda and begins to develop the content in discussion is influenced by the size of the group, the spontaneity of the group members, and their ability to express themselves. In one group, for example, the leader found to her dismay that the cooperating agency, in this case a school in an underprivileged area of a large city, had enrolled over thirty parents. They had done this because they wanted to be *sure* to have a group large enough to warrant setting up the program. The mothers were all eager to talk and the first session was a confused one, since it was difficult for them to accept the fact that everyone needed to be heard. It was also difficult for the leader to be sure that every member *did* have her chance. Despite all her efforts they interrupted one another and jumped in as they pleased, even in the first go-around. There is no rule by which the parents must identify themselves, their children, and their interests, and it does not necessarily have to be done in orderly progression around the circle. In a group of manageable size the leader can keep track of those who have contributed and those who have not, going back to have them fill in the gaps, if the order has been broken. In this case, the leader was herself confused by the numbers and left the meeting feeling that not everyone had participated as she had planned. Nor had there been any time to develop a plan by which to utilize the rich agenda they had formulated. She was deeply dissatisfied and felt that the members were dissatisfied, too.

In general, the procedure is so simple that, even when carried out with considerable flexibility, it serves to get the group started and eases the parents into speaking out. Even if there is very little time left for discussion of any particular situation or issue, the group has already begun to learn that matters will be discussed in some depth, from different points of view, and to see how guided discussion in group education is different from mere talk. They see that, while the individual is expected and will be helped to gain from the experience, the discussion is geared to the group as a whole as well as to the individual. They also begin to recognize that generalities or intellectualizations have little meaning unless they are related to the everyday happenings that lie behind them. Already, even in a limited way, they have begun the constant balancing of what may be true for a particular child or family as compared with what may be true for all children or families. And finally they begin to get a sense that although behavior is seen in the light of certain general principles, there are always significant differences in the individual, the family, and the community situation. Whereas they may be talking about a child or children in general, in each situation they also begin to sense the other parts of the interplay—that for each child there is a parent, just as for all children there are parents in general. And by the way in which they describe their individual situations they are building up a picture of the way they all live in their own special segments of the larger community.

Some Characteristic Snags

CHALLENGING THE LEADER. Occasionally first meetings run into characteristic snags. The most important of these is the challenging of the leader by one or more group members. He may be questioned because of his endorsement of this type of program or his role in it. Parents who come looking for specific answers, despite all the interpretations that may have been given them to the contrary, become quite restless during the usual procedures of a first meeting and feel that it is a waste of time. Somewhat allied to this feeling, but on a rather different note, is the idea that the leader is there merely as a policeman or traffic director and plays no real role in helping the parents achieve what they came for. This concept has been expressed in groups even where the interpretation given in the opening statement was quite specific on the very points the parents subsequently raised.

It is difficult to know what may have provoked such feelings in a particular parent or group of parents. Was it because they were so preoccupied with their own need to be "told" that they did not listen to the leader's interpretation? Was it because they doubted their own capacity to develop answers for themselves? Were they not yet clear about what new information and understanding they would acquire to enable them to make effective decisions? Was there some marked passivity in the leader, perhaps, that provoked such feelings? (Occasionally this issue has come up in first meetings led by workers holding their first group. Unsure of their own role, they may unconsciously have given parents the idea that they would play no part at all in the developing sessions.) Whatever the reasons for such a challenge, it is important that the leader be prepared for it, accept it as part of what may occur in a group, and not evade the issue but bring it out directly for the group to discuss. This can be done by asking whether other parents have similar questions. The leader can give his concept of the leader's role, as he may have done earlier, and the reasons for a "nonanswering" approach. Even though the words may be somewhat academic and too theoretical for the group to grasp all at once, a quiet, sure explanation is usually accepted if the leader has conviction himself. Some members are likely to support the leader, at least to be willing to give the experience a chance. Somehow, the very honesty shown by the leader, his willingness to be confronted with the issue, is likely to convince members that they can express themselves, even when they are not in thorough agreement with those who are in charge. Where such confrontation has occurred and the issue has been squarely met, most of the parents who objected have been quite willing to return to give the program a chance to serve their needs.

SILENCES. Many leaders say that their first meetings are difficult because of the occasional silences that occur. Often, as has been suggested, they do come after the "go-around," when the leader asks the group to say where they want to pick up the discussion. Actually, these silences do not happen as often as some leaders fear, nor are they as long as they seem to the leader. When they do occur, they suggest that the group members may not yet know how to take their part. This is quite understandable. To allow silences to go on until somebody breaks through is neither justified in theory nor helpful in practice. After a reasonable period of time to allow the group to think through what it wants to say, it is important for the leader to ease the way, without taking over. He may make a comment such as, "Well, it is hard to know where to start, isn't it?" Or perhaps, "So many suggestions have been made that it *does* seem difficult to make a choice." Or even, "What are you all thinking about now?" Any comment from the leader that, by its tone of voice or words, indicates his appreciation of the fact that this is not easy and that the parents are really working to achieve what is being asked of them, usually results in a breaking of the dam of silence. Or the leader may help them more specifically by saying, "We can really start with almost anything you've brought up" and may repeat some of the concerns they have already mentioned, suggesting they choose one of these as a take-off point. The talk then usually begins to flow.

THE END OF THE FIRST MEETING

No matter what the experience has been, it is important for the leader to give the first meeting some kind of suitable ending, rather than let it deteriorate into nowhere and end with a comment such as, "Well our time is up." (Such an ending may be appropriate for a later meeting, supplemented by the further comment, "We'll continue next time.") At the end of the first meeting it is important that the group be given some interpretation to let them know where they are, what they have achieved, and how this meeting may open the way for further sessions. If the session has been confused and stormy, like the overlarge group we have described, it is quite appropriate for the leader to say something to the effect that "The group is such a large one that we have not been able to hear from everyone, as we had hoped. We'll continue with this next time, and then see what all of your ideas add up to and where we can begin to talk them over together." Or, if the discussion has just barely begun after the opening procedures are completed, a leader might very well say, "We have just started to get into the whole matter of discipline (or fighting in the family or whatever) and are only beginning to see some of its many implications. We will surely be able to pick this up next time, or we can take it up at a later meeting, if the group wishes to talk about something else that seems more important when we come together next week." It is also wise to remind the group that they can bring in other ideas later that have not been mentioned in the first meeting, and that there is no set order in which they have to take up the topics that have been brought out. In this way, the leader adds the idea that future discussion will be fluid and flexible and can be adjusted to their most urgent needs.

A very brief review of some kind serves to underscore what has happened in the first meeting and put it in its place. Out of its very seriousness and relatedness to the parent members, this gives them some assurance that they will get something from the group process. It is surprising how quickly, even within a fairly limited first session, the members begin to feel that they are part of a group, and the leader recognizes that the particular assemblage of people who have come together more or less by chance are beginning to form a group, distinct from any other, with its own group life.

Reminder. See Appendix II. Excerpts from Group Records: First Meetings.

VII

The Practice of Parent Group Education:
Developing the Content of the Discussion

During the course of the meetings the content of the discussion, which is developed from material brought out by the group members, will include the contributions they make on matters closely related to their present interests, the comments they voice as they talk and think about relevant experiences in their own families. Added to this will be the perspective they gain from looking at the issue from different points of view and relating it to fundamental concepts of human development and interpersonal relations as these are seen against the background of their particular communities and cultural environment. And finally, it will include some discussion and thought as to various possible ways of coping with their situations, so that hopefully their lives with their families will proceed with greater satisfaction and fulfillment for all the family members.

If the philosophy and approach is valid and is carried out consistently, in each case the discussion will cover those areas which are of particular concern to the parents who come. At the same time, experience has shown that, by and large, many of the situations parents face in bringing up their children are similar to those of other parents, even when their specific problems are highly individual. So it is to be expected that the discussion will represent the concerns of parents in similar circumstances or at similar stages of their family cycle—concerns that indicate areas in which parents feel threatened in their ability to deal with the demands and needs of their families. In the content of the discussion in many groups there are recurrent general themes, if one is attuned to recognize them. At the same time, each group, with its own individual members, introduces these themes from a never-ending variety of individual approaches. These too need to be listened to carefully and thoughtfully, for their own special meaning as well as for their relation to the larger themes.

These are the general areas one would expect to have raised and discussed in various kinds of parent groups:

For expectant parents, the content of the discussion usually includes: the physiological processes of pregnancy, labor, and delivery and the mothers' and fathers' psychological and emotional reactions to the changes that take place; the stage of pregnancy in which the mother finds herself, and its meaning in the physical preparation for the birth of the new baby; the fears and anxieties of both parents about the coming infant and the mother herself; relevant aspects of sound medical and nursing practice in relation to the mother's physical and emotional needs; guidance directed to the mother's experience of giving birth and assuming the care of the new baby immediately afterwards and in the months to come; and some preparation for understanding the social changes that take place in the family with the addition of a new baby and the reactions of both parents to the emergence of a family of three. Usually included also is some discussion of child-rearing issues and practices in the first few years, such as the handling of thumb-sucking, toilet training, and "spoiling." All this is explored from the point of view of factual knowledge, ideas, and expectations, in very personal terms. Stress is also laid on what each mother or father can and wants to do on any special issue—and what she or he cannot do.

For parents of children of different ages, the content of discussion includes occurrences within the family that the parents find baffling or difficult. Out of the discussion comes a picture of the behavior of children at different stages, of the characteristic responses of parents to this behavior, of the way in which they mobilize their inner resources to meet these situations, and how, with wider understanding, they can meet them more effectively.

For parents of children with handicapping conditions or in situations of chronic illness or disability, the content of the discussions includes, again, the real-life situations they face and find burdensome. Discussion here leads to a knowledge not only of the characteristics of the particular age under discussion but of these children as they are coping with a special disability. Here, too, parents look at the complex parent-child relationships and the way in which the disability or illness may distort the relationship, out of feelings and attitudes of which the parents themselves may not yet be aware. In these groups, the content covers many of the issues brought up by parents of so-called normal children, but these issues take on a special coloration because of the additional factor which makes these children's lives so different and which, to the parents, adds an extra load which they understandably find hard to carry.

THE SECOND MEETING

In all these groups, as we have said, the tone and purpose have been set in a first meeting. But it is the second meeting that is quite crucial. Here the group really gets into the core of the educational experience and begins to see how it can have meaning for them. The way the leader gets the group started in a second meeting is often the key to its future success.

In a second meeting the discussion reinforces the exploration begun in the opening session and pushes on to a new dimension, developing one or more areas of content in detail and in depth. (As we have seen, such exploration is often not possible in a first meeting, when so much time is taken in getting acquainted and in setting up the structure in which the group will operate.)

Usually, leaders find it helpful to interpret the group procedure again, briefly describe its plan and purposes, and summarize for those who were not at the previous session the essential facts they must know. Going over these matters a second time often has value also for those who came to the first meeting, for repetition serves to bring the main points home. Group members frequently respond to a part of the interpretation they seem not to have absorbed before, and they comment or question more thoughtfully than they did in the first session. In this meeting, too, leaders will of course ask any new members to identify themselves and their children and state what they would like to have the group discuss. Having gone through all of this before, and feeling somewhat bored with it themselves, leaders are relieved to find that a second time around seems to go much more easily and quickly.

The leader's giving some idea of what went on before is particularly important for new members, of course, but even when no new members have been added, a general comment or summary is often helpful in a second session to get the group moving. In a brief recapitulation of what happened in the first meeting, the leader opens the way for the group to add new items to the "agenda," if they care to; it also allows him to group some of their concerns under more general headings, thus beginning to put their specific comments into a more general framework. Such a summary reminds them of what they have shared and gives them a springboard for moving ahead. If the leader feels that an area the group had started to discuss at the first meeting had not been explored completely, he can say this too. However, he should leave the group free to go on with this or not, as they wish. He and the group can consider this unfinished business to be taken up some time later, if they choose not to do so now.

Such a summary is often helpful at the beginning of a second meeting, but it is not always necessary to open it in this way. Nor are we suggesting that all meetings must follow this pattern. A regular routine can become artificial and dull; it can also leave the parents less free to think for themselves and cut off their chance to operate with greater independence and initiative. In any case, the leader must know why he follows such a procedure or decides not to, on the basis of his best judgment at the time.

Having cleared the way with these introductory measures, the leader usually opens the discussion, as he did in starting the discussion in the first meeting, with a question such as "Where would you like to begin today?" He may add that they should feel free to pick up on something that was talked about last time or not as they care to, or they may want to bring up something new. Following such comments, the group then repeats something of the process in opening the discussion that was described in Chapter VI.

ESTABLISHING A FOCUS

As the discussion enters into any new area, in whatever meeting, it is essential that the talk focus on some aspect of daily living with which they want to and can come to grips. Here the process involves limiting the field, in a sense, since discussion toward educational goals cannot be expected to cover everything that happens with parents and children. Obviously, some selection must be made to pick out those parts of their lives that are most in need of clarification and educational help. Deciding where to begin has sometimes been described as "establishing a focus," a term which draws from the field of photography, a concept that may be useful. Focusing on a photographic subject implies selection and concentration in order to establish clarity, so that the material looked at can reveal itself. "Establishing a focus," in group educational terms, means singling out a concern or interest that a parent sees as important at a given moment. This concern may be a central one for this parent and for others or it may be a peripheral one. The decision as to its real importance cannot be made at the first opening. To go back to the photographic metaphor, the focus may not be sharp in the beginning and the leader and the group may have to accept it in a somewhat fuzzy form until it has been explored more adequately.

Whether the focus is clear or blurred at first, it may be expected to shift as the many complex factors that are involved in it become more sharply outlined. The focus must, however, be meaningful not only to the person who introduces it but to the group as a whole. Any concern that reflects some aspect of parent-child relationships and interaction within the family can meet these qualifications and serve as a core around which the discussion is to be developed. The focus is most meaningful if the parent who raised the issue describes specific happenings in his current experience so that the others have a clear picture of what they are talking about. When the group discussion starts *where they are*, it gives the group an immediate entry into the lives of all of them. The real situations and their impact on all the family members can then be explored. In this way, parents are involved emotionally as well as intellectually, and move into active discussion more quickly than they would have if they had taken up a topic in general terms.

To obtain the focus, several steps are usually necessary. When a parent introduces a situation about which he is concerned, he can be asked to explain it a little more fully, so the picture will have more meaning. Frequently, without waiting to be asked for their comments, group members express their feeling that this is a common cause for concern, although the immediate situation in which they are each involved may not be exactly identical. Adding this factor of universality even in the face of difference immediately puts the issue into a larger perspective. The leader will probably not leave it at this, however, without exploring it one step further with the person who introduced it. He will want to find out what aspects are troublesome or even what part the parent would like the group to discuss. This step helps the initiating parent pinpoint his concern more clearly. At the same time it narrows the focus and makes the subject more accessible for the group to react to.

Before moving into a wider exploration of the issue, however, the leader will want to "check with the group." He will usually do this overtly. Sometimes, however, he will encourage the group to go ahead on the basis of his own judgment, if he senses that this is an area which is of sufficient interest to be productive to the members as a whole. In the latter case, however, he must share his judgment with the group in some way, to see whether they agree.

Throughout this process the leader makes use of his knowledge of the principles of child development and his understanding of the meaning a particular form of behavior may have for the parent who presented this issue as well as its relevance for the others in the group. The leader is aware that even though the issue may be a very specific one, it has many broad implications which will come clear later in the discussion. He knows, too, that parental concerns differ in nature, intensity, and emotional coloration in various socioeconomic, ethnic, and cultural groups. As these are suggested in the group, he is quick to recognize them and encourages the parents to express them more clearly and to examine their validity—for themselves and for other parents.

Sometimes a meeting will open with one issue which can be developed from different points of view. Often several such situations are presented, making it necessary for the group to select the ones that are closest to their own experience. It is incumbent on the leader to assure the members whose suggestions are not being followed at the moment, that the group will come back to their questions or interests later. They will then feel that they are contributing to the group even though their ideas are not being discussed just then.

After a group has shown its interest in pursuing one particular line of thought, the discussion may not proceed in a logical fashion as in a textbook. The situation with which they start may be one that is commonly met, but it may have quite different implications for individual parents in the group. The leader knows this. His important role now is to help the group explore the situation with which they have started, knowing that it will surely open up many different meanings. He will follow the discussion carefully, give himself up to what the group is saying, recognize their feelings as well as the facts they divulge and go along with the current of thought. At the same time, he tries, out of his own background of knowledge, to see what it may add up to, and uses his group skills to bring it finally to some resolution of thinking, even though this in no way entails a common plan for action.

Some examples may serve to illustrate the many possible meanings a subject may have, all under the same general "umbrella." Let us listen in to a young mother who reports that she cannot get her twenty-month-old girl to sit on the toilet; the youngster slips away from her hands, dancing around the room, even though she—and her mother—know that what she really needs is to urinate. As the mother introduces her story, other mothers nod vigorously and with considerable sympathy; they say they know such behavior, too, and how exasperating it can be. Obviously, this situation can have many meanings. The mother may be concerned because her child resists toilet training and continues to wet her pants. Or she may be upset because the child's lack of cooperation may be another sign that her child won't listen to her about anything, and does this mean that her child will always be defiant? It may also mean that the mother is at her wits' end, not knowing what to do about *any* situation with her little one. The group could discuss this from many different points of view, but what is the focus with which they should begin? In this case, it develops, the mother's prime concern is about "discipline," specifically, getting her child to "obey" her. This is what she would like to have the group talk about. As he places the issue before the group as a whole, the leader recognizes that they do see this as a "disciplinary" problem, since they bring in other situations in which their almost two-year-olds defy them, refuse to listen, and, even more annoying, refuse to "obey." If the leader had quickly decided, as he had been inclined, to use this as an opening for a discussion on toilet training—how to help children accomplish this step in their development—the discussion would have followed *his* line of thinking rather than that of the group and would not have been as meaningful to them at the time. The leader's responsibility, however, is not merely to let the discussion follow the line of the group's thinking without developing it further. At some point in the discussion, he will see that the basic issue—what the child is doing and why—emerges. This, in turn, will surely lead into the area of toilet training, which he knows is vital in the growing-up process.

Or take a situation introduced in an expectant couples' group: a prospective father states directly that *he* wants to know just when to take his wife to the hospital for her delivery. This opening, too, can represent many lines of thinking. It may be a direct request for information as to the signs of oncoming labor. It may show, as the discussions progress, that the young husband is not familiar with the whole process of birth. It may reveal the wife's anxiety, rather than the husband's, about being alone all day while her husband is at work, with no one to whom she can turn to go to the hospital with her when the time comes. It may represent a deep feeling on the part of the husband that he wants to be there at that time, and share as far as possible all steps of the experience of having a baby. Any of these possibilities can probably be elicited by specific questions such as: "How do you picture this is going to happen?" or "What will you have to do about it?" or "Do you think you'll have to deliver the baby yourself? If so, what would you need to know?" Or it may be enough to ask, "What is there about this that concerns you?" Such openings pave the way to find out what the father really needs to know from the group and/or the leader that will help him cope with the situation when it comes. When he has articulated more of his thinking, the group can then take hold of the problem if it is of interest to them. They can share their knowledge and ideas, and the leader can add information appropriately, if the group's knowledge is inadequate. An opening like this probably will be answered at many different levels, going beyond the stated "focus." The stimulating aspect of group discussion is that it rarely stays on any one level of need. In a fluid and endlessly fascinating way it reaches into many levels of parents' concerns, almost at the same time that it seems to deal with specific aspects of a situation.

In a group of parents of children with muscular dystrophy, a mother mentioned her great difficulty in getting her sixteen-year-old boy into the bathtub without having someone to help her. The leader recognized the practical aspect of the question and encouraged the group to share with this mother any experiences they had had in similar situations that could be helpful to her. At the same time, he realized that there was more to the question than appeared, and asked the mother what part of this was especially troubling to her. With very little prompting, she said that this was the most blatant example of her utter helplessness in the face of her son's overwhelming disability. As the discussion progressed, the focus shifted from the practical problem to a much deeper exploration of what the future held for the boy and the mother's anxiety about what the future would bring.

MOVING AHEAD IN THE DISCUSSION

The foregoing description indicates that one cannot separate the process of discussion into distinct parts without overlapping. Establishing a focus is merely the beginning of the discussion. Discussion itself, in any meeting, is a developmental process, in which the parents bring out and share their many experiences, ideas, and feelings, not for the benefit of one person but for the group as a whole. In the process, each has an opportunity to formulate more clearly his own concern, and so to see it better. He also learns to listen to others, as he wants to be listened to. He begins to compare, to sort out, and to take from the discussion what is close to his experience and throws light on his own questioning. And out of this, he comes to his own conclusions about more effective ways of coping with this—or any—situation and acquires more confidence in what he is doing or plans to do.

And so, as the group goes on to discuss a particular occurrence or area of interest, parents are encouraged to interact about many aspects related to the incidents that are revealed, rather than to topics. The process moves from the specific to the more general, toward resolutions that may be important for individual parents and that have some relation to general principles. Often it is only after considerable discussion of specific incidents that there emerge trends of behavior patterns that are typical, as the parents respond to various inner drives and external circumstances. Often they themselves recognize these patterns or relationships between one situation and another and bring them out as a possible interpretation. When a generalization of this kind comes from the group, it shows that they have been truly involved in the discussion and their comments take on real meaning.

It takes time, however, for this process to take place. Patterns and trends emerge slowly, only after considerable discussion and sharing of experiences. It is up to the leader to help the group enrich the "subject" area they have chosen by encouraging them to develop certain strands of their comments that seem most significant—sometimes a single poignant word gives the clue—and to bring out parts of their experience they had apparently overlooked in the telling.

Sometimes these aspects may not have seemed important to the parents. At other times one wonders whether they are holding back certain of their ideas and/or reports of their behavior, either deliberately or unconsciously. They may do so for a variety of reasons. Perhaps they feel uncomfortable about what they have done. Or they may be pushing important parts of the matter out of their own minds, unaware that these may be influencing their behavior and decisions. As the group sessions progress and as they get confidence in the group and in the educational experience itself, parents are freer to bring out negative experiences or negative feelings.

DATA GATHERING

For the beginning, however, the prime task is to get plenty of descriptive material as to what is going on within the parents themselves and in their homes. Even as in the first "go-around," these descriptions must come from many parents, as many as choose to enter in spontaneously. In the sharing, the spotlight shifts from one parent to several parents, to the group as a whole and back again, as each parent begins to participate. For all of them, there is a necessary process of clarification. Do they express what they really have in mind? Are their comments understood by the rest of the group? Are there any points that seem to be confusing? In order to facilitate true communication, the leader encourages the parents to say more clearly what they have in mind in language they all can understand and to elaborate general statements or casual side-comments, if these seem important, or strategic words.

Important words that should be further defined are those that describe a child or a situation in general terms; general terms, as we well know, may mean different things to different people. If a parent says his child is "stubborn," for example, what does this word mean to him? What kinds of behavior is the child showing that appear to the parent to indicate stubbornness? Under what situations is this happening: Is this behavior new in the child's life or has it been characteristic of him from the beginning? Without staying with the issue too long, it is necessary to get behind the term to the actual child as his parents see him, in order to have the group know what they are really talking about.

As they take part in this type of exploration, other parents will talk about their children, piling up a picture of what children are doing at a particular age. Out of this emerges some appreciation of the similarities in children, of what behavior is characteristic at certain ages and under certain conditions, and also of individual differences. There emerges, too, a concept of the wide range in what may be considered normal, both for parents and children, and of what constitutes behavior that goes beyond the limits of what is normal.

In gathering the necessary data as substance for the group to discuss, the group members learn a way of approaching an issue. What is the immediate situation or problem? With regard to children, it is important to know the age of the child, how he has developed up to this point, and where he is in the growing-up process. They must know the circumstances under which he behaves as he does, how often and for how long a period this behavior continues, the circumstances under which it starts, and when it is different. They need to know not only how the child is behaving but how he feels, and how the parents and others feel, about his behavior. Implied in all this are the assumptions which parents may be making about the behavior, assumptions which may or may not be valid. In the example just referred to, is a child generally "stubborn" if he holds out for something he urgently wants or needs at the moment, in a way that is not characteristic for him? Is a child's behavior to be interpreted as nasty or deliberately disobedient if he objects to doing something painful or distasteful to him? In other words, are our interpretations of behavior based on understanding what is going on inside the child and in relation to those around him?

Also inherent in all these discussions are the goals parents have for their children. To pursue the example somewhat further, is stubborness something that they wish to wipe out in their children, because they see it as bad or dangerous? Or is there a possibility that this strength of feeling in children may also have certain values, as a more aggressive way of responding to the world around them? More basically, what kind of child do they envision his being and becoming? And is this expectation compatible with the kind of child he really is?

This gathering of data from a single member and involving the group in expanding the material out of their similar experiences, does not come about quickly. Nor does the detailed picture necessarily emerge as a totality. Certain parts of it may be more significant for the issue under discussion than others. This the leader judges, based on his background and experience. He emphasizes certain information which he considers necessary, rather than attempting a complete coverage, as the above formulation would seem to imply.

In an expectant parent group, data gathering must also be quite extensive, starting usually with one parent but spreading to the group as a whole. Here, too, the group members need to know exactly what the parent is talking about in order to involve themselves in the subject and make appropriate contributions. In such an apparently simple statement as "I don't know whether I will want to breast-feed my baby," there are many aspects to consider, some that the mothers-to-be already have on their minds, and others they may not have thought of, that will influence their ultimate decision. They will want to be clear about the "facts" of breast-feeding, the extent to which it is essential or not for the healthy growth of the baby; their own feelings about breast-feeding, both positive and negative; the relation of breast-feeding to their physical well-being after the babies are born and to their social life and possible jobs; the implications for the baby, not only physically but psychologically and emotionally; and the implications for the husband, who may or may not have strong feelings about having his wife nurse the baby. Throughout such a discussion the group will certainly bring out some of their preconceived ideas and assumptions and will have an opportunity, through the comments of other parents and the contributions of the leader, to check them against reality. They will certainly bring out their expectations and their fears, to be looked at honestly and evaluated. They will consider not only themselves but the cultural and familial environment in which they live, the influence of neighbors, friends, and relatives—even in-laws—on whether they follow one practice or another. Hopefully, the discussion will end with a better understanding of what they may really be faced with later. They will know, too, that they do not have to make a final decision now, but that when the actual day comes they will make a choice based on their own honest feelings and convictions.

VIII

The Practice of Parent Group Education:
The Balances That Round Out the Discussion

On any aspect of parent-child or family relations, then, the discussion must open up for exploration many different sides of a subject or situation that has been introduced. When the group members initiate various aspects of a subject, they are contributing experiences and ideas they feel are needed to round out the picture. But sometimes the discussion does not develop spontaneously in this way; the group seems to continue along one line of thought. As we have seen, then the leader interjects a comment or a question that suggests that there may be other parts of the situation to be considered, too.

Sometimes he does this as a general opening, leaving it up to the group to contribute a new dimension. More often he does it directly, mentioning the aspect which he feels has been overlooked. He may say, for example, "We've been talking about the children in all this, but what about *your* side?" Or, in reverse, "We've been talking about the parents and what they are doing and feeling, but what are the children going through?" The group may not go along with his suggested opening, especially if it is made before they have gone as far as they want to along their original tack. (They may pick it up later when they are ready.) But if the attempted redirection is appropriate and well-timed, the group usually responds and the discussion becomes richer and more rounded.

To help leaders keep in mind some of the categories in which the many aspects fall, the material has sometimes been thought of in terms of a series of balances. These balances are seen somewhat artificially as opposites or rather as two sides of a coin that contrast and yet complement each other. This concept grew out of experience in which it became apparent that exploration of only one of two balanced aspects creates a marked *im*-balance and that discussion which centers around only one of the alternatives is bound to be incomplete. Some categories of balance are more basic to rounded discussion than others, yet they are all significant. Some have to do with the *form* the parents' comments take, such as whether they are generalizations or specific points; others with the *subject matter*, such as what a parent is experiencing or what the child is experiencing; or the *tone* or *mood* of the discussion, such as negative or positive feelings and attitudes. Let us take them one at a time, recognizing that while such balances are essential for all group education, they are being applied here to the substance of parent group education—to child development and parent-child relations in their broadest sense.

At the same time, we must be realistic and know that these balances cannot—and need not—be kept in perfect balance, either within a single session or through a series of meetings as a whole. If leaders try to follow these concepts too literally, the discussions become stilted and too controlled. They are suggested here so leaders can have them in mind as a general guide, to keep from neglecting one phase for the other over a period of time.

THE GENERAL AND/OR THE SPECIFIC

This balance is inherent in the entire process of parent group education and grows out of its philosophy and goals. We have already suggested that a generalization—even a general, abstract term—has little or no meaning without the specific examples or situations which cause a parent to raise the issue. Reality—the ordinary, complicated stuff of human relationships and interplay—must be brought into the meeting room to make an intellectual formulation come alive and be significant. On the other hand, to stay with specific happenings for their own sake limits the educational value of the meetings. It is not enough for parents to say, "Well, that's how it is," or "That's how kids are," or "I guess that's what happens in families," or even "All children seem to be the same" or the opposite, "No two children are alike." The substance of the discussion should move to new levels as specifics are described, compared, and evaluated. They should, of course, reveal both basic similarities and individual differences in children and families. But these should emerge not just as a general picture, but in relation to the characteristic phases of family development, such as the adjustments of the pregnancy period or the behavior of children and parents in relation to the psychological problems of each stage of growth (what Erikson calls the "developmental tasks") and in the face of special settings or special problems with which a particular group may be concerned. Within the area defined as the focus for the group, specifics must lead to general trends and concepts—interpretations that illuminate the dynamics of development and interaction and open up new possibilities or reaffirm previously established ways of dealing with specific behavior, in keeping with the principles of sound mental health. Here it is not a matter of either/or. It is rather a continuous process in which the discussion shifts purposefully from one aspect to the other as seems indicated, to further the group's learning.

THE INDIVIDUAL AND/OR THE GROUP

Parent group education is by definition an experience in which individual parents make active use of group processes for their own learning. This differs from learning in a kind of classroom procedure where the lines of communication run from a central figure or "teacher" to each "student." In parent group education the pattern of communication is a continuous circle of interchange. The "students" make up the rim and the leader is the hub of the circle. He relates to each and also facilitates their communicating with one another.

In parent group education, some balance between the individual and the group is essential. Each parent brings his special needs and demands, growing out of his special circumstances and temperament. But here the individual becomes involved in group sharing, in the belief that he will be able to draw from it what is significant for him. If a discussion is allowed to focus primarily on one person, there is little opportunity for the sharing that provides the rich texture of the discussion; and even though the other members may try to be helpful and add their comments about the individual's "problem," they tend to be less involved and feel less secure if they have to wait for *their* turn to come as the primary figure in the discussion. As in the interplay between the general and the specific, the flow of interest moves from the individual parent to the group as a whole and, often, back again.

In the interchange, a composite picture with general implications is gradually built up, against which each parent tests his own situation and his response to it. Hopefully, each parent will take from the general discussion some added understanding which he will apply to his own family in his own way. It is often helpful if the leader comes back to the parent who originally described the situation which became the focus of the meeting and asks whether the discussion was meaningful or useful to him. His response then challenges the other parents to think about their reactions, too, and to stay with the subject longer, if they feel that the basic issues have not been evoked. So the shift from the individual to the group and back again continues.

If properly explored, any individual family or parent-child situation has elements of significance for all the group. If it is close to the experience of many of them, parents gain relief from knowing they are not alone in having to meet it. They also begin to isolate some of the factors of inner growth and external environment that may be bringing it to the fore. When a situation in one family is "way out," quite different from what is happening with most of their children, they as well as the parent who introduced it get some feeling of what is "out of bounds" and may perhaps need individual attention of some kind.

The shift from individual to group and back again takes place at many levels: in relation to the content of the discussion, the feeling tones that are aroused, and the interplay of personalities as they take their individual roles in the group. It makes a changing, kaleidoscopic picture of great variety. The important thing is that it not get stuck and stay with one person, to the exclusion of others in the group.

Many leaders find it difficult to maintain this balance. Sometimes a leader who is a psychologist or a caseworker finds himself caught up with the individual and his problems; he becomes so absorbed in having the discussion meet one person's need that he tends to overlook the group as a whole. A leader who comes from the field of education may err in the opposite direction and try to meet the broadly educational needs of the whole group without giving sufficient thought to the concerns and growth capacity of individual parent-members. Leaders, from whatever field, become more skillful in providing for these two functions of the group experience if they remind themselves of the essential nature of the group educational process and the purposes for which it has been set up.

FACTS AND/OR FEELINGS

Another pair of contrasting qualities that must both be provided is that which is cryptically identified as "facts and feelings." Obviously, here we are not talking about facts in a vacuum. Facts that are isolated bits of information are valueless unless they have personal meaning for the people who are acquiring them. Education helps people to "discover the meaning of facts so that behavior is affected. People behave in terms of the personal meanings (perception) existing for them at the moment of action." [1]

Furthermore placing "facts" and "feelings" in opposite categories implies that they are quite separate, which of course is not true. As one listens to parents talking about "facts" of behavior, it is obvious that there is some feeling connected with the recitation. When a mother describes how

[1] *Perceiving, Behaving, Becoming: A New Focus for Education,* Yearbook 1962, Association for Supervision and Curriculum Development, National Education Association, Washington, D.C., 1962, pp. 67, 68.

Tommy persistently dawdles at breakfast and she just can't get him off to school on time, she shows her irritation in the tone of her voice as well as in the words. In a discussion of what expectant parents know and want to know about the "facts" of anesthesia, as it is used in childbirth, the underlying feeling may not be so clear. As the talk goes on, however, one usually hears—if one listens—suggestions of many possible feelings here, perhaps anxiety regarding pain in labor and delivery, or fear the mother may not come through unharmed, or even exhilaration at the thought that one might be able to do without any anesthesia and thus experience completely the ultimate reality of giving birth to a baby. In practice, however, groups often tend to focus on one of these sides of an issue and remain stuck there. Unless they are helped to expand the scope of the discussion, they may talk only about the facts of what is happening, or only about their feelings.

In watching and guiding the discussion with regard to facts and feelings, there is an added dimension. It is apparent that both elements are essential if the group is to have a more complete view of the matter under discussion. But these elements are more than two sides of the same experience: in a very real sense, they affect each other in a constant interplay. The irritation the mother feels with her school-age child at the breakfast table undoubtedly influences not only her perception of the boy's behavior but her ability to cope with it and help him. And her irritation may be lessened if she is able to get a clearer appreciation of the "facts" of the boy's behavior. Perhaps he just does not need the amount of food *she* thinks he should eat. Or perhaps he is postponing going to school until the last moment so he will not have to meet a gang of boys who are "picking on" him. Or there may be some other reason for his acting as he does. In the other example cited, a mother's apprehension about childbirth in general may cause her to accept having anesthesia—any anesthesia— without thinking through what it may really be like. For her, a greater knowledge of the various kinds of anesthesias from which a doctor will choose flexibly according to his judgment of a mother's need will certainly help to allay some anxiety.

Usually this cause-and-effect relation of "facts" and "feelings" flows back and forth as the discussion develops, though the group may not be aware of it. The leader sees what is going on, encourages this interplay, and at times, when he feels the group has reached the point where they can accept it, makes explicit what he thinks has been happening. In the case of the boy at the breakfast table, the leader may find it expedient to make a comment such as, "It *is* hard, isn't it, to see what may be going on in a child when one naturally finds his behavior so irritating," or perhaps later, after something has developed to suggest that there may be a special reason for his dawdling, "It is easier to be patient and to help a child, isn't it, if we begin to see what he is going through."

Contrasting "facts" and "feelings" may become more clear if we examine somewhat further how the words are used in this context. "Facts," as used in parent group education, includes chiefly two kinds of information: specific behavior, within the general range of child development and family relations, that seems of sufficient concern to be worth bringing up in a group; and knowledge about phases of growth and development and interpersonal and community relations. They, too, feed into and illuminate one another.

Take, for example, the behavior of children following the assassination of President Kennedy. In group after group at that time, parents poured out their concern about their children's responses to his unbelievable, tragic death. Some children were completely shaken, as were their parents. Others were excited but seemed not to appreciate the significance of what had happened, at least at first. Even these children, however, slowly began to talk about death and what death might mean in their lives. They expressed their questions directly and indirectly. But beneath their words, they seemed to be saying in many different ways: Would their parents die? Who would take care of them then? Would they feel lost, as the world around them felt lost when the young, shining leader was gone? Would they die too? Adolescent girls and boys seemed to ask even deeper questions. They talked about God and religion and what life was all about anyway if something like this could happen.

Although parents were struggling with their own grief, many were surprised and shocked at the intensity of these feelings. They wondered whether they should have protected their children from knowing about the catastrophe and how much they should have let them remain glued to their television sets. Some said they *wanted* their children to know and share the nation's tragedy. It gave them a sense of their country and of history, one mother said. As they talked further, they seemed better able to look at their children's responses in a more individual way, and to think about them in the light of the children's ages and stages of understanding. The discussions seemed most helpful in those groups where parents came to grips with the fact that sooner or later children do meet the reality of death in some form. They cannot escape its lurking presence, some said, and gave examples from their own families. Almost all of these discussions ended with parents talking about ways to help children face and cope with this ultimate reality, protected and supported by the parents' own attitudes and beliefs.

As the group develops a common basis of information from which to begin their exploration, they begin to recognize what they know and what they need to know, individually and as a group. The leader then helps them to correct misconceptions and also supplies additional information as they need it.

To take a rather simple example: a mother reported that her two school-age children were constantly quarreling, giving each other no peace. The group had accepted this situation as being of general interest and had begun to explore it, all members bringing in comparable episodes from their own homes. It soon became clear that the members had quite different ideas about the meaning of such behavior. They also seemed to have wide differences in their ability to tolerate and deal with it. Some accepted this as a "normal" sign of "sibling rivalry" and something you just had to put up with. At the other extreme, a few mothers felt that children in the same family should love one another and saw their children's bickering as something evil, something to be ashamed of. In between were two parents who understood that an older child might be jealous of the new baby but thought that in a few years these feelings would fade out.

This group knew what was happening in their homes, but their understanding of basic principles of child development from the mental health point of view was quite incomplete. After much patient exploration they came, as a group, to a better appreciation of the normality of tensions between siblings throughout childhood, the ambivalent nature of their feelings toward one another, how parents often stimulate feelings of antagonism between their children without being aware of it, and the many ways in which they as parents could help the children cope with their angry feelings and find other outlets and satisfactions. The discussion of this issue had many strands. In the process, the group's knowledge of behavior was expanded and certain false assumptions were clarified.

To accomplish this, leaders are careful to help the group examine the knowledge on which their reactions are based. In discussing thumb-sucking or masturbation, for example, they need to find out what these forms of behavior mean to a parent, to many parents. Is there some lurking idea that such behavior may presage mental deficiency or perversion? Will added knowledge of the nature of psychosexual development help parents see the behavior in a more realistic light and help them to help the children more constructively? The important point here is that the leader and the parents need to know what they know before the group can go ahead.

This question is more obvious in expectant parent groups where many of the parents' concerns—both husbands' and wives'—are closely linked to facts about the physical aspects of the pregnancy and postnatal period and the nature of medical-nursing practice. Here, too, many misconceptions often are presented in the form of "old wives' tales," which need to be examined for their validity. In such groups one can see more clearly how "correct" information often helps to lessen specific anxieties. It also increases the confidence of the couple in their ability to cope with their respective parts in labor and delivery and the care of the baby, when the time comes.

Feelings, on the other hand, cover an equally wide range. Sometimes, out of one's experience with many children and parents, one can almost anticipate what these feelings will be, especially in situations that are common in families. Yet sometimes they are surprising in nature and intensity. In such cases, they are usually found to be connected with unusual occurrences in an individual's life. They may include any emotional response to an issue under discussion: annoyance, frustration, anger, pleasure, pride, fear, elation, comfort, discomfort, sympathy. You name them.

Yet the word "feeling" is in itself apt to be misleading. It is often used, of course, in relation to physical sensations of pain or well-being. "How do you feel today?," a well meaning intern asked a patient in the hospital. She answered quietly, "Miserable," to which he countered, "Where is your pain?" To his surprise, the patient answered, "I don't have a pain. I just feel generally miserable at having to be here."

Obviously, there are feelings and feelings. Especially in expectant parent groups, physical feelings fall into the classification of facts or real happenings. Here young expectant mothers bring out the extent to which they are preoccupied with their bodily changes and the discomforts that often accompany them. For example, an expectant mother's backache in her ninth month is a fact which she needs to put into its proper perspective. She needs to understand its physical relation to her stage of pregnancy and its possible significance as a prelude to labor. At the same time, she may be reacting emotionally to the backache, perhaps with feelings of irritation that it persists so long, or dread of what is coming next, or fear that this may be with her forever, and on and on.

It is the subtle emotional responses that are of special significance in parent group education, for they are often unrecognized even by the person experiencing them. Parent group education concerns itself with those feelings that are conscious or closely accessible to consciousness, feelings that are connected with immediate happenings, but that may range far and wide. A parent, listening to another mother's description of how she felt about her daughter's staying out at night beyond the time they had agreed on, burst out with, "Oh, I guess that's just how *I* feel when Sue comes home later than she said. I'm not only worried about her but I'm mad at her, too, for upsetting me in this way. Only I never saw it quite that way before." The mother's face showed that she was shaken and yet exhilarated by bringing out in the open something she had only vaguely sensed. She had not talked about her feelings in an abstract theoretical way; she had *expressed* her feelings directly, in relation to and out of experience. The outburst seemed to clear the air for this mother and for the others as well. The group then began to examine more thoughtfully what went into such episodes on the parents' part and that of the young people themselves, and later found themselves thinking about what they might do in handling such situations.

The mere mention of feelings as an important part of parent group education frequently raises a significant question. If group members are permitted to express their feelings, does not this turn the group experience in the direction of therapy? Behind this question is the implication that feelings are dynamite and not to be touched or tampered with. This point of view, it would seem, is based on the concept that feelings exist primarily in the unconscious and, since they are largely repressed, are pathological in nature and should only be explored within a deep therapeutic process. Yet we know that people have many kinds of feelings which they handle in different ways, some with repression, some within their individual mechanisms of defense, some within the more accessible aspects of their ego functioning.

These accessible feelings are appropriate for and open to educational intervention: emotional responses that are close to the surface of consciousness and easy to tap; responses that are common to many, yet have shadings of difference for each individual; responses that relate to a parent's current experience (though undoubtedly influenced by previous happenings in his life, some of which he may remember and bring out spontaneously); in short, responses that, with his growing acceptance of the group and its approach to learning, he chooses to share with the other members for their mutual gain.

Tied closely to the idea that all feelings must be dealt with gently if at all is the concept that feelings usually mean anxiety and that anxiety has absolutely no place in parent group education. Parent group leaders and other parent educators often express this point of view. Yet here again, experience has shown that feelings are not always linked with anxiety but may be the direct expression of many other strong emotions, both positive and negative. (Is it perhaps our own fear of *any* strong feeling that makes us uncomfortable when we meet it in others or experience it in ourselves? And do we tend to project our own anxiety onto parents and decide it is better not to discuss it with them because of our reluctance to come to grips with the emotional aspects of everyday existence?)

This is not to negate the fact that parents do bring a great deal of anxiety to the groups—anxiety about their children, themselves, and their capacity to be adequate parents. Some of this may have deep roots in the personality and life history of individual parents, roots which are not deliberately uncovered or explored in parent group education. But much of it is provoked by the parents' daily functioning in their families and is therefore immediate and ever-present, though with shifting intensity. Parents know this; they bring it out in group after group. To avoid or evade it is impossible, even if one wanted to do so.

Furthermore, to avoid recognizing or facing anxiety is contrary to the basic principles of group education. If we honestly believe that any aspect of living in families is suitable for discussion, then we cannot exclude the feelings that are so much a part of it. If we sidestep anxious feelings even by indirectly turning the group's attention in other directions, this very avoidance inevitably gives the parents the impression that anxiety *is* bad and dangerous. On the other hand, if they are not deflected but are rather encouraged to express their anxious feelings as these relate to their preparation for parenthood or their relations with their children at different phases of the family cycle, bringing these reactions out within the safety of the group and with the acceptance of the leader can give them a new sense of their own power. They feel better able to meet whatever comes, the unpleasant as well as the pleasant.

In a very real sense, facing anxiety can be an important source of learning and growth. Moderate anxiety about one's functioning as a parent is one of the best stimuli to goad parents to turn to educational services. We are using the word "moderate" advisedly. Educational programs are generally of little help to parents whose anxiety pervades all aspects of their functioning or is so intense in the area of their parent-child relations that it paralyzes them in their dealing with their families. In such cases, treatment services are usually indicated, unless for special reasons it is thought that these might not be helpful.

THE PARENTS AND/OR OTHER FAMILY MEMBERS

This category is perhaps the most obvious. Its balances are the easiest to recognize and the simplest to develop. Their significance lies in the fact that the family is best understood if it is seen in its totality, as an entity in itself, made up of individuals whose very presence and behavior constantly affect one another in continuing interaction.

The Parent(s) and/or the Children

Since these parent groups are formed with the express purpose of dealing with parent-child relationships and family matters, naturally the bulk of the discussion is focused on the "problems" and relationships of parents with their children. Even the original formulation of purposes implies that parent-child relationships are a two-way process. Yet there is a strong pull on the part of some parents and some groups to focus primarily either on the children or on the parents, without giving adequate weight to the other partner or partners in the family interplay. So it is necessary that parents be helped to broaden their understanding by looking at the total picture from both sides. If they are preoccupied with their own struggles, difficulties, and inadequacies and their feelings about *themselves* in relation to their children, they must be given a chance to move away from their self-absorption and to think about their *children*, so that they can come to understand them better and to feel with them. If they are preoccupied with their children's behavior and attitudes, they must have a way opened to think about their own part in the parent-child interaction. Often a simple comment from the leader is enough to shift the discussion from one direction to the other side of the balance. He may say, "Well, what about the children (or you parents) in all this?" or perhaps, in a less directed opening, "It isn't easy for the children (or for parents) either, is it?" or some comment of recognition that breaks through the parents' single-track thinking and jolts them—even though it is done gently—to become aware that there is more to be taken into account.

This tendency to get stuck either with the children or with themselves is frequently apparent when the discussion is concerned with what parents call "discipline," a subject area that might be described more euphemistically as "exerting influence" over their children. Here both aspects are extremely important if a better picture of the problem is to emerge as a basis on which the parents may be able to handle it more wisely. They need time to give vent to their feelings, their hopes and aspirations, their disappointment or frustrations and to consider thoughtfully what they have done that seems to have "worked" or "not worked." But all this is meaningless unless it is accompanied by a better appreciation of the child who presents the disciplinary problem. What emerges is a composite picture of this child and other children in similar positions, a picture characteristic of the particular age and situation under discussion, but which also includes the many factors that may make a particular child behave and feel as he does. Only then can the individual parent come to any decision as to what he will want to do in relation to a particular child or problem.

This twofold approach applies to most if not all of the difficult management problems parents face: with the two and a half-year-old who plants his feet squarely on the ground and says "I won't" to any suggestion; or with the ten-year-old girl who finds all kinds of delaying tactics—washing or curling her hair, or watching a favorite television program, or chattering endlessly with her "best friend" next door—to avoid doing her homework;

or with the teen-age boy who goes out to wander aimlessly on the street with other boys, some of whom his parents are certain will lead him into "bad ways." In all of these fairly common situations, the parents' wishes, aspirations, and feelings are vital. But so are the needs, attitudes, and feelings of the children and young people. Out of a better feeling for both, parents come to work out plans as to what they will do.

With the teen-ager, for example, they may decide to be more accepting of his behavior—however they may dislike it—if they see that the boy is gaining a feeling of independence and confidence from being accepted in a group of his peers. Or if they decide that there is too great a risk that under the gang influence he will become destructive and even lawless, they will want to use every means in their power to keep him away from this particular group. Or they may decide on some compromise in between. Usually, a broad, balanced exploration of the situation helps the parents to involve the young people in their decision, listening to them, talking the matter over with them, and explaining their reasons for taking a stand—if this seems necessary. In discussions on subjects of this kind, parents have gone away from group meetings planning many different approaches, and they feel supported somehow in trying to see how they will work.

In expectant parent groups, the parent-child relationship is a peculiar one, since the parents are preparing for a new baby who has as yet no definite characteristics beyond the fact that he (or she) is known to be present *in utero* and growing. In the early months of the pregnancy, the mother has no direct knowledge of even this, except for the usual evidences of general bodily change. Often a mother will say that she never was really sure she was going to have a baby until she "felt life" around the fourth or fifth month. And yet expectant mothers and fathers come to groups to prepare themselves for the baby's coming and for his care.

In actuality, these young men and women give little real thought to the baby in the first trimester of the pregnancy. Since the group is supposed to give them anticipatory guidance in baby care, they often do raise questions in early sessions about the baby's bath and methods of feeding, but they do so without seeming to be really involved in these matters. Their discussion is much more vivid and personally significant when they talk about the mothers' bodily changes and discomforts, difficulties with diet, thoughts and fears about labor and delivery, and, running through everything, their awareness of the changes they foresee in their own lives because of the new baby. Husbands as well as wives share these concerns. As the pregnancy comes closer to term, the interest of the parents tends to shift more and more toward the new baby. The imminence of his arrival seems to bring home to them their need to know more about how to give him the care he will need. As they talk about babies in general, they seem to be turning toward *their* baby—and he becomes a little more real.

Leaders who are familiar with the usual psychological manifestations of the various periods in pregnancy respect these trends of interest. They know, however, that parents in these groups are preparing for a relationship. If they think only about themselves, they are missing an essential part of the learning they may need for the future and they are pushing away their entering into the relationship, almost as if they were denying it.

Total preoccupation in the group with the fantasy baby and even with the specific details of his future care are again incomplete preparation for the parents' role with him. This may also be a denial of their own involvement with him or of their wish and readiness to become involved. Or it may be evidence of some other denial—perhaps an inability to face the reality of the pregnancy and childbirth. Particularly in this category of balances, any extreme avoidance of one side of the relationship is suspect.

And so the leader takes responsibility to see that the group is helped in some measure to explore both aspects of this pairing—the parents and the coming baby. He does this without probing for the possible deeper meanings of one or the other preoccupation. He watches for any comment from the group that may suggest an opening which he can pick up for the group to explore further if they will. Or he may say something like, "We haven't talked much about the baby up to now, have we?" Or, as in the previous examples, "We really have been talking mostly about the baby so far. What about yourselves in all this?" Thus in a direct, realistic way he passes on to all the group members his understanding of what the group has done and still needs to do. If the parents do not follow his opening, he does not force them to, and he may have to reconsider whether his suggestion was well timed. Perhaps they needed more discussion before they were willing and able to move on. And so he may try again later on.

If the leader has been involved empathetically as well as intellectually with the group, the parents are likely to follow his lead, even though they may not always continue with it as far as he would like. Shifts into new areas may be brief and choppy at first and the discussion may still swing back and forth. This process, too, is significant and, if the leader points it out, it can enrich the parents' understanding of the way in which the two aspects of the family relationship are really inseparable.

The Mother and/or the Father

Despite the myths that married couples become as one, each person has his own individuality, of course, his own ideas and beliefs. The "united front" parents consider so important in facing their children is often dominated by one or the other of them; they have continued in this pattern without giving much thought to the way they have shared and reconciled their different views. In parent group education there is a great opportunity for parents to bring these differences to light, to see what it means for each to respect the other's views, and to see how the differences can be handled.

In mothers' groups the talk is usually about what *their* experiences have been with the children, but gradually the fathers' ideas come into the discussion in one way or another. Sometimes a mother will say, "My husband has other ideas about this and I just don't go along with him." This gives the group a chance to find out what his ideas are, how valid they may seem under the circumstances, and how his attitude compares with that of other fathers. This brings in a whole new dimension for exploration. Another mother will reveal that she wishes her husband *would* tell her what he thinks and take more of an interest in the children. Or, in another vein, a mother will announce that her husband has strict ideas of discipline, stemming from his own early experiences, and although she doesn't go along with them, she is afraid not to—except sometimes when he isn't at home! Any reference to the father-mother relationship is rich in potential meaning for all the group members and may throw light on similar situations in their own homes.

Exploring the implications of any situation involving both husband and wife does not mean that the group should become involved in a discussion of marital conflict per se, for this is not the purpose of parent group education. Unquestionably, parental differences and disagreements can have a great influence on the child, and it is appropriate to explore this, following the same educational principles as with other phases of parent-child relationships. Facing the fact of differences may be a first step. One would then want to see what the differences are about and to look objectively at the concepts on which they are based. Finally, the group might examine the effect these differences may or may not have on the children and ways in which the differences might be handled, if not resolved, in the best interest of the children and of themselves.

This brief formulation is not meant to suggest that the process is an easy one. This is an area in which one's educational principles and convictions are really put to the test. But if clearly understood and well carried out, they have been useful in bringing in a breath—or sometimes a gust—of fresh air on a subject parents often hesitate to discuss. They can and often do come to take a hard look at themselves as well as at their spouses, even where there is considerable frustration and antagonism, and think more clearly about how they both function, as individuals and as partners in the family enterprise.

Discussions about the relation of husband and wife to the children, or to the coming child, involve much more than their differences. Often they reveal a deep, moving relationship of love and closeness which the parents want to maintain at all costs. This was brought out in the very first session of an expectant mothers' group, when, after the first go-around, they began the discussion by focusing on their husbands and their wish not to have them feel "left out." To some degree their concern may have grown out of their half-conscious recognition that at this stage of pregnancy they tended to withdraw into themselves, as many expectant mothers do. Without expressing this openly, they talked about the fact that their husbands were, in a sense, observers, while they were in the process of producing the baby. They sensed that they would be holding the center of the stage for some time, and that after the baby was born they would be preoccupied with his care. They brought out some of their husbands' reactions to the immediate situation and thoughts about the future. They ended this session with a discussion of the many ways they felt they could include their husbands all along the line—to the extent they wanted to be included—in preparing for the baby, in being with them during labor (the hospital in which they met did not permit husbands in the delivery room), and in helping with the babies' care. Underneath the discussion was a strong feeling that they were trying to protect the husband-wife relationship in the face of the new demands that would be put on it.

In mothers' groups all this takes place, of course, for one person of the couple; hopefully, however, some of what transpires in the group is shared in some fashion at home. The processes are more apparent and sometimes more difficult when husband and wife are both present in the group. In many places both mothers and fathers come to expectant parent groups; fathers also attend some evening groups with their wives to discuss their children, most notably those of preschool age or adolescence. In groups, husband and wife appear as a couple: they almost invariably sit together and form a unit in which one or the other tends to be the family spokesman. This behavior is likely to shift as the sessions go on. Encouraged by other parents and by the leader, the quieter ones often get to the point of speaking out and begin to appear as separate individuals. Sometimes they themselves are surprised at the way they can talk up and at the things they say.

Husbands and wives are not always in agreement—nor should they be. This may be the one place where they have group sanction to speak out and appear as themselves. Unfortunately, there have as yet been no adequate follow-up studies of the effects of group participation on the husband-wife relationship. There is some impression, however, that seeing themselves and their marriage partners in a somewhat new light may be painful at times and call for considerable readjustment, but it can be a step toward a sounder relationship. At the very least, the presence of both parents is evidence of the involvement of both with their children, even though some fathers come reluctantly, under pressure from their wives. Once they are there, the process of the group can cement their interest and increase their understanding of the role of both parents in the family interplay.

The Parent(s) and Other Family Members

Other family members are often brought into the discussion almost as if they were actually in the room, lurking behind the chairs. The parents' own parents or parents-in-law are referred to many times and are described in many ways. Some parents, and not only the very young ones, are still very much under their own parents' influence and do not hesitate to say so. "My mother says . . ." or sometimes even "My mother-in-law says . . ." comes out again and again, as if the mothers or mothers-in-law were the oracles who know all there is to know about child-rearing. Some years ago one seemed to hear somewhat less respect voiced for older persons. Parents then were more likely to call their mothers "old-fashioned" and not "hep to new ways." Perhaps today the value of life experience is somehow being given more weight, although the state of the world would hardly indicate that this is justified. Perhaps the difference in attitudes between generations is less marked since young people are marrying earlier and the time gap between parents and their parents is decreasing.

Yet this attitude of at least listening to the older generation is scarcely universal; one still sees many young parents who do not go along with the ideas of their parents at all and are struggling to find their own guidelines. Some go counter to *anything* their parents may think or believe, without relation to the real meaning of the issue itself. In groups, one hears echoes of all shades of the struggle of young adults to free themselves from the kind of influence their parents exerted over them when they were children. They show that they are at different stages of maturity in this relationship. Some are completely dependent, uncritically so. Some are still in the throes of what seems to be a prolonged or late "adolescent rebellion." Others are striving thoughtfully to step out on their own in terms of their own ideas and values.

Some of these variations are suggested in the following excerpt from a session of a group of Negro and white mothers in a city school:

They were discussing how they might best prepare their preteen daughters for menstruation. A Negro mother brought out with great feeling what had happened to her when her mother found out she was menstruating. Without warning, the mother had hit her across the face, leaving her shaken and in tears, not understanding what her mother's behavior meant and certainly more confused than ever about menstruation. "I was so mad at my mother," she said, "that I promised I would be different. If I ever had a girl, I'd try to help her. But then my Ma didn't bother much about us anyway," she concluded with great bitterness. After a moment of stunned silence in the group, a white Jewish mother said gently, "You know, I had just the same thing happen to me and I was just as hurt and upset. It was only years later that I found out that what my mother did to me was part of Orthodox Jewish tradition and that somehow it was supposed to be for my good. Then I had a better feeling about it—but I am still going to tell my daughter ahead of time and no slapping for me." The group went on to discuss the possible meaning of the slap. Some said it was supposed to bring blood to a girl's cheeks, others said it was to guarantee her good health, still others said it was a kind of symbolic warning that a girl should not "get in trouble" now that she had matured physically. Even this limited exploration by the group suggested that their mothers probably had not meant them any harm but had been acting in ways they themselves had not understood. Some of the sting seemed to have been taken out of even the first mother's bitterness, possibly because another mother had had a similar experience. Of course she stuck to her plan to "be different" to her child but she talked about it in a quieter, more realistic way.

Fortunately, as in this case, there are usually some parents in a group who have worked out their parent relationships in a fairly satisfactory way and are able to choose where they will go along with their parents and where they will not, without feeling guilty about it. When the group does not provide this kind of balance by itself, the leader can help bring it in. As in the case of marital disagreement, the group would not be expected to focus on the relationship for its own sake; the discussion would be directed rather to the validity of the *ideas* attributed to the member's parents, whether or not there was a dependent or rebellious relationship. In a group educational program, the emphasis is on the soundness of the grandparents' attitudes and ideas about the children, in practical terms. A better understanding of the grandparents' beliefs and actions will, of course, not bring about any deep change in the parent-grandparent relationship but it may accelerate just a little the parents' maturing. This area lends itself well toward a more balanced exploration of a particular issue, not just in terms of "what my mother thinks"—that is taken either as gospel or as of no value at all—but directed consciously toward helping fathers and mothers find out what meets the issue most satisfactorily.

As one might expect, the influence of the thinking of older people seems to come out more in expectant parent groups since today many young about-to-be parents are not far in time from their own childhood homes. But the same overtones may come out in connection with all stages of child-rearing, even of adolescence. The struggle of parents to find and maintain their own ways goes on for a long time and is often reactivated at any period or in any special situation of stress. Group education can make a real contribution, if it helps parents with the difficult task of coming to an objective decision without being unduly influenced by their emotional bias. It sets up a process in which parents learn to extract what seems to them to be valid out of general knowledge and specific experience, by-passing as far as they can the emotional overtones that are connected with the source from which this knowledge comes.

INNER FORCES AND EXTERNAL CIRCUMSTANCES

Parents often do not fully recognize certain aspects of human behavior that have been illuminated by new scientific knowledge in the past half-century. This knowledge is concerned with the inner forces of personality and particularly with the dynamics of behavior (what makes Johnny—and his parents and siblings—tick), interpersonal relations (how people react on one another), and the feelings people have, both positive and negative, that influence their attitudes and behavior. In order to help parents assimilate this knowledge, group discussions have dealt to a great extent with the inner psychological factors in family interplay, helping parents sort out those that are most pertinent to their own needs.

Along with this, parents have also brought out the difficult problems they face because of external conditions such as poor housing, deteriorating neighborhoods, overcrowded schools, and the like. They have talked about how hard it is to do well by their children under these adverse circumstances. How can they arrange for a child to have privacy in doing his homework when there is no real privacy anywhere in their home? If he does not do his work, will this mean that he will become a "drop-out"? What priorities should be set up in buying clothes for the children, when they all need more than there is money to buy? Should teenagers be given a special break, since it seems to mean so much to them to dress just as the other teenagers do? What about letting these older boys and girls work after school, when they have so much studying to do, too? Questions of management have been raised on many issues and in many ways and the parents have benefited from the thinking and experience of other group members.

But perhaps not enough attention has been given to the effects of these difficult situations on family relations and on the personalities of the children. These effects have usually been implied, yet they need to be made explicit if the picture is to be complete. This is another area where balance should be maintained in the group by avoiding overconcentration on the inner forces of psychic struggle and interpersonal relations, on the one hand, and the nature of external circumstances, the outside factors that bombard the family, on the other. However, for the balance to be complete, the discussion must do more than recognize and explore both ends of the scale; it must point to the close and constant interplay between the two.

For reasons about which one can only speculate, some leaders find it difficult to have a group look into the deeper impact of social conditions. They find some issues easier to deal with than others, possibly because the parents themselves find them easier to talk about. Mothers often share with the group, for example, their indecision about whether to go to work and "go off" the welfare rolls. They are quick to point out their concern about making the proper provisions for the care of the children, either all day for the younger ones or after school for the older ones, and they are quite aware of how the children may feel about their going away every day and seeming to abandon them. They often know how such an arrangement will put an extra burden on them and extra strain on their relations with their children. Will they be able to have a good give-and-take with their boys and girls—of whatever age—in the short evening hours that remain after they get home from work? Will there be time and energy left for pleasant things or even for sharing the day's happenings after the evening meal is over? And, some mothers go so far as to say, will they be able to be firm with the kids when they need it and not "spoil" them because they want to pack only good things into their limited time together? With these openings, leaders have comparatively little trouble in helping the group explore some of the feelings that may prompt these fears and the extent to which they may or may not be valid, clearing the way for a better basis on which each mother will make her own decision.

Other situations seem to be more difficult for leaders, yet they come up time and time again. In two groups in different parts of the country, parents brought out their discomfort about their social position due to their limited financial resources. In one group, the parents talked about the way they were looked down upon in the community because they lived in a low-income housing project; in the other, the same attitudes were cited because they were "on relief." In both instances, the parents mentioned that they were very hard on their kids. They wanted to be sure their youngsters would do nothing to increase the feeling of the community that they were not only "poor" but also unable to control their children. Their fear for their children was mixed up with their wounded pride and the threatened loss of self-esteem which they wanted so much to maintain.

In both instances, the leaders, out of their wish to protect the parents from overexposing themselves, found it hard to encourage the group to articulate these feelings more clearly, examine the extent to which they stemmed from something in the parents themselves or from the outside world, and see what all this meant in relation to their children. In both cases, the leaders recognized the strong feelings these parents were burdened with, and knew how necessary it was to bring them out in the open. Each leader handled the group situation in his own characteristic way, not always feeling as free in exerting his leadership as he would have liked, and caught, with different degrees of involvement and identification, in the weight of shame and defeatism of the members themselves. Yet, by encouraging the parents to talk more about their view of the problem and by accepting what the parents felt in the social circumstances they shared, the leaders did help them in some measure. They were able, to some extent, to come to grips with their discomfort, their sense of guilt at being where they were, and the undue pressures they were putting on the children to be models of behavior so as not to draw attention to themselves in any way. To some degree the group saw what the external circumstances were doing to them and their children—and began to marshall their inner resources to meet the issues more realistically.

THE PRESENT AND THE PAST

Even though they are concentrating on the present, parents know that there is a continuity of experience and, on their own initiative, often bring out experiences from the past. Frequently the talk is about events that immediately preceded some occurrence, usually some change in a child's pattern of behavior. A small child becomes difficult to manage, for example, and on giving it some thought, the parent reveals that this behavior started soon after the coming of a new baby. Another child begins to night-wander around the house and the parent wonders whether this is at all related to the fact that the parents have begun to talk about separation and possible divorce; they had thought the child did not know a thing about the possible breakup of the marriage. The time-relation thus often suggests a possible cause for this new behavior, not recognized before.

The leader can suggest this line of thinking if the parents do not introduce it themselves. He may ask, in a specific situation, whether anything unusual had occurred in the life of a child (or of children) that might be related to this new or troublesome behavior. A simple question of this kind stimulates parents to think about the happenings in the recent past and even sparks their recognition of how they felt at the time. This exploration can be done without probing into the unconscious or exposing the parents' individually colored, emotional reactions. The stress is on the "what" of how they responded and not on the personal motivations that determined "why" they felt as they did.

Sometimes, as in some of the records already quoted, parents go much farther into their past and come out with surprising connecting links between happenings in their childhood and their present situations. In an expectant parent group, for example, the following discussion took place:

A group of expectant mothers were discussing natural childbirth. One mother said, somewhat angrily, that her doctor had commented that mothers who asked for natural childbirth were somehow special. She had not asked him what he meant but had been troubled by the remark. What was so special about them, anyway? The group was silent for a moment. Then, one after another, the mothers began to say why each of them had chosen to deliver their babies with natural childbirth. One mother said she thought it would be easier this way and that through exercises she might have her baby without pain. Although some of the mothers questioned the certainty of her conclusion, they went on to give other personal reasons for their choice. One mother said with great feeling that somehow she felt this was connected with her experiences as a child. She and her mother had fled from Eastern Europe ahead of the Nazis. Her father, however, was apprehended and died in a concentration camp. She had been spared, and her life had been comparatively easy. In choosing to have her baby by what she considered the hard way, she said she felt that somehow she was making up to her father for his suffering and also proving that she too could go through an ordeal. The mother next to her added that she herself had lived an easy, protected life and wanted to face the important experience of giving birth to a baby in all its reality. She was eager to know what it was all about. At last, another mother broke the tense, serious mood by saying somewhat sharply, "I don't *know* just why I want to do it, but I am going to try to have my baby this way. So what!" After a very brief pause the leader underscored the obvious fact that such a decision had different personal reasons for each one, and the group then went on to talk about what natural childbirth really meant.

In another group in an elementary school, mothers and fathers were discussing the enormous amount of fighting among their children. In most cases the five- and six-year-olds who were fighting were the older ones in the family, and they all had younger siblings. Several parents discussed how hard they found it to put up with this kind of quarreling. After some discussion, a father said he suddenly realized that he had been the oldest brother in his family and remembered how much fighting had gone on between him and his younger sisters and brothers. To prevent this in his own family, he had gone all out to support the older child when the next baby was born, concentrating on his needs so that he would not feel pushed aside by the new baby. Now he wondered whether he had perhaps gone too far and neglected the younger one. A mother seated near him added, with some feeling of shock, that she too had been the oldest in the family, had the same memories of fighting as a child and had behaved in quite a similar way when her second child was born. During all this, a mother and a father across the room, representing different couples, had been talking quietly. The father broke in at this point to say that he and Mrs. S. had discovered that they, who had seen very little evidence of rivalry in their children, had both been only children. They wondered whether this had in any way affected their attitude toward their youngsters. They both had felt deprived as children, because they had no playmates in the home and had envied their friends who had sisters and brothers. They were delighted to provide their first children with a sister or a brother. The father who had introduced this part of the discussion then volunteered, "Well, it certainly shows that our own feelings from our childhood play a real part in what we are doing with our children."

Revelations such as these do not occur very often. When they do emerge, there is sometimes a temptation to stay in the past, stimulated perhaps by the excitement of discovery. In both of the discussions just cited, however, this did not happen. Having recognized something of the way the past was influencing their current behavior, they were glad to turn back to their immediate situations. The flow from the present to the past and back again had accomplished its purpose.

This is in keeping with the focus of parent group education which sees the relevance of the past to the present but starts with the immediate. It recognizes that "the *historic* view and the *immediate* view are not mutually exclusive." They are both true. "A person's behavior is, indeed, a result of his past experience, his life history. How he behaves right now, however, results from his ways of seeing, learned from his past experience, to be sure, but existing in his present perception at this time. . . . If we can understand how a person is perceiving right now—we may be able to help him change his behavior even if we do not know how he got that way. That is, if human behavior is a function of perception and if perception exists in the present, then it should be possible to change behavior if we can change present perceptions."[2]

THE PRESENT AND THE FUTURE

Parents also have one eye to the future even though they are dealing with the present. When they talk about what Debbie and Jim are doing now, they are often concerned about the implications of this behavior for the children's future development. And so it is important that parents be-

[2] *Perceiving, Behaving, Becoming: A New Focus for Education,* Yearbook 1962, Association for Supervision and Curriculum Development, National Education Association, Washington, D.C., 1962, p. 75.

come aware of this and bring out both their fears and their aspirations in order to see how far they are based on reality. The fact is, of course, that the future reality cannot be predicted. But when parents recognize that some of these concerns for the future are largely in their minds and cannot be definitely resolved at this time, the way is opened for them to evaluate present incidents more clearly.

The future plays a large part in the thinking of expectant parents, of course, since they are preparing for a great new experience. The group sessions can give them a *general* understanding of what is coming, but the exact details of what labor and delivery will be like for each of them, for example, must remain unknown until the fateful hour. How a particular mother will fare, how she will act, what her feelings will be, cannot be anticipated—and mothers have many surprises, both bad and good. Fathers, too, cannot predict what they will do and what their feelings will be. The greatest unknown is, of course, the baby himself: his appearance, his temperament, his sex, even his normality at birth. No wonder expectant parents have so many questions and anxieties, yet they have to live with these until they are finally answered by reality itself. In the meantime, in the group, the parents get general information which increases their understanding of the processes of pregnancy and birth, and they get some preparation for what babies are like in general. Most important, they learn what they can do at various times, such as in getting to the hospital, helping during delivery, and beginning to take care of the baby in the hospital and when they bring him home. Through discussion, their attention is also directed back to the present. The mother may discover ways of making herself more comfortable during various phases of the pregnancy. Stimulated by ideas from other group members, she and her husband can plan how they will arrange their lives and their homes for the baby's coming to provide for the well-being of all of them. They may begin also to explore their relations with other members of their families a little more thoughtfully, even perhaps the extent to which they will or will not want to involve them in helping with the care of the little one.

Some of the aspirations and concerns of parents for the future are suggested by the traditional jokes about what they say and do at critical times. There is the young father who wants to buy a bicycle for his boy's first birthday. And the parents (fathers especially) who worry about enrolling their sons in the old Alma Mater even before the youngsters are in school. Many middle-class parents can justify this last concern today because of the heavy pressure to "get" children into the "right" college, and the feeling that one must begin to think about this early, by sending them to the "proper" nursery, elementary, and high schools so they will have the best chance. But the exaggerated emphasis on college in general and on specific colleges, regardless of the possible nature and interest of the particular boy or girl, places such stress on the future that the realities of the child's present situation and unique possibilities tend to be lost.

The concern about their children's educational future is not limited to middle-class parents. In a group of Negro mothers in a low-income housing project in a southern state, the mothers revealed this concern in a number of ways. One mother, for example, was worried because she could not help her child enough with his homework. Another was upset because her child, absent some weeks because of illness, was now dropping behind the rest of the class. A third mother, whose daughter was thinking of getting married at seventeen, said that her main objection to the marriage was that it would keep her girl from going on for further schooling. These parents were struggling to find what they could do to help their children develop to their utmost. Their concern was definitely to prepare their children for a future about which they were full of apprehension.

Another type of fear for the future is that of the parent who lives in a neighborhood filled with group tensions and fears that his boy of ten, who "speaks up" to his father angrily at times, will become a delinquent. Such fears need to be unraveled, for they have many overtones. Both the great expectations and the fears need to be made explicit and separated from what the children are today. When parents begin to do this, they can consider what they can do—now—to help their children develop their particular capacities in their own particular way.

This process of checking the present against the future and future expectations against the present can also be described as maintaining a healthy balance between fantasy and reality.

FANTASY AND REALITY

While parental fantasies are usually directed toward the future, both positively and negatively, fantasy sometimes enters into a parent's view of the present, distorting his interpretation of what is actually going on. Again, one can turn to caricatures for clues. Take the mother, for example, who sees an expression on Johnny's face which reminds her of Uncle Willie and convinces her that he is foredoomed to be like him in every way. (Since she thoroughly dislikes Uncle Willie and everything he stands for, this is a horrendous thought!) Or the father who, looking into the hospital nursery, suddenly thinks his newborn son is the image of Winston Churchill, as many chubby infants are, and predicts a great political career for him. Of course there are many less vivid fantasies as well. It may not always be advisable or necessary to expose them in the discussion, but if parents bring them up with any degree of seriousness, they should be explored.

Putting these ideas into words is often enough. Parents sometimes laugh at themselves even as they talk, when they see how foolish these ideas are, since Johnny *isn't* Uncle Willie and his behavior—or facial expression—is very much like that of other children under similar circumstances, as reported by their parents. So the reality of Johnny-as-Johnny takes over and the fantasy—or fear—of Uncle Willie-in-Johnny fades out.

There are times, however, when parents' ideas about possible heredity based on external characteristics may have more serious implications for a particular parent and may make it difficult for him to respond to a child normally for his own sake. If this is the case, the parent's reactions need to be explored outside of the group.

POSITIVE AND/OR NEGATIVE FEELINGS AND EXPERIENCES

Parent groups seem to function with distinctive moods and colorations. Some are active and sparkling, others tend to be slow moving and somber. Often a single session of a series will take on a special tone. Bright sessions are often superficial. The talk flits from subject to subject without giving the parents breathing space to consider the less positive aspects of the subject under discussion or the difficulties they are really facing. In the somber meetings, parents are often stuck in their feelings of discouragement and defeat, concentrating on the difficult, negative side of their situations, their failures and frustrations—and often with good reason. At both extremes the mood is sometimes broken by the parents themselves. A parent will say, "But it isn't all as gay and cheery as we make it sound," or, in responding to the other extreme mood, "Aren't we the gloomy ones today! And yet it isn't always that grim. We do have some fun." The leader then picks up these clues and asks the parents to say a little more about what he or she has in mind. If the parents themselves do not try to counteract such a prevailing tone, the leader can initiate the shift, hoping the group will follow his lead.

A vivid example of a group caught in a negative mood and staying with it for many sessions was one composed of mothers of young mental retardates in their twenties who were attending a sheltered workshop. As the sessions progressed, the leader was aware that the parents were utterly discouraged and even depressed. They kept talking about the burdens they faced, the heavy demands these young people put on the whole family, and their fears for the future, since they saw no way in which this burden would ever be lessened. The leader came away from these sessions discouraged as well. Suddenly she realized that the mood of the parents had been contagious and that she was caught up in it, too. As she thought over their situation, she began to see that these parents had, in fact, done very well with these difficult young people. After all, they had managed to live together not too badly for over a generation. At the next meeting, her own attitude had shifted to some extent and she was able to ask the parents how they had managed. They began to discuss what they had done that had helped these young people in their adjustment to their handicap and to the world around them and found that they really had done a great deal. This seemed to break up the depressed mood of the group. The tone shifted and they were even able to laugh at some of their mistakes. As the talk moved on to their handling of management problems in their everyday situations, their feelings about themselves seemed to have changed as well.

Even when they are not faced with such an extreme situation, parents naturally come to groups with some sense of burden and considerable awareness of the difficulties in their family relations. That is why they come. So one expects that in groups there will be a preponderance of their negative feelings, about themselves as parents, their children, and their handling of their home situations, feelings that are closely tied to a sense of failure. To cut off the expression of these feelings prematurely negates one of the most important values of parent group education. Whatever is on the parents' minds has to be explored far enough for them to gain relief at having shared their concerns and some understanding of the validity of their feelings in relation to the children and the rest of the family.

It is not easy for a leader to know the magic point at which "enough is enough." There are two clues to watch for. Is the group repeating the same content again and again without moving on to a different level of understanding? And is there building up a mood of wallowing in their common misery and self pity? The leader uses his own professional judgment and personal sensitivity to decide when to introduce the opening to a new line of thought. But the group response is the best indication of whether his decision was right or not. In any case, the parents should be free to respond as they are ready to.

Ultimately, however, if the group is to accomplish its purpose, the discussions should end on some corrective note. Experience has shown that when given the lead, groups are usually able to come through with positive feelings along with the negatives, as in the group just cited. If they did not have some of this balance already, the burden of their daily living would be utterly overwhelming. In less ominous circumstances, they are also able to report successes with their children along with their failures. Often they seem to accept their successes as hardly worth mentioning, but once they are given an opening, they are glad to talk about them. Then what is happening every day assumes a better balance—and a realistic one.

SIMILARITIES AND/OR DIFFERENCES IN REACTIONS OR OPINION

A final concept of balance which enables a leader to stimulate group interaction toward better learning is that of similarities and differences in feelings and ideas or agreement and differences of opinion.

Parent group education provides the educational framework within which parents consciously develop their own opinions, based on expanding knowledge and thought. This approach is in keeping with the basic principles of our democratic society. Yet the idea that they should work through to an independent way of thinking, even though they are in a group, is new to many parents. In the beginning they seem to feel that being in a group implies that their ideas should conform. Conformity of thought or consensus *is* the ultimate goal of other types of groups that are directed toward social action. Such groups work toward agreement at least on a general plan which represents the group thinking. In parent group education, the parents learn to think for themselves, to come to their own decisions on the basis of the group discussion, and they are free to carry them out in their own individual way.

As a rule, parents are hesitant to disagree with one another at first, unless they are persons who are accustomed to dominate others or who are inclined to argue for argument's sake. For the rest of them, it usually takes a little time to know that it is actually expected that people will have different ideas and will express them.

Usually the differences are seen in the varied experiences the parents are having with their children, the different interpretations they give to them and the wide range of feelings they have about them. These they report with comparatively little hesitation, once they are involved in the process of group learning and know how they can take part in it. Sometimes the leader can identify the fact that there are differences and underscore the wide range of variations. At other times it is unnecessary for him to do so. The parents' comments speak for themselves.

Parents are apt to be uncomfortable, however, when they find they do not agree with another parent's opinion. "I don't see it that way at all," a mother may say, when the mother next to her states that her fifteen-year-old has to be home by ten o'clock. Or a parent may say vehemently, "I think you are all wrong," to a father who announces proudly (yet somewhat defensively) that he uses the strap on his kid to make him obey. At such a point the discussion is often helped if the leader comments that apparently the parents here have many different ideas on this subject, or "This is a matter about which we seem to have many kinds of strong feelings." Putting into words the awareness of both strong feelings and opposing ideas points up the right of each person to think and feel as he does. It broadens the spectrum of responses both of ideas and of emotions. And it takes the issue out of the area of personal conflict into that of discussion toward greater understanding.

If, on the other hand, differences of feeling and disagreement in opinions are smoothed over, it suggests that these differences are undesirable and are therefore to be avoided. Actually, such an attitude does even more. It takes away an important stimulus to sharper thinking. It also slows the members down in the process of finding out what they really think, not only on practical issues, but on the basic values which guide their lives. A discussion of methods of discipline, sparked by the episode of the father with the strap, challenges each parent to think through just where he does stand in the face of such extreme variations in attitudes, and why. He will have to decide what his own goals are for his child and what means he will use to guide him.

Differences and disagreements then are not an end in themselves. They can be used as a stimulus to deeper learning. At the same time, the group should come to feel in agreement on the freedom to express differences. At least they are all working in a common framework toward a common purpose: growth in individual self-knowledge and individual competence for each in his parenthood.

❊   ❊   ❊   ❊   ❊

As one goes more deeply into the many forces, the people, and the events that affect the health, personality development, and well-being of children and their families, one realizes again and again how much might be explored in any group. Yet in eight or ten or even twelve sessions one can only cut into certain limited areas of these parents' family living, like taking small wedges out of a large wheel of cheese. But these pieces give the flavor of the whole.

The main categories that have been outlined here can be taken as some of the "wedges." They are presented as a general outline of concepts, a kind of checklist for the leader to keep in mind. They describe many dimensions that might be introduced around any starting point to broaden the material as it develops. Obviously, all of these balances will never be achieved in any one meeting or series of meetings. The choice is made on the basis of what is relevant at different times, in relation to the parents' contributions and the course the discussion has taken. They will be most useful if they are introduced flexibly and selectively. They are especially helpful when the group seems to be concentrating on only one phase of their special interest and excluding other sides of the balance that are needed to give a rounded picture.

But the balances are not expected to be equal in amount or time devoted to them. Sometimes even a single, telling comment from a group member will suggest the balancing of the scales and open up a new and much needed point of view.

The process by which an area or subject is developed, then, becomes itself an important part of the group's learning. Parents begin to see—and the leader may want to make explicit—that this approach can be applied to any situation they are in. Knowing this makes them accept more readily the fact that the material covered in the group represents only a segment of their many interests. They sense that they are developing a tool or a method by which they can continue this line of thinking on their own, not only for current matters that have not been covered in the group but for new situations as they come.

IX

The Practice of Parent Group Education:
Pointing Up the Learning Experience

GIVING ADDED MEANING TO THE DISCUSSION

Its Meaning for "Coping"

As the mass of material is "put out on the table," the parents begin to sort it out. Instead of responding to an issue as a whole, they usually break it down into separate parts and react to them. Sometimes one of the separate parts takes over and emerges as the main focus, even obscuring the original issue. This may be quite in keeping with the interests of the group. At some point, however, they can learn from seeing where the discussion started and where it has gone. Picking up the thought connections between the parts and the whole, they see how they are interrelated.

In a seventh session of an expectant mothers' group, the mothers decided they wanted to talk about baby care, so they would be able to "do all right." After some fumbling around, they said they wanted to begin with the baby bath. They talked about the equipment they would need, how they would go about giving the bath, at what time of day, in what temperature room, etc. Since they were so absorbed in the specific procedures, the nurse-leader pulled out the equipment she always had available, and gave them a brief demonstration. As she did so, she answered a number of their specific questions, pointing out that there was "no one way," no fixed order of sequence, and relating everything she did to factors of safety and the baby's comfort. She commented that this was one aspect of baby care but there must be others of which they had been thinking. They then brought up many questions about the baby's clothing, the number of diapers, sweaters, blankets, and so forth. She helped them explore what they needed to know at the practical level and then checked back with them as to whether this information made them feel more comfortable about being able to "do all right." The question led them to examine their own insecurities and need of additional support. Toward the end of the session she pointed out that they had started from the question of baby care and the practical handling of some of its aspects. They then had seen that their need for this information was tied up with their feeling that because of their lack of experience they might not do too well when the time came. A number of the mothers nodded their heads as they went along with her interpretation.

There were many ways in which this opening might have been developed, as there always are. The leader might have picked up in the beginning on their wish to "do all right," given them some opportunity to examine the feelings that prompted the question, and then gone on to the practical matters about which they felt ignorant. It is essential, of course, that both aspects of the matter be explored. Airing some of the young women's feelings of uncertainty and the reasons behind them seems to help them accept them with greater comfort. At the same time, giving them some specific skills to draw on helps to allay their anxiety.

To give the discussion added meaning, the leader does not lead it in any predetermined channel, but follows the group's lead, using his knowledge and skills to clear up their confusions and expand their understanding. He does this partly by opening up new aspects of the issue for their consideration. He also underscores comments or interpretations that he feels are significant and sound and relates them to principles of individual behavior and family dynamics. A mother says, for example, that her fifteen-year-old daughter is not telling her everything that is going on with her boy and girl friends; although the mother feels hurt, she guesses maybe this is a sign that the girl needs more freedom to work things out alone or with her contemporaries. The leader may say something to the effect that Mrs. X. has brought out an important point, thus giving it extra weight. After the other parents have had an opportunity to share their ideas and experiences in this area, he may add that what they have been saying is in line with current thinking on this subject, that such behavior is seen as one evidence of the need of young people to work things out on their own, as a step to becoming psychologically independent. In underscoring and restating in this way, he picks up and strengthens what he finds valid and pushes the interpretation a little further.

He also opens up for further discussion comments and interpretations that need to be questioned. This selection is vital, for if questionable interpretations are allowed to stand, the group will have no hint that they may not be sound. Of course, the leader will not contradict a member or say flatly, "That isn't so." But he may pick the matter up with a comment such as, "Many people do think about it in this way, but perhaps we should talk about it a little more to see what is really involved." In most instances, the parents themselves will come to see on what basis the statement is unsound, if they are given a chance. But sometimes they do not have the necessary information on which to base their judgment. This the leader must add, although he will do so in a way that shows clearly that he is contributing something which the group has not known about so far.

In groups of parents of preschool children a subject brought up again and again is the problem of children coming into the parents' room during the night, wanting to get into their beds. Parents voice their annoyance at these episodes, which tend to occur repeatedly at certain periods in the children's early development, notably when they are around two and again around four. Parents are confused about what to do about these performances, and usually settle for the easiest way out, which is to take the children into their beds. Yet they sense that this is not meeting the issue directly and only hope the child will eventually be able to stay in his own bed. Group discussions on this issue bring out some of the reasons why children may find it hard to stay alone at night during periods of developmental stress: their new awareness of what is going on around them and their wish not to be left out; their discomfort with some of their own strong feelings which appear with great vividness in their dreams or night fantasies and from which they run to their parents for protection.

Although many parents see that their children are upset in some way, they often do not understand the strength of the children's inner drives, drives of which the children are not really aware. Frequently young children are full of aggression coupled with fear of punishment for their very thoughts. Or they have a wish to control the people around them, coupled with fear of being controlled. Or they are swept by mixed feelings of love and antagonism toward their mothers and fathers. Parents often bring out evidence from a child's own words of his ambivalence toward one or the other of his parents, as he struggles to find his place in the family constellation. Without knowing the full details of the oedipal struggle, parents nevertheless sense something of what it means when the boy says to his mother, "I wish Daddy would stay away on business so I can be alone with you," or the little girl, in a similar vein, tells her mother not to come back too soon from the PTA meeting, because Daddy will put her to bed. Often the discussion moves toward linking the children's comments with their night restlessness. Even when they recognize the principles of psychosexual development involved, parents often have not thought about the effect on the child of taking him into their bed. They recognize that this may "set up a habit," but they do not appreciate the extent to which it may stimulate and reinforce the very feelings that may be causing a child to leave his bed in the first place. After a rather full exploration of what children of this age are going through, leaders can usually build on what the parents have given them and point up from clinical experience that children learn better the hard way, by being taken back to their own beds time after time and helped to stay there. By doing this, parents avoid being caught inadvertently in reinforcing the child's fantasies; instead they reinforce the reality that the child is a child who must learn to stay by himself and that he is safe in his own bed, too. Where this concept is developed slowly and tied in with what the parents are already observing in their homes, they usually find it an important piece of knowledge on which they can base a better procedure.

If a discussion is to be helpful, then, its many ramifications should all lead up to what is sometimes called the "coping phase." Kurt Lewin stressed this step as "one of the basic properties of group life"—the swings from "perception" to "action," from the "subjective" to the "objective" aspects of what he defined as "social fields"—and back again.[1]

In a sense this is the core of the group educational process. How—and at what point—do parents translate their understanding into performance? In what ways does it help them meet and manage their daily problems with better success? At some point, the group thinking must focus in this direction. It usually does, without any nudging.

Sometimes this happens *too* quickly, before the group has thought the matter through sufficiently. The leader can then point out that it might be helpful if they talked more about the situation so that they could understand it better and then think about how they would handle it. But he must see that the group comes back to the coping aspect of the discussion before they leave the subject. They need to conceptualize—and articulate as well as they can—what it means to them in terms of what they might do, even if they are not ready yet to map out a specific course of action. This last step may evolve slowly, out of their somewhat different feelings and better knowledge, and it is best not to let it be rushed.

In the discussion about taking the child into the parents' bed, it is not enough for the group to end on the note that they should not give in to the youngster; they must go on to think about the various ways in which they can handle the problem constructively for the child as well as for themselves. If they are really convinced that it is better for him to stay in his own bed, they will take him back there, despite their own feelings of annoyance at having to get up in the middle of the night. If they appreciate what the child is really asking for, they will handle it so that he is assured that they will not abandon him (to his dreams or bad feelings, although these words would probably never be used) and that they will be nearby if he really needs them. The exchange in the group will give

[1] Kurt Lewin in Dorwin Cartwright, Editor, *Field Theory in Social Science,* Harper & Brothers, New York, 1951, p. 199.

them some idea of a variety of procedures which they may want to test: staying in the room for a while, keeping a light on in the hall and the door open, leaving a stuffed animal or beloved toy in the bed, and so on. But the exact way in which they will help their youngster learn to stay by himself and cope with the situation more effectively, they will have to work out for themselves.

No matter what situations are brought up—whether problems of discipline, or training in toileting, or study habits, or whatever—the discussion should raise in the parents' minds new methods, new alternatives, or even new conviction about the methods they may already be using. They then can choose, thoughtfully and deliberately, what they will want to do.

Going on to Other Areas

When a discussion of a particular issue seems to have run itself out and has been reasonably broad in scope, the group may feel they have "had it" and want to go on to something else. Sometimes the points that have been made are so clear that nothing more needs to be said. In that case the leader acknowledges the group's wish to move on and helps them find another focus from which to begin again. Sometimes, however, leaders like to summarize before leaving a subject, to pull together and restate the concepts that have emerged and help the group see where the discussion has led them. Such a summary serves also as a check on the leader's evaluation of the process. Does the group see it as he does and, if not, what do *they* see as having taken place? A review often brings out more clearly than before certain ideas that may have been only half-expressed and which the group members acknowledge with appreciative shakes of the head. Sometimes in summarizing, the leader gives further dimensions by adding information, or pointing out that there may be other implications that could be explored another time, if the group wants to come back to the subject later.

But there remains the question of how the discussion should be ended, for it will come to an end at sometime and in some way. Sometimes, as we have said, the subject runs itself out. Sometimes the end of the meeting is suddenly here; whether the discussion is fairly well completed or not, it must stop because of the time. There are no general rules one can prescribe except one: no matter what is happening, the group is entitled to some comment from the leader, giving them his interpretation of where the discussion has led them. If the situation is obvious, it may take only a word or two, such as "We can pick this up again next time, if you want to," or "We didn't get too far with this, did we?" or even, on occasion, a simple "Well, that's that!" (What he will do at the end of a *series* is another matter. This is discussed later in this chapter.)

Continuity of Discussion; Coverage of Content

The foregoing may make it appear that the flow of the discussion consists of separate pieces, isolated, self-contained, which the group completes and then, looking around, finds another piece to which to jump, like Eliza crossing the ice. Actually, the process is much less clear-cut. Although areas are explored more or less completely and new areas are entered into, they are not rigidly compartmentalized. Nor are they finally concluded if the group moves on to something else. There is always the opportunity to go back to an issue, if situations arise that throw new light on it or if, on mulling the matter over, parents have come to new insights. This is the advantage of so-called "unstructured" sessions which are not bound by a prefixed curriculum. In going back to pick up an issue that has been previously discussed, however, the general procedures of parent group education are followed to ensure that the discussion remains in keeping with the wishes of the group as a whole and not of only one member. If an issue is reopened, the group usually is glad to follow the lead, particularly if other parents, too, have had additional second sights to contribute.

In going on from one issue to another, there is often a recurrent underlying theme. It may not be apparent at first but the parents or the leader may identify it as it emerges, at one time or another. Even when no such theme emerges, parents sense that they are moving along in a general area, and often refer back spontaneously to what Mrs. S. said earlier or what they had discussed in a previous meeting. The leader uses this approach consciously to help build the continuity that is an important part of the group experience. For this reason it is essential that he keep clearly in mind what has gone on from session to session, so he can relate the group's current discussion to what has gone before.

To facilitate this, leaders usually keep weekly records, or at least write skeleton notes immediately after the meeting, or as soon as they can get to it. Naturally, leaders vary greatly in their rate of recall. The details of a group session fade out quickly for most of us, yet the details are what keep the group alive in our minds. They need not all be recorded, of course. One selects those contributions that revealed an individual's need and his possible growth, or were significant in moving the discussion ahead. Sometimes jotting down a word or phrase is enough to revive the incident, especially if it is identified with a particular parent. (These are often words or phrases other group members pick up and refer back to, almost as slogans.) Notes, however, are of little use if left in a notebook. It is important that leaders look them over before each session begins. Even a quick glance provides the background for the continuity, the development of ideas, and the uneven process of group thinking that slowly creates a totality all its own.

At any point the leader can strengthen this continuity by relating not only to what has been discussed but also to the person or persons who have spoken. In underscoring an idea or picking up a comment, he too can say, "As Mrs. S. has said." Sometimes he may quote her directly. Or he may vary this by saying, "As Mrs. S. has suggested," and go on to state something she may have implied, which he feels needs to be made more explicit. Often his comments may be related to "What we seem to have been saying," or "What we've been talking about." If he does not in some way identify that the contributions on which he is making his comments were made in the group, he may inadvertently give the impression that he is "telling" them something new, as if from an authority on the outside, and the parents may become irritated, since they have heard this before. If he adds new knowledge or information, as he often must do, he also relates this to what has gone on before. He may say something like, "Besides what we have been saying here, it is generally known that . . ." or "What we have been saying is along the lines of what the psychologists (or others) tell us about children of this age, etc." Of course these procedures cannot be followed in a regular, uniform way; their form grows out of the content of the discussion. They are important as realistic evidence that the content of the discussion actually is determined by the group members themselves and is developed as a cooperative venture with the leader's help.

At the same time, the leader has an obligation to see that the parents have an opportunity at some point to direct their thinking to the main areas of concern they have identified. These include, of course, the points they brought up in the first meeting. But often parents do not mention in the first go-around the concerns for which they really want help. Some hesitate to talk out freely at first, not knowing how other parents will react, and mention only matters they think they are expected to talk about. Others are not able to formulate their real needs clearly at first; they become aware of them only in the course of subsequent discussions. At whatever point their concerns are articulated, however, the leader should add them to his "list." Then *he* has them in mind, at least. When any of the parents bring them up again—or something related to them—he can refer back to the original comment, linking the two. If they do not come to these areas spontaneously, he may remind them of their earlier interest and thus bring the issues back for members to explore, if they still feel they are important. Or he may decide to leave them alone, even though he recognizes that they are "unfinished business"; and he may say so at the end.

Sometimes a leader tentatively adds to the agenda himself, drawing on his knowledge of what parents usually bring up in similar groups. He may not have to do this overtly, but if he is aware of glaring omissions, the chances are that a parent will make some comment which he can pick up which seems to point in these directions. If his general knowledge is sound with regard to parental concerns, the possible foci of friction in families, and the special stress situations of the "target" population represented in the group, the questions introduced by the parents are likely to confirm his judgment, unless they are unusually preoccupied with special situations which, for one reason or another, are pressing and all-absorbing.

To take an obvious example, it would be unsual for a group of parents of school-age youngsters not to want to spend some time on their children's psychosexual development, if only to discuss such aspects as their boys' attitudes toward girls or vice versa. It has been said that there are always two general topics of interest to parents: discipline and sex. Today one would add education as a third category of universal appeal and urgency. Leaders often wait for these areas to be introduced. If no expression of concern related to these larger issues is forthcoming, they sometimes point out to the group that so far they have not mentioned this or that, as other groups sometimes do, and then wait to see whether the parents pick up the cue with any real interest. Sometimes, however, there may be neither time nor opportunity to do this appropriately and so a leader will decide not to introduce possible new areas. At the end, however, he may mention what he sees as omissions, hoping the parents will think about these issues by themselves or take them up in other groups.

In expectant parent groups, the coverage of subject matter has somewhat different imperatives. As in all group education, the discussion is directed toward two targets. First, there are the parents' immediate situations which they need to understand at every level: physical, psychological and emotional, and interpersonal. Second, there is the future for which they need "anticipatory guidance." This includes preparation for the birth of the baby, knowledge about the possible physical and emotional reactions of the mother then and afterwards, the possible responses of the father, elements of their joint care of the infant and their adjustment to the changes he will bring to their lives. Hopefully, group education provides knowledge that helps the parents meet both the present and future with greater ease. But the preparation time is self-limited to the period of pregnancy. Parents and leaders recognize that a great deal must be packed into a comparatively short time.

Naturally here, as in all parent group education, the sessions can take up only those issues about which the participants are most concerned or have little knowledge. One meets the specific questions as deeply and as thoroughly as one can, trusting that the discussion will lessen the parents' anxiety and increase their self-confidence to function in the future in areas that have not been explored. During the eight or ten sessions, expectant parents usually initiate many basic issues of the immediate present and of the time ahead. If they do not, it is necessary for the nurse-leader to encourage them to do so. The vital areas are sharply conceptualized in her mind and give her a general framework into which the particular aspects raised by the expectant parents fall in place. If one important slot is empty as the sessions go on, she points this out—and the group can move into the missing area if they choose to do so. Again, if her judgment of their needs is sound, based on her contacts with many parents, they usually follow her lead.

Not every aspect of the content can be explored in the same detail, but the leader helps the group see that there is a sum-total of things about which they may need to know. The overview gives a scope to the discussions, even though the group may have chosen to go into some issues more fully than others or to bypass completely those for which they felt they were already prepared.

The Use of Printed and Other Resource Material

With all the current books, pamphlets, and articles on child-rearing available to parents, it is natural to ask whether they should not be used in some way in parent discussion groups. In practice, their contents come into the meetings directly or indirectly, as parents refer to ideas they have read about or comment on pertinent programs on radio or television, in films, and the like. The question is: how can this material be dealt with most effectively, in keeping with the general approach of parent group education?

We have already suggested that group programs based on printed material—as some are—tend to be carried on at an intellectual level, remote from daily experience. On the other hand, building the discussion from the stuff of the parents' current living with their children does not mean that this must be explored in an intellectual vacuum, divorced from interpretations of family life that may be helpful. The heart of the matter is where to start: what is to be the primary source of the content on which the meetings are based?

Leaders sometimes wonder whether a reading assignment, either to be read by the group or reported by individual members, may not provide a good starting point for discussion. Undoubtedly, it can. But the suggestion often stems from a leader's uneasiness about how to begin and his fear that the parents will have nothing to contribute—and that he, in turn, will not be able to "get them started." Experience with groups of many kinds, with parents from many educational and cultural backgrounds, has shown that this fear is unfounded. It is true that parents who are not in the habit of expressing themselves or are hampered by language difficulties may be slower to participate than others, but once they understand the nature and purposes of the group, their experiences, ideas, questions begin to come through vividly. Their contributions bring the group to the core of their concerns more directly, with a quicker sense of relatedness than is usually possible when they start from something they have read. As a starter, then, printed material is usually unnecessary; furthermore, it may slow down the learning process by delaying the point at which the meaning literally comes home to the parents.

As a provocative secondary resource however, printed material can be of great value. A mother comments on a magazine article about thumb-sucking which, she says, she does not go along with. She is sure her little girl's mouth will be out of shape because she sucks her thumb so much, though the article says this will not affect her jaw at all. Other mothers who have read the same piece have gotten quite different impressions. Their varied interpretations become the basis for an interesting discussion.

Leaders cannot possibly have read all the current magazine articles themselves, and it does not matter if they haven't. What the author really says is not as important as what the parents get from it and how his material sparks their ideas about their own situations. If the leader has not seen the article, it is wise for him to say so; he can then underscore those parts of the discussion—whether they are in the article or not—which he finds in line with current thinking, or raise for further exploration those he feels are unsound. If he happens to have seen the article, he nevertheless draws from the parents their reactions to its contents and handles the discussion in much the same way. And he continues to make sure that theoretical concepts are tied to the parents' real experiences.

Parents often do reach out for books and pamphlets to supplement the group discussions. For this reason, leaders sometimes set up a "lending table" of pamphlets and books, usually at the side of the room, readily available but not so conspicuously placed as to make them appear a "must." The group members are then free to make use of the table as they wish. (This calls for advance planning by the leader, who chooses material he thinks would be most appropriate. In placing them on the table he auto-matically gives them his endorsement.) The selections the parents make are often most revealing, for they show the areas in which they know they want help. Sometimes they have already identified these in the group, sometimes they have not. It is perhaps not surprising that parents of children of all ages seem to pick up pamphlets on discipline first. One mother in a group of ADC families, apparently not satisfied with the discussion itself, brought a pamphlet on "Understanding Hostility in Children" from the library for the group to read. Her concern was clear. Although she had already mentioned it in the group, she seemed to involve herself more directly in the discussion after she had indicated her continuing concern.

Sex education pamphlets are of particular interest. In a housing project largely occupied by Mexican-American families in a southwestern state, several mothers had taken home copies of a paperback book, *What to Tell Your Children About Sex*,[2] to help them talk with their children. One mother reported she had found the words difficult, and there were some she did not understand, but the pictures helped, and she and her eleven-year-old daughter had gone through the section on menstruation together. In a number of the other families, the "children" (from about eleven to fourteen) took the books themselves and read them from cover to cover. One mother said she was amazed to find that her twelve- and fourteen-year-old sons were very much interested in menstruation and the development of girls. They asked her the meaning of words as they read. She said that at one point her fourteen-year-old son got red in the face, but "not half as red as I got." Soon her eight- and ten-year-old daughters got interested, too. In the end all five of them were sitting down poring over the books, trying to figure things out together. Another mother, who did not read well herself, said her husband had gone through the book and helped her with things she had not understood. Still another mother, who had also read the book with her husband, commented self-consciously that her husband said this discussion group had done more for her than anything that had happened since their marriage.

The group talked at length about the many ways in which the discussion in the meetings, supplemented by the printed material which they were now using, had loosened up some of their inhibitions regarding sex matters and helped them meet these matters more openly with their children. They talked about how they had felt when they were teen-agers and how, if they were honest, they would say "a lot of us did things we don't want our children to do." They went on to talk about some of their sex problems as adults, such as the temptations they faced when their husbands are away. (One was about to come home after a prison term.) They brought out some of their experiences with methods of contraception, which were so necessary in order to keep down the size of their families. One of the group commented on a *Life Magazine* picture-article on "Life Before Birth." The leader had brought several copies to the meeting and at this point passed them around. The material provoked many questions. One mother commented with great feeling, "Just to think, I've

[2] Child Study Association of America, New York, Pocket Books, revised edition, 1959.

had eight babies and never until today had any idea what was really taking place inside of me." They also discussed their fears during their pregnancies and how no one—either in the clinic or in the office of private doctors—had "explained" anything to them or helped relieve their fears. They wished they had had this kind of discussion then. One mother said haltingly that looking at the pictures made you feel that each time you had created a life, it was a kind of miracle. The meeting ended with their borrowing copies of the magazine to show their husbands—and undoubtedly their children as well.

In expectant parent groups, too, pamphlets and books are often helpful. Many agencies make available materials on the facts of pregnancy and childbirth, including the mothers' and the babies' nutritional needs. Lists of supplies, equipment, clothing for the baby, leaflets on formula making, and so forth, are also useful for the parents to have as a base of reference. These materials are usually offered free, especially in health centers; where necessary, they are in Spanish. They provide detailed, practical information that would take a great deal of time to cover in the group.

Parents should have a chance to discuss in the group their reactions to any part of what they have read. One never knows what ideas—true and false—may be touched off at any point. In one group, for example, discussion of the number of diapers required for an infant led into a fascinating discussion of enuresis in relation to toilet training for children as they grew older, and what this might mean in the parents' early handling of their children as infants. Lists of recommended diet items often provoke feelings that need to be discussed and sorted out thoroughly to help parents handle their food requirements on a realistic basis.

Printed materials on the nature of a physical handicap or chronic illness are also useful as supplements to discussion in groups of parents of children with disabilities. They are most helpful if the individual parents' reactions to the material are brought out in the safety and protection of the group and looked at from the viewpoint of many parents.

Groups vary, however, in their use of printed material. In some, where a table of books and pamphlets is introduced, it is almost untouched; in others, the pamphlets go in and out during the course of the group and are well thumbed over by its end. This variation does not seem to depend on the educational background of the parent-members. It appears to be determined primarily by the parents' awareness of their own needs and their eagerness to reach out for new information as one way to ease their discomfort. Even this generalization is not always true. Some groups, which are carried on with great purpose and involvement, function well without help of any outside material at all.

These implications of the value of the printed word apply to the use of audio-visual material as well. The showing of a film or a dramatic presentation can give a group a common experience from which to start the discussion and is extremely valuable in a single, large meeting. It is not needed to start the discussion in small groups that plan to meet continuously. Again, as supplementary material to fill in factual information on such matters as the physical care of cerebral palsied children or the physiological details of development during pregnancy or the birth of a baby, they sometimes have a place. Since their use has to be planned ahead, it is not always possible to show them at the time the group is most interested in their contents. If they are shown when it happens to be convenient, they may actually interfere with the natural development of the group's thinking. On the other hand, they may also stimulate the group members to consider areas of their experience they have not yet come to. Whenever they are shown, plenty of time should be provided for the group to talk out their reactions, not only to the presentation as a whole, but to its various parts. Many leaders prefer to use these media at a special session or series of sessions. The discussion meetings can then be used to develop and maintain a continuity based on the spontaneous interests of the members themselves.

But there is no doubt that any medium of communication which introduces new ideas can be stimulating in unpredictable ways. Where parents bring these new ideas into the sessions, the discussions are often sharpened and enriched, to the extent that they are made meaningful to all of the group. They merely add another element to the fluid learning process.

LAST MEETINGS

There is something special about a last meeting. Leaders often say they can feel its quality when they enter the room. They sometimes talk about the behavior of the parents in a last meeting as being "characteristic," but are hard put to describe just what they mean. Actually, the "characteristic" behavior may be of many different kinds.

Sometimes in a last session the members will jump from one topic to another, touching on each "once over lightly" and then jumping to something quite different. Leaders meeting this for the first time are sometimes discouraged, because it seems as if the group members had learned nothing in the previous meetings. On second thought, however, they begin to see that this behavior must be related to the other unique element of the session—it is the last. One can only speculate as to what this last-meeting superficiality may mean. Perhaps the parents are unwilling to involve themselves deeply in anything new at this point, since they know there is little time to follow it through. Perhaps they are feeling the sessions as a whole may have been incomplete and thus the topics they bring up so hastily are, in a sense, unfinished business. Sometimes they express the latter feeling when they begin a last meeting by saying that they have many things to discuss that have not come up yet, and they enumerate them with a feeling of great urgency. At other times they may revert to the kind of dependent attitude they showed in earlier sessions, asking many specific questions and pressing the leader to answer them. Sometimes, but more rarely, a last meeting may take on a slow pace and dull tone, as if the parents were already finished with the experience and were writing it off.

These different manifestations may all be evidences of the parents' difficulty in leaving the group. They seem to have "separation problems," perhaps somewhat similar to the ones they had when they were very young and had to separate in space from the person who had protected them so far, their mother. Certainly, parents are not aware of this parallel, but those who have observed many groups as they come close to the end feel that there is a girding of their loins, as it were, a marshalling of their own reserves, since from here on they will have to function on their own. Just as individuals vary in the emotional quality that accompanies any such experience, groups, too, show a wide range of feelings as they face the fact that they are leaving a kind of safety zone in which it was proper for them to learn, experiment, choose their own way. For some, this separation has overtones of sadness, others take it more philosophically, or, in a queer way, are even buoyed up at having to face the world and their home problems again in isolation. Some even refuse to recognize the situation altogether. And, again, they attempt to solve the situation in various ways. Many friendships that are formed through parent groups, for example, are maintained for a long period after the group is over. It is as if group members, even from quite disparate backgrounds, find not only pleasure and stimulation but also a kind of security in banding together in small units.

In the records of the Child Study Association, there is a report of the way in which one group reacted at the end of a series which points up some of the possible meanings separation had for this particular group of mothers. They had been an active, vivacious group of mothers of school-age children, coming from different parts of the city and with widely differing levels of schooling. Some of the women had outside jobs, some were staying quietly at home, some were active in school and community affairs. It had taken several sessions before they began to feel unified as a group. As the tenth and last meeting came near, the group asked the Association whether the number of sessions could be extended. After consultation with the leader, it was decided that this was impossible, since he had other commitments. (Besides, previous experiences in extending the length of a series had made the Association rather hesitant to agree to such a plan.) When the group was told that it was not possible to extend the series, the members were disappointed and frankly annoyed. As if in answer to this feeling, they decided to meet at lunch before the last session at a coffee shop in the neighborhood. They invited the leader to join them, but he was unable to do so because of a tight teaching schedule. Although he explained this to the group, they did not accept his statement with much grace and were frankly disappointed again. Their disappointment was understandable because throughout the series of meetings there had been a most favorable rapport between the group members and the leader, a recognition of his skill in his role and his warmth as a person, and a feeling on his side that this was an unusually responsive and alert group of women.

When the time came for the last session, the meeting room was empty until they all appeared *en masse*, chattering and excited at having had a pleasant social time together. The leader entered a moment later and said afterwards that he had never felt so isolated or left out! He felt he had literally to push his way through the cohesive wall that the group had built up around itself. As he began gently to assume some leadership in directing this last meeting, the group settled down and the session was reasonably productive. At the end, after the leader had shared with them his feeling about how the group had gone and, in turn, listened to some of their comments, they left, again as a group, stating somewhat defiantly that, even if the Association could not provide a leader, they would meet on their own.

Subsequently, the mother who had stood out in the group as one of the more active members was informally chosen to be the chairman of the group. She reported back to the Association that the group met in the evenings once a month at the homes of various members. At first the meetings were carried along on their own momentum, but they found that the quality of the meetings gradually changed. This was partly due to the fact that the husbands were introduced into these post-sessions without any preparation or guidance from a unified source. To a large extent the husbands' diversity and different levels of functioning in the group broke up the unity that had developed when the wives had met alone. These parents did get a great deal out of the experience; but they learned that they missed the direction of a trained person who could guide their discussions. They felt that the meetings never again approached the high quality of exchange and searching toward a purpose that had been so characteristic of the group's regular sessions.

If parents get a good deal from a series of meetings, it is quite natural that they may want to have the sessions extended, if it is at all possible. And yet, as we have indicated, in practice it seldom works out very well if sessions are added. Inevitably there are some who cannot attend longer than the period for which they had originally planned, and any change in its composition causes a change in the functioning of the group as a whole. There seems also to be something about the way group members see the group experience as having a particular structure, which makes them feel that the extra sessions are being tacked on and are perhaps not as important. On the other hand, there are a number of cases on record where groups have been extended without this sense of let-down. The reasons may be found in the enthusiasm of the group, their ability to work together, and the validity of their feeling that the discussions have not sufficiently covered the range of their interests.

If one looks at one's expectations for the group honestly, one must face from the beginning the fact that coverage of the material discussed will obviously never be complete. Helping parents accept this is a problem that runs through all the group sessions but comes out particularly at the end. Even though they may have discussed it before, now they are brought up sharply against the fact that, from here on, they will have to use their own resources and reserves, without the help of the group. They are then forced to question what they have gotten from the sessions. Have they a better understanding of the dynamics of behavior that lie back of immediate, outward happenings? Have they really learned a way of analyzing a situation which they can apply to situations that have not come up? Has their better knowledge of many situations and of themselves, as well, given them confidence that they will be able to manage?

Often parents put some of these feelings into words, without being asked. As they talk about the fact that this is their last meeting, they inevitably begin to evaluate what they have gotten from the discussions. It is unusual for a group to complete a series without at least some comments along these lines. Usually their remarks are quite spontaneous and positive, sometimes embarrassingly so. It is almost as if they were saying kind things as a present to the leader in return for what he has done for them. In such comments there is also apt to be a slight element of wishing to please the leader, just as they may always have wanted to please their teachers when they were in school. Usually leaders accept these comments gratefully and with appreciation, but they are seldom completely taken in by them. In any case, they tend not to let this kind of exchange go on too long. Sometimes leaders voice their feeling that though the members are talking about only their positive reactions, they must have had some negative ones as well. Such an opening often breaks the euphoric mood, and the members begin to express some measure of disappointment or criticism. (The chances are that if they had been deeply disappointed they would have brought their feeling to the leader before this or dropped out.) Here, even at the end, there is need for balance. The parents should be given an opportunity to express the full range of their reactions; but one would hope that the meeting would not close on a negative note. Usually the group itself will now point to things they have gotten from the meetings. If not, the leader can do so, without defensiveness, adding, as some leaders do quite naturally, that he enjoyed the experience of being with them and hopes to see them again. Such a comment reinforces the friendly feeling that is usually present in the group, and gives it a kind of seal of approval.

Frequently, the end of a series is marked by some extra festivity, initiated either by the agency or by the parents themselves. Coffee or coke and cookies usually at the close of the meeting make it "a party" and give the ending a pleasant sociable note. Expectant mothers in a group in a Texas city had planned with the leader to have their husbands join them at the last session, which was to be held in the evening. They surprised her, however, by bringing a full supper to start the meeting off and appeared in their best clothes, chattering from the moment they entered the door.

In some programs, formal methods of evaluation are introduced. This is essential where the program includes evaluative research as part of the total plan. The details of this kind of evaluation cannot be gone into here, but it should be pointed out that if evaluation forms are given to the parent-members at the last meeting, it should be done in a way that does not disrupt the flow of the meeting itself. They can be distributed before the meeting or afterwards; they can be filled out in the room or taken home and mailed in. If they are introduced before the session, the leader must be prepared to have the parents talk about their reactions to the form and possibly even to their being used as guinea pigs! Such reactions will be at a minimum if the general purposes of the research have been interpreted to the group well in advance and introduced from the beginning as part of the program. Inevitably, however, there will be some residue of discomfort that their private responses may be used for public (study) purposes. It is interesting to note how much of this feeling persists even when it is made completely clear that the evaluation forms are not to be signed. Every effort should be made to have the questions as general as possible within the purposes of the study, so that the participants will feel free to answer honestly and know that the study is not directed toward getting any "correct" answers.

If evaluation forms are to be used, it is important that the leader and the agency do everything they can to separate the fact-finding aspects of a study from the free, ongoing process of group learning. One would hope that the leader and the group members do feel that, even in the last session, they are going to use the bulk of their time to continue their learning.

Often in a last meeting, the group will ask about what further resources are available if they need them. Can they call the leader in the future about specific situations, for example? What other services does the agency offer? What counseling or treatment facilities are available in the community? Sometimes these questions express their feelings about "separating" from the group and being left to their own devices. (Often the parents find they do not need to turn to these services, after all.) But often, too, these questions express their legitimate feeling that in particular instances, group educational programs may not be enough. Their experience in the group may have helped them to evaluate their situations more clearly and to pinpoint their needs and prepare the way for them to make better use of other community resources. For some parents, this is an important outcome of their participation in the program.

The last part of last meetings can take many forms. Sometimes, as in first meetings, leaders may summarize briefly the areas that have been discussed (but not necessarily "covered") or, even better, survey the educational process that has taken place during the series. Sometimes—but not often—the parents do this. (They are usually more concerned, however, with where they are now.) Often it is unnecessary to take a formal backward look; the group may neither need nor want to do so. The actual words of an ending can never be predicted. Sometimes it may be a member who puts the final "period" to the experience, with some general comment. Both the leader and the members feel better satisfied if there *is* a "period," a final underscoring of the fact that their meeting together is ended and that the time spent together has been productive. Whatever form the ending takes, it is hoped the members will carry with them a feeling that they have gained in knowledge, understanding and strength— and have the impetus to develop their thinking further on their own.

X

Group Interaction: Its Meaning for Learning

The process of group interplay has been inherent in everything we have already described. Involved in the stages of group formation and group development are the live group members—the parents or expectant parents—who come together to learn and who are relating to one another from the moment they enter the door. By virtue of the kind of program in which they take part, the interplay between the members (member to member to member) and the members and the group leader is basic to their learning.

Of all the aspects of parent group education, this interaction is the most elusive, the most difficult to describe. Yet one has only to sit quietly in the corner of a room, observing the flow of conversation around the table in a parent meeting, to be aware that it is vital. One can almost *feel* it as a physical force, a flow of energy that moves from person to person, in and out, in ever-changing patterns. Sometimes the interplay increases as individuals make their contributions in words. The parents' attitudes influence the interaction, too, as seen in the friendly nods of support and agreement or frowns or restlessness or exclamations of differences. Sometimes the interplay is slowed down as the interest wanes, perhaps, or feelings of anger, defeat, or futility take over, stopping discussion dead in its tracks. Then the interplay must be picked up and given new momentum either by the leader or by group members, who for one reason or another feel the need to start the group into motion again.

The process of group interaction in parent group education is hard to describe because, as in other groups, it is subtle and complex. Here we have a number of separate individuals who, by meeting for a common purpose, form a group, an aggregation that in a sense is larger than its separate parts. As we have seen, different types of group programs vary in the emphasis they place on the group and on the individual, but both must be taken into account. Parent group education makes full use of the group itself and promotes the interaction of the group members in order

136

to open the way for the growth and change in feelings and performance of the individual members. That is the underlying purpose of the program. This statement, however, only confirms the fact that in this, as in any group experience, the activities of the individual and of the group are so closely interwoven that they cannot be isolated.

This close relation has been described by Hare, Borgatta, and Bales in relation to the small (usually leaderless) group, but the interpretation applies as well to parent discussion groups.

"The individual may at first see the group as a collection of individuals, all different, or may view the group as a kind of undifferentiated entity, or in both ways at once. But as interaction proceeds, both views become more articulate and refined. One result of interaction is the mutual adjustment of individual perspectives toward a similarity in certain respects, and toward a knowledge of similarity. The content of this overlap in perspectives and expectations we can call the common culture of the group. Another result of interaction, however, is that the members of the group become more differentiated from each other, both as to who does what kind of thing overtly and when, and also as to the picture of the group that each individual carries in his mind. The individual now begins to see himself as having a particular position within a differentiated structure or system of positions.

"The individual feels himself a part of the group and like other parts in his orientation to the common culture, but at the same time, different from all other parts because he has a particular position defined by the common culture, and also because he knows he has a life apart from the group—much or most of himself and his internal life is unknown to the others and is not part of the culture he holds in common with the other members of this particular group." [1]

In parent group education programs, the individual attempts to synthesize the common points of the group experience with his own particular background and needs and to use the group for his own individual purposes: to improve his functioning as a parent in direct, personal terms.

Group interaction is complex also in that the interplay takes place at many levels of response. Parents relate to one another overtly, sharing ideas, experiences, and feelings. At the same time, they relate and react to one another as people, whom they may like or dislike, respect or look down on or ignore. In this interplay, primarily unexpressed and almost never brought into full consciousness, the parents find themselves taking on different personal roles not as parents at all, but as individuals of different temperaments. Through their impact on one another, each is challenged to find his own place both in *ideas* and as a *parent-person*. (Since

---

[1] A. Paul Hare, Edgar F. Borgatta, and Robert F. Bales, *Small Groups: Studies in Social Interaction,* Alfred A. Knopf, New York, Revised Edition, 1965, p. 355.

these groups are formed for a specific educational purpose, they must be kept to their stated orientation: to help the parents build on their own ego strengths in relation to their role in the family.) The picture becomes even more complicated because parents' responses as persons and as parents are not separate, nor can they be made so. There is a constant interplay between the two.

WHAT PARENTS BRING TO GROUPS

First, when he enters the room each parent brings with him all kinds of individual experiences and needs which color what he thinks the group will be like, what he expects from it, and what part he thinks he will play. Parents bring memories of earlier experiences with other formal groups—in the schoolroom, in church, in social organizations, or in industrial associations—and with informal groups on the block or in the neighborhood, in social contacts and business activities. Inevitably, they respond to the new situation in terms of the emotional residue of these earlier experiences and the feelings that accompanied them: whether they were accepted or not, whether they were leaders or followers, whether they were pushed around and dominated, or whether they stood up for what they believed, in whatever position they happened to have had in the group.

In addition, since the groups here are relatively small and are conducted by a leader who is per se in a position of responsibility, they often arouse in the group members some echoes of their earlier experiences in the family. Without knowing it, in the group they may find themselves repeating patterns that were established in their earlier years at home, tendencies to be submissive or rebellious, critical or too accepting, fearful of being overlooked, jealous or competitive, or whatever. Since, in any situation with others, one's experience is rarely completely happy or completely unhappy, the chances are that they approach a new gathering of people with mixed feelings. Obviously, they would not come if they did not think the group would be of some value. But along with their vague hopes are often hesitations, fears, and biases that make some of them edgy and defensive at first. They are reluctant to do anything that will make them conspicuous or that will disturb the protection they sense they get from the group as a whole.

This backlog of sensitivity affects their attitude toward others in the group as they look them over, make quick first judgments, and sense whether individual members will be allies or enemies. Most parents, in embarking on a group program, want to be liked and accepted and are fearful that they may be ignored or rejected. As described by Mildred Rabinow in a session of a training program given at the Child Study

Association of America in 1964, they "waver between social hunger and fear of narcissistic injury."

These are some of the mixed emotions that often lie beneath the surface when parents come to groups, responses that have no real relation to the new project but which come from extraneous sources, mostly in the past. It is not the purpose of parent discussion groups to explore directly the idiosyncratic meaning of these many conflicting emotions, as might be done in therapy groups. Leaders know, however, that they exist in some form and they recognize the surface clues. Their leadership role is relatively clear. It is their responsibility to use their skills to further a non-threatening, cooperative group spirit and to stimulate group interaction by following the general procedures of parent group education. Put in simple terms, they do this by helping the members listen to one another and learn from one another, as they (the leaders) also listen and learn.

FINDING THEIR PLACE IN THE GROUP

Fortunately, in most cases the strong wish in the parents to be like and to be liked by the other parents in the group predominates and provides a basis for good group feeling. Parents usually find that they have had similar situations and have reacted in much the same way as others have done. This interaction process was described in a symposium on "Parent Groups in Education, Psychotherapy and Group Work" at a meeting of the American Orthopsychiatric Association in 1954, as follows:

"[In a group education program] parents gain (1) a wider objective knowledge of other children and parents, (2) a recognition that others experience similar feelings and situations. . . . and (3) a testing out of their experience against that of others for differences as well as similarities, to explore with what ideas they feel at ease or not. All of these serve as a wider basis for making choices as to ways of behaving. This process takes place in two ways: (1) by identification—either unconscious or in the conscious recognition of oneself in someone else and (2) by contrast, the recognition of difference on an individual basis. Both can take place within the formation of an education group.

"Identification with other group members is facilitated by the common purpose of their coming together and by the accepting atmosphere set by the leader, which allows them to express themselves as they choose, on any pertinent subject, assured that everything they say will be given due consideration. In such a climate they gradually come to express feelings as well as thoughts that they usually hesitate to reveal, and these revelations give courage to others who have similar feelings, which they may not have quite faced.

"In the third meeting of a group of parents in a small town, for example, one mother described in some detail her resentment during the weekend when her children were constantly under foot, interfering with work she and her husband were trying to do on their house. As the weekend wore on, her irritation became so intense that she finally came face to face with it, and realized that the situation might have been avoided—some of her feelings, too—if she had spent even a short time with her children or had planned some things with them so that they would not feel left out. The discussion went on to similar experiences of other parents. Some minutes later, a mother broke in with 'I can't help thinking of the resentment Mrs. S. talked about; we all have some of the same feelings and I think it is a tribute to this group that we can talk about it without feeling ashamed.". . .

"Such contagion does not always work out so smoothly, however. Even in educational groups parents disagree, contradict each other and argue, at times, quite heatedly. This usually takes place after the parents come to feel comfortable with one another and with the leader. . . .

It is out of such discussions that parents learn by *contrast*, rejecting interpretations and ways of behaving that do not seem to them to be sound, and slowly, by elimination, coming to those choices that seem right for them and their children." [2]

This process of identification and differentiation was exemplified in another group, when one mother, who had said she was quite uncertain about what she should do when her child left things strewn about her room, came back to the topic several sessions later and announced that she had decided some things were more important than others, and she added with an expressive gesture, "So now *I* pick up, no matter what other mothers do."

It is easy to see how parents identify with others on a personal level. Some choose to sit next to those to whom they are attracted. Others may be timid about showing their liking openly, but their feelings of empathy and often admiration shine through in their facial expressions, across the table. They also show their aversion to others, based perhaps on quite superficial initial judgments, and sometimes they sit as far away as possible from someone with whom they do not want to identify or be identified. The choice of seating is in itself a fascinating phenomenon which has not been fully recognized, but the initial random choice, which may not be really accidental, and the regularity and shift of seating from session to session often suggest significant emotionally colored relationships that influence the group interplay. The wish to be near another person in space or in communication may indicate that the parent senses "she is my kind" or "he knows what he is talking about." There is often the further implication that "since I like her (or him), I agree—or at least I want to agree—

[2] From an unpublished paper by Aline B. Auerbach on "Parent Groups in Education."

so I'll *be* like her (or him) in every way." It takes time and subtle guidance from the leader for parents to realize that even if they are drawn to people, they can have differing opinions. Sometimes they find that if they speak out on their own, they are even better respected (and liked) than if they always agree.

Finding their place in the group as independent people often goes by stages. Some group members find that they align themselves with one or two others for a while, forming a subgroup whose members function together. It is as if they need the support of a small cluster of their peers until they find out for themselves where they stand. They may not always stay with the same few and are likely to shift around until they are more sure of themselves.

Some leaders are bothered when a few people buzz together during the discussion, instead of talking to the group as a whole. Of course the group interplay is easier to follow and handle if this does not happen. But if the leader views subgrouping as an aspect of group development which may have positive value for the members, he can take it in his stride, even if at the moment it seems destructive to the unity of the group. Besides needing to group together for their own personal reasons, these parents may be reacting to the content of the discussion, perhaps critically, perhaps supportively. The leader can usually pick up what the parents say and bring it into the stream of the discussion for the others to react to. Without meeting the issue head-on, he uses his skills to make the subgroup function as part of the whole.

And so, through the uneven but continuing flow of group interplay, parents seem to pass from their original separateness through a phase of identification, consolidating the group and making possible the sharing of experience, which emerges as the group's "common culture." From this, it is hoped, each parent then finds his own identity again as a separate, unique person.

Slavson describes this aspect of the group interplay as a "mirror reaction" which serves in a sense to break through the process of identification in order to gain greater self-knowledge. He says:

"Parents do not normally stop to examine the validity of their ways of dealing with their children; being emotionally involved, they are not aware of the effects of their conduct and of their part in children's difficulties and anomalies. In these groups [child centered guidance groups] such matters are mulled over and over until awareness finally emerges. This awareness is greatly accelerated and enhanced through seeing one's self mirrored in the acts of others. While a parent in isolation may succeed, through his defensive mechanisms and fear of guilt, in blocking out and in denying or ignoring his undesirable behavior, this is not as easily accomplished when faced with similar behavior in others. Unless the defenses are too rigid, in which case the parent would not be acceptable for our guidance groups, his identification tendencies cannot but lead him to recognize reactions in himself similar to those presented by fellow members. Such mirroring of one's mechanisms and acts is one of the important dynamics in loosening up the crustification of conviction, behavior patterns and defenses and in laying the foundation for emotional detachment, objectivity and flexibility." [3]

THE INDIVIDUAL IN GROUP INTERACTION

While leaders watch and guide the flow and development of the discussion as a group phenomenon, they are also constantly aware of the behavior of the individuals who make up the group and who give it its special quality and mood. Their individual contributions—sometimes unique, sometimes banal, always unanticipated—obtrude because of their personal coloring. They impinge on the leader's consciousness primarily, however, because of the way in which they contribute or fail to contribute to the task in hand, which is to utilize the group to develop in parents new understanding and a better ability to cope with the many facets of their lives with their children.

It is the more active members, of course, who first stand out in the group and almost demand the attention of the group and the leader. They are always ready to talk, sometimes too ready, so they do not give the others a chance. Sometimes they seem to talk in order to keep the discussion moving and thus avoid thinking more deeply. (They succeed in keeping others from doing so, too.) Sometimes they seem to talk to get rid of nervous energy or to break away from their feelings of isolation. Often they are just "eager beavers" who want to be of help, who want to be "good children" and do what the "teacher" seems to want. But whether they do this to curry favor with the leader or to gain status in the group or merely to be helpful, they can be a great help if they do not overplay their part. They are quick to pick up suggestions from the leader about how the group is to function and to act on them. They talk about their own experiences and concerns—sometimes too much so—but at the same time they do listen to the others, as the leader does. Further, since these parents usually also want to please and be liked by the other parents in the group, they often encourage others to speak, try to get at the roots of their problems, and give them advice. Sometimes they also try to mediate where there are differences of opinion and act as peace makers.

Many of these efforts are of value since they follow the expressed and

[3] S. R. Slavson, *Child-Centered Group Guidance of Parents,* International Universities Press, New York, 1958, p. 287.

implied aims and procedures of the group. Where they are appropriate, again, from whatever motive, the parents seem to be taking on some of the leader's functions for which he has given them a pattern. Leaders report wryly that they sometimes can hear echoes of their own words in the words the parents use with one another. They often make the same opening gambits or raise the same questions. In the search for further information on a specific issue, for example, a parent may ask, "How long has your boy been doing this?" or, "What did you do about this?" or even, "What about this bothered you?" and "How did this make you feel?"

Such comments from parents in the group are not always helpful or well timed, however, and the leader must be alert to see what effect they have on the group interplay. Advice-giving, for example, presents many difficulties under any circumstances. It may be irrelevant, if it is not based on a thorough exploration of a situation, and often tends to cut off further discussion. Even if the advice-giver has a fairly accurate picture of what is involved and what one might do about it, other group members may not have arrived at this point. But most important, giving specific advice as a quick solution defeats one of the purposes of the group, which is to have the members involved in an active exchange of ideas and experiences, out of which each person will come to his own decision.

So the leader needs to redirect the talk of those who dominate the discussion into appropriate channels, and this may not be easy to do. There is always the danger of cutting a person off too soon, perhaps even before he has come to his main point. He may be building up to a sound and valid comment that can then be underscored, thus bringing him and his ideas into the mainstream of the group. Cutting one person short can also bounce off and affect the other members, who may feel that the leader may cut them off too when they speak. On the other hand, if one person takes over for too long, the rest have every right to feel irritable, as they often are, and angry at the leader for not helping the group to get on with its business.

There are times, then, when the flow just must be stopped. A leader may say directly, "Perhaps we should look at this a little further to see what it involves," and draw the others into the discussion. Or he may encourage an advice-giver to tell more of his own experiences in this respect, thus breaking the advice-giving pattern and hopefully getting at the real happenings from which this parent has drawn the conclusions he wants to pass on. This can then open the way for others to come into the discussion. In any case, the leader tries to shift the talk from one parent's "I would do this if I were you," or, "Why don't you do this?" Instead, he involves the whole group in telling what they have done or might do in similar circumstances. Such a move takes the discussion away from both the words and the tone of advice-giving. Instead, it brings in alternatives from several parents' experiences, which other parents can follow or not, as they choose.

In a recent meeting of an expectant mothers group, several of the members had expressed dissatisfaction with the attention they were getting from their physicians. Although they were private patients, they said they might as well be in the clinic for all the attention they got. The doctors were so busy they had no time to listen to their questions. At this, one of the more talkative members broke in—and the leader held her breath, for this young woman had given advice continually during the preceding sessions. She had already told the other mothers how to get comfortable in bed at night, how to control the queasy morning sensations, even how to tell off their mothers-in-law!

Each time the leader had tried to draw others into the discussion, to balance or supplement her "words of wisdom." This time, to the leader's surprise, the mother (to be) came in with "Gee, I guess it'd be easy to say 'just go to another doctor' but I found it wasn't that simple. I talked it over quite a lot with my husband, because I wasn't satisfied either and finally we did go to see another doctor and explained the situation and I liked what he said and now I am going to him. But," she added thoughtfully, "I know how hard it is to break off from someone." This time she had her say and let it go at that. The leader then helped the group to think about possible ways in which they might meet this problem. They talked about how they might discuss it with their present physicians and explain how they felt. They discussed ways to find out about other competent doctors. They also faced quite thoughtfully what they were really looking for in their patient-doctor relationships and whether this was realistic or possible. They left with many new ideas. The subject did not come up again directly in the sessions that followed and the leader never really knew just what course each parent had followed. She did know, however, that they had fewer complaints. And the talkative mother seemed to have settled into a new tone. This episode suggested that although people usually behave in characteristic ways in group sessions, they can often modify their behavior through the group interplay, as this mother did.

Some active, talkative members express their activity not in trying to be helpful but in rebelling against the leader or resisting the procedures that have been set up, thus delaying the establishment of productive relationships and interchange between the members themselves. As we have already seen, these challenges have to be met, and they can be, if the leader avoids answering back defensively or counterattacking or becoming involved in a cross-battle. Sometimes a member tries to dominate the session in an unpleasant, hostile way, as if to say, "I know better than any of you.

Just listen to *me*." His attitude often implies, in its tone if not in words, that the opinions and ideas of the others in the group are worthless. Such people seem to object to anything that is said and go out of their way not to belong to the crowd. They may be impelled by many hidden drives: the wish to show off, to dominate, to get recognition at any cost.

This kind of person is often a great problem for the leader who may feel threatened by the parent's attitude and struggles not to become competitive. His challenge is to see if he can extract and underscore what is constructive in this parent's comments, diverting attention away from the person to an objective consideration of his ideas. This makes clear that the aggressive member is still part of the group and the others can respond to his contribution—or part of it—on an impersonal level. If they agree with his ideas or have had similar reactions, they can now say so, without having to disagree just because they do not like *him*. If they really see things differently, they can say that, too, without seeming to be fighting him as a person. And they learn that it is quite appropriate and helpful to disagree in this way. Then the group interaction process moves ahead along more constructive channels and usually some better understanding comes through as a result. If the aggressive parent is sensitive and able to pick up subtle clues, he will see from these procedures that the group is not going to fall into his trap and battle with him, just for the sake of an argument. Instead, he is being treated as a member who makes his contribution for what it is worth, and, it is hoped, learns to behave more appropriately in the group.

But it doesn't always work out this way. In a group of couples, all parents of preschoolers, the first session was dominated by one father whose unusual name alerted the rest of the group to the fact that he came of a well-known family of educators. After the opening go-around, he took over. He knew all the answers, was prepared to talk in long words on any issue, and gave no one—not even his wife—a chance to talk. Gradually the other parents became intimidated and contributed less and less, despite the valiant efforts of the leader to draw them in and to break up the monologue. At the second and third meetings, the father continued in the same vein but his mood and that of the group shifted. The other parents began to get restless and showed their annoyance. He commented that he was not "getting much out of it," apparently unaware that his behavior was largely responsible for the lack of productive exchange among the members. By the fourth session, some of the parents had come to the point of wanting to talk him down, or at least to take part more actively in what they saw as the general plan. Unfortunately, by this time a number of other parents had dropped out, the dominating one (and his submissive wife) failed to appear, too, and stayed away from later meetings despite a call of inquiry from the leader. So there was no further chance to help him move beyond his need to expound in a one-way stream and to interact in a give-and-take relationship from which he too could have learned. The group—what was left of it—pulled itself together. The parents worked well for the remaining sessions, but the discussions seemed to have lost their impact. In retrospect, the leader saw that he too had been intimidated by the prestige of the family name. Hoping this father might come to contribute more appropriately in time, he had not been quick enough in trying to help him redirect or curb his need to dominate. He felt that, as a result, he had lost his group.

The silent ones, the watchers, present a different kind of interaction problem. Because they are there physically, one must assume that they want to take part and be part of the group. They are not contributing anything in words, yet their very silence affects the group interplay, often by throwing something of a damper on the group tone. ("Why don't they speak up?" may be in the back of the minds of the other parents as well as the leader, often accompanied by the vague fear on everyone's part, "Have I done anything to make them pull away?") One must assume, until one has evidence to the contrary, that they are merely shy, waiting until they feel comfortable enough to take part. The question is: How can one help them do so?

Whatever the real basis of their behavior, the leader uses his skills to bring them into the group when they seem ready. It is difficult to describe just when and how this can be done. Leaders sometimes sense "the decisive moment" when a friendly look in a parent's direction will encourage him to speak, even if only hesitantly at first. Sometimes a leader may say, "You seem to be smiling (or frowning), Mrs. X.," if the mother seems on the verge of participating. A direct approach of this kind, however, may misfire and cause the parent to withdraw even more, in embarrassment. Then it is apparent that the leader misjudged her tentative response. Perhaps she feels that the matter is a personal one and prefers not to talk about it in public. Perhaps she is not ready yet to speak out. It is safer to offer a more general opening, such as, "Some of you are smiling (or frowning) over this" or even more broadly, something like, "What do some of the rest of you think about this?" Sometimes in time the pattern set by the other parents carries over and the silent one begins to take his place as a contributing member of the group.

Often it takes a matter of special urgency to pull parents out of their apparent passivity. This was illustrated in a group of mothers of limited educational background in a midwestern city. They had spent several sessions talking about the sexual interests of their preteen-age boys and girls and the different ways they as parents had responded. At the seventh meeting, one mother, who up to then had not spoken *one word*, began to talk quietly. The discussions, she said, had started her thinking about her ten-year-old girl who seemed to be "developing" and who had not seemed to show any interest in these changes. Now, she said, she began to see that she had not been looking for an opening to talk to her daughter, though she remembered how hurt she had been because her own mother had not told her in advance about menstruation. Somehow she found herself having "a real good talk" with her girl. Although she felt she could have done a lot better, she consoled herself by saying "I guess there is more to sex education than just the words," and illustrated this by talking about the coldness of her mother and grandmother and her own lack of preparation for sex experiences. This mother's comments brought her into the stream of interaction of the group and the other members responded with support and interest, adding their own experiences. The mother was not consistently active in the remaining sessions, but she was now "with" the others and contributed occasionally with increasing ease.

Frequently parents who have been silent in the group come to the leader either before or after the session to raise a question or report an incident about which they are concerned. In general, such an interchange with any group member is not encouraged, unless the parent faces an urgent, emergency situation which cannot wait or unless he feels he is bringing up something that should be discussed privately. The extent to which it is wise for a leader to carry on private discussions with these parents is a delicate matter. Obviously, the process of group learning is diverted if the question is explored in detail on a one-to-one basis. The parent may gain some further understanding of the issue but misses out on the learning that comes from the group interplay. On the other hand, the parent's reaching out to the leader may be an important sign of movement, a step forward, and should not be rebuffed. The leader will want to explore the matter briefly to see what may be involved and then suggest that the parent bring it up in the group, since surely other parents would be interested and would be able to contribute. However, it may still be difficult for the parent to act on this suggestion. It is usually better for the leader not to call on this parent directly in the next session even though he may be tempted to do so. Left to his own initiative and responding to the leader's friendliness and the working atmosphere of the group, the parent often is able to follow up his contact with the leader with more appropriate and purposeful behavior in the group. If he is not able to, the leader can go to him later, to suggest that he may wish to talk to a counselor in a private interview. However this out-of-the-group contact is handled, the other parents usually are aware of the situation and are often relieved to know that the quiet one is being listened to and taken care of, just as they would expect to be treated if they too needed special help of some kind. In this way, their confidence in the leader and the group is reinforced.

It is difficult to classify individuals in rigid categories according to their behavior in the group. One kind of performance may stem from widely different emotional needs in different individuals, and, conversely, an identical inner drive may express itself in many different ways. Although it is important that the leader be sensitive to possible sources of a parent's behavior, in groups of this kind he responds only to its outward manifestations.

Take the matter of the overanxious parent, for example. Tension and apprehension may take many forms. Such a parent may be one of the silent ones, afraid to reveal his anxiety, but hoping desperately that the group will bring him some relief. Sometimes the group does just this, but it may also add to his anxiety by stimulating reactions in him that he cannot bring out to be looked at and evaluated. The trouble here is that neither the leader nor the group knows what he is feeling, since he does not tell them, and so he walls himself off from the very help he wants. In others, overanxiety may produce the kind of restless activity we have already seen, in which the parent uses his activity to cover up his true feelings. Or it causes a parent to be preoccupied with his own problems, unable really to wait, to listen to others, to share with them.

Sometimes an overanxious parent shows his conflict and upset by staying on one theme or one issue, bringing it up again and again, in different forms. It may be a teen-age boy's "insolence" or "stubbornness" which a mother reports in various incidents. It may be—and frequently is—an expectant mother's obsession with her fear of abnormality in the coming baby. It may be a father's preoccupation with the personal and physical demands placed on him by his handicapped child, a problem that he seems so immersed in that he cannot see beyond this. When these areas of anxiety and distress are brought out and explored, they contribute strength and meaning to the group interplay. As the discussion develops, one can begin to test whether this particular parent's response is amenable to educational intervention or is so personally motivated, so deep rooted, and so pervasive that the parent should be referred to casework or treatment services, if this seems advisable.

Sometimes the group interaction is interrupted by one member whose comments seem irrelevant, "off-beat," or even bizarre. To many workers, such behavior is not only difficult to handle but suspect, because it has implications or intimations of psychic pathology. Is this parent unable to maintain a logical thought sequence? Does this apparent lack of connection with the reality of what is going on in the group suggest that he may be psychotic? Does this behavior irritate the other members and make them restless? (Doctors often say they can trust a mother's judgment about how sick her child is when he has a physical ailment. In the same way, leaders can sometimes—but not always—take their cues from group members, who often sense the unhealthy quality in extreme behavior and pull away.) Obviously, there is no opportunity for psychiatric diagnosis, and it would be out of order at this point, in any case. While considering such a possibility for the future, the leader should make full use of his own professional knowledge and, without jumping to conclusions, try to find out whether the behavior is as irrelevant or bizarre as it seems. What did he or she have in mind? Was this related in some way to what had gone before? Usually the parent has some thread of association in his mind which relates his statement or question to those of the group. Sometimes there *is* no connection; the parent has merely brought out something because of pressure within himself. He may even say, "I guess there really is no connection; I just felt I wanted us to get to this." Then the leader can relax to some extent, since the parent shows he sees the reality. Certainly his point does not have to be picked up if doing so would take the group off the line of thought that has not yet been fully developed. Without seeming to be critical, the leader can say something like, "Let's hold that for a while until we've gone further into this." He must remember to come back to this point later, however, handling it as he would any other new material, in terms of the group's interest.

Only very rarely do we find a parent who speaks out in terms that are truly bizarre in the strict psychological meaning of the word. In one instance, in an expectant parent group, a mother repeatedly introduced odd comments that seemed unrelated to the discussion, bringing in information from scientific fields such as biology that was accurate but not applicable. Her manner too was bizarre, as were her exaggerated clothes—long, colored gloves that matched her extra gay hat, worn with one tight black dress, not a maternity dress, that grew tighter and tighter as the sessions went on. The leader tried to use any of her contributions that were at all valid, though there were very few. Aware that this mother was odd in many ways, the leader reported her impression to the doctor who had referred her to the group. They decided to have her continue, unless her behavior became troublesome. Interestingly, the other mothers accepted her in spite of her peculiarities and simply bypassed her comments when they made no sense. Although she contributed almost nothing that helped the discussion and it was not at all clear whether she gained anything tangible herself, she did not actively confuse or block the group's learning. She stayed on faithfully until the sessions were finished, seemingly at one with the others until the end of the group.

Any behavior in the group that is consistently exaggerated or remains on one tone needs thoughtful consideration and possibly some action from the leader. Since it suggests rigidity, at least, or possible denial of one aspect of a person's emotional reactions, the leader should give such a person an opportunity to take part in the group interplay and to recognize, from the contributions of other members, that there may be many mixed feelings about any situation and many different ways of responding to it. The mother who is always sweet, too sweet, in describing her children and in reacting to others in the group, may need to face up to the fact that things are not always that good or easy, that she, like the others, has her moments of irritation and her children are not always that good, either. The leader can help a parent toward such understanding, either directly, by saying something like, "But things aren't always this good (or this easy), are they?" or by underscoring a different statement of another parent, "As Mrs. T. has said, etc. . . ." Or, in reverse, a father who constantly belittles his son or who is always critical of his teenagers can be encouraged to talk about some of his boy's good qualities or some times when life with teenagers isn't all that bad.

We are suggesting here another version of the balances we have already discussed. This balance comes when the behavior of individuals is modified in the group interchange so that instead of being all black or all white, it takes on the quality of gray mixture. The blending which results is more in keeping with normal human behavior and therefore may be a healthier way of functioning, free from the strain that comes with a denial of a part of oneself or the pressure to live up to impossible and even undesirable standards. In other words, group education can to some extent break down set forms of behavior, as the responses of many parents bring into focus for each of them the natural ambivalences in their thinking and feeling about their children and family relations. As they come to accept their own mixed feelings, they become more tolerant of their children and often react with more understanding in the group. The group interplay affects them in other ways, too. Parents become aware of how they react to the actions of others in the group, such as when they are interrupted and cut off or encouraged and listened to. This, in turn, seems to sensitize them to how their children (or their spouses) may feel when they are interrupted or encouraged and causes the parents to modify their own behavior toward others. Finally, consciously or unconsciously, they respond to the leader's attitude of acceptance and helpfulness which they seem to take over and incorporate into themselves.

GROUP INTERACTION AND THE GROUP AS A WHOLE

While these developments take place in the parent-members, there seem to be characteristic changes in the group itself, as it emerges from the chance gathering of individuals who come together with a common purpose and becomes a cohesive entity in which the individuals work together toward their common goal. This integration takes place at various times and can never be precisely predicted. But there comes a moment, as reported by leader after leader, when one can say, "Now for the first time the group is *a group!*" The feeling of cooperative effort is in the air. The parents have begun to move out of their self-absorption. They are not only talking; they are also listening and are developing their ideas from what they have heard from others. And they are talking less to the leader directly, as pupil to teacher, and more to one another, across the table, back and forth. They have passed beyond the exploratory stage of getting to know one another and of finding out how the group operates and are settling down to their task.

Some of this exploration takes place each time the group meets. In a sense, the parents have changed since they met the last time. Many things have happened in their families that have influenced their thinking and their moods. So they need to get acquainted with one another all over again. This need decreases, however, as the series progresses, as parents learn to work together. Obviously, the cohesiveness that makes for active group interplay is strained when the make-up of the group changes because of absences. Then, at each meeting the group is literally different. It has to re-form and start over again. Parents are therefore encouraged to attend regularly, not just so that they will share in the continuity of the discussion, but so the group's working pattern of interaction will be maintained.

To help establish the group as a group as quickly as possible, registration in parent groups is usually closed after the second or third meeting. Under special circumstances, such as a small initial enrollment, new members are sometimes added during the better part of the series. Having new members come in late, however, slows down the group movement. They too have to go through the initial exploratory stage of learning about the group and finding their way of functioning. Sometimes the other parents sit back patiently until the new ones "catch up." Sometimes they are irritated by the presence of the new members, who seem to them almost like intruders, and they go on with the discussion as if the new ones were not there. Yet their coming into the group has its positive side, too: new members often give a different flavor to the group, by introducing ideas and experiences that are fresh and stimulating. Whatever reactions new members provoke, they have to be absorbed into the group interplay. And they usually are, although the process may take time and needs skillful handling by the leader.

In working through the various stages of group development, the parents have to come to terms with their relation with the leader and must learn, under his direction, to understand his proper function in this type of group and to make use of him in this light. This in itself involves considerable learning, since leaders are traditionally thought of as authority figures, like teachers—or parents—and the parent members often expect to be "told," no matter what interpretation they have been given about the way in which the group will proceed. Leaders must be prepared for the fact that they are the pivotal point in starting the group interplay and that their role must be truly clarified. This is essential so that they and the parent-members can take on the roles that make interaction productive.

While the group moves ahead at its task, the members continue to work out their relationships with the leader. These often take the form of transference phenomena, the transference to the leaders of members' needs and feelings that originated elsewhere, usually in their childhood or within the family. Leaders must recognize that at times the parents' responses to and need of them may run the full gamut of transference feelings: dependency, hostility, jealousy, competition. In the same way, members may react in transference terms to other parents in the group who may at the moment represent their parents or siblings or others with whom they have had intense personal relations. But whatever their source, the individually motivated feelings are handled in the group only in terms of their conscious, overt expression. The leader directs his efforts to meeting the transference phenomena on a factual, reality basis and uses his skills to stimulate the group interplay—member-to-member, with appropriate guidance from him as indicated—to provide the basis for the learning that is the task in hand.

This progress of the group members through a series of meetings is a phenomenon that has been described in various ways by group psychologists. Whatever their special orientation, they see it as one important aspect of group development, the process in which the group moves from one characteristic phase to another as it takes on a life of its own. Bennis and Shepard [4] found in their studies, for example, that the group as a whole moves from preoccupation with authority to preoccupation with personal relations. In its preoccupation with authority, the group moves from submission to rebellion and reaches a resolution in independence. In its preoccupation with personal relations, the group movement is from identification to self identity and finally to the acceptance of interdependence. In parent discussion groups these progressions are often recognized, though as each individual takes his place, he participates in the group process largely according to his characteristic pattern of relating to authority and his ability to work with others toward a common purpose.

[4] Findings of W. G. Bennis and H. Shepard, "A Theory of Group Development," *Human Relations*, 9: 415–437 (1956); summarized by Helen E. Durkin, *The Group in Depth*, International Universities Press, New York, 1964, pp. 46–48.

GROUP INTERACTION AND BEHAVIOR CHANGE

Much has been studied and written about group interaction in education, therapy, and social group work. As in many procedures that aim at producing "consciously induced change," programs have been studied primarily in terms of their demonstrable results rather than in terms of how they work and why. With regard to all methods of behavior-change processes, Mann, in his book, *Changing Human Behavior,*[5] states that evaluative research can document the method's effect but not explain it. He goes on to say that because of the inherent complexity of the vast majority of the processes used to induce behavior change, it is almost impossible to describe their nature precisely. Most methods are not that clearly formulated, and, as a result, one is at a loss to know what happened. The cause of any demonstrated effect can therefore not be determined. He suggests isolating a number of specific components that are shared in varying degrees by some or all the behavior-change processes, since these components lend themselves to precise description and measurement and can be used in experimental designs to attain interpretable scientific conclusions. From the experimental investigation of such individual components, he believes that the efficiency and generality of the investigation can be enormously enhanced.

Evaluative studies of specific aspects of group processes already have thrown light on factors that are important in parent group education, even though they do not contribute to a better understanding of the basic process itself. Among these are the studies of small groups already referred to, which were initiated in the late 1940s with the work of Kurt Lewin, and which have developed rapidly since then. Many aspects of group functioning have been investigated as they relate to behavior change, but we will refer here to only a few areas that are particularly relevant, either as challenging or as confirming the empirical findings of parent group education. These have to do with the composition of the group, the size of the group, and the participation of group members.

COMPOSITION OF THE GROUPS

Studies of the effect on group performance of the composition of groups have not yet been very helpful, although they have laid the groundwork for further work on this question. Here investigation has been difficult to execute because, as Mann has said, "The issue is complex, involving the nature of the task and the setting in which the group functions as well as the background and expereince of its members."[6] As this comment sug-

---

[5] John Mann, *Changing Human Behavior,* Scribners, New York, 1965, p. 12.
[6] *Ibid.,* p. 85.

gests, the groups studied were of many different kinds, set up with a variety of goals. The practical issue for parent group education is the effect on the group interplay of homogeneity versus heterogeneity of the group members. But these terms need defining. Homogeneous or heterogeneous in what respect? In parent group education, what common factors are significant: the age of the parents; the age of the children represented; the social, cultural, and economic backgrounds; personality traits; motivation; previous experience with groups, or what? [7]

As a partial answer to the question of personality characteristics deemed to be favorable for group interaction in the interest of behavior-change, Mann refers to the work of a psychologist, Richard Heslin, who reviewed a number of studies in this field. Although Mann states that "little objective knowledge exists as to whether different types of persons actually will function more or less effectively in the group," he mentions as significant Dr. Heslin's analyses which showed that both the ability and adjustment of group members significantly contributed to their capacity to function together effectively. He added that "while this conclusion is not surprising, it aids in distinguishing characteristics that are significant for effective group performance from those that are irrelevant." [8]

Mann raises the further issue that this conclusion is particularly relevant "when the small group is to be a vehicle for significant social or environmental rather than personal change." Yet this finding has definite implications for the process of personal change through increased understanding, as in parent group education. However, it is as yet impossible to select parents to participate on this basis, except where programs are set up primarily for the purposes of research. We would need to ask, too, what kinds of "ability" and "adjustment" are relevant for this type of group learning and by what personality test they can be best measured. As we have seen, members are usually not selected for parent group education as they are for group approaches which have other goals. For effective group performance, these programs must rely on those qualities of homogeneity that are in a sense self-selective: a common interest "in being better parents," a common focus of experience in "having children of similar ages," a common motivation "to join a group for personal growth through education." Implied, too, is the degree of emotional maturity in all the members that makes it possible for them to use the group profitably.

In the experience of the Child Study Association of America, these factors provide a homogeneity in groups of parents who often are widely heterogeneous in terms of age, personality make-up, educational experi-

---

[7] Edgar F. Borgatta, Leonard S. Cottrell, Jr., and Henry J. Meyer, "On the Dimensions of Group Behavior," in Hare, Borgatta, and Bales, *op. cit.*

[8] Mann, *op. cit.*, p. 85.

ence, and social, cultural, and economic backgrounds. The fundamental push to improve their handling of their life circumstances in the family cuts through these obvious differences and provides a vital common platform for group exchange and interplay. An outstanding example of this diversity is a group of expectant mothers that met in a hospital setting. It was made up of mothers who were receiving both private and clinic care, whose ages varied from eighteen to thirty-five, and whose educational backgrounds were as diversified as the Ph.D. in sociology of one and the grammar school education of another mother-to-be who was working as an aide on the maternity floor. There were only seven members in the group, and at the first session the differences were extremely marked, in fact, so marked that the leader was apprehensive that she would not be able to help them have a good group experience. Even in the first meeting, however, in the initial "go-around," the common quality of their interests and concerns began to be apparent. Under her guidance, these expectant mothers began to exchange their ideas and experiences with a feeling of friendliness and cooperation she would never have expected. In the exchange of ideas, the variations in their educational backgrounds faded as the members discovered they could really learn from one another—even from the young, relatively "uneducated" aide.

A similar blending was apparent in a group of parents of children with muscular dystrophy. Here, too, the parents presented a wide range of educational, social, and economic backgrounds. They also represented the three major religions. The commonality of their struggles to give adequate care to their chronically ill children asserted itself, despite the many differences in attitude that seemed to be identified with the various religious faiths. They were even able to surmount the difficulty of sharing experiences concerned with children of widely different ages. One family had a young child who had been recently diagnosed; other families had children in their late teens (one was just past twenty) and had consequently lived with their problems for many long and arduous years. The older parents were able to pass on to the younger ones some of the hard lessons they had learned—both emotional and practical—in living with their children. At the same time, the young parents reinforced in the older ones the courage to look to the future—a future which, at best, was dim for all of them.

These examples suggest that instead of being a hindrance to group interplay and group learning, heterogeneity within a common purpose can be a strong asset, for it can provide the richness and wide range of family occurrences that are so necessary for discussion. The leader selects and strengthens the elements of homogeneity, encourages the full exploration of the elements of diversity, and develops both elements in keeping with the principles and purposes of parent group education.

GROUP SIZE

The question of group size is also an important factor, but it, too, cannot be categorically defined. In parent education, how large should a group be to provide the needed variety, without decreasing the amount and quality of each person's participation? In other words, what is the optimum group size to allow for group interaction and the resulting personal growth?

Leaders have long been aware that group size affects the participation and contributions of the parent members, but exactly how and to what degree has not been sufficiently analyzed. Some light has been thrown on this problem in various studies of small group research which indicate that, as the numbers increase, the opportunity for members to speak is obviously diminished and they seem to be less satisfied when a limit is put on their participation.[9]

As groups get larger, there are more persons with whom each member relates. This factor is confusing at times, both to the members and to the leaders. Bales and Borgatta studied the effects of group size on the social interaction of members within the group.[10] They report that as group size increases, the relative talking time available for each member decreases and each person is confronted with a larger number of people who are under pressure to maintain a more or less adequate relationship with one another. "Thus as size increases, each member has more relationships to maintain, and less time to do so." They note that the larger the group, the greater the tendency for group members to give suggestions rather quickly and with less asking and giving opinions. They point out that giving suggestions is a more direct response to the demands of the group than is giving opinions and that when time is at a premium, members may feel under pressure to take the more direct approach, making suggestions without taking time to justify them with opinions or to ask others for their opinions. Leaders of parent discussion groups have observed this tendency, and have used their skills as best they could to develop the discussion in a way that would help the members be more reflective about the situations they are exploring, before giving suggestions or advice. Other studies have suggested that the larger the group, the greater the tendency to form the subgroups that are not always easy to handle within the total framework. This finding has also been confirmed in parent discussion groups.

[9] A. Paul Hare, "A Study of Interaction and Consensus in Different Size Groups," *American Sociological Review*, XVII (1952), pp. 261–267.

[10] Robert F. Bales, and Edgar F. Borgatta, "Size of Group as a Factor in the Interaction Profile," in Hare, Borgatta, and Bales, *op. cit.*, 1965.

Small-group research has focused largely on groups with membership up to twelve. The analysis of group behavior and of the advantages and disadvantages of larger versus smaller size within this limited range reinforce the experience that even a small group can function with valid and productive group interaction, if leaders maintain their goals and help the members take their appropriate part. This point of view is somewhat contrary to the feelings of some leaders who have been reluctant to hold meetings when, for one reason or another, the attendance on a particular night has been extremely low. They have been apprehensive that a meeting of only three or four people might become more problem-oriented or might probe too deeply into the personal, unconscious motivations of the members, in ways that are not consistent with parent group education. Wide experience with sessions in which there was a small attendance has shown, however, that the trends they feared did not happen, if they exerted their leadership properly. A small attendance can have a positive value for the few members who are there. This is especially true if any of these parents have been somewhat timid about speaking up in a large group. Participating in a "cozier" and less threatening atmosphere sometimes serves to open the way for their participating more fully in subsequent meetings. They find that it was not so hard after all to bring out their own concerns and to look at them with a few other sympathetic parents—and sometimes with some who even challenged them.

A leader's personal preference for a certain size parent discussion group probably plays a real part in his ability to keep the discussion moving and fruitful. Yet there is also no question that the group discussion can be most effective if the parents have an opportunity to exchange their ideas with enough others to present considerable variety.

MEMBER PARTICIPATION

Much attention has also been directed in small-group research to the matter of participation and specifically to the relative frequency and distribution of participation among the group members. The opinion has been held by many that members are influenced by a group experience to the degree that they participate in it. In parent group education, this has seemed to be true to a great extent, though there has been no specific research to validate this. Certainly, those who participate by speaking out involve themselves by their very activity in the group learning process. Furthermore, they are compelled to put their own ideas in order as they speak and, in doing so, to bring their thinking to a new level. Sometimes one hears a parent say, after making a comment, "You know, I never really saw it that way before." A member's spoken words also reveal for other members and for the leader where he is in his thinking and thus provide the basis for the development of other ideas by the group. Moreover, they reveal changes that may have taken place in his thinking, as well.

Regardless of the nature of the comments, participation is usually uneven in its distribution. Some people are naturally more volatile than others, more outgoing, better able to express themselves in any situation. These are the ones who from the beginning stand out and even dominate the group, sometimes overwhelming the more quiet ones and causing them to draw into their shells. As groups increase in size, this unevenness tends to become more pronounced, according to some studies. Then the discrepancy in the number of contributions between the smallest and the largest participators also increases.[11] This finding, however, is not substantiated in "A Study of Participation in Parent Group Education" conducted by Ambrosino.[12] In this study of nine parent education groups, attention was directed to patterns of participation, their relevance to the goals of parent group education, and the extent to which they moved in directions which practioners using the group discussion method have widely assumed to be desirable. The conclusions of this study are:

1. Different groups appear to establish a distinct rate of participation, which suggests that the members of a group arrive at implicit "rules" for the amount of entries they will permit in the discussions.

2. A comparison of the distribution of participation curves of these groups with studies of other types of groups suggests that parent groups distribute participation on a more equal basis.

3. Certain members can be characterized as high and low participators; it is nevertheless possible over the period of the series of meetings for the lows to increase their frequencies proportionately and come closer to the highs, thereby making the distribution of frequencies more equal.

These findings suggest that in parent group education the leader plays a significant part in shifting the patterns of participation so that more members contribute as the sessions progress. He consciously uses his skills to cut down (without cutting off) the contributions of the more active participators and to encourage those more timid, hesitant ones. In doing so, he seems to establish a more even balance of participation than is found in the leaderless groups that have usually been the focus of small-group research. If this conclusion is valid and if participation is, in fact, a positive factor in learning, it places even more responsibility on the leader. He must see not only that the members learn from the content of the sessions but

[11] Mann, *op. cit.*, p. 83.
[12] Salvatore Ambrosino, unpublished doctoral thesis submitted to Teachers College, Columbia University, 1960.

also that, in the process, they discover that they can change in their ability to make use of the group and can take part in the experience in a new way. It is hoped that this change will increase their self-confidence and will carry over into other aspects of their lives.

Ambrosino [13] points out that for the less active parent, the acquisition of new knowledge and changes in attitude can occur "especially if the situations under discussion are sufficiently close to ones which are familiar to him. In such instances, he can identify with one or several positions taken by the active participants and application of the discussion to his unique situation is possible. However, it must be pointed out that the private ponderings of the silent participator do not offer him the same chance for helpful development of attitudes that would be afforded by the group's reaction to his stated ideas or questions."

These general impressions are sometimes confirmed when previously quiet members begin to talk toward the end of a series of meetings. They often indicate then that their presence in the group had led to their learning, even though they had not been vocal. Each one has to progress in his own way.

The nature of the participation of the group members, then, is often more than appears on the surface. Leaders say they sometimes feel this "in their bones" as they react not only to the words but to the less obvious evidences of response that are recognizable if leaders are sensitive to them and look for them. These, too, contribute to the subtle process of group interaction.

Although group studies of different kinds have been directed to a number of variables that affect group interaction and its meaning for learning, the findings are still limited. We have referred to some of them here, not because they give us specific guidelines but because they suggest aspects of group life that seem to have bearing on parent group education. Much more research is needed in the small group field. The findings can then be applied to parent group education and their validity can be tested on a broad scale. What is missing is a more complete picture of how parents learn from the group interplay at all phases of the life of the group.

Each group, like each person, goes through its characteristic developmental tasks, from the beginning through the middle to the end. These tasks are for the members first to learn to take part appropriately in the group interplay itself and, second, to use the interplay for learning more about the parental role in the family. In both aspects, the individuals join together as a group which is more than its parts, to explore, work through, point up, absorb, and apply the concepts and approaches that have been developed together.

[13] *Ibid.*, p. 19.

XI

The Role of the Leader

We have seen that the leader in parent group education is part of a fascinating interplay of people and events in which he plays a decisive role. In taking on this role, he assumes responsibility to see that the group sessions become the learning experience for which the program is set up. The description of the procedures that facilitate this learning have naturally included what the leader does at various steps to help the parents achieve the group's goal. Obviously, his performance is not static or fixed. He acts in certain ways at certain times, as different stages of group development are reached and specific episodes occur. He acts as the particular moment requires and fits the immediate moment into the overall plan. Again, there are no prescribed formulas—many beginning leaders wish there were!

His leadership has different aspects. Yet these are never isolated. They merge into the total functioning of a helping person, with a consistent attitude and point of view. A beginner may push himself to take on one aspect of leadership at a certain point and then another, as he sees the need, and his performance may thus be uneven. As he becomes more experienced, however, his efforts—while still consciously chosen—become smoother and less effortful, as he responds more freely and spontaneously to the group's requirements. The separate parts of leadership become part of a whole, just as in any new area in which one acquires a new skill.

How can these functions be described? For purposes of summary, let us review them briefly, hoping they will be seen as supplementing one another and contributing to a well-rounded, whole role-performance.

ASPECTS OF LEADERSHIP

The leader in parent group education is neither a dominating, authoritarian teacher nor an exhorting preacher. Nor is he a passive, inactive auditor or mediator. Instead, he acts as a supporting, helping person who leads the group toward new knowledge and new understanding.

160

He creates an atmosphere for learning as he prepares the parents (and the community) for the group before it begins and in everything he does from the first meeting to the end.

He starts a process going by helping the parents to find their way in the group experience; he gives them a hand over the difficult humps in the group process such as the first meeting, the opening of any meeting, silences, arguments, and the like.

He guides the discussion, giving it form and direction by helping parents identify their concerns, relate them to the interests of the whole group, clarify them, explore their meaning for themselves and for the group, analyze the issues into their various components and synthesize them into a point of view based on an understanding of personality development and family interaction.

He deepens the discussion by making explicit the undertones of meaning and emotional response that are implied; underscoring material that is significant and putting the content into a broader framework by relating experiences to basic knowledge and knowledge to experience; opening up new sides of an issue or allied areas to be considered, emphasizing aspects that parents most need to understand or know about in advance, as anticipatory guidance; adding information which the parents do not have, to clarify assumptions about development and behavior and give more substance to the discussion; encouraging the expression and honest exploration of different points of view, without taking sides himself, so parents can find where they stand as individuals.

He fosters relationships and interaction between the parents and with himself, relationships which become the medium for learning and through which the parents gradually take more responsibility for the course of the educational group process.

He recognizes parents' problems of transference and countertransference in their relations with him and with other group members as he encourages group interaction for learning. He deals with the overt manifestations of these problems and does not expose them directly or explore their deeper meaning.

He sets an example in his acceptance of each individual parent as someone to be listened to and respected, and in his way of approaching life situations, as these are presented.

Some leaders feel that group members should pattern themselves not only on their attitudes and behavior but even on their appearance and stress the need to be neatly dressed and well groomed. To many, this point of view seems false, since every leader's appearance is part of his own self-concept and should not be artificially forced, beyond what he feels to be appropriate, within his own dignity and self-image. A leader's personal style may be utterly out of keeping with that of the parents, and by its very difference create a gulf between them and the leader. More important, they say, are the inner qualities of respect for others and a method of functioning that it is hoped the group members will choose to emulate and that cut through similarities or differences in outward appearance. Primarily, it is a leader's general attitude toward life that can be contagious. We have all seen groups that have been bogged down by a depressed, discouraged feeling on the part of the leader, just as we have seen leaders who are influenced by this attitude within the group. Similarly, we have seen how a leader whose approach is more confident and optimistic can influence his group in this direction, though this may not be effective at first.

If the group members are themselves burdened and depressed, it takes much more than a cheerful attitude on the part of the leader to pull them up to a more hopeful outlook. This, as we have suggested, comes about slowly, as the parents come to feel more competent to handle their lives and recognize that they do have resources to use—as they always have— to meet whatever comes. Certainly the attitude of the leader is an important factor in influencing the tone of the discussions; it must not, however, be so different that he seems unfeeling and causes the group members to be resentful.

WHAT KNOWLEDGE DO LEADERS NEED?

Leaders must have a reservoir of varied knowledge and skills on which to draw.

This should include first an understanding of the psychological background of family life and personality development at every stage, from infancy to adulthood and parenthood, when the cycle begins again with the new baby. This knowledge should be based on the psychodynamic point of view,[1] and should include a sensitive awareness of the "language of behavior"—the meanings, manifestations, and etiology of behavior in general and particularly within the family. The leader must also be familiar with characteristic emotional responses of parents, whether expectant parents or parents of young, school-age, or adolescent children, and must be able to evaluate what is normal and what is abnormal or pathological human behavior. He must know children of the particular age period which is the focus of the group—infancy, adolescence, or any other—and be aware of the effects of their behavior on their parents. If these are parents of children with handicapping conditions, the leader must be familiar

---

[1] Gertrude Goller, "The Place of Psychodynamic Orientation for Professional Leaders in Parent Group Education," *Journal of Psychiatric Social Work,* **XXIV**, No. 4 (September 1955).

not only with the nature of the specific disability,—mental retardation, muscular dystrophy, cerebral palsy, or whatever—but also with the impact of the disability on the family as a whole.

The leader, then, has general concepts of children's growth in the family and the community, knowledge of "critical" points of child-rearing, and understanding of those special issues about which parents may unknowingly hinder their children's development. Such typical questions as hampering a young child's freedom to develop in physical activities for fear he will hurt himself or failing to recognize when a child is literally begging his parents to "set limits" on his behavior are important for the leader to pick up. His knowledge of the developmental tasks that children and young people must master at each stage of the family cycle helps him open up questions for further exploration. These are areas where the leader introduces concepts about personality growth if the group does not come to them themselves.

Beside all this, the leader must have empathy with people. He expresses this by listening completely to what every parent says, searching out the special meaning this has for him. He does not see any parent as a stereotype. He lets himself feel with parents: he neither holds himself aloof nor becomes sentimental and overly involved. Such empathy is possible only in a leader who is not self-absorbed or very self-conscious. It may prove to be the one most important quality for effective performance as a parent group leader.

It helps if the leader is aware of himself and how he functions in certain situations and is thoughtful about his attitudes toward different kinds of group learning. He also needs to be thoughtful about his attitudes toward people of different kinds and personalities and honest about their effects on him as well as his effect on them. He should be able to tolerate discussions that reveal pain and distress in parents and to withstand the emotional impact of a number of people in the group rather than seeing parents in individual interviews. Above all, he must know the areas where he is inclined to make value judgments without sufficient thought.

And, finally, he must have a knowledge of the learning theories and skills of group leadership to which this book is devoted. If this seems a large order, we hasten to say that this is, of course, an ideal picture. All of us who have been active in group leadership know that we may be strong in some areas and somewhat lacking in others, knowledgeable about some phases of content and less knowledgeable about others. Added together, these requirements are undoubtedly what all of us would hope to achieve in order to carry on this kind of work. The main purpose of defining them in detail here is to challenge all of us to examine our performance and to see the extent to which we are making a disciplined use of ourselves, in a truly professional way. We are using the word "professional" here not in relation to whether or not we are being paid by an agency or a group, or have one professional background or another, but rather in the sense that we take our job seriously, and approach it with high standards of self-discipline and purposeful performance.

DUAL LEADERSHIP

Occasionally question has been raised as to whether groups can be conducted by two people who together guide the discussion and share the various aspects of leadership. In the experience of the Child Study Association, double leadership seems to present some problems, unless the two persons see eye-to-eye as to their goals and are completely comfortable with each other and uncompetitive. Even then, their "double image" may be confusing to group members who may intuitively turn to one of the pair as the person in command and thus upset the balance of their combined direction. Yet groups have been reported in which joint leadership has functioned well, with the two persons working together as a team, each supplementing the other.

A variation of this procedure is sometimes instituted by having two key people take different roles, clearly identified, as when one is designated "leader" and the other "resource person." Here the functions of the leader as we have defined them are compartmentalized and divided between two people. The leader is responsible for directing the group and guiding the discussion; the resource person contributes, where necessary, from his knowledge and experience, to fill in and enrich the content of the meetings. This arrangement is sometimes used in situations which call for specialized knowledge on the part of those conducting the program. Groups of unmarried mothers are sometimes conducted in this way, either with a nurse as the leader and a social worker as the resource person, or vice versa. Groups for parents of children with handicapping conditions occasionally follow this pattern too. When each person understands what is expected of him and plays his part appropriately, this approach can be effective. But a single, well-trained leader with a good background, who is well informed about the special aspects of these situations, can usually help the group achieve the same ends.

SHOULD A LEADER ALSO BE A PARENT?

This issue comes up frequently with regard to leaders in parent group education. Parents sometimes feel that anyone who has not experienced parenthood cannot begin to understand "what parents go through" day by day in living with their children. They may even ask the leader whether he or she has any children. Some leaders who are not parents feel that this question puts them "on the spot." Leaders without children of their own often bring many mixed feelings to their work with parent groups. Some are envious, perhaps, or uncomfortable with their own status in life and therefore uncertain of their own ability to be helpful to parents.

Certainly our personal experiences and life situations always have meaning in relation to the people with whom we are working. Being a parent can surely increase our awareness of the experiences and emotional responses of other parents, as we share with them some universal aspirations and satisfactions, fears and problems. But it can also limit our effectiveness if we see their lives only through our personal viewpoints. Then we may find ourselves responding primarily to those situations which are similar to ours, or we may read into their comments meanings that are not relevant for them. And there is always the danger that we may become overinvolved with certain parents, out of the sympathy that comes from "having been through it," too. In a sense, then, parenthood adds a dimension to leadership but also has potential dangers that must be safeguarded against.

On the other side of the question, leaders who are not parents lack the first-hand experience with all its implications. They do, however, have many other ways of knowing about children and what parenthood means. They have acquired knowledge from their professional training, whatever their specialized field, from their contact with families in the course of their work, from their own homes in relation to their parents, from their friends and relations. This they can say, quietly and with assurance, if the matter is raised in the group. They also have the advantage of looking at parenthood from a distance, without being directly involved. This adds a certain objectivity which often makes it easier to separate the various aspects of parental responses and help the parents look at them more objectively, too.

What we seem to be saying is that leaders can best help parents learn when they themselves are not so close that they are overinvolved yet not so far away that they are aloof and lose contact with the parents' human problems. From this point of view, whether or not they are parents is secondary. What is primary is that, whatever their family status and personal experience, they are able to use their resources and skills for the purposes of the group.

SPECIAL PROBLEMS OF LEADERSHIP

As they apply the principles of parent group education to practice, leaders sometimes find certain aspects of their leadership performance difficult. These rough spots emphasize some of the critical questions that arise in this kind of group guidance. They are summarized here with brief pointers that may help to bring the practice in line with the group's purposes.

How "ACTIVE" SHOULD A LEADER BE? This question implies that there are alternative choices of activity and passivity.

Each leader has to find his own way of functioning within the setting, structure, and purposes of the group. Some tend to be too passive, at least at first, in their wish not to "teach" but to help the parents learn for themselves. Until they develop more skills in how to do this, they sometimes do nothing, letting the parents flounder.

Other leaders tend to be too active, commenting on every comment, guiding and directing every moment, without giving the parents time to develop their thoughts—and relationships—at their own pace.

Obviously, these extremes *are* extremes. Leaders who fall into either category are overreacting to the situation, sometimes out of their understandable eagerness to do the best possible leadership job, or perhaps overcompensating in controlling their tendency to act in just the opposite way. The issue is in itself somewhat false. Activity and passivity are not important in themselves but only in relation to what they are being used for. Leadership calls for selective activity toward specific goals. Sometimes the group learning process calls for a leader to be active in ways that have been described, to help the group move ahead. At other times, it calls for him to be passive, in the sense that he may not be talking; but even then he is actively involved, listening, observing the course of the discussion and the behavior of the parents, and letting the group function "on its own" as long as it progresses well and does not need his intervention.

A leader discovers when to act (speak) if he keeps his eye on the content and the tone of the discussion and comes in *for a purpose*.

How CAN LEADERS BE SURE PARENTS LEARN WHAT THE LEADERS WANT THEM TO KNOW? They can't. One must ask, in turn, however, whether the parents always want (or even need) to know what the leaders think they should know! Or if they do, are these issues as important to the parents as they are to the leader? Are there other matters that are of greater concern to them at the time?

Leaders are often imbued by their own background and experience with strong convictions about the understanding they feel parents should have in order to function more effectively. And they are usually right. As we know, however, learning is acquired better and applied more relevantly when it is sought after and reached for, rather than imposed from the outside. A leader may be so eager to be the educator that he fails to pick up the cues to what the parents are really asking for. When a parent introduces a question that is related in some way to sex, for example, many thoughtful leaders take this as an opening for a general discussion on sex education and how parents need to meet their children's developing sex interest at every level. They lead the discussion in this direction without finding out just what part of the question the parent had in mind or what implications his original reference had for him or for the rest of the group. The original comment may have been connected with the mother's fear of homosexuality in her boy, perhaps, a fear that would never come to the fore if the leader pushed toward an academic discussion of sex education for children of different ages.

A mother in a group of parents of teenagers went into a long monologue after the first go-around, complaining about the irritating behavior of her two boys and the fact that there seemed to be no communication between them and their parents. The leader, who was just beginning her first group, saw that the parents were getting restless listening to this long tale, so she launched into a lecture of sorts, describing the needs of teen-agers and the reasons why they behave as they do. She was so eager to be sure that the parents got a picture that would help them communicate with their young people that she overlooked the fact that, in a sense, she was broadcasting to the group without really knowing where they wanted to begin. She failed to establish a reasonable focus with which to start, a focus that could have been established quite easily if she had asked the mother, and then the group as a whole, what part of their situations with their young people they wanted to begin to examine.

The leader serves the parents best if he does not impose on the group either his own "topics" or his quick interpretation of what a parent has in mind. These may be quite unrelated to the parents' thinking. If a leader has his own favorite themes, the parents will usually bring them up in time—if they are a part of their real concern. On the other hand, of course, leaders have a role to play in broadening the parents' sights, branching out from their beginning concerns and opening new implications for them to consider.

Leaders often report episodes in which they jumped to *their* conclusions —and were wrong. The following is a case in point. In a group of mothers of preschool children, one mother complained that her four-year-old girl did not talk and asked how she could help her. Because these mothers lived under depressed conditions and had many difficulties to contend with, the leader assumed that this child was not being stimulated to talk at home. She saw the mother's comment as a fine opportunity for the group to encourage this mother to have more interplay with the child in her daily activities. As the discussion continued, however, it became apparent that, if anything, the mother was "at" her child too much at home. The little girl apparently clammed up at home though she chatted busily when she was with other children. The discussion, then, served to point up that children do not talk when there is too much prodding as well as too little. This added a dimension the leader had not anticipated and had almost overlooked in her eagerness to make *her* point.

How can a leader help the group find a common basis on which to begin the discussion, when the parents' experiences have not been similar? The leader has to recognize what is "common." When a parent brings up a problem area he would like to discuss, leaders sometimes ask the group whether they have had similar experiences. If they say yes, there seems to be a sharing with which they can start. If they say no, the leader is stopped. Actually, he has taken the group up the wrong alley. It is the *concern* of the parents about the problem that provides the common basis for their thinking, rather than the exact events. It is this concern that they are likely to share, even though their experiences with their children are not identical.

In the second meeting of a group of ADC mothers, one member brought out this problem: her school-age girls took her cologne, jumped all over the furniture, and would not listen to her. She and her children lived with her parents and the girls apparently paid attention to the grandparents but not to her. She said she worried that she could not raise her children; her parents would not let her. The leader asked if any other members had had a similar experience and the group became diverted into a discussion of the influence of other family members on the children. In retrospect, the leader saw that her question had been directed to *similar occurrences* which the group picked up in terms of experiences with relatives, when actually the issue the mother had brought up was her loss of control. As it happened, several other parents had already brought up the same issue in the very same words but with different circumstances. The leader felt that if she had focused on this common response, the discussion would have been more meaningful.

How can a leader guide the discussion so that the concerns of each parent are met and at the same time keep it meaningful for them all? Leaders who have come from fields of work in which they have been concerned primarily with one person at a time often find this a troublesome problem. They have a tendency to concentrate on one person after another, almost as if in sequence. Thus parents get the impression that the group is there to solve one problem—or the problem of one parent—and then move on to another, with each person hoping that in time his turn will come. Leaders are less apt to follow this procedure when they begin to see that there are common threads of response from parents on many issues. It is the underlying theme that is more important than the actual form of the problem itself. The first attitude that "serializes" the problems parents present is rather pedantic and limited. As leaders become more experienced in seeing the way in which commonality can emerge, they become less rigid and are freer to move from one parent's problem to another—and back again—as they talk about a matter of mutual interest. In this way, the individual parent's concern becomes merged with that of the group. From the discussion in which all the parents take part, he takes what is relevant and meaningful for him.

To what extent should a leader limit the group discussion to one age period, when parents in the group have children of a wider age range? Sometimes a leader finds it difficult when the discussion involves children of various age levels all at once. If, for example, a group is set up around the problems of school-age children, the leader may be inclined to rule out the introduction of descriptive material about older or younger children, feeling it is not appropriate for this group. In terms of the original commitment with the group, it is right to try to keep the discussion primarily focused on the problems of school-age children. But the leader soon finds that if he cuts off material which at first seems extraneous, he may lose reports of behavioral tendencies that run through all age levels. These can be used to make more vivid the period under discussion, highlighting what went on before or, in some cases, what developed later in some of the members' families.

To what extent is it necessary to adhere to a focus the group has agreed to explore? Some leaders tend to adhere quite closely to a "focus," holding the group to its original commitment when the focus may already be shifting or spreading toward a wider area. The problem usually comes up in connection with a comment a parent makes that appears to take the discussion up another alley. When this happens, a leader sometimes indicates to the group that this seems to be a new topic, and asks the group if it wishes to pursue this or to go on with the earlier line of thought. But sometimes the alley is not a *blind* alley; rather, it may be a branching out of thinking that relates to the main theme, although the connection may not be apparent at first. In such a case, it may be wise to stay with the discussion until one sees where it is really going. Occasionally, the leader will ask the parent why he brought it up, or whether there was some connection between this and what they had been talking about before. Such a comment may bring out a connection the leader had not seen at all. On the other hand, the parent may say that there is really no connection, he merely wanted to have the matter brought in at some time. Then the leader can easily suggest that this be held in abeyance at the moment, but that surely the group will come back to it.

DIFFICULTIES SOME LEADERS HAVE IN INTERPRETING THE CONTENT PARENTS BRING UP. Sometimes, in his wish to accept everything parents bring up, the leader may accept the surface meaning of something a parent says without looking into it further. The leader may be right in his assumption, and the group may go along with this. But if he is wrong, the parent and the group are likely to be bewildered and not know how to continue the discussion. Accepting a member's words, then, is not enough. To be sure of what the parent has in mind, the leader must raise questions that will clarify the issue for everyone. An expectant mother's complaint about backache may mean merely that she is experiencing some of the usual discomforts of pregnancy and may be helped by suggestions of change of position at night and a better use of her body in the daytime. On the other hand, she may also be troubled that this may indicate some distortion of her body function that will carry on after pregnancy as well. Merely handling it on a mechanical basis, in such an instance, would not be enough.

On the other hand, leaders sometimes find they are being too clinical, dealing with every statement as if it were a symptom of pathological behavior when it may be only an expression of the parent's concern of the moment, a concern about something that may be quite normal. Of course it is important that the parents all find out something of the meaning of the behavior he is reporting and its causes. But one must first know what is in the parent's mind, and what the situation really means, in order to help them all understand and cope with it more effectively as they encounter it themselves.

For example, when a mother reports that her five-year-old boy wets his bed, the leader may have in mind that the child is already enuretic, in the clinical sense of the term. On closer exploration, however, it may appear that this little boy, who had already been well "trained," has been through a period of illness, in which he was not always able to maintain his bladder control. Thus his wetting was only a temporary regressive response to a period of stress. Viewed in this light, the group can understand the causes of the immediate behavior without delving deeply into the child's relationship problems or the situations that may be connected with enuresis in a five-year-old.

In line with the tendency to find evidences of clinical problems in such situations, there seems to be, for some leaders, a feeling that they are threatening and fraught with deep implications. Leaders sometimes hesitate to explore a particular situation where exploration seems justifiable and even necessary, because they fear they may expose the parent's weaknesses and ineffectiveness. When these matters are explored more fully in the group, the leader often finds that the situations may have arisen because of factors beyond the parent's control. He sees that, faced with the full implications of their problems, parents have strength and resiliency to call on, the strength and resourcefulness that they have shown in many other aspects of their lives.

And yet there is the other side of the picture. Sometimes leaders are misled by the frequency with which they encounter reports of a certain type of behavior and overlook the fact that it may very well be a sign of pathology, even though it appears to be common. For example, public health nurses who participated in a training program commented on the fact that they saw a considerable amount of head-banging in the infants and small children they saw in their home visits. When one mother in a group of parents of nursery-age children brought up her child's head-banging, a leader accepted this as being quite usual and failed to explore the circumstances or help the parents understand some of its possible causes and how to cope with it. Because the nurses had seen so much of it, they were under the impression that this was a normal phase of development that would fade in time. After some discussion in the training group, the nurses began to recognize that this manifestation suggested more pathology in the families they were visiting than they had realized. One nurse later reported that the next time head-banging came up in a parents' group, she helped the group examine it much more thoughtfully.

How can leaders get at the feelings that underlie parents' reports of situations? This question is often raised because leaders are aware that it is important for parents to examine the emotional as well as the factual aspects of the situations they are discussing. It often happens, however, that feelings are expressed in the very telling of an episode or description of an event within the family. They do not have to be "got at" because they are already out in the open. One need not ask an expectant mother how she feels about diet restrictions in pregnancy when she says she is always hungry and, by her very tone, implies that she feels deprived. Sometimes the feelings that are implied can be brought out more clearly when the parents are encouraged to do so. Given a chance, this hungry expectant mother will usually say she feels deprived. At least she will say it's hard not to eat the things she likes so much when she sees her non-pregnant friends eating rich pastries and other fattening desserts. When the other mothers in the group share her feelings and give her sympathy and support, she may be better able to stick to her unsatisfying regime and to accept the reasons for the doctor's orders.

Often the word-label a parent uses to describe a child or an episode reveals his feeling quite clearly. The mother who says her child of three is an "imp" or a "monster" may be half joking, but her very choice of the word shows how she feels about him. Such a comment from a mother in a group of parents of preschoolers provoked another mother in the group to say, "You don't really approve of your son, do you? You haven't said a good thing about him." After further discussion of what this little boy was really like, the second mother said with a smile, "Well, he seems pretty good to me. Let's swap!"

Putting feelings into words often helps parents in ways they hadn't expected. Sometimes they themselves have not been aware of the coloration of their own or their children's responses and they are surprised. Usually, they are surprised because they are not in the habit of recognizing their feelings. If the leader and the group accept them as they are stated, and the discussion perhaps shows that other parents or their children, too, have these feelings at times, of course the feelings no longer seem so horrendous. Furthermore, airing them gives parents a start toward evaluating what significance they really have and how they can be dealt with.

How should the leader frame his question in order to push the group's thinking ahead? The words a leader uses fall into place when he is clear about why he is using them.

Certainly the question that aims at a specific answer has a directing, schoolroom tone that is not helpful. If parents feel that the leader wants them to give him a particular response, they struggle to meet his request, but at the same time they may feel like children again, searching for the right answer. Group members sometimes express this by saying, "Is this what you had in mind?" In contrast, questions that open up a line of thinking which may take different forms are more likely to stimulate the group's thinking in new directions.

Leaders can be quite flexible in asking questions for additional information. For example, when a parent brings up something that happened, the leader may ask whether it was usual or unusual and raise other questions to bring out aspects of the problem which will clarify it for the group as well as for the member who brought it up.

Perhaps the most helpful questions are those which pick up ideas or responses that are only half-articulated, and those that are presented in a sharp, provocative statement or a particularly significant word. When the word or statement is made clear by the leader's question, it gives the discussion a vital push by adding vivid material to which the other group members can react.

How much do leaders really need to know about where a subject should go to see that it is adequately covered? Leaders are often uneasy when parents bring up an issue for which they are not prepared and which they may not have thought through adequately for themselves. One leader, for example, was floored when the parents in a group discussing school-age children brought up the question of masturbation. Although this leader knew that the prevailing attitude toward masturbation was much more accepting than was usual some years ago, she was uneasy because she did not know the extent to which it was healthy for children to be allowed to continue this "habit" and when—and under what circumstances—they might be helped to control it. Because of her own insecurity and lack of a clear position in her own mind, she did not follow and guide the group discussion as well as she might have otherwise.

In a situation of this kind, the parents themselves would probably have brought out many different points of view about masturbation, as they usually do. They might have indicated whether their children masturbated at first without self-consciousness, and at what point they began to recognize that this was not generally acceptable and might therefore have been helped to restrain themselves, at least in public. Some might have reported that their children asked for help in controlling these actions about which they really felt uncomfortable. On an issue as full of emotional overtones as this, as in any area of child problems, parents will want to explore the possible significance of this behavior in the child's development and the meaning—or threat—it may carry for the parents themselves. As a result of such discussion, parents usually become more understanding and less punitive in their attitude. They are better able to accept a child's masturbation as a natural part of his psychosexual growth—if it is not extreme and preoccupying. They are also better able to help a child control his behavior appropriately as he grows older, as our society requires. In this situation, the leader uses his customary skills for the group learning. If he is unsure that the issue has been adequately covered or uncertain that the general conclusions that have been reached are sound, he can look up pertinent research or studies on the subject after the meeting is over. Or he may want to consult another qualified professional person. In either case, he can bring back some interpretation of current thinking on the matter to add at the next meeting, if this is needed.

In other sensitive areas as well, even when leaders may not "know the answers" themselves, they can help the group share their ideas, their experiences, and their fears, and put them into some kind of order, in relation to the attitudes and ideas of their own cultural and social community.

Leaders are often uncertain whether to help a group move on to another area for discussion or stay with the current topic. This raises the next question about leadership.

How can a leader judge what is more conducive for learning? This question comes up when the group seems to have lost interest or feels they have had enough of a subject for the time, yet the leader knows that much more could be said from different points of view. Here, too, leaders have to feel their way. They try to balance their own knowledge of what may be involved in the situation against the group's interest and readiness to stay with it. They are free to suggest other approaches, other angles, to broaden the discussion or give it new life. But they should be prepared not to belabor the issue if the group does not respond.

In discussion groups that meet for a series of consecutive meetings, whichever course is followed need not be final. There is always time to come back to a subject if the parents are not satisfied, or if they bring in new experiences or new ideas that may further develop the thinking of the group. If, however, the leader feels that the discussion has been really inadequate or confusing, it is his responsibility to say so, pointing out that they may want to come back to it at another time, since there is much more that could be added.

HOW MUCH "INFORMATION" SHOULD LEADERS GIVE AND WHEN? This is always a burning question. As we have seen, it is tied up closely with the fact that parents do need information about the manifestations they are dealing with in living with their families. The question is what and how much information do they need from the leader, and under what circumstances?

This question has been raised at many points in this book, but it is brought up so often that it may be helpful to summarize a general approach to it here. Within the philosophy of parent group education, the group process provides an experience whereby parents can bring out all the information they have about the areas they want to discuss, sharing, testing it for its validity, and discussing its implications. Where their information, so-called, is false, it is the leader's responsibility to help them correct it. Where the information is incomplete, the leader adds from his own knowledge and experience. Information from the parents, clearly expressed, together with supplementary information given by the leader, provides an important fund on which the parents then develop their ideas.

In practice, leaders tend either to pour out too much information too soon or to withhold information because they so much want the parents to gain it from each other for themselves. The middle ground here, as in other delicate leadership areas, is determined by the way the particular group functions. Certainly, if the leader is too quick in introducing material, the parents may be kept from exploring what they know themselves. On the other hand, withholding information which the leader obviously has may irritate the group and prove extremely frustrating. Again, the leader must judge when his contribution is needed.

Sometimes, particularly in expectant parent groups where the questions are often related to a physical matter, a simple answer will clear the air and help the group go on to something else. Even here, however, the leader first makes sure whether other group members may not have the "answer," in which case he needs only underscore its validity.

WHAT SHOULD LEADERS DO WHEN THEY ARE ASKED FOR THEIR PERSONAL OPINION ON A MATTER? This situation comes up frequently. Parents often say, "What do *you* think about it?," particularly when there is a difference of opinion. Leaders are puzzled about what to do with such a question. If they give a straightforward answer, will this throw the weight of their authority on one side of an issue in a way that may not be helpful? On the other hand, if they merely withhold their opinion, will they seem precious and difficult?

Probably the leader does have an opinion on an issue and occasionally— very occasionally—he may decide to say what it is. But he should be sure to state that it *is* a personal opinion. He makes clear that what he thinks as an individual is not the issue; that his point of view is based on considerations that are valid for him but may not hold for others in other circumstances. What *is* important is for the group to know that he is there to help them think matters through for themselves, as these apply to their families and to their own goals. All this he can say quite honestly. Usually, group members accept such an interpretation, and go back to developing their own ideas, with his help. Handling the question of the leader's opinion in this way is consistent with the principle that leaders are there to strengthen the functioning of the parents on their own, without exerting undue influence over them in an authoritative way.

As we have seen, many leaders struggle against their tendency to be authoritative. They sometimes inadvertently suggest an authoritarian attitude by the frequent use of the words, "I think," which many of us often intersperse in our sentences without noticing that we are doing so. Where this phrase introduces a tentative statement, such as "I think we're saying . . . ," it does not interfere with the feeling that the leader is working with the parents. Yet the same purpose can be accomplished if the leader uses an impersonal form, such as "What you seem to be saying is. . . ." It is when the words come out with the emphasis on the "I" ("*I* think") that leaders put themselves into a more authoritarian position than they intend.

TO WHAT EXTENT IS IT WISE FOR A LEADER TO DRAW ON HIS OWN PERSONAL EXPERIENCE TO ENRICH THE DISCUSSION? Many leaders are tempted to bring into the group episodes with their own children or their own families, to illustrate points that the group may bring up. On the whole, this does not work out well. By identifying the material in this personal way, the leader somehow becomes involved in the group in a way that is not always constructive. It is as if he entered into the group interplay as a group member, since his material, added to theirs, is open to their reactions, either of agreement or disagreement. Actually, because of his position in the group, parents react to his comments more intensely, either for or against. By identifying something in which he has been involved, he may divert the group's attention away from the issue and direct it to his performance instead. Then, too, since he is the leader and a person in authority, there is always the possible implication that what he does is also what they should do. But it may not be the right way for them. Leaders can certainly enrich the discussion by bringing in anything they have experienced, but it is better if they do not identify it as based on their personal lives. They can merely say "I know a child who . . . ," suggesting they may be talking about a neighbor or a relative or someone they have known in their work. Then the material is presented objectively, without the emotional overtones that may attach to him as a person or as the leader.

SHOULD LEADERS MAKE USE OF THE INFORMAL CONVERSATION THAT OFTEN TAKES PLACE BEFORE A MEETING ACTUALLY BEGINS? Leaders sometimes feel that what takes place outside the group is not part of the group discussion. In a sense, this is so, since exchange of ideas between members (two, perhaps) before the group is assembled does take on a rather informal, cozy tone. Certainly, it is not shared with everyone, and it may even have been offered in confidence. Where several people have been involved, as often happens, there is no reason why the leader should not refer to the conversation which he has obviously overheard while waiting for the group to begin. He might ask those parents whether they would like to share with the group some of the matters they were talking about while they were waiting. This gives them an opportunity to do so or not, as they choose. If their conversation grew out of some immediate interest or concern it may be a valuable introduction to a group meeting.

CAN LEADERS CONDUCT COUPLES' GROUPS IN THE SAME WAY THAT THEY CONDUCT GROUPS FOR MOTHERS ALONE? Leaders raise this question because they sense that having fathers and mothers or expectant parents together in pairs creates a different set of dynamics. They find that a group of twelve mothers and fathers is made up of twelve individuals, but these individuals tend to group themselves into six subgroups of two with each couple serving as a separate unit. At times the group also may divide into two subgroups according to sex. Each subgroup has its own internal relationships and complicated interplay. At the same time, the subgroups break up and re-form in a constantly shifting pattern, as their members find members of other subgroups with whom they can identify—or disagree. Some leaders find this interaction confusing and also unpredictable—and so it is.

Within the couple-pair subgroups, there are many kinds of interplay. In some, both partners are equally involved and work together, eager to do their respective and joint best for their children. In others, one finds different degrees of involvement, stemming from their individual ideas about maternal and/or paternal responsibility in child-rearing. Their attitudes are also affected by the relation of the two partners to one another, whether there is mutual trust, shared purposes, and freedom to communicate or hostility, disappointment in the other partner's handling of the children, and the wish to prod him or her into better performance. In the discussion husbands and wives sometimes reveal other characteristics, such as self-doubt that may not yet have been resolved in the marriage relationship and that spreads into any area of their functioning, or greater or less capacity to extend themselves in any relationship.

Although there *is* more for the leader to take into account when couples are present, he carries out his role in much the same way as in other groups. He recognizes the interplay between the two parts of the couple and listens to each one with respect, as he hopes the other parents will. He encourages each to have his say, without being too obvious about it, and is particularly attuned to any comment made by the quieter of the two. (Usually, one is apt to do most of the talking, especially at first.) He is not afraid to have couples disagree between themselves, even when they do so heatedly and with some bitterness. He focuses on the differences of *opinion* (but without taking sides) and involves other parents in expressing their relevant ideas. Thus he bypasses the intense feelings, though he may recognize that they exist by making a general statement, such as, "This seems to be something about which parents have strong feelings." In short, he handles the parents' comments primarily as if they came from individual members of the group and follows the practices he uses in any educational group.

Even when both parents are not in the group, the presence of the other parent is often felt *in absentia,* as a member reports his or her perception of the other's attitudes and behavior toward their children. This is difficult to deal with, for there is inevitably some distortion and it is hard to filter out the true picture. When both parents are there in person, each partner speaks out directly. His contributions are then subjected to the reality testing that goes on in the group interchange. The group reacts to his perception of himself, rather than to his partner's view of him.

A leader's performance is greatly influenced by his feeling about the make-up of the group. Some prefer to have only mothers or only fathers, although groups of only fathers occur rarely. Some women leaders are not sure in advance how they will respond to men in the group, or how the men will respond to them. Nurses leading expectant parent groups are occasionally concerned about this, especially if they have devoted their professional attention to women patients in maternity services. Actually, their fears usually melt away when they start their couples' groups. Then they begin to look at the husbands' and wives' behavior and comments as part of the total group interaction, subgroups and all. The members emerge as individuals who are sharing in a learning experience, rather than as males and females.

LEADERS RAISE FURTHER QUESTIONS. *Do fathers play a different part in parent groups? Are they concerned more with immediate or with far-reaching results?*

These questions cannot be answered definitively, with the present state of our knowledge. There are some suggestions from small-group research findings that men may tend to play a more task-oriented (instrumental) role, concentrating on achieving a goal and adapting to external demands; women, in contrast, tend to react on a social-emotional basis, concerned with matters of internal integration and adjustment. Experience with parent discussion groups has seemed to support these findings, though only on an impressionistic basis. Leaders often say they find fathers more practical and down-to-earth, more interested in finding "solutions" to situations, more likely to ask for specific answers to specific questions. Yet there have been many examples of fathers who are "social-emotional" in their points of view and mothers who are more "task-oriented." And many fathers who are eager to have an immediate problem met and resolved quickly are also concerned about the long-range development of their children, as they face the future.

For practical purposes, such theoretical considerations, although interesting, are not vital. Leaders deal with these different types of behavior as they appear, no matter where they come from. To provide the diversity so necessary for productive parent group education, both points of view are helpful and supplement each other. Either approach alone is limited and sterile without the other.

It is not enough, for example, to concentrate on a child's achievement in school and how to help him, as fathers sometimes seem to do; the group must also take into account the social-emotional factors for both parent and child. The kind of things to buy for the expected baby—folding carriages, plastic wash-basins for bathtubs, and the like—and discussions on a practical level are helpful as far as they go, but even these matters have to be considered in the larger context of the baby's total well-being and the parents' reactions to all phases of his care.

Here again, the leader sees that all the implications are considered, as far as this is possible in the time available.

✿   ✿   ✿   ✿   ✿

These examples of troublesome spots in leadership performance indicate the need for leaders to be certain about their purposes in whatever they do. At the same time, they need to see that there is danger in following any general procedure too rigidly, if it cuts off the free flow and development of ideas and responses from the group members themselves. The test of a leader's skill in any part of the group meetings is the way in which the group members perform together and the way in which they carry out the group plan and accomplish the purposes for which they come.

XII

Group Education for Parents in Special Situations

The approaches and practices of parent group education described in this book have been presented as they applied to three kinds of parent groups: parents of children of a particular age, expectant parents, and parents of children with physical handicaps and chronic illnesses. All of these groups, focusing on different situations their members meet as parents or prospective parents, are based on the same general concepts and follow the same general group procedures. Yet they seem to have unique characteristics.

Naturally, much of the *content* of the discussion differs in these various groups, since the concern is with the special problems of a specific situation or phase of family development. But they differ also in the intensity and tone of the discussions. Some of these qualities have already been suggested in various excerpts from group sessions, excerpts which have been chosen because they seem characteristic of many groups in many settings. The usual parent discussion groups—those organized around the particular age of their children—serve as a kind of norm, against which groups of parents in special situations present some typical variations.

GROUPS FOR EXPECTANT PARENTS

It is not surprising that the discussion in expectant parent groups turns largely to factual information, particularly at first. There is much pregnant women and their husbands need and want to know about the pregnancy itself, the accompanying bodily changes, and the physical processes by which the baby grows and is born. This is often a great mystery, even to women and men who have had biology courses in school or college; mothers who have already had several children are sometimes not clear about such matters as the menstrual cycle and how conception itself takes place. Not infrequently it has been found that mothers of six or eight

180

children attending a parent group ostensibly to prepare for the coming of the next baby are motivated to come to the group by quite different needs. What is often present in their minds is the need to find out about birth control, so that they will not have any more children. In some communities this subject is now being given open sanction in the announcements of expectant parent group programs, which state that the groups will discuss matters pertaining to pregnancy, labor and delivery, the care of the new baby, and family planning.

Discussions have revealed an amazing ignorance of bodily processes and functions, in some cases extending to ignorance of the exact relation of intercourse to conception. Small wonder then that parents-to-be come to groups with many questions, questions that reveal the large gaps in their knowledge. To a great extent the information they are looking for is part of medical-nursing knowledge, so it is natural that these groups should be conducted by nurses, many of whom have been specially trained for this kind of group teaching.

This factual information has been the main substance of expectant parent classes for many years. Leaders in the field of maternity and public health nursing were aware, however, that learning about the processes of pregnancy and birth and the physical care of the baby was only part of the educational job that had to be done. Expectant parents—husbands as well as wives—needed an opportunity to understand and come to terms with the psychological and emotional aspects of the experience. These cover a wide range. They include the emotional fluctuations of pregnant women that seem to be closely connected with the physiological and hormonal changes of the prenatal and postnatal periods, their psychological reactions to the coming of the baby, their fears for his normality and well-being as well as their own, their expectations—and anxiety—about the new kind of life his presence will bring, with its physical and psychological demands and possible changes in their husband-wife relations and social activities. So discussion groups for expectant parents, making use of the procedures of parent group education, have taken on an expanded scope. As young parents-to-be explore what is happening physiologically, they find that the accompanying emotional experiences are just as real; they too need to be aired and examined. These two interwoven aspects of their concerns are, in a general sense, not too different from parental concerns about children of different ages. Both deal with problems of growth and development and their emotional concomitants. But there the growth and development is that of the children, rather than parents. The growth experience of pregnancy is the mother's own and is obviously more intense and preoccupying to her and, in a lesser degree, to her husband. Group discussions for expectant parents take on a vivid, personal quality, beginning often in physical terms, about many intimate matters that are usually not openly brought out. The group sanction breaks down the parents' reserve and the professional background of the nurse gives parents-to-be the confidence to talk frankly. They usually respond with a strong feeling for one another, brought about by this rare shared experience.

Yet sometimes these groups start more slowly than parent groups in which the parents identify with one another quickly in connection with their children. Expectant mothers and fathers still see themselves very much as individuals, not knowing just where they stand in relation to the other expectant parents. Gradually, the common quality of the pregnancy and their planning for the new baby takes over and they lose themselves as they learn together and from one another.

Because they realize that they need a great deal of information and have many specific questions, expectant parents often are skeptical about learning through discussion. They often want *answers*, especially the husbands, and they need to be helped to see that there are different ways of finding answers and that answers have many dimensions. The main point is that they come to understand that they will get what they are looking for, with the nurse-leader's help, although the "answers" do not always have the simple quality they expected.

Nurses need a rich background for this kind of work. They draw on all of their experiences in maternity and public health, the knowledge that they received in their nursing training, both academic and clinical, plus added sensitivity to the emotional needs of their patients and their patients' families. This emotional component is being increasingly stressed in professional literature and seminars, and is rapidly becoming part of general nursing background. In addition, they turn to group leadership training, in Masters' and post-Masters' courses (with supervised practice leadership) now increasingly available in schools of nursing, and in in-service seminars in some agencies. They familiarize themselves with the current obstetrical practices which the patients of their groups will encounter in their communities. They also find they need to be alert to the newer concepts of infant and child care, since expectant mothers and fathers often raise questions about the "training" of their babies as they grow, such as how to "discipline" them and how not to "spoil" them. The young parents' advance thinking along these lines is a further indication of their wish to succeed as parents and their hope that their children will grow up happily, able to meet what life offers them. Nurse-leaders who have led discussions of this kind have come away feeling that they have played an important role in helping the group think realistically about these general matters, even though they were doing so in advance. Although the discussions could not lead to any specific rules for the parents to follow, they were productive. Parents were given a chance to think ahead about how they might react under certain circumstances, such as if the baby should cry a great deal; and they developed some guidelines as to possible meanings of special kinds of behavior and different ways they might cope with them.

Nurse-leaders of expectant parent discussion groups find that they have to get accustomed to the fact that the order of content discussed by the parents is unpredictable. This is in marked contrast to maternity classes that proceed in a set curriculum in which the sessions usually follow a time-logical sequence from conception through the stages of pregnancy to labor and delivery and the care of the baby. In parent group education the discussion may start almost anywhere, depending upon issues which seem important to the members at the time. Their choice of issues is usually influenced by their stage in the pregnancy. Yet even the characteristic concerns to be expected in their first or third trimesters, for example, are not always forthcoming. Expectant mothers are, of course, quite preoccupied with themselves during the first months, sometimes to such an extent that they feel uncomfortable about their self-absorption. It may be their discomfort that makes them hesitant to talk about this at first—until someone breaks through the wall of personal reserve and they discover that others are preoccupied with themselves, too. Until they get to this point, it often seems safer to talk about baby care, although they may do so without great interest. Besides, many of them think that is what they are supposed to be coming for—and talking about a far-away baby somehow also postpones facing the reality of the whole experience. But they do begin to talk about themselves, too, as they have the need to do, either in terms of their physical problems, their psychological reactions, or the free-floating anxiety so common in pregnancy, anxiety that takes many forms and can attach itself to almost any aspect of the pregnancy and birth. Then the discussions usually lose their pallid quality and take on a new sincerity and vitality. On the other hand, these concerns may come out directly in the early sessions. Leaders deal with them in whatever sequence they come up.

For those who are accustomed to conducting so-called "structured classes," it is not easy to see how an understanding of the physical course of pregnancy and childbirth can be developed out of the specific interests of the members. Leaders find, however, that this whole area can be approached from any point. The parents-to-be may start with questions about hearing the baby's heartbeat in the sixth month of pregnancy, and through this get into a discussion that can give an adequate overall picture of the process of growth of the embryo up to this point and may even be followed up to the time of birth itself. Or a part of the story may come out at one session and other parts at others, building up gradually the continuum of understanding that is needed. Nurse-leaders have to remind themselves that expectant parents do not need to go into every detail of every stage or know every technical term. It is their familiarity with the course of the experience that is important, along with some knowledge of what they can and need to do at critical points to make it proceed more comfortably. The total picture develops by piecing together different parts of the discussion, not only of the physical processes but of the personal, emotional, and social overtones that accompany them.

Doctors are sometimes uneasy about the course the discussions may take if they are not specifically preplanned. How can they be sure the discussions will cover the items they would like taken up and which they have approved? Will they produce unnecessary anxiety? Will they go into specific medical problems not pertinent for laymen? A maternity nurse in a large city hospital was asked these questions by the chief of the obstetrical service. She assured him the group would take up the points he had authorized; she said, however, that they would probably not discuss them in any specified order, nor would they go into them all to the same degree. The doctor had great respect for her professional competence and her conviction convinced *him*. He did not question her again about the subject matter of her "teaching."

The content of the discussion in expectant parent groups is often permeated by reports of misconceptions of all kinds, sometimes partial truths, sometimes superstitions, which are passed on to expectant parents as advice or warnings, always with the best intentions. These ideas are often loosely lumped together as "old wives tales," ideas that in themselves seem to have been based on primitive concepts that have no scientific basis. Leaders are prepared for a wide range of such ideas, which seem foolish enough on the surface but which often center around a core-concept or interest, a fear or wish, that is fairly universal.

Sometimes these ideas have to do with the mother's fear of possible injury to herself. Women on some Indian reservations, for example, wear string-cloths around their waists until after delivery, even though by that time the articles are anything but clean. A perceptive nurse in an Indian county hospital discovered that for the mothers this practice ensured, in a magical way, that their babies would not seriously harm them by their kicking.

Other tales, perhaps not so extreme but nevertheless widespread, have to do with possible harm that may come to the baby. Many mothers are afraid that if they raise their arms, they will cause the cord to become wrapped around the baby's neck *in utero*. A young woman in one group said her mother-in-law had warned that the same thing would happen if she wore beads around her neck. There are many echoes even today of ideas that the baby may be "marked" by experiences of the mother during pregnancy: strawberry marks on the skin if she eats too many berries or red streaks if she sees a fire. And one still hears vestiges of what we usually think of as the Victorian attitude of "prenatal influence," that one can establish a child's positive qualities in some way while the embryo is growing—make him musical by exposing him *in utero* to fine music or make him good and gentle, if the mother thinks only good thoughts during her pregnancy!

One cannot say today that nothing that happens after the baby is conceived changes the course of his growth. Experiences with the drug thalidomide, for example, made it only too clear that certain chemical elements *can* affect the embryo's cellular growth, in this case by stunting the development of his arms and legs. The wide publicity given to cases in which this occurred has intensified the common fear of birth anomalies that expectant mothers bring out time and time again. It also has tended to reinforce their vague, general idea of prenatal influence, which some parents believe or half-believe, without differentiation. So leaders often find it necessary to help the group distinguish between the physical changes in the growing embryo that may be produced by the introduction of some new chemical factor such as a drug, or by a specific illness of the mother, such as German measles in the early weeks of pregnancy, and possible changes in the baby's psychic endowment, which are not thought to be influenced at will.

The tales and superstitions parents bring up are fascinating and challenging to unravel in the group. Although leaders are tempted at times to make light of them and to brush them aside as nonsense, nevertheless, they know it is necessary to listen to them thoughtfully. For these concepts indicate areas in which parents are confused, at the very least, and usually anxious as well. Because of the general approach of parent group education, it is possible in this type of group to pick up these cues and to help the parents look at the issues they raise realistically and examine their true meaning.

One would expect to find more of these myths in families with lower educational background. To some degree this is true. But the echoes of these tales come unpredictably from mothers of all socioeconomic and educational levels and reflect the same basic anxieties. In expectant parent groups, as in parent groups, however, one finds increasing evidence of disturbed behavior—if not in personality makeup—in low-income families living under continuing stress. Where expectant parent groups are part of the programs of comprehensive maternal and infant care such as those sponsored by the Children's Bureau, for example, the leaders anticipate that the members will be more problem-ridden, since these projects by definition have been established for families "at high risk."

In these and other groups in similar settings, the mothers-to-be reveal severe crises in which they have found themselves and the means they have used to try to cope with them. They report efforts at abortion, even an occasional suicide attempt, and there is a high degree of illegitimacy. Although the mothers sometimes bring these situations into the group discussion, it is apparent that they are signs of severe difficulties which group education cannnot be expected to resolve. Other resources must be made available to help these prospective parents as they need it: mental health nursing consultants, mental health clinics, psychiatrists, social workers, and the rest of the battery of treatment services, either within the agency or in other places to which they can be referred. The nurse-leader helps the parents-to-be continue to get what they can from the group, if this seems wise, but at the same time she draws on these other resources to pick up those aspects of the individual problems which are outside the scope of this type of group. Toward this end, she is quick to recognize indications of greater need, is familiar with other services in the community, and uses her skills to help the parents accept and make use of them.

GROUPS FOR UNMARRIED MOTHERS

The large number of unmarried mothers giving birth each year through-out the country includes a high percentage of teen-agers. This serious social problem is being approached in a variety of programs. Some provide maternity care, placement services (where requested) for the baby, and casework or treatment for the mother. Some give special academic instruction for mothers who have not been allowed to complete their schooling. Some approach the problem from the point of view of prevention, through better family life education, including sex education in schools and church settings. Basic to all these special projects, are, of course, the measures needed to improve social conditions for all families in our society, to ameliorate those unhealthy environmental, family, or personal situations which bring about crises of maladjustment of which illegitimate pregnancy is often one.

Obviously the problem cannot be explored here in its many implications.[1] What is relevant, however, is the role of group education in helping unmarried mothers go through pregnancy and childbirth as well as pos-

[1] See Leontyne R. Young, *Out of Wedlock,* McGraw-Hill Book Company, New York, 1954.

sible for themselves. In other words, what can group education be expected to accomplish for these mothers—and what can it not?

The fact that the mother is having her baby out of wedlock is a special circumstance that makes her pregnancy different, because it is out of step with the accepted social pattern of our society. And yet she is just another mother, having a baby. What implications does her special circumstance have for her participation in group education services?

Such pregnancies are often the result of disturbed family relations, but —regardless of their cause—they are inevitably accompanied by emotional upset. The first question to be raised, then, is whether young women in these situations can be expected to benefit from educationally oriented groups. Experience has shown the answer to be yes, if one defines what part of her need the group is designed to meet. Following the general criteria for group education, unmarried mothers can gain a great deal from sharing their reactions and concerns about the immediate situation with other mothers. Often unwed mothers have joined groups of married mothers, and their status has not been identified. They have entered into the discussion on many questions as the others have done, and have remained silent at other times. When a question concerning the husband's reactions is brought in, for example, they either make no comment, or on occasion, fake the situation, to be like the rest. One cannot but wonder how helpful the experience can be under such circumstances, since the unwed mother must of necessity block out—or at least keep to herself— problems that she alone is facing. On the other hand, if she chooses to be part of the group, one may assume that she has enough ego-strength to take from it what is helpful to her, in spite of constant reminders that her situation is different. Although she does not get help here in working out the practical and emotional problems created by this difference, she may get a great deal from sharing with the others her and their reactions to the universal aspects of pregnancy and childbirth. If she can take it, the group may to some extent reinforce the universal aspects of her feminine identity.

In practice, however, the number of unwed mothers who join expectant mothers groups with married women seems to be small, though there is no way of knowing how many register without being so identified. More usually, groups are set up expressly for unmarried mothers, in connection with special maternity services,[2] public health programs, adoption agencies, or residential homes where they live until they deliver. Here the situations are clear and accepted; the group operates within this frame-

---

[2] See Grace A. Day, "A Program for Teenage Unwed Mothers," *American Journal of Public Health*, **55**, No. 7 (July 1965); Philip M. Sarrel, "The University Hospital and the Teenage Unwed Mother," *American Journal of Public Health*, **57**, No. 8: 1308–1313 (August 1967).

work. The question is: How should these groups be similar to those for married mothers and how should they be different?

Probably there should be—as indeed there are—different kinds of groups for specific purposes. The more direct question must be: What should be the content of parent group education for unmarried mothers, and how does it work out in practice? These issues were explored in one session of a three-day nursing conference for nurses on "Developing Preventive Group Educational Services in Federally Aided Maternal and Infant Care Programs" given in September, 1964, by the Child Study Association of America under the sponsorship of the Children's Bureau, Department of Health, Education, and Welfare and the New York State Health Department.[3] At the meeting it was felt that group educational experiences for unwed mothers can meet many of their immediate questions and concerns. It can and should provide, first of all, the opportunity for them to learn about the physical aspects of pregnancy, labor, and delivery. Many of the young women in these groups, as in other groups, have been found to need this information badly. It is difficult to prove that an unwanted pregnancy resulted from ignorance of the facts of reproduction, since there are so many reasons (sometimes unconscious) why women get themselves into this situation, even with the best knowledge about conception and contraception. But certainly in many cases ignorance is a contributing factor and sometimes the determining one. We must therefore expect unmarried mothers in groups to reach out for this information. And in many groups they do, particularly in groups of unmarried young teen-agers. It is not uncommon to find fourteen- and fifteen-year-old girls in groups offered by public health agencies for out-of-wedlock pregnant young women. This trend has been increasing. Some of these girls may have seen films on menstruation or reproduction in their family life education classes in school, but they seem not to have applied their information to themselves.

They want to know such things as where the baby comes out and all about labor and delivery. They have many of the same fears as older girls have—fear of pain and what will be done to them. But their fears seem exaggerated by their ignorance and youth. Some confuse the normal "discharge" of pregnancy with signs of venereal disease about which they have been taught in graphic terms. Others are concerned about their own sex practices and are afraid in some instances that they may have harmed the baby by masturbating. Besides needing direct information on matters such as these, they also need to unburden themselves about some of their feelings, and this they often do, too, once they get started. Some are

[3] Aline B. Auerbach and Mildred Rabinow, "Parent Education Groups for Unmarried Mothers," *Nursing Outlook,* **14,** No. 3: 38–40 (March 1966).

deeply resentful because their mothers had made so many demands on them during their childhood and early adolescence. These girls sometimes say quite openly that they are having a baby to get back at their mothers and now give *them* extra work to do, since they expect their mothers to take care of their infants. Often their feelings of resentment are increased by their mothers' punitive attitude toward them now, because they are in this fix. This attitude on the part of parents and other family members only serves to exaggerate the poor self-image which often played a part in their having been unable to resist sexual advances in the first place.

In contrast to these groups of young teen-agers, other groups of unmarried mothers, usually somewhat older, seem to concentrate less on pregnancy and the coming delivery and more on the way the physical experience of having a baby will affect their ability to have a normal future life. In other words, they are deeply concerned about such matters as whether, because of striae or episiotomy scars or other physical manifestations, their having a baby will leave its mark on their bodies forever. Unwed mothers can also be helped to understand what they will be facing not only in labor and delivery but later in providing for the baby. Obviously, the information given them is influenced by the rules and procedures of the hospital or home in which they are to deliver their babies. If the hospital does not show the baby to the mother except on request, it is essential that she knows this so she can ask to see her baby if she wants to. Many unmarried mothers do want to, even when they are going to give the baby for adoption. They have a real need to know the facts about the baby and to have the final answer to any doubts they may have had about their ability to have a normal child. Although they may not come to a decision in the group as to what plans to make for the baby—if they are free to make plans on their own—some of the implications of what they might want to do can be brought out and the discussion may point up the fact that they have certain choices of which they may not have been previously aware.

It was generally felt, in the conference session previously referred to, that the young women should also have a chance to examine their anxieties against the background of the anxieties most women experience during pregnancy. They can be helped to see something of the way in which their special situation may increase or distort these feelings. These matters can be explored without probing into a particular girl's past to uncover the roots of her individual problem. In general, the value of group education for these mothers seems to be the same as that of all groups, to help them bring out whatever they are ready to, in order to understand and live through the present more realistically and purposefully. It is the specific content that will necessarily be different.

Basically, taking part in such a group can and should be a corrective, educational experience through which the mothers come to see themselves in a new light. Each one is treated as a human being who happens to be in a difficult situation at present but still has a whole life to live. In the group they are seen as individuals, each with her own capacity to make decisions growing out of greater awareness; they are treated as women who are entitled to know whatever they want to know and are regarded as persons capable of understanding and moving ahead independently. These goals can only be accomplished if the nurse-leaders feel with the individuals in the group and approach them nonjudgmentally. These attitudes are essential if unmarried mothers are to be helped through this crisis and made to feel that it need not be a devastating one, but that it can be an opportunity for growth and maturation.

On the other hand, it was felt that there are limitations to what one can accomplish in such groups. While everyone who works with these young women hopes that they may be helped so that they will not become involved in any more out-of-wedlock pregnancies, the question was raised as to whether it is feasible to make this a goal of the group educational experience. At best, one may hope that some added awareness of the reality factors they are facing may influence these young women so their behavior will become mature and less destructive. The extent to which this can be achieved will vary from individual to individual, group to group, and even nurse-leader to nurse-leader, and it will need much further study.

This conference highlighted the complexity of the problem and pointed up the need for many kinds of services from persons with different professional backgrounds. To supplement the necessary medical services, nurses and social workers seem to be the most strategic as helping persons, for the focus of their respective activities emphasizes the two chief elements of these mothers' needs: the medical-nursing aspects of pregnancy and childbirth and the social-emotional problems connected not only with childbirth and child-rearing but with their special situation.

The kind of expectant parent group on which we have concentrated here is usually led by nurse-leaders. They prepare for this type of work by becoming more familiar with the emotional needs of the mothers and by developing the group skills that are needed to help young women meet all phases of this experience, whether they are married or not. Nurses have been effective in work with unmarried mothers when they have defined the group's goal and have used their leadership flexibly toward its broad educational purposes.

In leading groups of unmarried young adolescents, for example, the youth and immaturity of these girls present problems that call for some modifications of leadership procedures. Along with others of their age group, these girls are likely to be impulsive, often unable to stick to a subject with any consistency. One wonders, however, whether their current situation may not increase these behavior manifestations. Often they are unable to conceptualize and find it hard to state their concerns. These qualities may be characteristic of the culturally disadvantaged groups from which many of them come, rather than of their stage of development, but they must be taken into account nevertheless. Because of these tendencies, these young group members seem to respond better—at least at first—to a more directed approach both in content and methodology. Instead of leaving the areas of discussion to be determined wholly by the group, the leader takes more initiative in opening up subjects to be explored, since the members may have no clear notion of the issues that need discussion. The leader is also more directive in keeping the discussion within a focus that has meaning for the group. With these adaptations the groups can be carried on in keeping with the purposes and general practices of group education. They help their members look realistically at their present and future and realize there are choices they can make: about continuing in school, caring for the baby or giving it for adoption, finding a permanent life partner, or other aspects of their future lives.

Social workers, too, sometimes lead such groups, bringing to bear their own special skills. Their need is to expand the scope of their knowledge to include a thorough familiarity with the physiological aspects of the experience and the characteristic emotional responses of pregnancy as well as to develop relevant group skills.

In some cases groups have been conducted by a nurse and a social worker, functioning as a team, with each serving, in a sense, as resource person in his area of competence. In the experience of the Child Study Association, however, unmarried expectant mothers, like married ones, seem to accept nurses more readily as group leaders since they feel they can get help from them in the areas of their educational needs. The social worker is usually the logical person to offer help on an individual basis, in resolving both the practical and the deeper emotional implications of the out-of-wedlock pregnancy with all it entails.

GROUPS FOR PARENTS WHOSE CHILDREN ARE PHYSICALLY OR MENTALLY HANDICAPPED

Parent group education is particularly suited to the needs of parents whose children have handicapping conditions or suffer from chronic illnesses. Here the chief aspects of what it can accomplish are particularly relevant: helping the parents gain factual knowledge and self-awareness and at the same time providing emotional support, which these parents desperately need. They want factual knowledge about the disability and its effect on the child as he grows, they want help in understanding their own problems in caring for their boys and girls under these conditions, and they want emotional sympathy and support to carry on their demanding daily responsibilities. These factors, in combination, seem to enable parents to help their children grow up more satisfactorily despite the disability, with greater self-fulfillment and with less strain for themselves, their parents, and other members of the family.

More and more families have children growing up with chronic illnesses, birth anomalies, or disabilities of one sort or another. Largely because of improved methods of medical care, many such children, who formerly were lost, survive today, but they survive with many kinds of physical and mental impairment. Medical services for these children have increased dramatically with the development of specialized skills of diagnosis, treatment, and rehabilitation. Understandably, attention has been directed primarily to the children themselves and to ways of helping them develop physically, intellectually, and emotionally. The parents, on whom rests the burden of care, day by day, around the clock, have been expected always to be there to carry out medical orders, to play an important part in their children's education, and to make some provisions for their social and recreational activities, where possible. Despite their fatigue and their own complex feelings, these parents are supposed always to be steady and patient, sympathetic and supportive, resourceful in meeting the daily needs of the child under all circumstances. They must be physically as well as emotionally strong. And in a most moving way, somehow most of them manage to be all these things. But often they are managing this on their own, with very little help. They say time and again that doctors, nurses, social workers, physiotherapists, and the rest, all mean very well but they have so little time to listen to them and to tell them the things they so very much want to know.

Because parents play such a basic role in the development of their children during illness as well as in good health, a conference was held in Boston, Massachusetts in October, 1959, sponsored by the Children's Hospital Medical Center and the Child Study Association of America with the support of the Sara T. Winthrop Memorial Fund. The conference devoted two days to discussion of many aspects of the subject "Helping Parents of Handicapped Children—Group Approaches." Realizing the urgency of the parents' problems, this author made a strong plea at the 1960 White House Conference on Children and Youth to bring the parents "out of the shadows" and give them the variety of services they need for themselves.

Parents of children with disabilities have not waited for services to be handed out to them, however. In recent years there has been a growing number of parents' organizations centering about specific disabilities— mental retardation, cerebral palsy, crippling conditions, epilepsy, muscular dystrophy, brain injury, cystic fibrosis, familial dysautonomia, hemophilia, and the rest. These organizations are primarily action groups that concentrate on fund-raising for medical, educational, and recreational services and for research, case finding, and public information about the disability.[4] They have had an important impact on the public at large, spreading information about the nature and toll of these conditions and, as a result, dispelling much of the secrecy that surrounded them in the past. Attitudes toward the afflicted children seem to have changed too. Children have been brought out of the backrooms where they were so often hidden and are accepted somewhat better in the community. Above all, they are being looked at less as freaks or objects of distaste and horror and more as children who are unfortunately handicapped but who are children, nevertheless.

Although these action organizations have had great influence and have accomplished many important tasks, they usually have not been geared to meeting the immediate needs of parents. And so parents have often found missing what they need most: a better understanding of the living reality of the illness, its effect on the child, and its personal meaning for each parent himself. Working with other parents to help all children who have the disability their children have has been valuable in directing these parents' energies into constructive channels; and being with others in the same situation has brought some measure of relief, some easing of their personal pain. But they have wanted more. Some parents, deeply disturbed by the impact of their children's illness or disability, have needed and sought out individual casework or treatment services themselves. Others are turning to group educational services where they are offered, and making good use of them.

Many of the group programs offered by parents' organizations and health and rehabilitation agencies take the form of large meetings, usually devoted to explaining the disability itself and/or the services available for the child. These are important, for parents want, first of all, up-to-date and accurate scientific information, in language they can understand, regarding their children's illness, its effect on the usual chart of normal child development, its emotional aspects, and the way in which it may affect the child's personality and behavior. Some of this they can gain through lectures given by medical authorities, usually at large meetings.

Some agencies also offer small parent discussion groups, such as those

[4] See A. H. Katz, *Parents of the Handicapped*, Thomas, Springfield, Illinois, 1961.

described in this book, when there are persons available who are equipped to lead them. The Child Study Association conducted a number of demonstration groups and gave consultation to several others which were set up to serve parents of chronically ill or handicapped children. It also gave several programs of training for parent group leadership to medical and psychiatric social workers who are working in this special field. (See Chapter XIV.) The material that follows has been drawn from the experiences in these projects. The groups were for parents of children with the following disabilities, respectively: blindness, mental retardation, cerebral palsy, brain injury, muscular dystrophy, orthopedic handicaps, Cooley's anemia, epilepsy, and familial dysautonomia. The parents in some of these groups had children who were multiply handicapped.

The discussion in such groups is quite diverse, depending on the nature of the handicap or illness, its causes and prognosis, and the special meaning it has for the parents. Parents react to a particular disability in individual ways, according to their earlier experiences and perhaps previous accidental exposure to the condition, their feeling about disabilities in general, and their ability to meet and cope with unusual life situations of many kinds. Beneath the differences, however, there are common threads that characterize them all. If one could change the specific content of the discussion, the underlying tenor and tone of one group would appear much like that of the others, for the parents' basic concerns about their handicapped children are very much the same. These do not come out in any regular order or at an even level of meaning. In the course of the group sessions, they reveal the many facets of the parents' needs and discover how, through the group interplay, these needs can be met.

What do they talk about, then, in discussion groups? Since the sessions are not preplanned, the discussion may start at any point. Often the early meetings of these groups center around practical problems of routine care, problems that are compounded by the child's disability. Parents of young children who are mentally retarded or cerebral palsied, or both, bring up their constant struggle to help these children in the developmental tasks they must accomplish: feeding, toileting, dressing and undressing, climbing stairs. Parents of teen-agers who are orthopedically handicapped talk about the constant chore of seeing that their children get where they are supposed to go: to school, the clinic, the recreation center, or just out.

Everyday problems continue in many forms as the meetings progress and the parents get many ingenious ideas and much practical help from the experiences of others. One parent, for example, has tried a new way of bathing a severely crippled child or has found a different approach to getting a cerebral palsied child to feed himself. Following the lead given by other parents, another may decide to give up his idea of an orderly living room and push the furniture around, out of the way, so that his blind child can have more room in which to play. Inevitably, members of the group compare their children with those of the other parents, sometimes to their satisfaction and at other times not, but always in the attempt to set up some kind of timetable of reasonable expectations for their child's growth and development. Unfortunately, for many handicapped children there are no set guidelines. Each child has his own timetable, in relation not to his age but rather to his capacities, as far as it is possible for him to develop them within the limitations of his disability.

At every point, parents reach out for all kinds of information which will help them with their children. The basic information they need, of course, is knowledge about the illness or disability itself. They need to understand the nature of the disability, its causes (as far as they are known), its cure (if there is any), and the prognosis, clearly stated and honestly faced. Beyond this they need to understand the impact of the disability on their individual children, on themselves, and on their other children if there are any. And so they raise questions such as: How much can my child really do? What is the true extent of his disability? What does this mean for his ability to take care of himself as he grows older? What does this mean for me? How much should I do for him and how can I learn to help him do things for himself? What does the future really hold? And will I ever be freed of this endless demand? And often, at any time, to what extent was I —or my husband (or wife)—responsible for the illness or disability? (In most cases, of course, the causes of the difficulty were outside of their control.)

The feelings that accompany these questions are implied in the very words the parents use, and sometimes are more openly expressed. They have been described quite extensively in recent literature.[5] All who have listened to these parents are shaken by the extent of their feelings of loneliness and isolation. Some of this of course comes from the fact that they are so burdened with the immediate care of a disabled or handicapped child, and find themselves so absorbed in their home chores, that they find it difficult to go out to be with other parents or friends. Their feeling of isolation is compounded by the fact that they are constantly aware of the difference between their children and those who are healthy and normal, and are understandably embarrassed when their child becomes an object of pity or is ridiculed by other children. Sometimes parents will say that rather than face this embarrassment and difficulty, they

[5] Of particular help are the following: Eugene P. McDonald, *Understanding Those Feelings*, Stanwix House, Pittsburgh, 1962; Allan O. Ross, *The Exceptional Child in the Family*, Gruen & Stratton, New York, 1964; Benjamin Spock and Marion O. Lerigo, *Caring for Your Disabled Child*, Macmillan, New York, 1965.

prefer to stay at home. They also say that they feel pulled down by having a child who is not normal, whether his condition was present from birth or came later. It is as if in some queer way having such a child decreased their own worth as people. (Fortunately, this kind of feeling can often be eased if it is aired and examined realistically, provided it does not feed into a more basic personality difficulty.) They express their fears for their children's future, physically, socially, and vocationally, and they talk about their own fear that they will never be free to consider themselves. The anxiety for the future is all-pervasive and colors much of their thinking, whether or not they are conscious of it.

In groups there is a great need for them to pour out feelings they have so little chance to express in their daily lives. And the feelings pour out, when they come, with great intensity. This is true not only of parents who have recently faced the problem of having a handicapped child, but also for parents who have lived with the problem for many years. Perhaps these parents have never let themselves fully face the shock of knowing their child was handicapped and so have not thoroughly lived through the crisis that comes with this knowledge. It is as if they had not allowed themselves the mourning that comes with any loss, and they did not realize the extent to which an expectation was shattered by the unforeseen and unfortunate condition that, out of the blue, hit their particular family. No wonder, then, that in their confusion they often turned their energies into all kinds of activity, shopping from one doctor to another, trying all kinds of remedies, realistic or not, avoiding the issue in their conversation with their friends— in other words, using the many mechanisms of defense which we know people resort to when they are faced with difficult and even impossible situations. These parents, living from one crisis to another, seem rarely to have time to sit down and take stock of the situation and their feelings about it. Perhaps, too, they have never had the chance to express what they feel.

There are periods, however, when the impact of their children's condition seems to hit harder than at other times, and it is at these critical points that parent discussion groups can be extremely helpful. Parents rarely come together when they are first faced with the situation, usually mustering their resources as best they can alone, coming to groups only later on. One would hope that services might be set up to which parents could come when they are first given the diagnosis of mental retardation, let us say, or cerebral palsy, or whatever. It would be important to find out whether they might not make a better adjustment to the whole situation and develop more quickly their capacity to handle it effectively, if they were to face their problem together with others early, close to the time they first knew about it.

Certainly, by the time handicapped children become ready for social activities, either in the preschool or school years, the parents are particularly aware of their need for additional help, both to understand the situation and to handle it. When the young people reach adolescence, the problems are compounded by the impact of their social and sexual development and the inevitable comparisons with the healthy children in their world. Experience has shown that at any of these critical points, parent group education seems to provide supportive and educational help. It is hoped that the field will develop such programs on a differential basis and that they will be studied carefully.

How do groups for parents of handicapped children differ from those for parents of normal children? The experience of the Child Study Association seems to indicate that while there is a basic similarity in the nature of experiences for all parents, there is a marked difference in the intensity of the feelings expressed by the parents of children who are disabled and in the urgency and degree of the parents' needs. Although the range of anxiety that parents voice about their children's future is actually not very different from what is expressed in groups of parents of normal children, there is a difference in the reality behind the words, in the factors connected with the disability with which parents struggle day by day. The burdens these parents carry are infinitely greater and the reality is much more threatening, both now and for the future. The practical choices that are open to these parents in such matters as schooling, family mobility, and social activities for the children and for themselves are far more limited. The satisfactions of parenthood for them are less obvious, though they can and do find satisfaction if they move a little past their difficulties and are able to recognize what they are accomplishing. It is as if for them the concerns of other parents are present, but in a greatly magnified form, with less room for adaptability.

For the progress of the groups themselves, we have already commented on the ease with which these parents identify with one another. This often brings with it a feeling of group cohesiveness on which leaders have commented time and again. There seems also to be a second development which is more marked than in the usual parent group, in which a parent moves away from his sense of identification with the other parents as if he needed to maintain his separateness again, in order to deal with his problem. Parents show this in a variety of ways. They compare the extent of their children's illnesses with those of the other children represented in the group, sometimes almost with a feeling of rivalry, at other times with a suggestion of superiority.

"My child is not nearly as retarded as yours," a mother may bring out in her tone if not in these exact words. Or, in regard to a cerebral palsied child, a mother may say, "My child gets around very well with his braces," comparing him with a child who can move around only in a wheel chair. Whatever the realities in these situations, it is as if the parents had to use shades of difference to make themselves feel better, to see that their children were not as unfortunate as others. During the course of a number of sessions, however, this attitude usually breaks down and the parents are more concerned with drawing closer to the others again and examining more honestly the variations of their children's handicapping, approaching this with sympathy and trying to learn from it what can be of value to all the parents.

Some leaders have felt that although the group discussions started easily because of the group cohesiveness, and moved ahead quickly into the area of feelings, the discussions were slower to come to any depth. One can only speculate as to the reasons for this, if it is generally true. Perhaps the depths are too painful, perhaps they need to be approached more slowly until the parents gain strength by sharing their difficult experiences with other members in the group.

It is the impression of many leaders that these parents are so preoccupied with the disability and the problems it brings that they find it difficult to talk or think about the child. And yet, as groups proceed from session to session, many report that it is here they see spectacular changes taking place. From talking about the child only as if he were a disabled child, and then talking about all children who have the same disability, parents do come, in time, to see their child as distinct from other children who have the same disability. At the same time, they begin to see him as a child who is basically like all other children, having the same needs and the same potential responses. It is then that leaders feel the group has accomplished one of its most important goals.

Throughout many of these sessions, parents talk about the effect of a disabled child on the other members of the family. Usually they bring this up in connection with their own discomfort about having to neglect the other children because the handicapped one takes so much of their time and energy. Their realization that other members are equally important in the family is not enough, however, to help them develop specific courses of action. But raising the issue does, at least, take away some of the guilt they feel on both counts, either because they give too much attention to the handicapped child or if they withdraw a little from his care to meet the needs of the rest of the family. This issue comes up most vividly in connection with the possible need to institutionalize the child, a matter which parents approach with deep feelings of agonized conflict. The exchange of ideas about this against the background of the realities of many lives in many families sometimes helps parents to make a decision about whether to institutionalize—or not—with a little more ease.

In general, there is no question that leadership of groups of parents who are in this situation places an unusually heavy demand on the leaders. They must have strength within themselves to withstand the emotional impact of the various difficulties and disturbances in all of these homes. They must be able to see that while the situations carry with them constant, heavy burdens, at the same time, they seem to bring out in many parents resources they did not know they had. They must also be able to apply to these parent groups the balances that are necessary in any group but that here seem to take on even more weight. Primarily in relation to the mood of the discussions, the balance is extremely important. Undoubtedly the tone of these groups, compared with those of parents of normal children, is more depressed, more problem-ridden, more full of self-blame and, at times, self-pity. And yet, without seeming to be cold or hard-hearted, one can very well introduce the point of view expressed by Beatrice A. Wright in her pioneering book, *Physical Disability—A Psychological Approach.*[6] She questions the extreme emphasis placed in this country on deviations of one kind or another, whether they are physical or mental. She points out that people have many deviations from the normal and that perhaps in the conditions we have been talking about, we see here only a matter of degree. Her point seems to be that all people are handicapped in some way or another, limited by some circumstances or conditions so that they may not easily fulfill their true potential. The implication of her book is that if parents can possibly see their children's physical or mental deviation in a broader perspective, they themselves will not feel so devastated by them and will be more able to help their children develop to the best of their abilities.

Some measure of swing in this direction is often accomplished in parent group education when parents are able to shed, at least for a few moments at a time, their preoccupation with one problem-ridden child, so that they can see him growing and developing as other children do, even though he may be doing so on a slower timetable and toward a more reduced goal. As one of the parents so poignantly said in a group, "I see now that he isn't doing so badly—in his way."

GROUPS FOR PARENTS OF CHILDREN WITH EMOTIONAL PROBLEMS

Group programs have been offered in different settings for parents of children with emotional problems, but they have not been uniformly reported, nor have their goals always been well clarified.

Many agencies have been reluctant to set up educational group programs since they are not sure that these will meet the parents' basic needs.

[6] Harper and Brothers, New York, 1960.

Because of the long-held opinion expressed in the slogan "Behind every problem child is a problem parent," there has been a strong feeling that parents of children with emotional problems are themselves apt to be emotionally disturbed and are therefore in need of treatment rather than educational services. But today there is a wider understanding of the many factors, both constitutional and environmental, that may cause emotional disturbances in children. This knowledge has brought about a shift of attitude toward parents of these children. They are no longer automatically stereotyped as being seriously troubled themselves and are approached much less dogmatically and consequently with less prejudgment and condemnation. There is also a growing appreciation of the effect on parents of having an emotionally disturbed child and living with him day by day. The burden of meeting the constant demands of children of this kind together with feelings of guilt because they feel that they may have been responsible for the child's condition may well contribute to emotional difficulties in the parents. Thus their disturbance may be the result and not the cause of the child's difficulties.

This more individualized evaluation of the parents of such children naturally is bringing with it a change in the attitude about the services they require. These services, whether educational or therapeutic, are being set up in terms of what the parents need and can make use of, not on the basis of broad categories of possible personality make-up. Some of these parents may indeed require therapeutic services, but experience has shown that others may well make use of educational programs even though they themselves may have some emotional problems. We must remind ourselves that

"therapy directs itself to the deviant aspects of personality, the symptom of a character disturbance, with a view toward effecting change in the individual pathology. It approaches conflicts in order to free energies bound within them, making these energies available for further growth. Education is aimed at those faculties of the ego, undisturbed by conflict. It appeals to the ability to judge, to learn by experience, to gain understanding, to plan, to adapt to changing circumstances. . . . We need not stress the tremendous importance that educational experiences have assumed in the lives of people, despite their troubled souls." [7]

Sometimes group educational programs are being offered on a kind of individual trial basis in settings where there is no exact knowledge of the individual needs of the parents who come to the group, as in the program

[7] Peter B. Neubauer, "Basic Considerations in the Application of Therapy and Education to Parent Groups, *International Journal of Group Psychotherapy*, 3, No. 3: 316 (July 1953).

conducted by a public health nurse in a child guidance clinic for parents of children who are waiting for clinic appointments. Here the educational purposes of the program were clearly stated and the parents seemed to make definite progress toward the group's goals. They were able to get a better perspective of their children's behavior against the behavior of other children of the same age. They were also able to gain some general principles of child growth and development and guidance for themselves which applied not only to the children who were identified as having problems but to other members of the family as well. In his book *Child-Centered Group Guidance for Parents*,[8] Dr. Slavson also based his observations on educationally oriented groups offered to parents of children in a child guidance clinic. These parents also were not subjected to any diagnostic evaluation; whether they were considered appropriate for the programs was determined by the way in which they were able to make use of them.

In the Child Development Center in New York City, a center which studies and treats emotionally disturbed children from birth to age six as well as their parents, a differentiated program has been offered to parents over a period of some years. Here "individual treatment, therapy groups, and educational groups are available for parents and each has been employed successfully. No one group, however, attempts to combine education and therapy. A parent's problems are studied, and when we know them well enough, a treatment plan is recommended. Often we recommend that a parent obtain individual therapy and participate also in an educational group. Only with a clearly outlined treatment plan can we hope to make this combination effective. . . ." [9]

In this program, then, the educational experience is seen as an additional tool, one of a spectrum of services which can be used selectively for parents of children with emotional disturbances, according to their own needs.

GROUPS FOR ADOPTIVE PARENTS

The goals and procedures of parent group education are also applicable to work with adoptive parents. Here the content of the sessions understandably concentrates on the special, subtle problems and complexities of the adoption situation for the adults and for the children. But in programs that use the dynamics of the group for broadly educational purposes, the basic principles—and the generic questions raised—are still very much the

[8] S. R. Slavson, *Child-Centered Group Guidance of Parents*, International Universities Press, New York, 1958.
[9] Neubauer, *op. cit.* (fn 9, *supra*), p. 317.

same as in other groups. What is it that these parents need to understand about their specific situation as it affects their children and themselves? At what stages of the adoption process should group programs be made available? And what relationships do such programs have to other parent discussion groups?

For adoptive parents, the first two questions are closely related. They need to know different things at different times, and so in a number of settings discussion groups have been set up at points of special need. Some are offered at or soon after application for a child. These generally focus on acquainting the families with adoption procedures and with the philosophy of the particular agency. In some of these groups parents are encouraged to discuss their own emotional responses to the idea of adopting and their conscious reasons for doing so. Their feelings about their own inability to have children are usually discussed in the casework relationship, but they sometimes come out and are explored quite appropriately in a group. Here they are discussed in terms of the parents' response to the immediate reality, without opening up the individual-personal significance of their feelings. Thus the focus of preplacement discussions has been placed primarily on the facts and procedures of the adoption process, the prospective parents' emotional reactions to the process, and those aspects of the emotional needs and developmental predictability of the child that are relevant for the parents' choice of him and his final placement.

These concerns, with some variations of emphasis, seem to preoccupy parents up to and during the period of legal adoption. Some agencies therefore have offered discussion groups for parents during the supervisory period (before legal adoption is finalized) as a supplement to their casework contacts. These groups serve to give the parents anticipatory guidance, to prepare them for the fact that adoption itself will not be a totally positive experience. Inevitably there will be problems—for themselves and for the children—in facing the difference between their families and the usual biological families around them. Experience in these groups has confirmed that "parents in the group situation are freer to acknowledge their perplexities and fears" and that "parents are likely to continue their examination of their perplexities alone and with the caseworker in subsequent contacts."[10] Furthermore, unburdening their doubts of themselves and their capacity to deal with these real differences in the group, with other parents who have similar feelings, often brings a deep sense of relief and releases the parents to take a step forward in handling the complex process.

[10] See Sylvia E. Biskind, "Helping Adoptive Families Meet the Issues in Adoption," *Child Welfare*, **XLV**, No. 3: 145 ff (March 1966).

The need for counseling and support, individually or in groups, does not stop at this point. As stated by Dr. Viola Bernard as early as 1953, "Adoption is experienced progressively through a series of general stages such as . . . the moment of the child's actual entrance into the home." [11] Others too have pointed out how the different stages in the child's development in the family life cycle bring different problems which call for supportive help.[12] It is the parents' own recognition of crisis points in the progress of the adoption and integration of the child into the family that often brings them back to the adoptive agency or to other casework agencies, and has caused these organizations to provide groups for them, usually for a short number of sessions, at such critical points.

Parents often turn for help when they apply for a second adoptive child, when the children begin to ask questions about birth—as all children do —or when a child, sensing something unusual about his situation, pushes for knowledge about his natural birth. The idea that children must always be told the truth is not easy for parents to carry out. It is as if the need to explain the situation reactivates their half-buried distress about their inability to have a child of their own. In addition, they often are afraid that the child will be upset when he is "told," and they are understandably puzzled and unsure as to how they can explain the circumstances of the child's birth when it occurred out of wedlock. These questions have many overtones which each parent must work out in relation to his child's age and readiness for information and his own acceptance of the situation. If he has been able to achieve relative peace and calm, the chances are that the child, too, will accept whatever facts are necessary, just as he—and all children—learn to face stress situations that vary from family to family, but seem inevitable.

Workers in the adoption field are constantly questioning the most desirable way of handling this part of the adoption problem. What is the most favorable timing of this information, for example? They are particularly concerned with whether it is wise to expose a child to the knowledge that he is adopted when he is in the oedipal phase of his development. Is a child's ego sufficiently mature at this time, they ask, to cope with the idea that he was rejected by his original parents? Will the knowledge of this rejection increase his uncertainties about his place in the family? Will he be afraid he may be rejected a second time, especially if for any reason he feels that he may not be worthy? Would it be better to tell him

[11] Viola W. Bernard, "Application of Psychoanalytic Concepts to Adoption Agency Practice," in Heiman Marcel, Editor, *Psychoanalysis and Social Work,* International Universities Press, New York, 1953, p. 172.

[12] Allen O. Ross, *The Exceptional Child in the Family,* Chapter 8: The Adoptive Child in the Family, Grune and Stratton, New York, 1964, pp. 164–172.

when he is younger, before he can absorb the full impact of the story, or wait until he is a little older, when his inner turmoil will have settled down somewhat and he will have had more evidence that his new parents really love him and will protect and care for him?

Circumstances in any individual family may be such that children will get hints of their adoption at times that may not be the most favorable, and then parents have to meet the question as their best judgment suggests. In any case, it is a touchy and important issue which comes up frequently in the child's early preschool years, with a different impact in early adolescence, and often in the years in between. Adoptive parents need the chance to discuss this and other issues as they come up at different periods and they seem to profit by doing so in groups, when these programs are offered as part of a continuing contact with adoptive families.

Questions have also been raised as to whether groups for adoptive parents should concentrate on matters growing out of the adoption or whether they should also take up the usual matters of child development and child-rearing. Although one cannot arbitrarily draw a dividing line between the two, there seems to be a growing feeling that these groups may serve the adoptive parents more effectively if they are conducted for a limited number of sessions—perhaps three to five—to explore the important issues of the adoption experience and their emotional overtones both for the parents and for the children. It has been pointed out that joining with other parents in such an experience has a positive value, in that parents identify with one another as *adoptive parents,* facing their situation quite openly.[13]

After thinking through the implications of their special situations, these parents then often turn to regular parent groups for help with the general concerns of parenthood. Participation in these parent groups helps them break down their feeling of difference as they work together for the best development of all their children and discuss the common, universal problems of growing up. In these groups, adoptive parents move over to take their place as *parents,* deeply interested in the care and development of children.

It is not at all unusual to find adoptive parents registering and taking part in regular parent groups along with natural parents. Some never reveal their special situation; others, however, do so naturally and easily, just as they bring up any other situation which may be somewhat different from that of the other parents in the group. Adoption is so common today that this does not pose any real problem for the rest of the group members. Usually they are interested, recognize the shades of difference in the

[13] Rael Jean Isaac, *Adopting a Child Today,* Harper and Row, New York, 1965, p. 193.

emotional as well as the practical demands of having an adopted child, and accept the adoptive parent's concept of himself as a parent like themselves.

GROUPS FOR FOSTER PARENTS

Many child welfare agencies have set up group programs for foster parents, but we have not seen detailed records of these groups and cannot attempt to give a clear picture of their purposes and accomplishment. From reports in professional journals and conversations with workers in a number of agencies, however, we have gained a general impression that these programs are largely experimental and are varied in their goals and scope. Some seem to concentrate on concepts of child development and the problems the foster parents are apt to meet in the children who are placed in their care. Others provide basic orientation to the services of the agency and to community resources for the children's health care and educational needs. Still others, stimulated by increasing awareness of the hazards to children of repeated changes of foster home placement, are eager to help the foster parents achieve a most stable functioning. They are therefore directing their groups to helping the foster parents with their own problems, especially as these are likely to be accentuated by being a foster parent.

Faced with a widespread shortage of trained social workers, some foster placement agencies have spread the outreach of their trained professional personnel by assigning them to conduct groups in which foster parents discuss their problems with their foster children and their role as foster parents. Untrained workers, usually called case aides, are then freed to concentrate on other aspects of the agencies' services, such as supervision of the foster homes, arranging for practical matters of the children's health care, and the like.

It would seem that much more could be done for foster parents along the lines of group education as outlined in this book. Such groups would focus on the immediate reality of their jobs as foster parents and the problems they are having in living with the children in their care on a day-by-day, around-the-clock basis. In discussing these situations, the groups would inevitably expose and explore the children's needs at different stages and how best to deal with them. Such discussion would also challenge the foster parents to examine their own reactions to the children and their own feelings and behavior—as substitute parents or at least temporary caretakers—rather than as parents. From limited experiences along these lines, it seems clear that such discussions can be of great educational benefit and can help foster parents carry out their work more effectively for the children and more comfortably for themselves.

OTHER GROUPS

The possibilities for the use of group education for other aspects of family living are endless. The techniques can be used in any number of special situations which have many different kinds of emotional coloration, and they can be appropriately adapted as necessary. We cannot list all of the possible situations or subject areas or even those for which discussion groups have already been offered. No such list can possibly be complete since there is no clearing-house for this information and the number and variety are growing every year. (Undoubtedly, many of the readers of this book will know about groups that have not come to our attention.) In concluding this chapter, however, we would like to mention three fields which seem particularly significant and full of promise.

First, educationally oriented small discussion *groups for parents of premature infants*, which are usually offered under hospital auspices. Such groups seem to be especially helpful if the parents meet together soon after they go home from the hospital, while the babies are still under hospital care. This is a painfully difficult period in these parents' lives. Although they are now parents, they are not able to act like parents and, as a result, cannot feel like parents. Under these circumstances, a group can give them much needed emotional support and important anticipatory guidance in the special care of prematures. They can share some of their feelings of disappointment and frustration. They can become familiar with the characteristic ways in which prematures may be expected to develop. They can be somewhat prepared for possible variations in the development of these babies compared with the usual patterns of infant growth, while at the same time they can recognize that each baby will be unique. They can face some of their fears for the future of these babies and so anticipate to some extent the fact that these fears may persist but will ultimately be worked out as the babies hit their particular rhythm and tempo of growth. Where such groups have been offered, they have helped tide the parents over the difficult period of adjustment and have given them greater confidence in their ability to care for their babies.

Second, *groups of older people*. With the growth of interest in the problems of the elderly and the aged, attention is being directed to new ways of providing services, both individual and group, that will meet their different needs. An interesting example of group education for older persons was undertaken by the Manhattan Society for Mental Health, and the results have been presented as a practical guide for others who wish to initiate and carry on such programs.[14] This project applied many of the concepts of group education set forth in this book to the mental health needs of older persons. Weekly discussions were held with small groups who came to established centers. Based on the conviction that "by providing information as well as influencing attitudes, the Mental Health Education discussion group helps its members recognize and attempt to meet their own individual problems in their own individual ways," [15] these discussions dealt with things they themselves wanted to talk about: their concerns about the present and the future, tied in with some exploration of the past. Some of the subject matter was of a practical nature, such as how to improve their living conditions, the best arrangements to maintain health, or the problems of living on fixed, limited incomes. Other subjects were more general though colored by their individual experiences: relationships with grown children and with grandchildren, attitudes of society towards the aging, the pace and changes of present-day modes of living. Throughout, the leader maintained her "basic respect for the capacities of the members, their desire to conduct and manage their own affairs as fully as possible within their means and capacities. . . . This approach was clearly appreciated by the vast majority of those who participated, as was demonstrated by the variety and richness of their response." [16]

We share the hope of the authors of this monograph that their "experience will serve to enrich the information and understanding of others working with the aged, (and) encourage others to use the tools of mental health education in helping groups of older people to find themselves and each other, and through their own thinking and sharing to find new ways of fulfilling themselves for living creatively all the days of their lives." [17]

Finally, in discussion *groups for teen-agers,* some experimentation is going on in many places in which group educational approaches are adapted to the special needs of the group members. In Chapter XIV, brief reference is made to a program which prepares school health nurses to lead teen-age groups in family life education. (See page 222.) In the groups now being led by these nurses, the techniques of group education have been adapted to the characteristic behavior and needs of these young people. As in the groups of pregnant teen-agers already referred to, here

---

[14] Wilma H. Klein, Eda J. LeShan, and Sylvan S. Furman, *Promoting Mental Health of Older People Through Group Methods: A Practical Guide,* published for the Manhattan Society for Mental Health, Inc. by the Mental Health Materials Center, Inc., New York, 1966.

[15] *Ibid,* p. 26.

[16] *Ibid.,* p. 15.

[17] *Ibid.,* p. 155.

too the impulsiveness, volatile emotionality, and lack of concentration of the group members often make it difficult to develop lines of thought in a consistent way. Accordingly, the nurse-leaders have found that they have to be more in command, as it were, quicker to bring the group members' comments into line with the subject the group has chosen to discuss. They have found that doing so need not block or dampen the spontaneity of the group interplay and the sharing of the wealth of ideas and experiences. The key to success in this kind of leadership seems to lie in the leader's ability to listen carefully to what the young people are saying, to accept honestly and without criticism whatever they choose to bring out, no matter how confused or "far out" it may seem, and to help them better understand the issues under discussion and the meaning of these issues *for them.*

The discussions are provocative and rewarding for the young people and for the leaders too. They open up many aspects of the teen-agers' lives and thinking: their concerns about the physical changes they are going through and their new upsurges of strong feelings: aggressive, altruistic, as well as sexual; their struggle to find themselves as individuals and with their peers; their confusion about boy-girl relations, steady dating, early sex experiences with all these imply; their relations with their parents and siblings; their constant struggle for independence and recognition at home, in school, and in the community; and their hopes and fears for their future, educationally, economically, socially, and personally. These concerns are close to the surface for many of these boys and girls and in the discussion group they are given a chance to bring them out.

XIII

Other Uses of Group Educational Concepts for Parents and Those Who Work with Parents

OTHER TYPES OF MEETINGS FOR PARENTS

The concept of parent group education as a method of learning has developed primarily in relation to groups meeting for a continuous series of from eight to fifteen sessions, in which the content evolves in an on-going process from meeting to meeting. Some leaders make use of the same approach in shorter series, which usually consist of from four to six sessions, but the different structure changes the pace and the depth with which the group's thinking can be developed. Inevitably, there is a feeling of urgency in a shorter series. Both the leader and the group members sense that there is much to cover in a limited time. In order to move more quickly into the meat of the discussion, some leaders help the group set up a "topic" agenda for the series in the first meeting, based on what the members see as the important issues. As a result, the sessions tend to start off with a greater emphasis on intellectualized categories. These may be topics such as discipline, independence, sex education, or sibling relations, along with other special topics that relate to definite age groups—as diverse as toilet training, "spoiling," or play and play material for the pre-preschooler; school achievement and the development of good study habits or the influence of friends for the school-agers; rebelliousness versus independence and how much "control" a parent should exert for teen-agers. Similarly, in a brief series for expectant parents, the group may decide in the beginning to use the sessions systematically to discuss the physiological changes of pregnancy, weight gain, labor and delivery (including anesthesias), and the care of the new baby. Within a chosen subject area in any group, however, the material can be developed from the experience of the parents or expectant parents. They can share their ideas and feelings in somewhat the same way as in a longer series.

In the shorter number of meetings, the leader usually moves in more quickly to help the group explore different sides of a question. He usually also summarizes more quickly, relating the discussion to general principles of behavior and of growth and development. He knows the group will not be able to bring out the full range of the members' questions and concerns, nor will there be time to build up much understanding of particular difficult spots in family interaction. He tries, however, to introduce some of the "balances" in order that the group may learn that problems of behavior have many facets and need to be looked at from different angles. With this approach, an attitude can be developed about the complexities of human affairs and the many possible solutions to a situation. This is important and far-reaching in that it can be applied by the parent to any issue long after the group has ended.

A similar attitude can be established in other forms of meetings as well. Instead of building up the content of the discussion from the group, some programs present a series of talks, films, or brief plays or skits, followed by a period of discussion. These presentations give the group a common experience or situation to which they can react at the beginning of each session. From there they can go on to ideas and experiences in their own lives that are stirred up by what they have just seen or heard. It is best to have some of the parents involved in the planning of such series so that the areas presented will be closely related not only to universal family situations but also to the interests of the particular community. Because the presentations cut down the time available for the parents' reactions, the discussion part of the meeting often becomes extremely condensed and calls for great skill on the part of the leader in pulling the material together. However, here too an attitude or point of view can be developed, sometimes implied in the discussion, sometimes conceptualized and clearly stated.

Even in a brief period of time the group can begin to see: (1) that certain concerns people have about themselves and their families are universal, but that individuals differ considerably in their response to similar life problems; (2) that human development is marked by characteristic developmental stages in the family, each with its specific tasks; (3) that the response of individuals to these tasks takes different forms, depending on their personality make-up, their families, and the cultures in which they live; (4) that most problems of life adjustment are not met with easy answers since they are complex in nature, but need to be looked at in their complexity; (5) that reasonably healthy people, if they are not blocked in their learning by areas of emotional conflict, *can* acquire some insight and knowledge about themselves and their children through educational experiences in groups and are able to face and deal with situations more effectively.[1]

Some of this can also be accomplished in the single meetings which are held in many settings. Such meetings may be as much as an agency or organization thinks the community will respond to, or they may be trial balloons to test the reactions of parents to a new program. Because single meetings are usually open to all who want to come and are set up in the hope of attracting a large audience, they usually are in the form of lectures or film showings or dramatic presentations followed by discussion. In such meetings, an atmosphere can be created that opens up for parents new awareness of the meaning of their children's behavior and of their relations with them. Some parents experience this awareness for the first time in such sessions. Although providing no pat answers, a single meeting can provide information which is new to parents, information which may stimulate their thinking and challenge stereotyped points of view. If the session suggests a new interpretation of the trying behavior of a two-year-old, for example, or the remoteness of a ten-year-old busy with his own ideas, or the critical attitude of a teen-ager, the session can be an important eye-opener. Furthermore, even the limited contributions of members of the group give other parents a chance to identify with those who speak out, though they themselves may not open their mouths. To a limited degree, they begin to find themselves in relation to the ideas of others just as they do more fully in a series of discussion meetings.

Yet their interaction with others is on a random, hit-or-miss basis. Here there is no opportunity for them really to get to know one another, no wide sharing of experiences, no time for the group to develop their thinking slowly and soundly. If the group is large, the participation of individual members of the audience will naturally be limited to those who are most articulate, most aggressive, and sometimes the most troubled. The more reticent parents often do not get a chance. The leader and the group members have to accept the fact that there is only so much that can be explored in a single meeting or part of a meeting. They have to use it as well as they can. But it can have meaning for the parents if the discussion, even around general issues, is closely related to their lives.

In discussions following a film or a play, the parents' responses to the ideas that have been presented give them their real meaning in personal terms. It has been said that the players in a story are in a sense also members of the group. They serve as live people with whom the audience can identify or empathize and whom they can reject or not. If they serve only

---

[1] Adapted from Aline B. Auerbach, "Varieties of Purposes and Methods in Film Discussion Meetings," *Mental Hygiene*, **41**, No. 3 (July 1957).

as mouthpieces for intellectualized ideas that stimulate similarly intellectual responses, they may spark a pleasant intellectual excercise, but the opportunity for learning "in one's guts" as well as in one's head is lost. Leaders are therefore often careful to avoid general openings such as, "What do you think is the main point of this presentation?" and use instead a more personal approach such as, "What parts of this had special meaning for you?" This emphasis brings the discussion right where the leader wants it to go—to the personal reactions of each person in the room. This gambit is consonant with the purposes of parent group education, no matter what its form. It gets directly to the individual and opens a way for him to recognize and, it is hoped, begin to express the ideas and feelings that are rooted in his own experience. These are the raw materials with which he will work, refining them as he gains greater understanding of himself and the situation with which he deals, and they will give him an ever-widening basis of choices on which to act.

And so the leader adapts his discussion techniques realistically to what the setting offers—even within one short discussion period.

GROUP CONSULTATION IN IN-SERVICE SEMINARS FOR THOSE WHO WORK WITH CHILDREN AND FAMILIES

Many people who participated in the various training programs given by the Child Study Association have made use of their newly acquired group skills in their contacts with their own staffs. They did this spontaneously, feeling, as some of them have expressed it, that they could not handle a group conference in any other way, once they had seen the effectiveness of group discussion techniques. Nurses, for example, who had taken part in the programs, conducted in-service seminars sometimes as consultants, coming from outside agencies, sometimes with their own staffs, as supervisors, helping them to enlarge their general understanding as well as to develop greater competence in their own professional work.

The skills of group education have also been used by the Child Study Association staff in conducting seminar sessions with such groups as nursery school teachers and day-care personnel in ongoing seminars [2] and with other professional groups such as caseworkers and child care workers in welfare departments, public health personnel, and religious educators, meeting for a limited number of sessions. Child Study Association staff members came in as consultants whose contact with the agency staffs took the form of seminar-discussions for which they were the leaders. In this capacity they made use of group methods to enrich the participants'

[2] Greta Mayer, Alaine Krim, and Catherine Papell, "Contributions to Staff Development in Understanding the Needs of Children and Their Families," *Child Welfare* XLIV, No. 3:143–9 (March 1965).

understanding of content that had emotional as well as behavioral implications for the particular client population they were serving. The role of the consultants (and seminar leaders) was advisory and largely educational; they had no responsibility to implement any plans developed by the seminar participants in regard to their work problems, nor were they in a position of administrative authority over the seminar members, a relationship which may carry with it a feeling of constant evaluation and judgment of staff performance. Since Child Study Association staff were called in because of their knowledge of children in the family, and since the family aspect of children's growth and development had often been underplayed in the services of the agencies who requested this kind of consultation, emphasis in the seminars tended to be placed on the relation of children to their parents and parents to children, the part that parents play in the family picture, and the ways in which the agency staffs could better understand them and help them.

For day-care personnel, for example, the discussion centered around a better understanding of the children in the agencies' care and the significance of their behavior in the centers, constantly evaluated, however, against the background of their home and community settings; day-care staff were also helped to examine the nature of their contacts with the parents and to make better use of them. Thus the functioning of the agencies' personnel was part of the seminar discussions, but with certain limitations. They discussed their role in the situations they encountered in their work and drew general conclusions which had value for all the group, but at no point was the emphasis on the details of a staff member's specific performance. In other words, the group did not deliberately examine the personal psychodynamics of the workers' job performance. Nevertheless, the group leader here, as in all forms of group education, had to be alert to the characteristics of the workers' individual responses and their possible effect on clients and clients' families. He did not open up this aspect of the workers' relationship with the families of the children in their care, although often it was brought in spontaneously by the workers themselves. During the discussions, some workers learned about their special idiosyncrasies and problem areas and were able to apply this self-knowledge to their work, as was to be expected. But the group conferences were conducted with emphasis on the educational implications of the problems of the staff, implications that had meaning for all of the group and were not directed toward resolving the personality problems of the individuals who participated.[3]

[3] See Gerald Caplan, *Concepts of Mental Health in Consultation: Their Application in Public Health Social Work*, Children's Bureau, Department of Health, Education and Welfare, Washington, D.C., 1959, p. 149.

The purpose of this kind of consultation through the group conference, then, is to give staff workers additional background content and knowledge of specialized helping skills which they can incorporate in their practice. Whether it is conducted by someone from an outside agency who comes in as consultant, or by someone within the agency who is in an administrative or supervisory position, it adapts the principles used in parent group education to help staff members improve their on-the-job experiences. The use of group discussion methods in in-service seminars follows the time-honored social work principle of meeting staff members "where they are" in their work and their thinking. The discussion is developed from the worker's own immediate experience. The thinking of the group is directed to the psychodynamic understanding of the needs and behavior of their clients and various ways in which staff members can best serve them. These are some of the basic principles on which parent group education is based, and they serve well in these settings, too.

Yet in-service seminars of this kind are different in many ways from parent discussion groups. In the first place, the relation of the leader-consultant to the group members is that of one worker with other workers. Although the members may not always be fully professionally trained, they are expected to take part in a professional way, examining their job performance and not the way they function personally. Already encouraged to be aware of their "use of themselves" in their work, they tend to be more ready to examine their effectiveness in applying whatever new knowledge they are absorbing in the group. They are usually also able to conceptualize the general implications of the discussion and to apply them beyond the immediate situations on which the discussions are based. As workers, they are expected to meet their agencies' demands, to live up to rigid standards of performance, all of which seem to contribute to a special kind of involvement of themselves. They therefore tend to come to these seminars with a high expectation for themselves. This response is, of course, not universal. Some workers seem to feel that the sessions are being imposed on them, and they approach them with feelings that may range from disinterest and lethargy to active resistance. With skillful handling and with discussions that are closely related to the workers' immediate work problems, these reactions are usually overcome as the seminar members find their knowledge and competence increasing.

Similarly, parents move in these directions as a result of group discussion, becoming more knowledgeable about their children and themselves, more conscious of their responsibilities, and more aware of the results of what they say, feel, and do with their children. But they cannot be expected to maintain the level of self-scrutiny and awareness that is expected of workers in the helping professions. The previous educational experience of parents within the make-up of any single group is inevitably more varied and uneven. This makes for an uneven participation of the parent members, since they are not all ready to participate in the group experience to the same extent or in the same way. By comparison, agency workers usually—but not always—have a more uniform background of learning and experience on which to draw.

There is also an important difference in the nature of parents' involvement with the subject matter under discussion. Parents in groups are usually deeply caught up in the emotional interplay between their children and themselves and, as a result, often find it difficult to be objective. Professional workers, devoted and dedicated though they may be, are generally better able to approach their work on a different plane, their very aloofness giving them a basis for a more detached and constructively analytical method of working in the group seminars.

This brief summary cannot adequately cover the many variations professional people will meet in this kind of in-service consultation. The personality variables are unpredictable, of course, as they are in parent groups, and may contradict such general statements as those just given. Here, as in parent group education, the leader-consultants must always keep in mind the nature of their goal, some of the hazards of the relationship, and areas of content which they will want to have stressed and those they may wish to avoid. In doing so, they will consciously draw on group skills they have generally found to be effective.

XIV

Training for Parent Group Leadership

The philosophy of parent group education and its translation into a conceptualized methodology came about gradually in the work of the Child Study Association. Parent groups have been at the core of the Association's work since it was founded in 1888. In the early groups, thoughtful parents met to discuss current findings of philosophy and education in the hope that they could extract from them ideas they could put into practice in rearing their children. These pioneer group members were deeply involved in digging out concepts that were personally relevant. Gradually these groups became "child study groups" in which the "leader" appeared as a teacher or lecturer, imparting the best current ideas and findings for the group's consideration. (The Association also offered single meetings and series of meetings—identified as lectures—on psychoanalysis, psychology, and education.) In time, the emphasis shifted to allow parents again to become more active participants in the learning process rather than passive listeners. Lectures were shortened to allow planned periods for questions and answers. Recognizing the learning value of group interplay, "study groups" became "small discussion groups" and emphasis was placed less on the intellectual content of the discussions and more on the potential ability of parent-members to attain personal growth and greater competence through increased knowledge and self-awareness. In addition, increasing stress was laid on the need for parents to work out their individual interpretations of this knowledge and their individual ways of applying it in their respective home situations. At the same time, the Association continued to hold large meetings and conferences, as it still does today, in which new concepts, new interpretations of individual and family problems in the larger community and in the world are offered to parents and professional workers.

The shift in emphasis to the small parent group, however, was an important new development and began to be reported at professional meetings, as part of the evolution in parent education that emerged under the long, pioneering leadership of Sidonie Matsner Gruenberg as director of the Association. At her retirement in 1950, the new director, Mildred Beck, challenged the staff to conceptualize the change in group methodology and approach and to formulate its rationale. At the same time, requests came from workers in various professions for help—and, in fact, teaching —in the development of the skills of parent group education which they might then apply in their own agencies. Under this stimulus, plans were drawn up for a program of training in group leadership. Mrs. Beck played a key role in its initial formulation and design. She was assisted by the Association's staff and a technical advisory committee which continued to function for a period of fifteen years as the programs developed. This committee was made up of Dr. Marianne Kris and Dr. Peter B. Neubauer, psychoanalysts, both of whom were deeply interested in the possibilities of group educational methods for parent learning. In addition, the committee included Dr. Katherine M. Wolf, psychologist, of the Yale Child Study Center, and Dr. Philip Zlatchin, Professor of Education, New York University, both of whom made important contributions to the training programs until their untimely deaths.

The pattern established in the first training projects proved sufficiently sound and workable to form the basis for a subsequent series of intensive training programs that have continued to the present. They were developed and carried out with the continuing support and encouragement of the subsequent director, Gunnar Dybwad, J.D., and of A. D. Buchmueller, the present director, who has headed the Association since 1957. These training programs were made possible by grants from the Field Foundation, the Good-Neighbor Federation, the Grant Foundation, and the Hoffheimer Foundation, which all supported the work at various times and to which the Association is greatly indebted. Of later programs described in this chapter, some were given under the sponsorship of the Children's Bureau, United States Department of Health, Education and Welfare, together with various state Health Departments; others with support from the National Institute of Mental Health and the United States Office of Economic Opportunity.

From the beginning, these programs introduced basic concepts of mental health, stressing their theoretical and practical implications for parent education. As the programs developed, they made clear the place of parent education and especially of parent group education in the larger field of mental health education which is being directed increasingly toward the prevention of emotional difficulties and family disorganization by helping build the sound, positive mental health of children and families.[1] Placing

---

[1] A. D. Buchmueller, "The Place of Parent Education in Preventive Mental Health," unpublished paper presented at the VI International Congress for Mental Health, Paris, France, 1961. Child Study Association of America, New York.

parent education within the mental health movement in this way reflected the direction of the philosophy and work of the Association established through the shared thinking of the Board of Directors, staff, and administration.

FIRST PROGRAMS FOR SOCIAL WORKERS

The original training program, begun in 1951, was a truly experimental one. It was offered to social workers, since their background—either in case work or group work—seemed most suitable, and since they were the ones who seemed most interested in learning the skills of parent discussion leadership. Many of them were already being called on to meet with parent groups and were raising questions individually and through their agencies as to the kinds of programs that offered the greatest opportunity for parents to learn and grow. The initial program therefore was planned with the needs of social workers in mind. It was carried out in keeping with the strong conviction of the advisory committee that a new, experimental program such as this should move slowly and should be offered to one professional group at a time, so that it could be adapted to the special needs of that group. The committee felt strongly that one would need to know the particular assets and gaps of knowledge of various professional groups for this kind of work before considering a program on an interdisciplinary basis. Although members of the Association's training staff raised some question about this recommendation at first, it soon became apparent that this was a sound approach which would increase the effectiveness of the training programs. At the same time they saw that it would not only serve to clarify the broad range of background information and skills required of any leader for this kind of work but would also throw light on the way different professions could be expected to contribute to this form of educational endeavor.

Two intensive programs were offered in successive years to social workers from a variety of community agencies, fifteen in each program. They came from family agencies in several large cities and nearby suburban areas; child guidance clinics: the guidance clinic of the Board of Education of the City of New York, a special clinic in the public schools maintained by the Youth Board, a private interracial clinic serving children in and around Harlem, and a treatment center for preschool children with emotional problems; the nursery education unit of the same treatment center; a variety of community projects interested in the prevention of delinquency; group work agencies in neighborhood centers; several medical social service departments of large hospitals, one in a general pediatric service, another in the department dealing with premature babies; and agencies serving the needs of children with special handicaps. The families served by these agencies covered a wide range of social and cultural backgrounds and many levels of economic status, from families with low incomes living in depressed areas to those in white-collar and professional groups. All of the agencies were concerned with having their staff representatives develop group leadership skills to work with parents of children of different ages and different special situations.

The agencies invited to join the program were those working with families and interested in developing programs of parent group education as part of their general services. The agencies made their own selection of staff representatives to participate on the basis of their capacities and their suitability for this kind of work.

The programs were intensive and were set up to provide contact between trainers and trainees over a period of about a year. These first programs consisted of an initial sixteen-week period during which the trainees attended a weekly theoretical session and group seminar and observed weekly meetings of parent discussion groups conducted at the Association headquarters. This part of the training program was followed by a period of field work in which the trainees conducted parent groups under the auspices of their own agencies, observed and supervised by the Child Study Association's training staff. During this field work period, the trainees had individual, supervisory conferences with their Child Study consultants. They also participated in an ongoing biweekly group seminar in which they discussed their own experiences in working with their respective parent groups.

The program faculty included, in addition to the Child Study Association's staff, leading experts in the fields of psychiatry, psychology, education, anthropology, and other social sciences. They contributed primarily to the theoretical sessions that dealt with the content of parent group education: the complex processes of child growth and development within the family, parent-child relations, and the critical points in the child's development which call for special understanding and wise guidance. The child's growth in the family was always discussed within the framework of the larger community and the various pressures of cultural, social, and economic factors on the lives of individual families. In addition, theoretical sessions dealing with the techniques of parent group discussion were conducted largely by the Association's staff, sparked by presentations from Dr. Neubauer, a member of the advisory committee, who contributed his formulations of the place of parent group education in the total spectrum of supportive services for families. Group seminars were generally conducted by this author, who was director of the programs, and who provided a thread of continuity and helped the trainees integrate contributions of outside faculty members with concepts introduced by the training staff. Observation of parent groups was considered to be extremely important as demonstrations of the kind of program the trainees were expected to carry out in their own agencies.

It is the opinion of many trainees and of the Association's staff that probably the most important part of the training program was the work carried on by the trainees in conducting their practice groups. The type of supervision that was offered by the training staff was developed from concepts of supervision in the social work field. Its purpose was primarily to see that "through sensitive guidance and practical help geared to the known requirements of jobs and the needs of workers holding them," the workers' efforts became progressively more effective. The supervisory process was not focused toward the growth and development of the workers as persons as a primary goal, although personal growth and development undoubtedly "can, should and frequently do accompany a sense of increased ability, opportunity for creative use of self and satisfactions gained in the doing of the job, and it is not difficult to see how sensitive and skillful supervision can contribute to this desirable experience of personal growth." [2] The focus, however, was to help the trainee develop competence in his assigned task.

In the training programs, supervision was especially adapted to the rather unusual circumstance in which a member of an outside organization supervised one part of a worker's activities in his agency. It was made clear from the beginning both to the trainees and to their administrative officers that the Child Study training staff was interested only in the way in which the trainees conducted their parent groups. Since the Child Study supervisors were not part of the trainees' agency staffs, they were not involved in a wider evaluation of the workers' competence in other parts of their regular work assignments; this remained the domain of agency supervisors or administrators. This distinction was made clear at the outset and, somewhat to the surprise of the training staff, the possible conflict of supervisory roles rarely presented any problem. As the programs developed, however, it became necessary for the training staff personnel to play a double role: as supervisor of the trainees' work in leading their parent groups, on the one hand, and, on the other, as consultant to the trainees and more significantly to the trainees' agencies in matters connected with the project, such as methods of recruitment, timing, and interpretation to the community.

The support the training staff was able to give as these experienced workers moved into a new area of activity was vital to their developing

[2] Margaret Williamson, *Supervision: New Patterns and Processes*, Association Press, New York, 1961, p. 20.

additional skills and competence and, as a result, increasing their feelings of self-confidence. In leading their practice groups, the trainees began to appreciate the interrelation of subject matter and methodology, a concept that was at the core of these training programs. They saw for themselves that group skills alone can accomplish very little unless they are directed toward an identified area of knowledge, with all its factual implications and emotional overtones. They began to have proof from their own experience that with a relevant background of knowledge, leaders are prepared for the many major and minor issues parents may bring up. They are then able to choose which to pick up and help the group develop and which to let go by, judging their significance for parents and the extent to which they can be adequately and appropriately dealt with in this framework. And, finally, they are able to add, where necessary, and tie the discussion together so the parents can apply it to themselves and make use of it. They recognized, too, that however rich their own background of information and understanding of the subject areas to be discussed, this cannot be made available to and usable by parents without the necessary group techniques. Their field-work experience brought vividly home to all the trainees their need for thorough familiarity with both aspects of the program, *content* and *methodology*.

Some of the agencies that were eager to have their staff representatives participate in the program found that they had to devote much more time and thought than they had expected to problems of organization of groups and recruitment of group members. They found that it was not enough merely to want to have a program of this kind as one of their agencies' services; they had to develop some of the skills of community organization that have already been described in Chapter V. They also found that in most instances it took the combined efforts of their total staffs to interpret the program properly, to set it up under the proper auspices and give the leader the necessary moral as well as practical support. One leader cannot develop such a program alone. For an agency to take on an added program of this kind requires a true commitment on the part of the agency itself—its administration, staff, and Board of Directors. Without such a commitment, one cannot expect such a project to succeed.

TRAINING OF WORKERS FROM THE FIELD OF EDUCATION

In the fall of 1953, a training program was offered by the Association for workers in the field of education, including special teachers, guidance workers, and psychologists in the public schools, directors of nursery schools and day-care centers, workers in neighborhood centers, and directors of religious education in churches of different denominations. The general pattern of the training program was continued. The presentations of techniques of group discussion remained more or less the same, although greater emphasis was given to those aspects of group skills with which earlier trainees had shown they had some difficulty. The content on child development and family relations was shifted somewhat to meet the needs of this particular group, as compared with the previous groups of social workers. Whereas social workers had seemed to need more information about *normal* child development and family relations, the group of trainees from the educational field seemed to need further knowledge of what was *unusual* and pathological in growth and development within the family. They also needed to know much more about children as they appear to their parents at home on a 24-hour basis.

Already, then, the original three years of training programs pointed up the validity of the initial premise that workers from different professional backgrounds required different kinds of knowledge to supplement their previous professional training and experience; each of them needed to add different areas of content to what they already had, in order to be equipped for this specialized work.

The earlier training programs had provided a considerable body of information on the way in which these training groups made use of the programs in which they participated. This knowledge was reported at professional meetings in papers prepared for such organizations as the American Orthopsychiatric Association, the American Group Therapy Association, the National Council on Family Relations, the Groves Conference, and the International Mental Health Congress in 1961.

PROGRAMS FOR PUBLIC HEALTH AND HOSPITAL NURSES

Before the work of the Association with educational personnel could be further developed, an urgent call came from a totally different professional area. In the spring of 1954, the Association began a demonstration training program in parent group leadership for public health nurses. This program was requested and sponsored jointly by the United States Children's Bureau, Department of Health, Education and Welfare, under the leadership of Miss Ruth G. Taylor, then Chief of the Nursing Section, Division of Health Services, and by the Bureau of Maternal and Child Health of the New York State Health Department, under the leadership of Dr. Alfred Yankauer, at that time its director. Both agencies wished to make available to selected nurses new methods of group learning so that the classes for parents conducted under public health auspices might reflect newer concepts of how people learn and how individuals can be helped to function more effectively by mobilizing their own inner resources. Plans were made at the outset to study the effectiveness of the program in a research evaluation project. (For the results of this study, see Chapter XV.)

The first training programs in parent group leadership for public health nurses were modelled after the earlier programs given by the Association and were intended primarily to train public health nurses to conduct discussion groups for parents of young children, thus offering a program which might tie young parents more closely to public health services after their children grew past the stage of infancy. In practice, the nurses soon began to apply the principles of group discussion to the work many were already doing with groups of expectant parents. The Association had thought initially that this would be a second area of group leadership, one which could be developed later, after the nurses had learned to use group discussion methods with parent groups. It soon became apparent that the general public looked to nurses for leadership of prenatal groups much more than of parents of young children, a role which in the public eye seemed to belong more conventionally to teachers and psychologists.

Subsequent programs were therefore shifted to focus on work with expectant parent groups first, helping the nurses to develop their skills in this area and later giving them support and encouragement to adapt their group skills to work with parents of young children as a second step. Before going into the field of expectant parent education, however, the Child Study Association tested the validity of the group educational approach in this special area in a number of experimental groups conducted by their own staff, with public health nurses as resource persons. On the basis of this experience, carefully evaluated, the Association felt justified in extending the training programs into this new subject area.

Beginning in 1955, two training programs were conducted for public health nurses under the auspices of the New York State Department of Health, always with the support and sponsorship of the United States Children's Bureau. The following year, a special group of twelve hospital nurses was added to the program, focusing directly on work with expectant parent groups. In 1956–1957, the New York and New Jersey State Departments of Health joined in sponsoring a program for some twenty public health and hospital nurses from both of these states. In this way, the work began to spread out into new geographical areas. The emphasis in all of the nursing programs was on adding to the training of the nurses special sensitivity to the emotional and psychological aspects of pregnancy, childbirth, the care of the new baby, and the problems of parents in caring for and rearing young children. In addition, as with the earlier groups, the nurses learned techniques of group discussion which they applied to these important areas of family life.

As the focus of the programs shifted into these new areas, the content of the theoretical sessions changed accordingly. Medical persons were added to the list of guest faculty to reinforce the nurses' knowledge of the medical-nursing aspects of the interests of expectant parents and parents. Obstetricians reviewed current practices in obstetrical care; other obstetricians discussed some of the psychological aspects of pregnancy during the antenatal and postnatal periods as they saw them; psychiatrists introduced the new but growing body of information on the psychological and emotional aspects of pregnancy from their point of view. In all of these programs, the trainees were given a general survey of growth and development, psychodynamically oriented. It covered the life cycle from infancy to the time when the growing young people became adults and took on the responsibilities of parenthood. As the programs went on over a period of years, these general surveys of development became more condensed and schematized; more attention was given to the prenatal and postnatal period and the years of early childhood with which the parents who came to public health services seemed most concerned.[3]

By 1959 the training programs moved in new directions. These were established to answer demands for programs to meet special needs and provided the groundwork for important further developments. The first was the initiation of programs of training for *supervision* of group leadership, offered to selected nurses who had participated in earlier programs. This step was taken to prepare these key nurses to play an important role in projected training programs to be established under the auspices of their own State Departments of Health. These programs would be modelled on the training given by the Child Study Association and conducted initially with some consultation from the Association staff. Three such programs were later established in New York State—in Rochester, Syracuse, and Albany—all drawing on local medical and psychological personnel as they were available, supplemented by nurses who had been in the original Child Study programs and who served as auxiliary faculty and supervising staff. This was the first region in which the experimental and demonstration program of the Child Study Association fulfilled one of its original purposes, namely, that of providing a model for other training programs and preparing people to conduct such programs.

The second development was the establishment of a training project away from the Child Study Association's headquarters. This project,

---

[3] Aline B. Auerbach, "Public Health Nursing and Parent Education: A Pilot Project of Training for Parent Group Leadership," *American Journal of Public Health*, **45**: 1,578–89 (December 1955).

Aline B. Auerbach, "New Approaches to Work with Expectant Parent Groups: A Report on a Pilot Leadership Training Program for Nurses," *American Journal of Public Health*, **47**: 184–91 (February 1957).

sponsored jointly by the Texas State Department of Health, Texas Woman's University, and the United States Children's Bureau, was offered for fifteen nurses from five states in the Southwest region—Texas, Louisiana, Oklahoma, Arkansas, and New Mexico. Because of the changing requirements created by gathering a group of nurses together away from their home bases and introducing a training staff from the Child Study Association's headquarters, the scheduling of the project took a different form from that of previous training programs. An initial intensive three-week institute was offered at Parkland Memorial Hospital in Dallas, Texas; this was followed by an extended period of supervision of practice groups, on a weekly basis by mail and with one field visit; a final one-week follow-up institute given six months after the program began, with an additional week's work for those who wanted to apply to parent groups the methods used with expectant parent groups. Again this was followed by a period of supervised field work, the contact with the trainees continuing as in earlier programs, for a period of approximately one year. In evaluating this plan, the Association felt that there were definite advantages in offering concentrated teaching institutes without the distraction of other professional duties. In addition, the nurses seemed to form a cohesive group more quickly, thus facilitating their own learning.

An important new feature of this regional program was the combined use of communication by correspondence and field visits in supervision. Here, too, the plan grew out of the time-and-space requirements of the project and differed greatly from the continuing face-to-face contact with the trainees maintained in earlier programs. As anticipated, the more diffused contact had certain disadvantages. The give-and-take of a personal interview was supplanted by the more tenuous interchange of ideas that depended on the written word, without the additional overtones that come from the tone of voice and facial expression of both trainee and supervisor. To many trainees the very idea of supervision by correspondence suggested impersonality and distance and therefore doubtful support and helpfulness. Besides, many found this much writing difficult and a distinct threat. The mail exchange, however, was only one part of the spectrum of supervisory contacts out of which the relationship was established and maintained. It was preceded by personal interviews during the period of the opening institutes and was supplemented by one field visit in each practice period, during which the leaders were observed conducting their groups and different aspects of their work performance were discussed in detail.

Although the Association was skeptical at first about the possible effectiveness of this plan for supervision, it proved to have positive values as well as limitations. The nature of the exchange forced both parties in the

relationship to sharpen their thinking about the process of group education and the way in which the leader used himself in all aspects of his
leadership. The leaders' own questions about their performance opened
the way for the supervisors' comments and suggestions that had educational meaning and helped them increase their skills along with their self-
knowledge. The supervisors (or consultants, as they came to be called)
were free to raise their own questions about the leaders' performance,
partly for further specific information but also to challenge them to
evaluate more clearly their own performance. In this interplay, the
trainees were encouraged to explain, clarify, reflect, and question. The
concerted effort to get to basic leadership problems and to conceptualize
them in relation to the philosophy and goals of the work seemed often to
speed up the learning process, even though long-distance communication
sometimes spread out the timing of the responses on both sides.[4]

This project provided the testing ground and opened the way for a
further five-year project sponsored by the Children's Bureau, given for
public health and hospital nurses at the Association's New York headquarters. This program drew on personnel from strategic areas all over
the country where public health or hospital services were eager and ready
to have their nurses acquire such specialized training. Originally begun
in 1959 as a yearly program that would be repeated for three consecutive
years, it was repeated another two years in order to complete its long-
range goals. These included not only the training of small groups of
nurses from different parts of the country, but also the building of a
reservoir of people who would be equipped through additional training
in supervision and in conducting training programs to begin to establish
training centers in various schools of nursing or of public health. These
centers would then carry on their own programs of training to meet the
increasing demand for nurses trained to conduct group services for parents and expectant parents. This project was reported in some detail in
Nursing Outlook [5] and in a more extensive report available from the Child
Study Association of America.[6]

During the five years of this special training project, 93 nurses participated in one year's training, practically all completing the first half of the

[4] See Franklin C. Cohen and Mildred Rabinow, "The Consultation Process in
Training For Mental Health Education Through the Use of Correspondence and
Direct Observation," unpublished paper, Child Study Association of America, New
York, 1966.

[5] Aline B. Auerbach, "Training for Leadership in Parent Group Education,"
Nursing Outlook, 14, No. 4: 35–40 (April 1966).

[6] Aline B. Auerbach, "A Five Year Project of Training of Nurses for Parent Group
Education Leadership," Child Study Association of America, New York, 1965, available at 50¢ per copy.

program. For a variety of reasons—changes of administrative policy, ill health, job promotion and personal reasons—ten of these were unable to complete the second half of the program. In all, these nurses conducted 329 groups under supervision during the training periods, reaching approximately 3000 expectant parents or parents of young children. These figures do not include additional groups conducted by a number of the nurses without supervision during this period, nor does it take into account the groups which they led after their training was completed. The nurses came from thirteen different states, Puerto Rico, and the District of Columbia. They held responsible positions in state, county, and local public health settings, in hospitals, in Visiting Nurse Associations, the American Red Cross and the United States Army Nurse Corps. Thirty-four of these nurses received a second level of training for supervision of group leadership, many of these having additional preparation for setting up and conducting programs in their own academic settings.

The first such program, begun in February, 1964, at the University of California School of Nursing in San Francisco, is being offered as continuing education at the postgraduate level. The Child Study Association's staff participated in its first year's program and gave continuing consultation as the project developed. Similar programs were established in 1965 and 1966 at the Boston University School of Nursing and the Indiana University School of Nursing. All of these programs followed the general pattern of training used by the Child Study Association, offering intensive institutes, followed by supervised field work. At the same time, each program is being carried on with some innovations and additions to meet new needs as they are being identified and to improve its educational effectiveness.

Understandably here, too, the content of these programs has shifted as the programs have developed. The nurses entering such programs were more aware of group processes and their meaning for learning. Some nurses who had been exposed to certain types of group experiences in their nursing training have not reacted with much enthusiasm, expecting that parent group education would be similar to what they had known as "group dynamics." Their skepticism has been overcome, however, as they came to realize that both types of programs make use of the dynamics of group interaction, but toward different end goals. In general, the nurses were already more familiar with the group discussion method as it was being used in expectant parent and parent classes. Because they were less naive in this respect than earlier groups, they were able to move more quickly into some of the finer points of group skills, and to relate them more consciously to the content of learning which the parents seemed to require. The nurses also were more sophisticated in their appreciation of the psychological and emotional aspects of pregnancy and the postpartum period, since these factors have now become accepted as part of nursing training. Less time therefore had to be spent on these aspects, though it was felt in each program that a review of newer interpretations in this field was essential to provide for those nurses who were less familiar with these concepts.

In each program, there was an interesting and consistent pattern in the way the nurses approached their practice work. In general, they were hesitant about using group discussion as a way of teaching, afraid that they would not be able to give their patients the needed information through this approach. They were unsure about when they might appropriately add this information and when they might wait and see if the group could develop it out of their own ideas and experiences. They recognized that their dilemma in this respect was probably the result of much of their earlier teaching, plus the attitude of the public toward the nurse as an authoritarian figure giving out information much as doctors give out prescriptions. Once they overcame their hesitancy and clarified some of their confusion in this respect, these nurses became most skillful in encouraging their patients to bring out their true concerns and in helping them explore and understand these more adequately.

As a result of their participation in these programs, the nurses often applied to other aspects of their professional work the method of group education gained in their training. They began to use it in in-service sessions with their staffs, around such areas as their increasing role in giving out birth control information, for example. They also began to use group discussion with teen-agers in family life education classes, which many of the nurses were being asked to conduct in schools in their areas. In Colorado, interest in preparing nurses specifically to enter this field led to setting up a program under the sponsorship of the Colorado State Health Department, again with the sponsorship of the United States Children's Bureau. This program was instituted in 1966 to prepare school health nurses to lead groups of teen-agers in discussion of some of the difficult sexual and other personal adjustments adolescents face. This program is significant as another outreach within the public health field, one which holds great promise for the future.[7]

The expansion of training programs for group leadership in the field of public health and hospital nursing provides a dramatic story. It was largely sparked by Miss Taylor's imaginative vision of this program as making an important contribution to comprehensive maternal care and also to nursing education. Its outreach has been extensive and gratifying.

[7]Ada M. Daniels, "Training School Nurses to Work with Groups of Adolescents," *Children,* **XIII,** No. 6 (November-December 1966).

Nurses who have been exposed to this point of view are using it creatively in their own ways; although they may not be reporting it to any central clearing place, they are continuing to develop new aspects to meet the needs of their communities. As an interesting sidelight: there has been built up a rather special *esprit* among those who have participated in these projects and have come to know people from other parts of the country who are doing work similar to their own. Many of these nurses are keeping in touch informally with the Child Study Association and with individual staff members with whom they have worked in the supervisory and consultative relationship. Occasionally they report or share their experiences, wanting, it seems, to maintain a contact with others who are continuing to develop new ideas in this field.

Another outcome of these five years of the training project was a three-day conference for nurses on "Developing Preventive Group Educational Services in Federally Aided Maternal and Infant Care Programs." This was held under Children's Bureau auspices at the Association's headquarters in September, 1965, for nurses who had completed the earlier programs of training for leadership and for supervision. Twenty-seven nurses attended this conference together with five regional nursing consultants and the nursing consultant for the care of mentally retarded children of the Children's Bureau. The purpose of this conference was to enable these key public health and hospital nurses to examine the implications of their work in this field for the tasks that lie ahead in comprehensive programs of maternal and child health.[8]

TRAINING FOR CHURCH LEADERS

In the meantime, the training programs had already moved into other fields. Picking up on the interest shown by ministers and directors of religious education in one of the earlier programs, training programs were given by the Association for three consecutive years for the Department of Christian Education of the Protestant Council of the City of New York (1957–1959). Forty-two persons representing various denominations within the larger Protestant group were trained in these programs. They were held on a weekly basis for a semester and then biweekly for another period. These religious leaders had come hoping to develop new skills to use with the parents of children in their church schools so that they might be able to strengthen family life and thus counteract the breakdown in family relationships and the increasing amount of juvenile delinquency in the neighborhoods they served. These representatives came from churches

[8] Copies of a report of this conference are available from the Child Study Association of America at 50¢ per copy.

in many different settings in all areas of New York City, including those in which racial tensions were high and extending also into a number of suburban areas around metropolitan New York. These religious educators, including some ministers who were responsible for the religious education in their churches, came primarily to develop group skills. However, they were also eager for additional content which would give them a better understanding of family relations and of children as they grew within the family and in the community. In a few cases, the additional knowledge of subject matter they gained found its way into the curriculum planning for church schools on a wide basis and into a number of pamphlets which have been widely distributed.

The most consistent difficulties encountered by this group of trainees were organizing and maintaining the parent groups for which this training prepared them. Many of the churches had a fluctuating attendance, particularly in the disadvantaged sections of the city. Many of them had no regular church registers and their contact with their parishioners was on a random basis. Groups were slow to form and difficult to maintain over a period of time; however, these difficulties gradually were overcome to some extent. Some leaders in these training groups found it difficult to add the organizing and conducting of parent groups to their regular responsibilities within the parish. But they continued to do so at great personal sacrifice.

These leaders, too, had considerable difficulty in taking over the enabling-leadership role with their groups. As had been anticipated, their positions in their churches as ministers or directors of religious education naturally caused them to be looked on as *the authority* and many of them were accustomed to functioning in this way. The conducting of their groups was, as usual, supervised by members of the Association's staff during the training periods, and it was primarily here that the trainees had the opportunity to talk out and work through their conflicting feelings about this (to many of them) new way of working with their parishioners. For some, it took time before they were able to help the parents move ahead in the discussions at their own level of need and interest, by means of leadership that guided and opened up new directions without preaching or being authoritarian. And it also took time for the parents to accept their functioning in this way. Several groups led by trainees in this program had to be conducted in Spanish, and supervision was complicated by the need to have an interpreter present at meetings observed by the supervisor-consultant. (Weekly reports were, of course, written in English.) There was considerable evidence that the leaders-in-training gained a point of view which they applied not only to those who came to their parent group programs, but to all their parent contacts. Many of the religious educators who took part in these programs continue to attend conferences and institutes given by the Child Study Association, thus evidencing their wish to remain identified with this field.

TRAINING SOCIAL WORKERS TO CONDUCT GROUPS OF PARENTS OF CHILDREN WITH HANDICAPS

At the conclusion of the programs for religious educators, the Association moved into another special field, that of training social workers to work with parents of children with chronic illnesses or physical handicaps. To prepare for this new direction, staff members again conducted experimental groups, this time in a variety of health and rehabilitation settings. These included a group for parents of children with muscular dystrophy given under the auspices of the Institute of Physical Medicine and Rehabilitation, a group of parents of children with Cooley's anemia, given at Kings County Hospital, and a group of parents of children with cerebral palsy, conducted under the auspices of United Cerebral Palsy of New York. Largely spurred by the interest of this latter organization in developing trained personnel for parent group leadership, the Association conducted an initial program in 1960 and a second in 1961 for twenty-six social workers connected with hospital clinics and a variety of health agencies. In each case, the Child Study Association staff worked closely with the agencies whose representatives participated in the program, giving consultation regarding the organization and conduct of groups as well as supervision of the groups led by their workers. Some of the implications of the work carried on in connection with these training programs have already been described in Chapter XII.[9]

The trainees in these programs conducted groups of parents of children with cerebral palsy, mental retardation, orthopedic handicaps, muscular dystrophy, blindness, deafness, and some with multiple disabilities. The social workers who conducted these groups, like the social workers in the earliest programs, had some difficulty in transferring their focus from individual parents to the group as a whole and in adapting their social work practice to make use of the dynamics of the group for the parents' individual growth in understanding and competence. They needed a great deal of encouragement, support, and guidance in the supervisory relation-

[9] See also Aline B. Auerbach, "Group Education for Parents of the Handicapped," *Children,* **8,** No. 4: 135–140 (July-August 1961).

Salvatore Ambrosino, "A Project in Group Education With Parents of Retarded Children," *Casework Papers, 1960,* Family Service Association of America, New York.

Ada M. Daniels, "Parent Group Education: Its Meaning for Parents of Mentally Retarded Children," unpublished paper, revised 1966, Child Study Association of America, New York.

ship before they mastered the techniques and used them for the group purposes. Once they overcame the initial hurdles, however, they felt that the programs were rewarding, though difficult to carry out, and that in many cases the parents gained more from groups than they had from their individual contacts with the workers.

The programs of training for workers in the handicapped field had also reverted to the original schedule in which the training sessions were held once a week for a period of some fifteen weeks followed by a period of intensive practice groups under supervision and an ongoing seminar that met biweekly. The content of the theoretical sessions for these training programs had, of necessity, to be shifted to meet the needs of this special field. Although it was felt that the social workers could well profit by a review of normal child development and of parental concerns, these were introduced as a background to the way in which chronic illnesses and special disabilities upet the usual timetable of growth and affect a child's ability to cope with developmental tasks. Considerable attention was also paid to the profound effect of these deviations on parents and the anxieties they arouse. The theoretical sessions were full of rich content and drew on a variety of medical and psychiatric personnel who had had experience in the fields of special disabilities. At the same time, the training programs offered intensive training in group skills, adapted here to the particular coloration and subject areas most characteristic of parent discussions under these special circumstances.

As indicated earlier, one of the most difficult aspects of parent group work of this kind proved to be the atmosphere or tone of the group sessions themselves. Understandably, parents brought to these sessions deep feelings of frustration and defeat; these, in turn, affected the attitudes of the leaders, who occasionally were also caught up in the same mood. One of the important contributions of these training programs was the emphasis they came to place on the fact that parents faced with these severe problems had great inner reserves to draw on and often accomplished enormous feats of guidance and support in the daily care of their youngsters. What they accomplished fell far short of what they felt they should accomplish in many cases, but a change of emphasis in the group sessions seemed to bring about a more realistic attitude on the part of the parents, which enabled them to cope more effectively with their day-by-day problems.

A conference given in Boston in October, 1959, by the Child Study Association and the Children's Hospital Medical Center of Boston, Massachusetts, on "Helping Parents of Handicapped Children: Group Approaches," already referred to in Chapter XI, was an extension of work in this specialized field. This conference grew out of the interest of several organizations in furthering the mental health of handicapped children and their families. The conference gathered together a group of some 200 workers from different disciplines to discuss many aspects of group services for parents of children with handicapping conditions. There were addresses by medical, psychiatric, and educational personnel, followed by workshop discussions. The conference pointed out the great need for services of this kind, the advantages parents could gain from them, the responsibility of the agencies sponsoring such programs, and the need for special training for workers to undertake them. It was difficult to evaluate the impact of this conference on those who attended beyond noting their great interest in the subject and occasional reports that indicate they are making use of some of the ideas projected there in the agencies in which they are employed.

It is the opinion of the Child Study Association that work in this field is as yet comparatively undeveloped. Much more can be done to improve group services for parents of handicapped children and to train workers from various disciplines to play their respective parts in such programs. A promising step for work in this field is a program of training, beginning in 1967, conducted by the Schools of Public Health and Social Work of the University of California at Los Angeles under the general direction of Dr. Alfred H. Katz. This program, again sponsored by the United States Children's Bureau, is making use of the services of the Child Study Association in conducting the program in conjunction with faculty from the university.

JOINT FSAA-CSAA TRAINING PROGRAM

Throughout all of the work of the Child Study Association, stress has been laid on meeting the needs of parents of all social, economic, and cultural backgrounds. In addition to parent groups conducted at its headquarters, the history of the Association reports many groups conducted in neighborhood centers, settlement houses, and public housing projects in all areas of the city. Furthermore, a large number of the trainees in the various training programs were working with low-income families. The staff and leaders who conducted the parent groups were well aware of the special needs of the parents in these families and the ways in which economic and social pressures complicated their child-rearing. In recent years, with the increasing emphasis on the need to serve families in this category, programs have been set up to serve them directly. In 1963, the Child Study Association of America and the Family Service Association of

America received support from the National Institute of Mental Health [10] to carry on an "exploratory project in parent group education."

Under this grant, the Child Study Association of America would conduct a program of training in leadership of parent discussion groups for case workers on the staffs of selected member agencies of the Family Service Association of America within a 1000 mile radius of New York City. In connection with this training program, these caseworkers were to conduct multiple series of parent education groups under the auspices of their local Family Service agencies. These groups would be offered to people in the community not previously served by the agency through parent group education methods. The long-term goal of this joint effort was "to extend the quantity and improve the quality of group educational programs for parents offered by Family Service agencies, in the interest of sustaining and strengthening the mental and emotional health of parents and children." Through this project, it was hoped Family Service agencies would be stimulated to initiate, extend, and improve the quality and number of group educational programs for parents, and especially for parents who had not been reached in such programs. This 1963 training program was repeated in 1964–1965 and was followed by a year devoted to a study of the findings. Thirty-seven case workers, representing agencies from twenty-one states, received training. Since the geographical area was extended in the second year of the project, the states represented ranged from Massachusetts to California and from Minnesota to Florida. While the Child Study Association conducted the training programs and supervised the practice groups of the trainees, the Family Service Association was involved throughout—in selecting agencies to send their representatives and in interpreting the program before and during the course of the project in order to smooth out any possible difficulties and maintain the agencies' interest. They also assisted with problems of community organization that arose here, as they had in other training programs, in connection with the organization and recruitment of parent groups. Since here the emphasis was on reaching out to new clientele, this aspect of the program was particularly important. The training institutes focused, as in other programs, on the basic content and techniques of parent group education. Additional emphasis was placed, however, on ways of reaching all levels of the parent population and on increasing the leaders' sensitivity to the special needs of low-income families, seen in the context of their various cultural and social environments.

The project was a demonstration of the way in which the special skills of two national agencies combined to develop and extend services for families on a broad scale. A summary report of this project and of the

[10] Under Grant No. MH684–A1.

evaluation study which accompanied it is available from the Child Study Association of America.[11] Pertinent here is the study's conclusion that the major objectives of the program were carried out: a new group of social workers were trained to conduct parent education groups; family agencies were encouraged to develop parent discussion group programs as part of their agencies' services; and, as a result, contact was made with many new families who had not had previous contact with social agencies nor been involved in educational programs. (For results of the research evaluation of this project, see Chapter XV.)

PROJECT ENABLE

The results of the Child Study Association of America-Family Service Association of America project challenged both these agencies to extend these services on a wider scale and to adapt them particularly to the needs of the poor, as part of the "War on Poverty." Based on the experience of the earlier program, the two national agencies invited the National Urban League to join them in a project which became Project ENABLE (Education and Neighborhood Action For Better Living Environment), supported by the Research, Demonstration, and Training Departments of the Community Action Program of the Office of Economic Opportunity in September, 1965.

The plan was based on the assumption that many of the antipoverty programs for children and young people would fall short of their goals if parents were not thoroughly involved and if, through this involvement, parental attitudes, home situations, and the community itself did not change. It seemed to be generally agreed that parent education has a key role in the War on Poverty. Accordingly, the new program made use of a team approach which brought together in a program of parent education the skills of group leadership and community organization. A training project was developed to teach social workers in Family Service agencies and Urban Leagues throughout the country the necessary skills for working with groups of parents. Its goals were to enable these parents to carry out their parental functions more effectively in a difficult and often hostile environment and find constructive ways of changing the environment through their own efforts—alone or in collaboration with others.

The Child Study Association staff of training specialists assigned to Project ENABLE had the key responsibility for planning and conducting

[11] "A Three-Year Project of Training of Social Workers in Parent Group Education Leadership" conducted by the Child Study Association of America under the joint sponsorship of the Child Study Association of America and the Family Service Association of America, 1963–1964–1965 (unpublished report).

the training programs given for members of the national and local staffs of the project. They worked closely with representatives of the other two national agencies under a project director chosen from the staff of the Family Service Association of America. Twelve of the original thirty-five family service workers who had been trained in parent group leadership in the joint FSAA-CSAA project became part of the National ENABLE staff. They were called area supervisors and were now trained by the three sponsoring agencies to become trainers, to teach others what they themselves had learned and to incorporate into the teaching the expanded concepts of this project. Working in teams of two or more persons under the guidance of the training specialists, they conducted regional training institutes for local project staffs from Family Service agencies and Urban League branches in their assigned areas. Also involved in each institute team was an area coordinator, drawn primarily from Urban League staffs, who contributed his knowledge of the community and of community organization. These regional institutes prepared local ENABLE teams to set up and carry on parent programs in their own communities for education and social action.

Local ENABLE teams were usually made up of caseworkers, who served as group leaders of the parent discussion groups, community organizers and social work aides, all of whom received special training for their respective roles and who collaborated in their various responsibilities. The community organizer was, in a sense, the link between the parents and the community and was identified in this project as the primary agent for change in the community. He strengthened those programs which helped to motivate parents to become involved in community action. Since action was seen as emerging from the discussions and decision-making processes in the parent groups, he worked closely with the parent group leader as well as with the other member(s) of the team. The social work aide was the nonprofessional member of the team and was drawn from the neighborhood population. He (or she) assisted in such matters as recruitment, interpretation of the program, reporting and research interviews, and in specific duties connected with the parent meetings. The social work aide was an important link between the parents and the project and between the parents and the community and also played a part in promoting social action.

As this project reached out further into local communities and neighborhoods, the Child Study Association training staff maintained close contact with the project at all levels. They participated in regional institutes and gave ongoing consultation and supervision to the area supervisors in *their* supervision of the work of the local teams. Staff members of the Family Service Association of America and the National Urban League also gave consultation as needed in their areas of special competence.

Six training institutes in six centers were held in the spring and six follow-up institutes in the summer of 1966. More than 150 professional staff from approximately 100 Family Service agencies and Urban Leagues in 62 communities took part in these institutes. Thus, in less than a year after the second year of the joint CSAA-FSAA training project, the number of communities using the learning from that project had doubled and the number of staff in training had more than tripled. It was conservatively estimated that approximately 10,000 parents would be involved in the ENABLE program in the first year. Thus Project ENABLE was a dramatic extension of the NIMH Project. As such projects develop and extend into new fields, their added complexity presents special problems which cannot always be anticipated. This project included plans for careful evaluation, so the lessons learned from it could be made available to others engaged in similar projects throughout the country.

The ENABLE project consolidated and expanded many elements that were present in the Association's earlier programs of training. First, it built on the Association's previous experience in working cooperatively with other national agencies in large teaching programs with wide community implications. Second, it followed and developed further the various steps whereby persons trained in parent group leadership were prepared to become trainers of others, in order to spread the outreach of such training in widening circles. Third, the pattern of training remained largely the same, with institutes made up of teaching sessions and seminars and the use of extensive case material from earlier group records. Emphasis continued to be placed on consultation and supervision in helping people develop new group skills.

The content of the training programs in this project shifted in keeping with its special focus, which was to concentrate on the needs of people from lower income groups and limited educational backgrounds. The aim was to help parents use the understanding they gained in the parent groups to bring about change not only in their families' functioning but also in the social environment. But the basic attitude still remained that of helping individual parents, in groups, to develop their capacities and resources through educational intervention so they might use these constructively in all aspects of their family and community life.

* * * * *

This chapter has recorded, in skeleton form, the way in which a simple program offered to a small group on an experimental basis was expanded and extended into many areas of content and made available to a variety of professional groups who are using its concepts and techniques in many services to parents. It is not possible to estimate the extent to which these programs and the publications and reports that have been based on them have influenced the thinking of professional persons regarding their work with families. We do know, however, that the ideas and procedures formulated here are being adopted and adapted in many places, as individuals and agencies do their own experimenting and set up their own programs. It is hoped that this record of more than fifteen years of training and consultation will challenge many more to enter this field.

XV

Research

In its early days, parent education was generally accepted as a worthwhile endeavor per se. It was assumed that parents needed only to have a feast of information about children laid out before them and they would partake of it and incorporate it into their child-rearing practices. The results, however, were soon seen to be uneven, unpredictable, unclear, and sometimes even doubtful. Different approaches were then tried, as we have seen, in an effort to fit programs to the needs of parents, and the results were gauged in a broad overall way, based on empirical evidence. Only in recent years has parent education been subjected to critical, evaluative scrutiny as a whole and in its various aspects.

The problems involved in such scrutiny proved to be subtle and complex because of parent education's vast scope, varied methodology, and sometimes undifferentiated goals. Brim described these problems in his comprehensive study of parent education.[1] He raised questions as to the possible effects which could and should be studied. He singled out first the effects of parent education on the mental health of the children, who are the end recipients of educational intervention with parents; at the same time, he pointed out the difficulty of measuring a condition that until now has been defined usually in general terms and that needs to be analyzed into its specific characteristics if it is to be measured in social research studies. Brim mentioned also the effects of parent education in bringing about changes in knowledge, attitudes, and behavior of parents, since these changes are presumed to influence the children's mental health. He pointed out the need for studies that would clarify the relationship between the parents' factual information, attitudes, and behavior and the children's mental health—a relationship which he said was "an open question." (Research studies in this last category have been increasing,

---

[1] Orville G. Brim, Jr., *Education for Child Rearing*, Russell Sage Foundation, New York, 1959; paperback edition, The Free Press, New York, 1965. See Chapter 9: Evaluating the Results.

however, and are summarized in two volumes of comprehensive research overviews prepared by Russell Sage Foundation and the Society for Research in Child Development.[2])

Brim also pointed out the many aspects of parent education programs that have to be studied: the methods they employ and their comprehensive effectiveness under varied conditions, such as type of leadership and group size, the nature of their content, and the background and characteristics of the parents who participate. He outlined the kinds of evidence that should be admissible in keeping with the accepted "cannons of science" as developed in evaluation research methodology. He surveyed several hundred studies that had been made in parent education along any of these lines up to 1959, when his book was written, and found that nearly two dozen of these met rigorous standards of scientific evaluative research. However, he came to the sobering and challenging conclusion that his survey of these two dozen studies "leave(s) little doubt that their results are inconsistent and inconclusive." [3] This he felt was true even in those relatively few which were conducted with a complete experimental design, including the use of control groups, with adequate sampling and the use of objective, standardized instruments. This conclusion applied whether the studies related to the effects of different methods of group procedures, the mass media, individual parent counseling, or multiple procedures. He was careful to point out many possible reasons for this lack of positive scientific findings. On the other hand, he said,

"There are those who argue that there is no reason to expect any important aspects of the adult personality to change as a result of parent education" and "we do not even know if the adult individual ever undergoes any important changes other than changes in factual knowledge even when exposed to educational experiences much more impressive than parent education. . . . On the other hand, an argument presented by many is that the educational programs for parents do produce changes but that for several reasons they will continue to escape detection, given the current measurements procedures. The changes which occur are alleged to be too subtle to be captured by other than clinical techniques, or too small to show up in the sparse examples of parents utilized in most evaluation studies; or are delayed in their occurrence so that they are not discernible except through a longitudinal study." [4]

He concluded that since the issue of the effectiveness of parent education is still unresolved in terms of scientific evaluative research, one looks

---

[2] Martin L. Hoffman and Lois Wladis Hoffman, Editors, *Review of Child Development Research*, Vol. 1, 1964, Vol. II, 1966, Russell Sage Foundation, New York.

[3] Brim, *op. cit.*, p. 310.

[4] Brim, *op. cit.*, p. 312–313.

forward to further studies in order to give "a deeper understanding of the significance of this modern social movement."

In the introduction ᵗo the 1965 paperback edition of this book,[5] several points are added to this interpretation. While research on the growth and development of children continues to increase and is of the highest order, there are also more studies of the influence of parents on the personality development of their children, with special reference to the "content" of child development, such as how boys and girls learn their sex roles, how children develop morality, what are the sources of creativity and autonomy, how attitudes toward death evolve. This is in contrast to earlier research on the control of primary drives such as sex and aggression.

There are also a number of new studies of marital and family interaction, from which we now have a better picture of the way the relationship of husband and wife influences their behavior toward their children. A clearer picture is also emerging of how "this husband-wife relationship evolves through time, passing through different stages at different periods in the family life cycle, and how the intersection of the lines of development in the marital relationship with stages in the parent-child relationship work to make easier or to complicate the task of the parent, and to create in the parents differing degrees of receptivity to outside information about child-rearing." [6] The authors add:

"We see more clearly the fact that education is but one of several kinds of activities necessary to help parents achieve full effectiveness in their parental roles. In recent years we have seen greater stress laid on intervention in the economic and physical aspects of family life situations. Providing additional services for working mothers or single parent families or for the poverty stricken, such as more readily available day care programs or homemaking services, is often essential to relieve the emergency aspects of daily living; this has the added benefit of permitting parents to take greater advantage of educational services."

" . . . [W]e now may understand better how the mass media, in transmitting information about human development to parents, tend to have a cumulative effect so that, from one generation to the next, significant change in knowledge and attitude occurs without this effect being measurable in any single experimental evaluation of a mass media program. The great array of information about child-rearing, available in any given day in this country in its books and magazines, its radio and television programs, is an almost constant resource or information bank, easily accessible to the motivated parent. The occasion which impels a parent to reach out for this information, or to be highly receptive if

[5] Orville G. Brim, Jr., and Aline B. Auerbach, Introduction to New Edition, in Brim, *Education For Child Rearing*, The Free Press, New York, 1965.
[6] *Ibid.*, p. v.

exposed to it, appears to be unpredictable in nature. . . . A particular parent, in response to some concern which has unpredictably arisen in his child-care tasks, is ready for information relevant to his question; information has become necessary and meaningful at this particular time in his parental career. At this moment relevant information can produce an increment in his knowledge, a change in his point of view, a shift in his attitude, so that his child-rearing henceforth is altered. Such instances, multiplied by the millions, can easily account for part of the shifts in child-rearing practices in the direction suggested by professional groups through the mass media during the past decade." [7]

Finally, some progress is reported in research studies of the effectiveness of specific types of educational programs, both in their outreach and their results in bringing about change. Two studies in particular are cited as examples: the first, carried on under the auspices of the Hogg Foundation, reports significant changes in parental attitudes brought about through participation in a discussion program conducted by trained lay-leaders; [8] the second is a joint exploratory project of the Family Service Association of America and the Child Study Association of America under a grant from the National Institute of Mental Health, in which a study was made not only of the parents who participated but also of the impact on them of their experience in the groups. Other studies are beginning to explore the comparative effectiveness of various educational approaches used in parent groups. But the conclusion still remains that until more comprehensive evaluative studies are completed, services will have to be developed—as they have been in the past—largely on the basis of sound judgment of persons of professional competence, integrity, and creative imagination.

It is impossible—and unnecessary—to review here the studies that Brim has summarized so well or even to select from them those that deal with group approaches in parent education. What can be added is a brief report of the evaluative efforts undertaken by the Child Study Association of America, the pioneer parent education organization. The Association has had no permanent research department, nor has it been funded to carry on the extensive research studies the field so desperately needs. Nevertheless, it has been able to conduct some limited evaluation of parts of the parent education process, either in connection with specific program activities or as special limited research endeavors. Some are merely descriptive studies; others follow, in whole or in part, accepted procedures of evaluative research.

[7] *Ibid.,* pp. vi–vii.

[8] Carl F. Hereford, *Changing Parental Attitudes Through Group Discussion,* Hogg Foundation for Mental Health, University of Texas Press, Austin, Texas, 1963.

In their operation, these studies encountered some of the difficulties already mentioned as being inherent in work in this field. Although they too were often inconclusive, their history shows a progressive development which is encouraging and which may open up areas for future study.

These studies fall into two categories: those that deal with training for parent group education leadership, and those that examine various phases of the group experience itself.

STUDIES OF THE EFFECTIVENESS OF PROGRAMS OF TRAINING FOR PARENT GROUP EDUCATION LEADERSHIP

From the inception in 1951 of the programs of training for parent group education leadership, the Association envisioned long-range goals for this endeavor. Considered from the outset was the need to (1) establish standards of professional practice in parent education, (2) define personnel qualifications for group leadership, and (3) delineate broad areas in which essential research was needed. On the last point, Mildred Beck, then the Director of the Association, stated that appropriate tools must be devised to help measure the nature of the modification that occurs in the attitude of parents toward themselves and their children after exposure to educational experiences of this kind. The earliest evaluation study, however, was not directed toward this problem but was set up indirectly to throw light on the first two purposes. In a sense, they became secondary goals of a research project conducted in connection with the first two years' program of training of public health and hospital nurses in 1954–1955 and 1955–1956.

As stated by the research staff of that project, the primary purpose of the research was to determine the effectiveness of the CSAA Leadership Training Program in the realization of its goals. These goals were to increase the knowledge of selected public health nurses and hospital nurses with respect to pregnancy and child growth and development and parent-child relationships, and to impart the skills required for successful leadership of expectant parent and parent discussion groups. It was hoped that modification of child-rearing attitudes in certain directions stressed by the training program might be a secondary gain. It had also been hoped that the research might throw some light on the personal qualities that seem to make for good group leadership.

A number of instruments were used on a before-and-after basis, eighteen in the first year and thirteen in the second. These instruments were employed to obtain a wide variety of both qualitative and quantitative data regarding the trainees' level of information, attitudes, personality characteristics, and leadership behavior at the beginning, and, where appropriate, at the conclusion of the training program.[9] Data were also obtained concerning the trainees' professional history, including their previous experience in group education, academic background, age, marital status, and a number of other characteristics. The instruments consisted of questionnaires, observational forms, interview guides, rating scales, and checklists. Some of these instruments were adapted from forms that had been pretested and used in similar projects, such as the Personal Opinion Questionnaire, which was based on the "F" scale designed by Adorno et al. and the "Opinions on Parent-Child Relations," which was adapted by the training and research staffs from the scale designed by Harris, Hough, and Martin for the measurement of child-rearing attitudes and practices. Others were developed for this particular project and were designed to provide data from which "movement" might be inferred.

During the second year of the project a control group of public health nurses was introduced, selected from nurses throughout New York State as candidates for a possible future CSAA training program. They were given six of the instruments, the others being appropriate only for those who actually participated in the program. These questionnaires were then readministered following an interval of time (four months) comparable to the length of the training program. They were completed by the nurses in the control group in their own familiar job settings; members in the experimental group completed them in group sessions at the CSAA training center. The control group was set up to be able with greater confidence to ascribe any "movement" in the trainees (positive or negative) to the effects of the training program.

Despite the extensive use of detailed instruments for different aspects of the program and its careful administration under the guidance of a distinguished research advisory committee, the results of this study were inconclusive, with respect to both the experimental and control groups. (Although the use of a control group was an important addition to a good research design, the general results were not sufficient to warrant continuing this procedure in future training programs, in view of the difficulty in establishing a satisfactory, comparable population.) As is often the case in a new field, the instruments used in these two programs were found to be not sufficiently sensitive to pick up any statistically significant changes in the nurses' attitudes and leadership—if any occurred—as a result of their participation in the training programs.

In the third program, one instrument (Leadership Questionnaire, CSAA) was refined and others were replaced by substitutes, including an

[9] The conclusion of the training program was defined for the purpose of this research as the end of the trainees' first field experience. Actually, the training program extended through a second and, in some cases, a third field experience.

adaptation of the Parent Attitude Research Instrument (PARI) (Schaefer and Bell) and the Edwards Personal Preference Schedule, thus making use of a different battery of tests. As reported at the time,[10] the results obtained were based on a small number of participants (twenty in all) and needed further validation. On the basis of these before-and-after measurements, however, the nurses showed a statistically significant change in the direction of greater *autonomy* (ability "to stand on their own two feet") and a markedly significant lessening of *nurturance*. The former change seemed important when compared with the nurses' initial concern about their subordinate relationship to physicians. The latter suggested an increase of faith in their patients' strengths. These findings were not statistically confirmed, however, in subsequent programs, although in the judgment of the training staff the shift of attitudes they suggested seemed to occur to some extent in many of the nurses who participated.

The research instrument that showed significant results on a group basis in the evaluation of all the programs was the leadership questionnaire, which was designed to test the trainees' knowledge of the theory and practice of a group educational approach to leadership of discussion groups for parents and expectant parents. This finding was confirmed in an evaluation study of a group leadership program given by the New York State Department of Health for nurses in the Syracuse region in 1958, which was modelled after the training programs conducted by the Child Study Association. It would appear that the reason this instrument proved effective in measuring change was that it measured the nurses' role performance, a concept that was not widely used at that time. This instrument was used for some years in subsequent training programs as well.

The extent of "movement" it recorded diminished somewhat as the trainees who participated were more sophisticated in their understanding of content and methodology. They had started at a higher level when they came into the project and therefore had less far to go. These findings, however, contrasted with reports from many of the trainees themselves who said, either spontaneously or on questionnaires, that they had gained enormously in knowledge of both content and methodology and were making use of both in many phases of their work.

The results of the various personality tests, including that of the "F" scale of authoritarian personality, were generally disappointing. There were no clear correlations between various personality characteristics and the adaptability and progress of trainees from various disciplines. This finding was confirmed in the experience of the training staff, who found it

[10] Aline B. Auerbach, and Gertrude Goller, "How Do Nurses Take To 'New Ways' In Leading Parent Groups?" *Nursing Outlook,* **6** (December 1958).

impossible, on the basis of their early judgment of the trainees' capacities and personality make-up, to predict who might become an effective group leader. They recognized that the intangible qualities that make for good leadership of the kind required for programs of group education are difficult to define. Since this is an important element to be considered in setting up programs of this type, we quote from the summary report of the Five Year Project of Training of Nurses, believing that although this is directed primarily to one professional group, it has implications for others as well:

"Although the training staff has been aware of the need to define those characteristics that are essential (for good leadership of programs of group education), as yet they have been able to come up with nothing conclusive. Such a quality as personal maturity, for example, seems crucial, but this seems to be present in persons irrespective of age; some of the younger nurses, with relatively little direct experience in life themselves, have seemed to have a quality of this kind more than others considerably older. The matter of flexibility seems important too. Again this is not necessarily tied in with age, contrary to the traditional belief that older people who have been accustomed to working in a certain fixed way find it very difficult to change. Some of the older nurses in the program have shifted from traditional academic teaching methods with relative ease, whereas some of the younger nurses, perhaps less confident of their own capacities, have found themselves more inclined to lean on a curriculum approach which gave them a structure. Intellectual curiosity and the wish to experiment in new methods of work seem to be essential for good leadership; these qualities are found in varying degrees with people of all temperaments. The most important quality, perhaps, is a fluid non-dominating attitude toward people, which respects them for what they are, regardless of their circumstances in life, and which carries with it the conviction that there is a strong potential for learning in everyone. In general, it seems that the nurses who had this particular quality have been most successful, particularly when it was combined with a sound professional background of knowledge." [11]

These earlier studies of the general effectiveness of various programs of training, exploratory and inconclusive as they were, served as the background for the evaluation of the subsequent training programs in the Child Study Association of America-Family Service Association of America project of 1963–1965, supported by the National Institute of Mental Health. In this project, evaluative study was made of two processes, the effectiveness of the training on the trainee and the impact on the parents of their experience in groups led by the trainees, which will be discussed later on.

[11] Aline B. Auerbach, *A Five Year Project of Training of Nurses for Parent Group Education Leadership,* Child Study Association of America, New York, 1965, available at 50¢ per copy.

STUDIES OF VARIOUS ASPECTS OF
PARENT DISCUSSION PROGRAMS

While the succession of training programs conducted by the Child Study Association of America was underway, a number of scattered studies were undertaken by staff members of the Association or by individuals and agencies who used the facilities or materials of the Association, either individually or in cooperation with the agency.

Shapiro's Study of Parent Group Education

Shapiro had based a parent group education project on the philosophy and techniques outlined by Neubauer in a booklet published by the Child Study Association.[12] In this study,[13] Shapiro described the philosophy and procedures of the group discussion method he used, clearly conceptualizing his educational methodology in such a way that it could be used as a basis for comparative studies of the effectiveness of different techniques. He also used both experimental and control groups, carefully matched.

The experimental group met for a series of twelve discussion group sessions, in which leadership procedures were controlled and analyzed. Attitude scales based on the work of Shobin and Harris, Hough and Martin were administered to both groups on a before-and-after basis. The results showed the experimental subjects to have improved to a significantly greater degree than the control subjects on three of five scales measured: authoritarianism, good judgment, and possessiveness. Among Shapiro's findings were the fact that parents attending four or more meetings changed more than those who attended less and, significantly, that those experimental subjects who initially held more desirable attitudes changed more than those holding less desirable ones. This was the first study which, using a sound research design, demonstrated the effectiveness of group discussion techniques as a means of learning and change in parents.

Rabinow's Study of Recruitment

Recognizing the need to understand the problems of community organization if programs of parent education are to be successfully estab-

---

[12] Peter B. Neubauer, "The Technique of Parent Group Education: Some Basic Concepts," in *Parent Group Education and Leadership Training: Three Reports*, Child Study Association of America, New York, Revised edition, 1953.

[13] Irving S. Shapiro, *Changing Child Rearing Attitudes Through Group Discussion* (unpublished Ph.D. dissertation, Columbia University, 1954), University Microfilms pub. no. 10,801, Ann Arbor, Michigan, 1954; also Irving S. Shapiro, "Is Group Parent Education Worthwhile? A Research Report," *Marriage and Family Living*, **18**: 154–161 (1956).

lished and maintained, the Bureau of Maternal and Child Health of the New York State Department of Health sponsored a study of recruitment methods used in organizing parent discussion groups in public health centers. This was conducted by Mildred Rabinow of the Child Study Association of America staff and was reported under the title, "Community Organization and Parent Groups." The study was based on the experience in recruiting parent groups in various local health offices, whose nurses participated in the Association's training programs. It was hoped that out of the study would come a better understanding of the factors that might account for successful and less successful efforts in recruitment, to help other public health centers as they inaugurated group programs.

This project was based on interviews with the health officers in centers whose nurses were participating in the program, as well as interviews with representatives of other community agencies and mailed questionnaires. The study pointed out certain general conclusions, such as the importance of involving administrative personnel from the outset in the planning of group programs and the need that they have conviction about the value of the project. It also reported specific recruitment techniques that had been found to be productive, such as the use of volunteer committees of community representatives, possible co-sponsorship of a program with other interested organizations, and a variety of methods of communicating not only with parents but with strategic persons and organizations who have contact with parents. Conclusions from the study stressed the importance of having programs led by well selected personnel trained in group leadership, who could set up an expectation of a sound professional program, since this, in turn, would attract more parents. Both the general conclusions and the specific recommendations have been used extensively in other projects.

Daniels' Study of a Parent Education Group [14]

This was an empirical study of a parent education discussion group of fathers and mothers of preschool-age children held at the Child Study Association of America. Its purpose was to determine, if possible, the attitudes of these parents toward major areas of child-rearing practices and how much and in what ways these attitudes were changed by an experience of group education. The methods used included a questionnaire given at the beginning of the group sessions, the use of the leaders' records and impressions, and a personal interview by the investigator with each parent at the close of the series of meetings. Admittedly based on the

[14] Ada M. Daniels, "A Study of a Parent Education Discussion Group," submitted in partial fulfillment of the requirements of the degree of Master of Science in Education, Bank Street College of Education, 1957.

experience of only a small group of parents, with no control group, and using instruments prepared for this study together with subjective material given in personal interviews, the conclusions were only suggestive. The investigator's familiarity with the purposes of parent group education led her, however, to raise questions about the nature of the group experience in relation to educational goals that were provocative and called for further study.

Westport-Weston (Connecticut) Mental Health Association Evaluation Study of a Parent Discussion Group [15]

This study conducted in 1957–1958 was a joint project of the Child Study Association of America and the Westport-Weston Mental Health Association. The objectives of the project were twofold: (1) to offer the parents of Fairfield County a sound group educational program, and (2) to plan and execute an evaluation study which met high social science research standards in order to ascertain whether or not parent education discussion groups do effect changes in the attitudes of parents toward child-rearing.

The program was described as one in which parents would discuss the common problems they met in their day-to-day experiences with their children. They would explore these concerns, sharing their ideas, experiences, and feelings about them, and thus be helped, with the guidance of the group leader, to gain a better understanding of their children and their relationships to them. The program was clearly presented to parents as a group educational experience in which the leader would help them to develop their own curriculum. It was based on the general procedures of parent group education as defined by the Child Study Association of America; the leader was a psychologist who had participated in one of the Association's training programs.

The design of the study was based on the immediate establishment of an experimental and a control group from the total number of parents who expressed a wish to attend. From the outset, it was explained that not all of them would participate in the first group; those who could not be accommodated in the first group were promised a group the following season. A number of instruments were administered to the parents in both the experimental group and the control group before the parent education program began; the same instruments were administered again to both groups after its completion. It is interesting to note that when those parents who made up the control group were contacted later to participate

[15] "Evaluation Study of a Parent Discussion Group," Child Study Association of America and Westport-Weston Mental Health Association (December 1959). (unpublished report)

in a group, a number had moved away and others were no longer interested. The second group therefore did not materialize.

All parents who registered for the program were asked to attend an orientation meeting and at this time to fill out the preprogram questionnaire forms. The parents were assigned by random selection, sixteen to the parent discussion group (experimental group) and twelve to a waiting list for a parent discussion group to be held at a later date (these parents comprised the control group). The parents were individually informed of their respective assignments after they filled out the pre-questionnaires. All the parents were again assembled (experimental and control) after the parent education program ended, to fill out the post-questionnaire. It was felt that this plan was significant in that, in this instance, the control group was made up of parents who had applied for membership in the group and were assigned to the control group on a random basis. Both the experimental and control subjects were self-selected and therefore seemed to be equally motivated.

The instruments used in this study represented an unusually wide range of criterion variables pertaining to changes in the parents' problem-solving and decision-making skills. A number of standard attitude and information inventories were also used, including several that had been used in earlier evaluation projects conducted in connection with the Child Study Association.

The overall analysis of the findings in terms of the group as a whole indicated that the parent discussion group failed to exert any statistically significant influence on the characteristics of parent decision-making or on a variety of other personal and social characteristics of these participating parents. There was evidence of change in certain members of the group on selected variables examined in the instruments, noticeably, in connection with the decision-making process, but the analysis indicated that the amount and direction of change on the dependent variables were unrelated to the personality characteristics that were measured in this study.

Here again the results consistently indicated an absence of change in the variety of measures used, but the meaning of these findings is not at all clear-cut. First, it may mean that parent discussion groups are not successful in effecting change. (Since the experimental and control groups were matched in that they both chose to participate, it may be that the *motivation to change* was the significant factor for both groups, regardless of the group discussion experience.) Second, parent education groups may result in change but not on the variables which were included in this study. Third, even though some changes may have occurred, the statistical tests were not sufficiently powerful to detect these changes, due to the small size of the sample. And, finally, the post-tests may have been administered too soon, before the parent-members had a chance truly to absorb the content of the discussions and translate them into their every-day practices.

Although here too the results were inconclusive, the project exemplifies a high level of competence in evaluation research in parent education. The research design in itself seemed to have set a new standard, and it could profitably be developed in projects that cover a wider population range.

Ambrosino's Study of Participation in Parent Group Education [16]

This study was concerned with the nature and patterning of active participation of parents in discussion groups throughout series of meetings. Its purpose was to determine whether parent groups follow patterns of interaction generally considered desirable by practitioners of the discussion group method. The investigator reviewed some of the assumptions about the significance for learning of active participation by members, but the study did not attempt to test these assumptions. Rather, it concentrated on the patterns of participation that occurred in nine discussion groups meeting at the Child Study Association of America. The data were gathered by recorders who followed a set procedure and whose results were checked against tape recordings for scoring consistency and reliability.

In general, the findings confirmed certain hypotheses gathered from small group theory: that the average frequencies of participation of the members increased during the series, for example, and that participation of individual members was distributed more equally in the end meetings. It was also found that the initially high and low participants maintained similar rank position (in the order of distribution of frequencies) over the series of meetings, but the "lows" increased their frequencies at a greater rate than the "highs" and thus closed the gap between them. On the other hand, the curve of distribution of participation in these parent groups seemed to have a definite characteristic that was different from that of other small discussion groups, in that here the participation was more evenly divided. This would suggest that skilled leadership may have a favorable effect in encouraging the participation of all the group members on a more equitable basis. This would also suggest that as the parents interact in discussing their common concerns, they may implicitly create a set of rules for one another that are different from those set up in other types of groups and that seem to develop spontaneously out of the special purposes and procedures established in these parent groups. This study did not attempt to relate the rate of interaction to the learning progress of the parents but indicated that this is an important next step to be undertaken by evaluation research studies.

[16] Salvatore Ambrosino, "A Study of Participation in Parent Group Education," submitted in partial fulfillment of the requirements for the degree of Doctor of Education in Teachers College, Columbia University, 1960.

A STUDY THAT EXAMINED BOTH THE EFFECTIVENESS OF
TRAINING PROGRAMS IN PARENT GROUP LEADERSHIP
AND THE IMPACT OF THE GROUP EXPERIENCE
ON THE PARENT-MEMBERS

The Child Study Association of America-Family Service Association of America program of training begun in 1963 has already been described in terms of its historical development and purposes (see Chapter XIV). The evaluative study connected with it had three purposes: to explore (1) the effect of the training program on the trainees (in this case, social workers from Family Service agencies); (2) changes in the parents who attended groups led by the trainees; and (3) the impact of the program on the family agencies themselves. Thus by directing itself to the first two areas within one and the same project, the evaluation gave recognition, though only by implication, that they were both theoretically important and related. The third area was also important and related to the success or failure of the other two, but it had more pragmatic than theoretical implications.

The various foci meant that the study examined many areas of response to the project and became of necessity somewhat scattered and limited. To quote from the final report:

"It should be noted in this connection that it was not the intention of this project to undertake a formal evaluation of pragmatic effectiveness. Such an evaluation would have required control groups and a degree of precision in the manipulation of the program that did not seem feasible. Thus no claim can be made to have scientifically proven the efficacy of the approach. Such a test must await a further study. It would, in fact, seem highly desirable to undertake such a study in view of the apparent success of the program. But since that was not the intention of the project, it is not fair to expect from it what it was not intended to produce.

"A related issue which needs to be mentioned concerns the research strategy that was pursued. The complexity of the operation and its developmental quality made it appropriate to use extensive questionnaire material with heavy reliance on open-ended statements in order to elicit full expressions of reactions and opinions. These kinds of data were suitable for answering the general questions that were at issue. However, they did not lend themselves to more precise comparison. . . ."

Within these limitations, however, the study developed interesting and significant instruments which produced findings valuable for the practical purposes for which the project was set up, and it suggested interesting correlations between various parts of the program.

Effect of the Training Program on the Trainees

The trainees were the object of extensive studies, including several sets of self-ratings, ratings made by the trainers and the trainees' agency supervisors, a background information form, a personality test which was the product of a considerable amount of research in personality assessment and measurement and which condensed into a concentrated instrument items that had been found valuable in four well-established and well-designed personality scales, coordinated here into one. Use was also made of the Parental Attitude Research Instrument (PARI). The questionnaire on techniques of leadership designed to measure the adequacy of leadership behavior in parent groups, which had been used extensively in previous programs, was found here not to be sufficiently discriminating to warrant its continued use. The use of these instruments did not pick up evidence of significant trainee change during the period of the first institute (the first three weeks of the program). As might have been expected, however, the material gathered after the training period was completed and practice groups ended, was more positive, although not definitely conclusive.

These findings were supported by the leaders' reports of their own reactions after they had put the theoretical concepts into practice in leading their parent groups. At the conclusion of each year of training activity, the three groups most closely associated with the project—the trainees, the trainers, and the agency administrators—were questioned about its outcome and asked to give their evaluation of its worth. These responses represented a reaction to the total project and its long-range impact, rather than, as in other material, its short-term aspects. The findings indicated that the demonstration program was successful in terms of its stated goals.

It is interesting to note that the trainees who had the highest final rating, both by the agency supervisors and in their own self-ratings, tended to have changed the least during the training process. This finding highlights a basic dilemma in the selection of candidates for such programs. As questioned in the final report, would it be better to look for persons of superior ability who will not be influenced to any great extent by the training program but who can become more effective workers as a result of it? Or should persons be selected for training who come with lesser accomplishments but who may be more amenable to change? In other words, is the purpose of such a program to prepare initially superior trainees to do this kind of work, or is it rather to select those on whom the program might have the greatest influence? These are some of the questions that pose difficult decisions for administrators in future projects.

The Effect of the Group Discussion Experience on the Parent Members

Information about the parents and their reactions to the parent discussion group experience was gained through two sets of instruments. The first was a detailed background questionnaire which gave information as to race, parental status, job activity, ages of the parents, their educational level, religion, number and age of the children, and previous attendance in parent groups or previous use of any similar services. Some 1600 parents took part in the groups studied in this project, approximately 83% of whom had never had any experiecence at all in a parent education group. Approximately 1100 had never availed themselves of any services of either a family agency or a mental health agency. Between 400 and 500 parents fell into the category of "low-income." The impression gained from these statistics was that the parents who came to the program covered a broad range of background and educational experiences and suggested the possibility that the implications of this project might apply to a wide population.

A second body of material was gathered on standardized forms given to the group members at the last group session, asking them to evaluate the effects which they thought the parent group meetings had had on them; a similar form was filled out by each trainee-leader concerning all the group members individually. In this way, two separate estimates were procured regarding each parent.

These data suggest the following conclusions: First, both the parent group members in rating themselves and the trainees in rating the parent group method felt the experience was more than moderately helpful in increasing their knowledge about, attitude toward, and behavior related to parent-child relations and also their self-understanding. Second, the parents were slightly more positive in their reaction to the experience than the trainees thought they were, the trainees thus showing a more conservative bias. Finally, there was a reasonable rank ordering in both trainee and group member ratings on the variables that were evaluated: in the judgment of both, most improvement was experienced in relation to new knowledge and least in terms of new behavior, as might have been predicted. A further analysis of three groups made up exclusively of low-income members and compared with all the groups on eight specific ratings showed, somewhat surprisingly, that all the low-income groups evidenced greater change on all variables than the total sample of the study. This finding seemed to indicate that when such groups are formed they are unusually successful, although the previous data on recruitment had indicated that such groups are inherently more difficult to form.

The Effect of the Parent Group Discussion Programs on the Agency and the Community

Information was gathered from a variety of sources as to (1) its general effectiveness, and (2) its specific outreach into the community. Information was gathered from trainees, trainers, and agency administrators, all of whom seemed in general to agree that the programs had enabled the agency to reach new groups of clients, had given the agency unusual publicity, and had helped it to provide needed preventive services on a wider basis. On the whole, the administrators felt that the project had been helpful in fostering the trainees' professional growth as well as increasing their contributions to the agencies' programs. In general, the information gained from the three different sources seemed to confirm the impression that the program helped the agencies realize a number of goals which they held to be relevant and important in the nature of their own community task, made a positive contribution to the skill and effectiveness of the workers in various parts of their work as well as in group leadership, and reached out profitably into the lives of many of the families in their community.

PROJECT ENABLE

As described in the previous chapter, the FSAA-CSAA project in parent group education was followed by the larger Project ENABLE, developed jointly by the Family Service Association of America, the Child Study Association of America, and the National Urban League. Begun in the fall of 1965, it was planned to have the results evaluated by an independent research agency, working closely with a project research staff selected by the three sponsoring organizations and the Office of Economic Opportunity. The research study was directed to an evaluation on a wider scale of the last two aspects explored in the FSAA-CSAA project: (1) changes in the parents' behavior and attitudes as a result of their participation in the program, and (2) the impact of the project on the agencies which sponsored the parent group in terms of institutional change. Study was also made of the characteristics of those parents who attended the program as compared with the characteristics of those who had the opportunity to participate but did not take advantage of it; also, of the characteristics of those who continued as members of the group as compared with those who dropped out before the series of meetings was completed. The research was also concerned with factors operating at the level of the group and of the individual that affected the achievement of the goals of the Project. Upon completion, the results of the research study will be obtainable from the sponsoring agencies.

No attempt was made to evaluate the effect of the training itself on the group leaders and members of the local project teams and to correlate the results with changes in the parents. This, then, remains to be done. It would be a vast, complex procedure but it is essential if the many different parts of the parent education process reported in this chapter are ultimately to be tied together and evaluative research in parent education is to reach a new level of significance.

Appendix I

Suggested Outline for Registration Interview for Enrollment in Parent Groups*

The following material has been worked out as a basis for personal or phone registration interviews for applicants to CSAA Parent Groups:

1. Content of Interview
   a. Parent's knowledge of group
      1. How did he learn of the group?
      2. What does he know of its method, content and goals?
      3. Has he had any previous exeprience in groups here or elsewhere? Of what nature and with what response?
   b. Parent's expectation of CSAA group
   c. Brief clarification of method (*discussion as distinct from lecture*), and realistic goals, including extent to which individual's specific problems can be explored
2. Criteria for Acceptance of Group Member
   a. Acceptable
      1. Those wanting an opportunity to share their experiences with other parents to get a better understanding of their children and themselves in relation to their children.
      2. Those who indicate some problem in parent or child that may be helped by an educational experience and is suitable to the goals of the program and the needs of the group.
      3. Those who indicate some problems which suggest the need for counseling, but who for a variety of reasons want a group experience, either in addition to counseling or until they come to see more clearly their need for counseling. In the meantime, they accept the goals and methods of the program even though they are aware that it may only partially help them with their problems.
   b. Refer to other services
      1. Those who have a specific acute or long-standing problem that

* Child Study Association of America, New York.

257

seems to need exploration in individual interviews and/or a different type of service.

2. Those with an adult problem that is apparent (even in this brief contact) and that seems likely to interfere with the functioning of the group.

3. If indicated, those who do not accept the goals or methods of the program.

Appendix II

Excerpts from Group Records: First Meetings

1. Parent Discussion Group in a Day Care Center
2. Discussion Group for Parents of Children Two through Four
3. Discussion Group for Expectant Mothers
4. Discussion Group for Parents of Preschool Cerebral Palsied Children

These reports are from records of continuous series of discussion meetings conducted by leaders who were staff members or trainees participating in leadership training programs conducted by the Child Study Association of America. These records are the leaders' own narrative accounts of the meetings. They have been selected to demonstrate many aspects of leadership and indicate the kinds of questions that parents and expectant parents are likely to bring up in groups of different kinds. Identities of the group members have been disguised for purposes of confidentiality.

These reports are not given here as "perfect" examples of leadership, since no leader's skills are ever perfect—least of all in his own view. We suggest that readers go over these records carefully and try to put themselves in the leader's place to see whether they would have met the leadership problems as these leaders did—or differently.

Record 1
PARENT DISCUSSION GROUP—DAY-CARE CENTER

Session I

This day-care center is located in a public housing project in a large city. During the summer, I had met with the director to discuss the possibility of having a series of parent discussion group meetings at the center in the fall. I interpreted to her the discussion group approach, the sharing of interests and concerns on the part of the parents, and the role of the leader in the discussion. We talked of other discussion groups that had been held in the center in the past, but which had been on a much more didactic level. She felt this could be a valuable experience in the nursery and it was decided that the group would be chosen from among children who would enter first grade in the neighboring public school and who would be in the after school program at the center.

It was felt that since the center is open until 6 P.M., remaining open later one evening a week could be worked out. We predicted that since so many mothers worked, we could not really start the meetings much before 5:30 and planned to end at 7. We talked of arrangements for extending care of the children, with a snack, and the director felt this could be worked out on an alternating basis with her own staff.

The director and I planned a flyer to be given to parents as they called for their children, she and the teachers to provide additional interpretation in order to recruit members for the group.

Total registration at the time of the first meeting was seventeen mothers, although both parents were asked to join. The director explained when I arrived that there would be some absences due to illness of children or parents or overtime work. Some parents who had registered would begin next week. Attendance at the first session was eleven; eight mothers were there when we started at 5:40 and three more arrived during the meeting.

As the mothers came into the lounge and were introduced to me by the director, I gave them large place cards which had on them their names and the names and ages of their children. The response to having the cards prepared in advance was noticeably warm, each mother pleased when she saw her own name and her children's names. I began the meeting by stating my name to the group, identifying myself as a social worker interested in getting together with parents for a series of meetings in order to talk over things that are going on in the family, with the children, in the neighborhood and the school—anything that could help us to figure out how we can have a good family life and help the children to grow up so that they, too, can look forward to a good family life. I commented that each mother here has a child who has just entered the first grade and that together we will be talking about how the kids are doing, how the parents and the rest of the family are doing now that this big step is here (laughter). I commented that we would not necessarily need to talk about the first graders, but could expand, each mother as she wished, into other areas of interest or concern that had to do with family life in general.

I indicated that I would try to keep the discussion in one place at a time, with one interest or concern, in order to keep us from jumping all over the place. I mentioned that we find that if we stay with something instead of rushing, we can come up with more ideas from everyone in the group about how to manage, and how our feelings as parents affect the children and vice versa. I would be adding information where it might be helpful, and I would also try to point out where we are in the discussion so that we could figure out where we want to go with other important ideas related to improving things in our families. I talked of taking notes for my own use, so that I could review what we had been talking about and help the group decide where to move on. I mentioned that our talks would be confidential as far as each individual mother and her family situation is concerned. I would be having a couple of meetings with center and school staff in order to learn from them how things seem to be going on a general level with the children and to share with them in general what we are seeing here as meaningful now that the children are in school a few months. Maybe we could get some ideas about how school and center can learn from our discussion, and how the teachers of the school and the center can work more closely with the parents in order to help towards better family life, good school experiences, and good neighborhood experiences.

With this, I turned to my left and suggested we start with Mrs. Otero, who might tell us what is going on with Myra or the rest of the family—anything that she feels she would particularly like to talk about here in the group.

Mrs. Otero is a fair, pleasant Puerto Rican woman who has three children: Myra, 6; Ariel, 8; Gabriel, 2½. She said that when Ariel, a boy, started school he wasn't after her every minute with questions, but Myra never stops. Most of Myra's questions are about the teacher, a young woman, and Mrs. Otero finds it hard because she just can't answer the questions: Is she married, where does she live, does she have any children, etc. Myra is so excited about school that she doesn't stop talking about it.

Mrs. Ball, a young Negro woman, said she was Manuel's cousin, that everything was OK. Manuel is very curious about school, learning all about Lincoln, etc. Mrs. Ball said nothing else for the duration of the meeting. (I learned later she came in Manuel's mother's place because she had to work late.)

Mrs. White is a dark, heavy set Puerto Rican woman, with two daughters: Elaine, 6, and Diana, 7. She is concerned because Elaine whimpers practically every morning about going to school, wants to go to the nursery instead. Mother gave her a penny once, and now Elaine feels she has to be bribed with a penny or a nickel each morning to go to school. Mother refuses, convinced that "it is wrong." I wondered if Elaine had said why she didn't want to go to school, and mother said the teacher screams. Elaine is frightened when the teacher screams, and mother tries to tell her it's a good class and the teacher has nothing against Elaine. The group laughed when mother said she herself screams on occasion, but that's different because Elaine knows mother loves her even when she loses her temper. Also, mother is concerned about Elaine's refusing to accept her help in learning to write. Elaine insists that in school they just print, they don't write, and she wants to do what they do in school. Some of the mothers started to reassure Mrs. White, indicating that children are taught to print so that they will not be confused over learning to read. Mrs. White said she had never thought of that before and it seems so simple. I indicated we could go into that and other questions about school which the group might have.

Mrs. Castero is a tall, fair Puerto Rican woman with three children: Julio, 6, Sylvia, 7, and Kim, 4. She is concerned because Julio forgets things every day. She calls for him and has to remind him that he doesn't have his cap, his jacket, his pencil case, etc. Nothing like this ever came up until he started school and she is annoyed because she thinks he is old enough to remember to bring his clothing and homework without her checking on everything.

Mrs. Gonzalez is a slight Puerto Rican woman whose children are Antonio, 6, and Ricardo, 7½. She said quite poignantly that Antonio misses his nap, that he is so tired at night she is worried about homework in the future. So far he hasn't had much to speak of. He wasn't too happy about school at the beginning, but now he goes willingly. I asked if they have a rest when they come to the center and the group jumped in to say no, that they go out to the playground as soon as they put their books down. There was some questioning around Antonio's not having had homework, one mother saying that her child has a great deal and I indicated that I would also list this as an area we would want to go into.

Mrs. Rodriguez is a very young Puerto Rican woman with one child, Raymond. He loves school but comes home filthy. Raymond is very restless, likes to play rough, is crazy about the center. Mrs. Rodriguez indicated Raymond was only at the center one year before entering public school; before that he went to a Catholic nursery where the sisters were very strict. She thinks he is reacting to his new-found freedom but is worried that he'll never settle down to do any work. He just goes and goes "flying." I commented that it sounded as though Raymond was kind of like a bird out of a cage and she nodded emphatically, adding that it was more like his being released from prison when he left the Sisters. There was sympathetic laughter from the group. Mrs. Castero said that her son suggests that she send Gabriel, 2½, to the Sisters to be straightened out (general laughter). (Father is out of the home; Mrs. R. lives with her mother.)

Mrs. Torres is a plump, personable Puerto Rican woman, whose frequent sighs and "Dios Mios!" are most endearing to the group. Her children are Jose, 6, Odette, 9, and Jeanette, 4. She brought the house down when she announced that Jose has the world's record: he played hookey the second week of school. She was home from work, ill, and a neighbor told her that Jose was in the project playground kicking a ball around. She sent for him and slapped him twice. He had no idea his mother was at home and was pretty surprised. Mother told him he was never to skip school again, sent him on with a note. He said very feebly he was late but then indicated he hated school, hated the teacher, wished he didn't have to get older. Mrs. Torres said that Jose had a very hard time getting adjusted, but he is doing much better now. She wants to be sure, because she works, that the teacher is aware if he is not in school and has set up a communication system with her. (Father is out of the home.)

Mrs. DeJesus was bundled up in slacks, a heavy sweater, and a winter coat, even though it was quite warm in the staff lounge where the meeting was held. She was the only member who was shy about English and who had trouble finding words. I indicated, haltingly, that I did speak Spanish although I was much less fluent than I should be. This seemed to encourage her to continue in English (perhaps she couldn't understand my Spanish!). Mrs. DeJesus has three children: Brenda, 6, Nestor, 7, and Elizabeth, 5. Mrs. DeJesus said that Brenda is already having a hard time with homework, seems not to understand what the teacher expects, and Mrs. DeJesus finds it frustrating to try to help figure out what the assignment is. (Father is out of the home.)

Mrs. Scott had arrived late, so I returned to her at this point. She is a very fair, young Negro woman more elegantly dressed than the others, with three children: Nina, 6, Margret, 5, and Kevyn, 4. Mrs. Scott created a kind of aura of antagonism in the rest of the group when she said that Nina was much happier in school now than she was the first two weeks because she had known how to read since she was two and she was placed in a class much more related to her capacity. You could almost see the back hair of the group go up as they exchanged looks. Mrs. Scott told the teacher how bored Nina was, and that it was probably because of the elementary material the class as a whole was getting. She commented on how cooperative the teacher was in informally testing Nina and then placing her in the top first grade group. Mrs. Scott said she had nothing else to offer this time since everything was going extraordinarily well with her children. Margret, 5, is in the Day-Care Center kindergarten and Kevyn, 4, goes to a nursery school. (Mrs. Scott is a widow.)

Mrs. Shaw, a very slender, Negro woman in a white uniform, also arrived late and suggested we not stop for her, that she would join in later. She has one child, Gerald, 6.

Mrs. Andrew, a heavy, fatigued Negro woman, mentioned that her biggest problem was that all of her children had a lot to say, many questions, and she is so tired when she comes home from work she just isn't up to it. Her children are Irene, 6, John, 11, Livingston, 10, Thomas, 9.

I said that they had mentioned a few things that they and the children were experiencing and some of them seemed to tie in together. What the group seems to be saying is that now that the kids have made it into the first grade from all their years in the nursery, there are many changes going on: some children can't stop talking about school, others are not too thrilled about it, some of the children can take it, and others would just as soon leave it alone and return to the Day-Care Centers where teachers don't yell, there's no homework, you have a nap every day, the class is smaller, and there's so much playing. At the same time, the mothers seem to be saying that there's quite a reaction in them about their children going to public school, concerns around homework, keeping the children clean, answering their questions, making sure they have what they need when they go to school and leave school, making sure they *get to school*. As the blue announcement said, it would seem the first grade is a big step for everyone.

I indicated we could talk about all of these areas, but that it occurred to me that mostly the parents seemed to be very much at ease, even though their children were making a big change and they were making a big change, also. At this point Mrs. Shaw, one of the latecomers, said that she didn't think that things were going that well. She realized that everybody has to get used to a new situation, but she's not sure she can get used to one particular situation. I asked her what it was and she talked of lunch time at school. The lunch hour is from 11:50 to 12:50. The children are out in about 10 minutes. Since 300 children or so need to be fed during that one hour, they're rushed out into the project playground. There is construction of a new part of the school going on so no playground at this time is attached to the school and they're left pretty much on their own. The group began to talk at once, with much nodding and much sighing. Recognizing that this was a neighborhood problem that might have particular importance for this group of working mothers, in relationship to the difference this year in protection for their children when contrasted with the few years the children were in the center all day, I went on to pursue with the group what the situation was.

What did the mothers mean by inadequate supervision? Here, each mother contributed to the pool of information about the particular situation. There is one teacher aide provided to supervise about 300 first-grade children. Since this is impossible for any one person to do, the children are left pretty much to their own devices, free to wander in the project grounds, out onto main avenues, and into the project buildings to loiter in hallways and in the elevators. After quite a good deal of exploration of what actually exists in the lunchtime situation, I began to explore with the group what concerns them about this lunch period as far as their children were concerned. I commented that one mother said that her child was like a bird out of a cage, and I wondered what there was about this "freedom" that they saw as worrisome. I did have to exert some firmness, smiling firmness, in order to have each mother speak and be heard. Mrs. Otero said that her neighbor had told her that Myra was going up and down in the elevator and she had had to tell Myra that this was not a good thing to do since Housing would be after her. I asked if Myra had used the elevator freely in the past. Mrs. Otero said that she had never permitted Myra to use the elevator alone, that she always takes her to the center or to school. What was the concern about the elevator? At this point the group laughed, as though to say that I seemed to be putting them on, as though to say that I really knew what the problems were. I commented on this, saying that I knew there were many problems in city living and in crowded areas, whereupon Mrs. White interrupted me by saying that it's kind of hard to talk about things like that. Mrs. Scott said that she wasn't afraid to comment that there are perverts in the area who can molest children. After she had said this, others joined in with their fears for the safety of their children with regard to something happening to the elevator, the possibility of sexual molestation, the fear of narcotics addicts approaching the children.

During the course of the discussion, we also explored what a pressure this thing could be for the working mothers who were a distance away. One mother commented that Mrs. Castero is lucky, since she works nearby and comes to be with her child at lunch hour. Mrs. Castero said that was all very well but she wished she didn't have to do it. Another mother suggested that Mrs. Castero had older children who could look after the younger ones, and she wished this was her situation. Mrs. Castero very vehemently stated that she would never do this to her children.

At this point there was a discussion of how the mothers, some of them, felt they must interrupt a pattern of having brought up siblings to take care of the younger ones (as many of them have, in fact) in order that their children approach maturity and family life with a little more enthusiasm and less anger. At this point I posed the question of judgment of 8 or 9-year-olds to cope with 6-year-olds. How did they feel about the ability of young children to care for slightly younger children? This led to an exploration of what they were expecting children to do who were not yet able to care for themselves. What emerged was that the mothers were worried about *all* their children at lunch time.

At one point, I asked Mrs. Otero if she had involved Ariel, 8, to help care for Myra, 6, when she was concerned about Myra's going up and down in the elevator at lunch time. Mrs. Otero said that she had enough problems with Ariel, who was very proud when 10- and 11-year-old boys asked him to cross the street or go behind the nursery kitchen. One of the other mothers said that her 7-year-old daughter feels like a big shot when an older girl is interested in her. Many mothers gave similar examples, indicating that they could not depend on children so young to care for the first graders when they were trying to make a place for themselves.

At this juncture, I articulated for the group that their major concern about this change, then, seemed to be around the safety of these younger children and that perhaps underscored for them their ongoing concern about the safety of the others as well. There was much nodding here, with one mother speaking up about how sometimes they're able to do something to relieve the pressure. I picked up on the "pressure" and explored with the group the factor of particular worry working mothers had which related to their not being able to be on the spot. The mothers referred to the hour between 12:00 and 1:00 as the zero hour, some of them mentioning that they watch the clock and get a belly ache while they're eating lunch on the job, and how they sigh with relief if they haven't been called to the phone by 1:30. I picked up on what happens at 3:00 o'clock, whereupon we explored the pattern of the children's being called for, returned to the center to put their things down, and go out to play in the playground. The mothers expressed in a variety of ways how productive they could be from 3:00 to 5:00 because they knew the children were cared for.

I commented that this must be hard on the mothers and I wondered how the children were experiencing this. There were quite a few examples of how some of the kids were very fearful at lunchtime, staying close to the one teacher aide, some of them wandering over to the Day-Care Center, where they cannot be cared for since the after-school staff is not there at that time, others sitting on the curb. There was discussion regarding how a petition helped to have one block on a side street closed off. I asked if the children could mill around in the street, then, and many mothers spoke of how ridiculous the system was. The older children are released after lunch onto the side street; the first graders are released onto the avenue where they can go right out onto the open street. One mother said that it was almost like a plot, whereupon everyone laughed.

I picked up on this, from the point of view that it did seem kind of silly and I wondered if the parents had made inquiries. What emerged here was a good deal of feeling on the part of the group that when it came to deploying school personnel, this was a touchy issue in which parents could not involve themselves because of rejection and abruptness. We then began to talk of the possibility, if funds could be provided, for discussing with school administration hiring some of the local mothers who do not work to help with the children at noon. Mrs. Scott said that there seemed to be so much money from the government that she felt that maybe this could be done if the need were demonstrated. I wondered what went on at another school nearby and learned that there are six teacher aides for the children. They are escorted out and escorted back, always in the charge of a teacher aide. It was felt that probably it's up to the principal to decide about aides, and one of the mothers remembered that I said I would be talking with the school staff generally. I asked what in particular I should clarify on this and she suggested that maybe I could figure out how one school got six aides and another one. We all nodded and felt this would be a good area to explore.

We returned to the fears of some children and the new-found freedom of others and discussed, with several examples, how children could get into all sorts of situations because they simply didn't understand that they were dangerous. One mother said it was like the story of "wolf, wolf." She suggested that if you yell over everything, then the important things don't make any difference to the children. We discussed informing children of dangers as limit setting but were not able to take it beyond this since it was time to close the meeting (the maintenance man was knocking at the door). I summarized briefly for the group. Mrs. White commented that she had been so fascinated she forgot to leave at 6:00 o'clock and many of the mothers said that they looked forward to returning.

Record 2
DISCUSSION GROUP FOR PARENTS OF
CHILDREN TWO THROUGH FOUR

Session I

Seventeen of the mothers who had enrolled for this series came to the first meeting. Only two were absent. Eleven of them brought their children to the play group, one mother bringing two children. Only one mother mentioned to me that she had left her child home because she was ill. Several of the mothers whose children were not used to playing with others came early and stayed with them in the playroom. We were able to start with about ten mothers present by ten minutes past ten, all seated around a large table.

Each person was given a folded piece of cardboard on which to write her name and the names and ages of the children, and it was explained that this was to facilitate our getting acquainted with each other. I then opened the meeting by explaining briefly how a discussion group functioned, with the members sharing experiences and ideas, while my role as leader was to keep the discussion focused and to implement with information where this seemed needed. I mentioned also something about the play group, the fact that it might be difficult for some of the children to adjust to being in a strange environment without their mothers in a short time, and that it might be expected that some of the children might need them, in which case the people in charge would bring the child to them. (As it turned out, only Mrs. Gi.'s child had any difficulty, and she spent some time holding the child on her lap and some time in the play room with her.)

We then went around the room at my suggestion, each one saying what her major concerns were in coming to the group. At first go-around, Mrs. M. said that her child would be 3 in April, and she was expecting another child in September, so she was interested in talking about preparing the child for the coming of another one. Mrs. S., whose boy is 2, was concerned about his dependence on his pacifier and his bottle, and the fact that he struck out at other children more than she felt he should.

Mrs. A., with R., 2, was also concerned about his "aggressiveness," and certain problems around toilet-training—he preferred to play in the water in the sink, rather than sit on the toilet. (Laughter)

Mrs. Sch. (who had informed me before the meeting began that she had previously attended a group for adoptive parents) was concerned about K., 2½, who had been difficult ever since her baby brother, 8 months old, was born. The child was very preoccupied with the fact that the baby had a penis while she didn't, and though they had explained and reassured her, she had many problems which they associated with this concern and with sibling rivalry in general. Sleeping problems especially—she often had nightmares and woke her parents frequently.

Mrs. G., with a girl of 2, said laughingly that she had thought she had a sleeping problem until she just heard Mrs. Sch.; her child had a tendency to awaken several times in the night.

Mrs. O., with a girl, 2½, who had been in a previous discussion group, and who had not spoken much there about K.'s difficulties, now indicated that she was concerned about her "aggressiveness." She was greeted with laughter when she added that she feared for the life of the family dog.

Mrs. Sh., whose A. is 2 years old, indicated that she had "no major problems," toilet-training was not a concern because she had not really started it yet, but was concerned about his eating, as he often gagged on food or vomited.

Mrs. H., with C., 2½, was concerned about his "negativeness" and also about sibling rivalry.

Mrs. D., with K., 2 years and 8 months, had no real problems, but "many questions." Mrs. D. had also been in a previous group, where she had been a most active participant.

Mrs. C., with M., 3 years old, and J., 20 months, was concerned about sibling rivalry and how to handle it.

Mrs. Cr., with D., almost 3, who had also been in a previous group, said that she had no problems with D., but found it helpful to hear about what other children did; also, she had postponed having another baby because of her concern about what this might do to D., and her own uncertainties about handling two small children, and would be interested in hearing more about the considerations around this.

Mrs. K., with T., 4 years old, who had also been in a previous group, and who was now obviously pregnant, said she had "gotten so much out of the other group, she had come back for more."

Mrs. T., with A., 2½, is concerned about his toilet-training, as the toilet seems to frighten him. Also, he worries a great deal when she leaves him. She doesn't know whether this is due to the fact that his father is away a great deal, and he doesn't see much of him.

Mrs. K., with A., 2 years old, is also concerned about negative, aggressive behavior.

Mrs. L., with J., 2½, and a baby girl, is concerned about his toilet-training, as he will urinate, but will not do BM's, can withhold for 48 hours sometimes.

Mrs. G., with B., 2½, says he is very independent and very active, and she wonders about how to discipline him, when to encourage his independence, and when to be concerned about his disobedience. Would like to discuss discipline.

Mrs. Gi., who was the only mother who had to take her child on her lap during the meeting, drew a laugh with her statement that the child had difficulty leaving her, and she was concerned about toilet-training and, since she expects another baby, about how to handle this with the child.

After we had gone around, I indicated that there seemed to be a number of concerns which they held in common—chiefly questions about toilet-training, discipline, and aggressiveness. When I raised the question of where they would like to start, Mrs. M. added that there was one thing she would like to add which she had not mentioned, which was, "how much time do we have to give them?" She went on to say that she spent some time with the child in the mornings, the child helping her to dust and do other chores, so that they were constantly together. What troubled her was that the child would not play by herself in the afternoon so that, since the child did not nap, she had not a minute to herself. She wondered if she was expecting too much to expect the child to play by herself more.

Several people reacted to this statement immediately, saying that they had children who wanted to be with them constantly, and they had reacted in various ways. One mother said that she had finally "put her foot down," and when she had made up her mind to have the child play alone, had devised games for her, and had been very firm about only being willing to start her on these projects and then insisting that she proceed by herself.

Since they appeared to be launched on a discussion of this question now, I pointed out that a number of them seemed to be quite involved in this last matter that Mrs. M. had brought up. Did they want to start with this and leave the various matters that they had originally expressed a common interest in? There was general head-shaking to this, so I suggested that Mrs. M., who had brought it up, tell us what she was most concerned about with this. Mrs. M. went into considerably more detail about her day with her child and the group then reacted with a variety of questions and suggestions. Mrs. C., who has two children, M., 3, and J., 20 months, said that she felt that by the time the child was capable of some quiet activities by himself, around 2, he should be encouraged to do these things, even sitting at the mother's feet, but that "discipline had to begin somewhere" and the child must learn early that the mother was entitled to some life of her own, too. (Mrs. M. had indicated that she felt aggrieved because she liked to read, and felt the child should allow her time for this.) Mrs. K. indicated that it was very interesting to her, that a previous group of which she was a member had also found it necessary to talk about this subject before it could go on to other things; it was hard for all of them to be so cooped up with a 2-year-old, who was not much of a companion. She reiterated her own experience with T., her mounting irritation and resentment at being with him and at his beck and call constantly. She reached the point where she felt if she didn't have some interests and life of her own, that she would be a very poor mother, not enjoying her time with the child and just being angry. It was at this point that she began to reorganize her life so that she was not with the child all day, every day. She described the changes she had instituted, and felt that both she and T. had profited.

Other people talked about the trying times in their day, and how they handled them—raising here further questions about T.V. and how they allowed the children to watch programs that they really preferred them not to watch because they involved a lot of violence. When they got off on a sidetrack of the virtues and evils of television watching for small children (some of them saying it was educational, others foolish, etc.), I tried to help them look at when they felt comfortable about using the T.V. as a temporary diverter, so that they could get chores or some reading done, and when they began to feel guilty about this. On the whole, they agreed that most of them felt it was all right if the children watched the cartoons for a short time, but that they needed to think of other means to keep them amused during the difficult hours when they felt they could not give them undivided attention. They talked about colored pictures in magazines, large picture books; others contributed ideas about coloring macaronis and letting the child string them. They contributed, in fact, a number of interesting and imaginative ways of helping a young child get started on an activity which he was capable of carrying through and getting some satisfaction from doing.

Several of them expressed the belief that it was helpful to them and to the children to have carefully adhered to routines. Mrs. K. particularly felt that it was important for children to "know what was expected of them," and that to have their lives routinized helped. Others felt this was fine, if the pressure of adhering to such a routine didn't "get one down."

At one point in the discussion, Mrs. S. brought in the question of whether one should allow a child to have a bottle or a pacifier to comfort him during the periods of stress in the course of a day. A number of people then related their own experiences; further questions elicited the information that the group felt that this problem related to Mrs. M.'s original question of, "just how much do we give in to them?"

After further discussion, I was able to point up that they were really saying that they were seeking a kind of balance in all the various aspects of handling the children, which would take into account the children's growing desire in some areas to express their *own* ideas and needs and still feel they were keeping them within bounds that were acceptable to themselves. This is what we would be looking at in a variety of ways as the sessions progressed.

Note: For another first meeting of a parents' group, see opening session of the extended record of a group for parents of elementary school age children, Appendix III, Record 2.

Record 3
DISCUSSION GROUP FOR EXPECTANT MOTHERS

Session I

Prior to the start of the discussion group today the mothers paid their fee, presented their doctors' written permission, and were given fifteen minutes of exercises.

At the beginning of the class I asked them to fill out registration cards and their name tags. As they finished, I welcomed them to the class and told them when we would meet, the hours, and the number of weeks. I introduced myself by name and as an R.N. and explained the class by telling them that in our discussion during these eight weeks we would be covering information concerning pregnancy, labor, delivery, postpartum, and care of the baby. I stated that the subjects for our discussion would be what they wanted to discuss: how to care for their baby at home, how to know when they are in labor, what they might be feeling, and what to know about any phase of this new experience. Then I explained my role, told them where the bathroom and drinking fountain were, told them there would be a co-worker visiting next week, and explained my reason for note-taking. I stated that since we would discuss the subjects the group wanted to discuss, I would jot these subjects down as we went along and then would have a record of them.

At my suggestion the go-around began. (There were nine of the ten expected women there. One had written a card saying she would be out of town but would be there next week. All had stated that this was their first baby.) Mrs. N. stated she would like just anything. When asked if she could explain more, she repeated, "Just anything. This is a new experience for me." Mrs. H. stated she would like to know about the baby and caring for the baby—also what to bring to the hospital for the baby. Mrs. B. stated she'd like to know what goes on in labor and the delivery room. Mrs. DiC. said she'd like to know what baby supplies they'll need the first few months. Mrs. M. said she'd like to discuss breast feeding and bottle feeding, the pros and cons. Mrs. C. said she didn't know—anything was fine with her. Mrs. W. asked to discuss the difference between labor pains and gas pains and how to know when to go to the hospital. Mrs. S. stated she would like to know how to care for the baby and how to make the father feel included during the pregnancy. Mrs. E. said she'd like to know how to care for herself now.

At the end of the go-around I restated that we would try to cover all of these subjects and asked what they'd like to talk about today. Mrs. W. stated, "Let's start at the beginning [classic phrase!] where we are now, I mean, pregnant." I asked if there were any other suggestions. Mrs. W. spoke again, saying, "Let's talk about what Mrs. S. said—I mean how can we help our husbands feel more a part, feel more included." At this point several women chimed in with their husbands' responses to their pregnancy. Mrs. N. said her husband was afraid to let her do anything. Mrs. S. said her husband didn't seem to feel like he was experiencing this, too. Mrs. E. said she found it helpful to refer to the baby as "our" baby and this helped. Mrs. H. said her husband was overseas and hadn't seen her since she showed, so she kept him up-to-date with letters. I suggested that it sounded as if they were concerned with their husbands feeling a part of this pregnancy experience and their (the husbands') responses to the wives' pregnancy. I asked if this was the subject they'd like to discuss today. Several people shook their heads.

Mrs. W. stated her husband wasn't pregnant, she was, and she hadn't felt any changes except gaining weight. She had never been sick at all since she became pregnant. Mrs. C. stated softly that she had been sick the entire time and still was. Mrs. H. chimed in with how sick she had been and she felt her husband got sick of her being sick. I asked how they felt nausea or morning sickness was related to their husbands' responses to their pregnancy. Mrs. H. said if you're sick he knows you're pregnant and can help you. Mrs. S. said her husband kept asking her how she felt and she felt fine. Mrs.E. said she hated to complain and tell him each little ache and change. She felt like she would always be complaining. Mrs. W. said her husband expected her to do all sorts of things and has even suggested a power mower so she could continue mowing the lawn. Mrs. N. said she wished her husband would not be so protecting of her. She said he wouldn't even let her wash the dishes and she believed he'd be happiest if she stayed in bed all the time. Mrs. H. said each man and wife was an individual and each pregnancy was different so everyone might respond differently each time.

I asked if any of their husbands had stated how he felt about this individual experience. Mrs. B. shook her head slowly and said the fellows at work had been talking to her husband and telling him things would be different. I asked if she could tell us what they had been telling him. She said they had told him he would be getting up at night and spending his Saturdays and Sundays playing or walking with the baby. Mrs. W. interrupted saying that things *would* be different; after all, he won't be the only one she would be taking care of. She added that supper wouldn't always be on time as it is now. Mrs. B. returned with a statement of how she felt this wasn't necessarily so. She said all you have to do is organize things. Mrs. H. said it depended upon how you wanted to feed the baby— by demand or by schedule. She went on to say different doctors recommended different ways and each person had to decide the best way for them. Mrs. B. said she told her husband it would be just the same except that they'd have a baby. Mrs. W. stated she didn't feel that way. She felt it would be different and they'd all have to get used to the change.

The discussion went on in this vein, with several members bringing in the variables that could cause their husbands to feel concern about this pregnancy experience. Added expense, their wife no longer working, the age of the husband (one was 36 years old), the change in living, the added responsibility, the lack of knowledge, and their lack of involvement in office visits and parents classes were mentioned.

I asked if they had heard of any ways or had tried any ways that were helpful to their husbands. Mrs. N. said she felt it was important to have her husband feel the baby when it moved. Mrs. J. said that some doctors welcomed the husbands in the office but it depended upon the doctor and the husband. Mrs. S. said she felt you should let your husband know about what you are feeling. Mrs. W. interrupted, saying she cried so frequently and her husband didn't understand why she was crying. I asked if any of them had the same experience. Two spoke, saying they had. Mrs. H. said she had read all about it and the books all said this depression happened in pregnancy at various times. Mrs. N. said sometimes she felt so unattractive—she felt like a slob. She said when she and her husband were out she watched him to see if he looked at the pretty girls as they passed. Mrs. H. said sometimes she felt that way but she remembered how glad she was to be pregnant and how much she wanted a baby. I asked if they felt their appearance had an effect on their husbands' response to the pregnancy. Mrs. N. said she felt her husband felt he had proved his manhood. Mrs. W. said her husband acted like he had a rose on his chest. Several women smiled and nodded or laughed and repeated that he felt like a man.

During the discussion I underscored the universality of their feelings—their husbands' and theirs. I also underscored the individuality of responses and of overt involvement of their husbands in the pregnancy experience. Then someone suggested that a film showing the birth of a baby might help the father's knowledge of the experience. Mrs. W. polled the group to see if their husbands might be interested in seeing the film after I asked if anyone else thought this might help the husbands. About half said their husbands wanted to see a film on normal delivery and about half said no. Mrs. B. said her husband would think it was "icky." I asked her to explain "icky" and she stated that her husband couldn't bear to see her have pain and the film might frighten him. Mrs. M. said some men might have seen it before or not be interested in seeing it. I stated that the variations in feelings they were experiencing and that their husbands were experiencing were common among parents.

We ended with a summary of what they had said. I stated that they had discussed how their husbands could feel more included in the pregnancy experience and how he responded to the pregnancy of his wife. I restated their husbands' responses and feelings that they had mentioned, such as their changing moods, the added expense, added duties, change in routines, and age of the husband, and then I reiterated ways they had suggested that might be helpful to their husbands, for example, books, telling him what and how they're feeling, concern with how he's feeling, visiting the doctor's office with them, and the use of parents' classes. I then added the individuality of time involved in the husband's responses to becoming a father.

The discussion closed as I stated that we hadn't necessarily covered this subject so they might want to discuss it again and reminded them of the other subjects they had brought up.

Note: For quite a different first meeting of an expectant mothers group, see opening session of the complete record, Appendix III, Section 1.

Record 4
DISCUSSION GROUP FOR PARENTS OF PRESCHOOL CEREBRAL PALSIED CHILDREN

Session I

The meeting began at 8:20 P.M., by which time three parents had arrived: Mr. and Mrs. D. and Mrs. S. The remainder of the group arrived within the next 20 minutes.

I introduced myself and explained the purpose of our meeting. I said that this was going to be a discussion group and that therefore we were limiting attendance to a small number. I explained further that we would have an opportunity to exchange experiences and ideas and raise problems that we would like the group to discuss. I said that I would act as the leader; that I would direct the discussion, add ideas and information when appropriate. I said also that we had had such groups in the past and the parents had found them helpful. I also explained the composition of the group—some of the children were already attending the recreation program, others were still on the waiting list—and that we had invited primarily the parents of the younger age groups. I said that we would have a series of eight to ten sessions on a weekly basis. I asked whether this night would be convenient for the parents who were here, and one or two raised problems about transportation, at which point we decided that we would discuss this after the meeting since some of the parents had volunteered that they would be able to give others a lift.

I suggested that we begin by introducing ourselves; that each one tell us the age of their children and make any suggestions as to what they would like to have the group discuss. We started at my left with Mrs. S. Mrs. S. seemed rather tense and controlled much of her feelings as she spoke. She said R., age 10, is the handicapped child and that she has two other children, ages 3 and 1. R. is moderately handicapped on his left side. He cannot use his arm or hand very well and there is some involvement in his walking. Her concern is that he seems to resent his handicap very much. She said her husband and she had explained to him that it was the result of an accident that they all had and R. keeps saying that he was very unlucky. The mother seemed very disturbed about this. I asked about the accident (because most frequently cerebral palsy is associated with birth or prenatal period). Mrs. S. then explained that while she was pregnant both she and her husband were in an accident and she was in a cast when she delivered R. She added, "how can you tell this to a child, so I tell him that all of us were in an accident when he was very little." (I made no comment, but later in the meeting one of the parents, who had not yet arrived, also questioned Mrs. S. about the accident and kind of raised her eyebrows at the explanation.)

Mr. G. then introduced himself and said his child, P., age 4, is the oldest. Mr. G. is concerned about P.'s "emotional development." Now he is fine, but the father is worried about how he will react when he starts school. Now he has children close to his own age in his family to play with, but Mr. G. worries about how the child will react to strangers, or how they will react to him.

Mr. and Mrs. C. said I., age 3 years and 5 months, is now attending the program at the Center and loves it. I. has a sister, age 5. The mother described the child as having a hearing loss, plus mild cerebral palsy. Also, her attention span is very short and she does not speak. The parents are not clear about whether her lack of speech is due to the hearing loss or her general condition, namely, cerebral palsy. The child attends a speech and hearing service where they tell her that her lack of speech is due to the cerebral palsy. The doctor in the Cerebral Palsy Clinic, on the other hand, tells them that the child's slow speech is due to the hearing loss. The parents are concerned because they do not understand this. I said that it seemed to be a problem of clarifying the diagnosis and that there was confusion perhaps because the child was being treated in two different agencies. The parents nodded agreement.

Mr. L. said that J., age 4, has an older brother, age 8. J. is mildly involved, has poor balance, began to walk late, but is very bright. He goes to the Hospital for therapy and also attends a Special Clinic for speech. He has just applied to have the child enrolled in the Center program and is on the waiting list.

Mrs. Sa.'s child, J., age 7, is on the waiting list for the Center program. Her big problem is the child's shyness. He understands everything. He attends a hospital in their community and gets some help at home through the visiting nurse.

Mr. and Mrs. D. said J., age 5, has a sibling of 8. He is under the care of Dr. C. He is ambulatory, mildly handicapped, and has difficulty with speech. He also attends a Speech Clinic. The child's attention span is very short and he roams around constantly. His hearing is good but his eyes are crossed. The child seems to get angry because he cannot speak. Mrs. C. asked if the Speech Clinic had helped her child and Mr. D. said that it had not helped him very much and that they were told to discontinue the child for six months to a year because he does not seem ready yet for a speech clinic.

Mrs. R. came much later in the meeting. Her child, S., age 3, has an older brother of 13½. S. is on the waiting list for the program at the Center. Mrs. R. said that her main concern is the eating problem. S. had difficulty with his tongue and this interferes with his eating. However, she said he was never a good eater and still takes baby food. He is starting to speak.

I enumerated some of the problems that had been raised: the child's attitudes and feelings about his handicap; the child's social relationships with his peers; the parents' concern about clarifying the diagnostic picture; speech problems; eating problems; and more. I asked which of these the group would like to discuss this evening. Mr. G. said that probably each one was interested in discussing his own problem and since I was the neutral person, he thought I should decide which of these the group would discuss. I turned this back to the group and explained that we would try to get around to all of these problems before the end of our series of sessions. However, I added that each person's problem, as he presented it, was not as individual as it appeared, but that there was considerable overlapping and that we could begin with any of the problems that was of interest to the group.

Mrs. S. seemed most anxious to discuss her problem and she again told about her child's resentment about his handicap and said that this was particularly noticeable when he went to school. He had difficulty in adjusting to the other children, who ridiculed him. Mrs. C. questioned the mother about the teacher's attitude. She said she felt that this was important in setting the tone for the class and having the other children accept a child with a disability. Mrs. S. explained that some of the teachers were helpful but then it was always the problem of after school when the teacher was not around. There was some back and forth about the importance of how to explain the handicap to other children so that they will be a little bit more understanding. Also, some parents commented about how most children are rather cruel and unfeeling about teasing and that this, too, was part of it. Mrs. S. also brought in that R. feels even more resentment when he sees his younger siblings doing things that he had difficulty doing, such as, when he saw the baby brother walking. Mr. and Mrs. D. mentioned another part of this problem, namely, that of the older, normal siblings. Their daughter, age 8, is concerned about bringing her friends to the house because they ask questions about her handicapped brother.

Mrs. S. continued about her son's problems with his peers. She said when they first moved to where they are now living, the problem was even more serious because none of the children knew him. She described again how he tries to play ball with the boys in the street and has difficulty keeping up with them. Mr. C. suggested that they should try to develop some of his strengths, such as his ability to read or anything else he did well, and that this would help in getting along with other children. I made some general comment about compensating for one's handicap. Mrs. S. seemed interested in this suggestion and said she had never really thought about it. Mr. L. thought that it was good that R. was interested in trying to play baseball. Mr. L. described how he tries to get his son interested in such sports. (Mr. L. was himself once a professional baseball player.) He also suggested that they invite other children into the house to play with J. as a way of helping him to socialize. Several of the parents commented that it seemed healthy and normal that R. was trying and fighting to do the things his peers do. Mr. C. said something about having to treat these children like normal children.

Mrs. D. asked if their child will follow commands. Mrs. C. said that she can never be sure if I. hears her and so she usually assumes that the child does not, and she will help her to do whatever she wants her to do. She added, "I don't want to test her and, therefore, I don't tell her what to do." Mr. and Mrs. D. both thought this was a mistake. They had never known some of the things their child could do until they asked him to do things. Mrs. C. implied that she was fearful of making any demands on the child because in a sense they really did not want to know what the child's deficiencies may be. Mr. C. seemed a little surprised at this point and laughingly added, "I did not know that we had this problem."

The group continued the discussion about giving the child responsibility; how much responsibility to give them; where to set limits, and so forth. Mrs. S. said that she could not let him do the things that a normal child does, that is, she did not feel she could let him go to the movies alone, which is what his friends do. Mr. and Mrs. D. commented that they, too, had some problems about letting their child go out to play unsupervised. Mr. L. said that these children have to be given some responsibility. He expects his child to put away his toys after he has finished playing. Mr. G. again expressed his concern about what will happen to his child when he is ready to go to school. Right now he is very well adjusted because he plays with his cousins and gets along with them very well. The father seems to feel, however, that this is a sheltered environment and strange children will not be as accepting of him. Mr. G. spoke about this in some detail and the group had the feeling that he was expressing concern for the future when actually he was saying the child was adjusting very well at present. They commented about this and one parent asked why he was worrying now when in reality the child would be older and will have learned more about taking care of himself when the time comes for him to go to school. Mr. G. then told the group that his child was recently admitted to the Rehabilitation Center for four weeks' evaluation and the parents thought they would have a problem with him about separation. However, the child apparently made the transition very well and the father said, "We were upset because he did not get lonesome or cry for us." Then he added that the problem seemed to be more with the other children in the family who were concerned about P.'s leaving. With this the father laughed and seemed to gain a little more perspective on the problem. Several members of the group, however, responded with interest to the evaluation at the Center and there was some discussion about medical resources.

Since the time was growing short, I commented that many of the parents seemed to be interested in the various medical facilities and that we could talk about this more at a future meeting. I summarized some of the problems that were mentioned at the latter part of the discussion: the whole area of how much responsibility to give these children; how we set limits; how we help them take the next step. They had also talked about the child's own attitudes about his handicap—and the attitudes of other children—how to help the child in his social relationships as well as within the family. I pointed out that many of these problems were also ones that we face with our so-called normal children and that we needed always to try to separate how the handicap makes a difference. I also said that we could pick up on any of these problems at our next meeting and discuss them more thoroughly or we could discuss others, depending upon what the group wanted. One parent suggested that I include on the list hygiene habits. In exploring this further, she meant activities of daily living—how to help children take care of such things as buttons and, particularly, toilet training. Another parent picked this up and felt it was very important to discuss this, particularly since children cannot go to school if they are not toilet trained. I agreed that these were appropriate problems to discuss.

Appendix III
Summary Records of Series of Group Meetings

1. Expectant Mothers Group
2. Discussion Group for Parents of Elementary School Age Children

These leaders' reports have been somewhat condensed in the interest of space.

In the second record, selected meetings are presented in detail, whereas others have been summarized by the author to suggest something of the way the content was developed from session to session and the interplay within the group. The author's summaries are given in brackets ([ ]).

Record 1
EXPECTANT MOTHERS GROUP

Meeting 1

Nineteen expectant mothers were recruited. A representative of the agency contacted each one by telephone and notified them of the meeting-place and time of meeting. We have an attractive, spacious, and well-lighted room to use. It is convenient to water and toilet facilities. The room is equipped with cabinets for storage of supplies and equipment.

Of the nineteen who had registered for the course, sixteen arrived at the first meeting. One called in and cancelled because of transportation and another had already said she could not come until the second class.

As the women arrived, I introduced myself, said I was a public health nurse, and asked them to fill out the registration card and to sit as they wished at the table. I had a place card for each person. We had four long tables joined together, so that we could all sit comfortably together as a group. By shortly after 10 o'clock all were assembled and ready to go. They looked so young, bright, and eager.

I explained the purpose of the meetings and that it was not to be a lecture or structured class. I gave a number of illustrations to try to clarify in their minds why the discussion group would be of greater value to them than for me to get up and "teach." I also explained my role, what they could and could not expect from me. I told them why I would maybe be taking a few notes.

Next, I asked them to introduce themselves and give their estimated date of delivery and anything else they wanted to say—such as how many children, if any, they had. All but two were to deliver within the next three months and only *one* had had any children before.

I had explained that they would make the agenda (which would be flexible) and decide what we would talk about. At this point I asked them to each tell what she was interested in, so that we could decide what they wanted to talk about during the course, either now or later.

Mrs. Arkin (26 years) said she wanted to know all about baby care. How to take care of the baby, how to make formula, when she should get a pediatrician, and so on. Mrs. Arkin is a mousy little thing and surprised me with her response and contributions to the group all through the meeting.

Mrs. Roth (28 years) vivacious and cute, said she also wanted to know about baby care, how long should babies' bottles be sterilized, about exercises, and so forth. After everybody had said what they were interested in, she also mentioned wanting to know about clothing needs for baby and also later about some of the "old timey" ideas about using "Mother's Friend" (a medicine for rubbing on abdomen) and all such. She was just full of herself.

Mrs. Paul (age 25) said she wanted to talk about the position to put the baby in the crib. She had heard disturbing things about the baby being apt to choke and strangle on his back.

Mrs. Bensen (age 20) said that she had never been around a little baby and didn't know a thing. She was worried because she had to move out of state when the baby would be three weeks old. She wanted to know how to handle feedings, clothes, and so on.

Mrs. Barks (age 40) is the only one in the group who has had a child. This child is now 12 years old and she says she wants to know how to give the baby a bath and care for it.

Mrs. White (age 31) said she wanted to know how to bathe the baby ("Aren't we going to have a baby bath demonstration?"). She also was concerned about types of baby bottles and nipples, sterilization. Later she said she would like to know what to take to the hospital. In answer to her direct question about the baby bath, I assured her that we would do this if they decided that this was what they wanted as the class progressed.

Mrs. Louis (age 23), a very quiet, small person, said she just wanted to learn about the baby care, and did not have anything definite in mind.

Mrs. Penn (age 34) said that she felt all right about her pregnancy and that her doctor answered all her own needs and questions, but she wanted to know a lot about baby care and how long should a mother keep her baby in her room to sleep at home, when would the baby be safe alone in a room, and the like.

Mrs. Walsh (age 19) also wants to see a baby bath demonstration and what is the reason for concern about whether a baby is breast fed or given a bottle. She knows some can't breast feed. She said her doctor was taking good care of her.

Mrs. Fulton (age 23) said she just wanted to know all about taking care of the baby.

At this point I was wondering if any of them wanted to talk about themselves instead of the baby. I thought surely that somebody, out of all these women, who were so near to term, had some interest about labor, the hospital, or something related to themselves.

Now Mrs. Dunn (age 21) said she was wondering about her weight-gain problem. Her doctor was concerned over her weight gain. Right now she wasn't nearly as hungry as she used to be earlier in her pregnancy. "Why is that?" She also was interested in pros and cons about breast and bottle feeding. The group perked up considerably at the mention of diet and food.

Mrs. Johnson (age 31) was the first to mention labor. "How can I help when in labor?" "I want to know stages of labor," . . . The group began to look interested in this idea. I assured her we would get around to her interest.

Mrs. Field (age 40) said she had expected a straight lecture class and I couldn't decide whether she was expressing disappointment or antagonism. She didn't say much as the class progressed. She said she had no special topic to suggest for discussion at this time.

Mrs. May (age 22) is really going to be my standby. She is always "in there pitching." She at first said she wanted to know about baby care because she was so "green" that she didn't even know how to change a diaper. She also was concerned about the lines that she had heard pregnant women were supposed to have on their abdomens and about some of these old wives' tales that were confusing to women (marking the baby, and the like).

Mrs. Carlson (age 31) came back to the area of baby care again.

Mrs. George (age 21) also is really anxious to know about taking care of the baby because she will be delivering next month.

After we had gone around the table, I assured them that all suggestions were good and that we could also add to these as we went along. I summarized for them their suggestions and mentioned every area that had come up. I asked what they would like to talk about during the remainder of this session.

Mrs. Roth said that it seemed to her that they were getting the horse before the cart (I was thinking the same thing but letting the group decide), and that we ought to talk about something besides the baby at the first class. She said it so pleasantly that the group smiled and seemed to think she had a point.

At this stage, the group was directing remarks to each other so that I honestly would have been hampered by note-taking and it is not possible to remember every remark made by individuals. Strangely enough, the group latched on to diet at this point to talk about.

The group now had the situation well in hand. They discussed diet from every angle with only a minimum of questions directed at me. There were only two or three occasions where I had to give information that the group couldn't answer, and once I had to tactfully clear up some misinformation. At one point Mrs. Barks, the one with the 12-year-old child, when talking about weight control, said that she heard that salt was really poison and if one had too much in one's diet it was dangerous and should be omitted if one was too fat and gaining too rapidly. Before I could say anything, Mrs. May said she was so thirsty all the time and was afraid she was drinking too much fluid and wanted to know if it were possible to drink too much—and would it hurt her. The group all looked puzzled as if they didn't know. At this point, I cleared up the idea about salt being a poison by briefly explaining why there might be medical reasons at times for limits on salt and that salt is needed in normal amounts. But under certain conditions it might be restricted by a doctor, because it could tend to cause fluid retention in tissues, and that under usual conditions fluids did not need to be restricted because the body (kidneys, and so on) could take care of excretion. This seemed to satisfy the group.

The group continued to talk about weight control and they began to give each other ideas on how to eat wisely but still cut down on calories. Many contributed now. Mrs. Carlson said that she ate a lot of yogurt to get her calcium and it wasn't as fattening as whole milk. Mrs. Moore told the group about how she learned to like skim milk, which had helped her. One member said her doctor had told her that he didn't care whether she drank milk or not because she was taking calcium tablets. Others nodded their heads. This pointed up that many decisions between a woman and her doctor may be right for her and may be different for others. Another member said that she had had leg cramps and that her doctor increased her milk. He told her that she was having these cramps because she needed more calcium in her system. Her cramps were relieved by adding more milk in her diet. Another said she had a "charley horse" at night often and seemed to wonder about this. I suggested that cramps could be caused by several things.

It was brought out that a pregnant woman needs a well-balanced diet, but, if gaining too much weight, she should restrict calories by restricting things that are more fattening.

Mrs. Bensen, who is in her first trimester, said her problem was nausea. She was concerned with this more than the others, who were long past this stage and problem. The group smiled with understanding, but offered her no help. Mrs. Bensen looked so young and helpless that I just had to suggest that maybe the group could give her some pointers and comfort— that "This too shall pass away." The group laughed, but didn't go any further with the matter of nausea. Mrs. Bensen, being the only one not far along in pregnancy, has some different needs and I hope the group will help her.

Several (Mrs. Dunn, Mrs. May, and others) wondered why they now were not so ravenously hungry (during the last three months) as they had been earlier in pregnancy. I asked if they had any guesses as to why this might be true. One said, "they didn't have as much room" as before. This led into reports of increased pressure in upper part of abdomen and the like. I briefly added a few things, such as decreased peristaltic action. I used simple words to explain this.

Somehow, but wisely, they got into special diet needs of pregnant women. They knew about increased calcium needs and why. They brought out that a developing baby needs calcium, especially for bones and teeth. Mrs. May wanted to know if women had any special needs during different months of pregnancy for the baby's proper development. No one seemed to know, and I clarified for her this question. Later we also discussed briefly other increased diet needs, such as increased iron content.

They began to talk about the benefits of exercise in weight control. Mrs. Bensen said her doctor said she could skate (she loves it) for a few more months. Another said her doctor told her she could continue bowling as long as she felt like it. The group brought out benefits of exercise; they also said that it doesn't cause much weight loss but helps and is generally beneficial.

The time was about up and they were still chatting. Once or twice I suggested that they might have plans and I didn't want to keep them overtime. They just weren't in a hurry.

I summarized what the group had done today. They really had done a fine job of talking about diet needs in general and its relation to weight control, general health, special needs in pregnancy, and needs of baby.

I asked what they wanted to talk about next time. Some wanted to talk more about diet. Mrs. Arkin said she wanted to have abdomen marking (stria) discussed. I don't know why this is of so much interest to two members. I told the group we could decide definitely next time what they wanted and that it was up to them. They finally decided to go home. They left "chattily" and in apparent good spirits.

Meeting 2

Sixteen arrived at class. Two members were new: Mrs. Walk (age 21) and Mrs. Case (age 20). They fitted in like "old timers" and participated well. Three women were absent today. The "I expected a lecture" woman returned and participated well. I started the class by recognizing the new members and welcoming them to our circle. (As the members came in, they picked up their name cards and placed them in front of their seats, which they selected. I was glad to see that nearly everybody sat by somebody else today.)

I repeated the purpose of the classes for the benefit of the new members and to be sure that the entire group would again know what they could and could not expect from me and what they could get from each other.

Next, I summarized briefly the accomplishments of the last class and then reviewed all suggestions for topics that the group had given during the first class. I told them that each topic would be recognized and discussed at the time they desired. I reminded them that at the end of the last class they had made two suggestions for discussion today. Some had wanted to talk more about diet and one wanted to talk about "stria" or body markings. I asked for a decision.

Mrs. Johnson said she wanted us to talk about this business of labor. This was her suggested topic at the first lesson. Mrs. Walsh agreed. The whole group looked interested.

At this point Mrs. May said she still wanted to have a few more minutes on diet. Others seemed to feel that they, too, still had a few more questions on their minds about diet. I checked with the group and all seemed to agree to settle these matters. As it turned out, they really did have further concerns.

Mrs. May said that her doctor wanted her to eat an egg a day and she just couldn't do it. She hated eggs. Mrs. Arkin suggested that eggs could be used in cooking and other foods and she could still get her egg a day. She was given many suggestions for recipes to use eggs. Next, the group came to the conclusion that eggs are really for their high value of protein and iron, which could be gotten in other foods. (Aha! They see different solutions to needs.) They suggested substitutes.

Mrs. Paul brought up again the increased desire for water and liquids. Strangely enough, this seemed to be a common problem and several wondered if it was harmful to them and/or the baby. A peculiar thought (and fear) came out. Mrs. Brown had heard about babies with "water head" and wondered if drinking too much water could cause this. The group looked thoughtful and concerned about this. At this point I felt it necessary to allay this fear and to also point out possible reasons for increased thirst, but also to point out that all didn't necessarily feel this desire.

At this point a fascinating thing happened. The group had said at first that they wanted to talk about labor after a brief clarification and discussion of diet. But a member made a statement that started things in a direction that I could not have stopped if I had wanted to.

Mrs. May wondered if others had been as emotional and "mean" as she had been. This statement really brought forth response. They were really as one at this time. The group members never interrupt each other and are courteous, but the discussion was flowing so freely now that I couldn't possibly take notes on what each member said.

Mrs. Cass said that everything has irritated her. She gets mad with her husband and even his snoring irritates her. She said her husband is "happy-go-lucky" and bears with her. She later said she had been nervous and had worried about the baby. She said she had had one miscarriage and was so afraid she would lose this baby. She was scared to even lift things, because then she would just "wait for pains and things to happen." "How long will I have to wait to see if I will lose the baby?" (This wasn't a directed question but an expression of the feeling she has.)

Mrs. Walk says she fusses and is cross with her husband. Many members said that they, too, were ugly to their husbands and that it makes them feel so guilty.

Mrs. Roth said that pregnant women feel so unloved and that most people seem to pity pregnant women. She said women know they look ugly and their figures are awful. "Why do most people feel sorry for pregnant women and always think a baby is an accident instead of a planned affair?"

Mrs. White said that she was even irritated by her cute poodle, which she loved.

Mrs. Roth said she shared all these nerves and emotional upheavals. She said she had been worried about whether baby would be all right. She had thought about all ancestors and everything, such as "cross-eyes," "buck teeth," and so forth. Others chimed in and thought these fears had added to their nervousness.

Mrs. White said she believed her nausea was largely caused by nerves. Her husband was overseas and she didn't have anyone to talk to about her problems. Her family "thought she was awful." She elaborated more fully than this, and with feeling. She seemed to feel so good to say this. In fact, all of the group looked so relieved that they could say these things.

One member said she had thought something was wrong with her because she was so cross and emotional. She had talked to her neighbor who was pregnant and she was such a placid soul with no nerves. Several members expressed surprise that most in the group had been nervous or were now emotional and upset at times. One member said she really felt better now after hearing so many who had this problem.

Mrs. Roth said some doctors talk to husbands and tell them what to expect from their wives. Another said husbands should get a medal after putting up with them. Many expressed appreciation for help and understanding from husbands. They also freely expressed guilt at their crossness with husbands.

One member said that it seems we get nervous and take it out on those we love the most. Her Daddy's cough, her husband's walking too heavy, and "the silliest things" make her crabby. Several said they felt sorry as soon as they did blow off steam and vent their spleen.

Mrs. Arkin said she had calmed down a lot recently and was much better. Mrs. May said the middle three months were the worst. Two others said they were better since they stopped work.

Practically all of the group had participated. I asked if they had any thoughts as to why a lot of pregnant women go through these periods of emotional upheavals, nerves, crabbiness. Many suggested resentment to body changes as an irritation to them. (They really went to town on giving illustrations of how upsetting this was.) Some suggested that they can't do the things they used to do (such as athletics) and that is nerve-racking. One suggested glandular and hormonal effects. (This was good, too. They then referred to similar feelings when they were menstruating before pregnancy.) Others suggested that waiting for others to do things for you that you can't do yourself is irritating (can't lift, tie shoes, and the like). Some thought that fears about having an abnormal baby made them nervous. Adjustments of all routines were considered. One said you just didn't feel as well and that made you nervous. Such things as discomforts of pregnancy and load of baby add to stress. One also is more easily fatigued. It was pointed out by many in various ways, although not verbalized as such, that they recognized this as an adjustment to a new experience. Things are now different and there will be other different and new things to face.

When they seemed to finish giving reasons for feeling emotional and nervous, I tried to pull their reasoning together by briefly summarizing what they had said. We pointed out similarities of experience and feelings, but also pointed out how individual our own experiences and feelings may be, and that not just pregnant women but all must constantly be making adjustments to changes. I tried to say that *recognition* of needed adjustments was helpful and that each adjustment successfully made, made the next one maybe easier.

Now Mrs. Cass, our new member who has really contributed today, said, "How about the 'after baby blues?' Can we expect them?" Several members knew women who had a worse time with nerves after the baby came than before. I said, "How about this, *might* one get these blues?" Some of their reasons were:

1. One suggested that she felt the baby was all hers while she was pregnant, but afterwards she would have to share it and would be jealous. This would upset one.

2. During pregnancy she gets so much attention and after delivery the baby would get all the attention. She'd feel jealous and left out.

3. Another member said, "Drop of hormonal activity" . . . "let down feeling."

4. Someone else suggested fatigue and added work as causes of "nerves."

5. Another said, "One might be nervous and feel one didn't want the baby." Group surprised me by recognizing that one might actually feel a rejection of baby at times. Guilt feelings were recognized as making one nervous.

6. Several recognized that activities as before could be curtailed and cause adjustment problems (going out often with husband, traveling, and so on).

7. One said that after nine months of carrying a baby, the body would be a vacuum, she would no longer be pregnant, and she would have anti-climax feelings.

8. Another said that it would hit them like a hammer all of a sudden, that they now had the care of this baby (new responsibility, fear of adequacy to do a good job, and the like).

9. One said that for a while after delivery, one would not feel so strong and would have to adjust to this.

Again I summarized briefly for them what they had said and pointed out that they certainly had done a tremendous job of thinking and exploring. I suddenly realized that we were running overtime and suggested that they might want to go, but there were still some "just one more thing" remarks.

I asked what they wanted to talk about next time. Mrs. Johnson said she still wanted to talk about labor; others agreed. I laughed and pointed out that at the beginning of the class labor was suggested, but the group itself took off on another topic. If they wanted to talk about labor next time, I was right with them. I again pointed out that *they* planned the agenda. I hope the group will get around to this next time.

They left in good spirits.

Meeting 3

Fourteen mothers were present today.

This meeting did not seem as smooth to me as the others, and there were many detours instead of a straight direction as before. In this class they got into information areas where they needed more help from me as leader. The members directed more toward me during this class and I had the difficult but fascinating experience of trying to handle this situation. I can see now that the "detours" always took them back to the "main" road again, when I was able to keep the signpost pointed correctly, and that the detours were what the group apparently wanted.

As the group members came in they picked up their place cards and all but two took a different seat today. They all seem to like each other and I don't have any "groups within the group" yet.

At the beginning of the class I reminded them that I had told them to feel comfortable about standing up or moving around if they desired, because "I realized that most of them are so near to term and that sitting in a straight chair for one and a half hours might get uncomfortable." Mrs. May straightened me out by saying that really they were most comfortable in a straight chair (and how reasonable to understand after she said it). She then said what a miserable night she had had. She was so uncomfortable lying down and had been up and down all night and couldn't figure out how to get in a relaxed position. Mrs. Wall said she was at her doctor's and fainted. He explained the cause as due to increased "pressures on something." He told her not to lie on her back, but always on her side. Mrs. Johnson described in detail the position she assumed in bed and use of pillows in relieving pressures that were uncomfortable. Another suggested an exercise that was helpful to her now. As usual, they gave each other ideas, help, and support. I could have given them some suggestions and reasons for pressures and discomfort, but they were all having the same discomforts, difficulty with breathing, and so on, and could actually help each other better than I, who wasn't pregnant. I did at some point ask them why they thought they had these particular discomforts now. They came across with the facts of increased pressures on diaphragm (breathing difficulty) because baby is now up so high, and also pressures on other organs. They later used this knowledge in understanding other discomforts. About this time they seemed to settle down as if to say, "Let's go."

I reminded the group that they had said at the end of the last class that they wanted to talk about labor. I also told them that we could talk about anything they desired. There were no further suggestions of topics for discussion so I checked with group to see if they wanted to discuss labor.

There was unanimous assent either by nods of heads or smiles of approval of the topic.

Next, I asked what they would like to know about labor. Mrs. Dunn remarked that she lived thirty-eight miles away from the hospital and her obstetrician. She wanted to know how she would know when she was in labor so she might get to the hospital on time. Before saying anything I waited to see the reaction of the group. Someone suggested that since the first baby usually didn't come so fast, she would probably be able to make it OK. Another said she should call her doctor as soon as she had any signs and he would advise her.

Somehow the group began to go into the signs of labor. I believe it was at this point that Mrs. Roth said, "How will I know if I am in false labor or not? I'll just die if I go to the hospital and then have to go home." She is stimulant to the group. When she asked about false labor, Mrs. Bark said the pains would be far apart and not regular if labor was false and described also how the stomach would feel when one was having a contraction. The group laughed and called her "the voice of experience." (She is the only one who has had a child.)

I felt it was time to focus their thinking on signs and symptoms of labor. I asked the group if they had thought about these things that would forewarn them of approaching labor. Mrs. May suggested backache as a sign. I asked why this might be significant. Mrs. May again responded by saying that the pressure of the baby and muscles contracting could cause this.

Next, Mrs. Roth suggested "show" as a sign of approaching labor. I asked if she would tell us what she meant by "show." She had "read the books," I believe, because she mentioned the dilating of cervix and passing of mucous plugs. She said, "Show is caused by stretching of cervix, isn't it?"

Someone next mentioned "the water breaking" as a sign of labor beginning. This matter of rupture of membranes was of much interest and we detoured back and forth a number of times on this during the meeting. Interesting thoughts were being pulled out at various points. One person wanted to know origin of the sac and its formation and growth. I supplied this information. Another was puzzled about the amount of amniotic fluid in the sac. I discussed how fluid amount could vary some from person to person and at different stages of pregnancy. I threw out to them for thought why fluid might be less near term. One said, "There isn't as much room now as before, baby takes up so much space." Later someone was interested in the function of this bag of water. One said it is a "shock absorber." Another said, "It protects baby from germs." Yet another said, "It stays at the right temperature for baby." Someone said, "Doesn't it do something for the baby's skin?" We agreed it did. This last question brought forth a remark about vernix caseosa and its value to the baby's skin. As I said, this interest in the amniotic sac didn't all come out at once, but we came back to it at many points. I also remember that one group member wanted to know what happened to the fluid in the sac when it varied in amounts at times and what was in this fluid (chemical composition). I tried to explain this simply.

At one point I remember Mrs. Roth, again in a humorous way, saying how horrible it would be to have membranes rupture when not at home, and she did this so feelingly that we could almost see her in this predicament. She followed this by expressing her feelings about the indignities of this whole labor business and the embarrassments that one must suffer. (I should have picked this up and found out if others shared this feeling. I'm sure some must.)

At some time I pulled the group back to further thinking on signs of approaching labor. I reminded them of what they had mentioned and asked if there were any other thoughts. Someone suggested "lightening" as another clue. I checked to see if group knew what "lightening" was. One suggested the baby was settling down and changing position to get ready to be born. I asked if they could see how this might make them feel differently from now. They remembered that pressures were causing them to have difficulty with breathing and that when the baby dropped down they could breathe better and be more comfortable. Someone saw that she might also have more desire to go to the toilet because of pressure on bladder.

All of the detours fitted in when they occurred, but right now I can't remember how we got into the problem of nausea and heartburn. Someone mentioned her present problem of being nauseated often. Another often had heartburn and acid stomach. The group related this somewhat to increased pressure on stomach and intestinal tract. I reminded them of our reference in an earlier session to decreased motility of intestinal tract, and I pointed out that to some people regurgitation of stomach acid could be troublesome. At this point someone expressed her concern over an article she had read about soda. She had found soda so helpful for her indigestion and "it scared her to death when she read this article." She was afraid she had hurt the baby. I checked with group to see if others had heard this business about soda being dangerous. Several had. They had heard they should "never take soda." I checked to see if they had any ideas about this. None knew why "soda was bad." I explained the possible reasoning in this matter about which they had incomplete information. I explained about the "sodium" part of sodium bicarbonate (soda), sodium chloride (salt), and such, as something that could cause fluid retention in excess under certain conditions. I pointed out that soda and salt restriction could be discussed with doctors and why on occasion it might be limited.

We were still detouring, so I reminded them that they had covered signs and symptoms of approaching labor and asked where they would like to proceed now. Somehow we now got into the function of the placenta. When I asked what they thought the purpose of the placenta might be, they recognized that it served to get nourishment to the baby and helped remove waste products. Although they rambled in getting it, they finally got the uterus and its contents fixed in their minds.

With all the detours, the group kept talking about things of interest and I was struggling with how to get them to gather together and package up this process of labor. They either didn't want to package it up as I did or I wasn't keeping it focused for them. I see now (but not then) that my thinking on the three stages of labor and the unique differences of each stage was so structured in my mind that I let the group throw me off because they didn't see it 1-2-3 right now. I must learn that maybe it can be approached 3-2-1 and still be clarified.

A member now posed somehow the question of delivery positions of the baby. (Here's where I could have got them heading to second stage of labor.) Mrs. May made reference to the shoulder presentation. Mrs. Cass mentioned the face presentation. Mrs. Walsh came in to say that the doctor by abdominal manipulation could put the baby in the proper position and inferred that they did not need to worry about the presentation problems of the baby.

This led right into discussion about the cord. One member related the delivery position to the possibility of the cord wrapping around the baby's neck. Several mentioned that this rarely happened, but the members recognized that it could happen. One member said that the doctor would watch out for these kinds of things. They all seem to have such confidence in their doctors. In another session Mrs. Johnson mentioned that the doctors were "co-workers" in this whole business.

One member wanted to know how long the cord was. No one seemed to know and I supplied this information. If I wait a few second without saying anything, this group will supply information when a question is asked by a group member, without my having to pose a question, if they know the answer.

Now Mrs. Bensen asked, "What about babies being born with 'a veil' over its face? What is that?" Another member said, "That's the caul." Another said, "Isn't that part of the afterbirth?" I supplied this information and this led the group into further discussion as to the different times that the membranes might rupture. They arrived at the knowledge of the most usual times but the less usual and individual differences were recognized.

Naturally, the group followed on with "after birth." They got right into the third stage of labor. They had me somewhat bewildered as to my role because they hadn't satisfied me. I knew that they hadn't gone through the other stages completely. (My structured thinking about the process of labor was in the way and I had missed opportunities, I know.) I asked what they thought was meant by "after birth" (when it was mentioned). One member then mentioned "placenta" and the group again made reference to its purpose. Another mentioned "lining of uterus." Another mentioned "sac" and that all these products weren't needed any more.

Mrs. George said she would like to see a film on delivery of a baby and others agreed. Mrs. Dunn said she'd like to be absent that day. She wants no part of seeing the baby born. A few others smiled as if to say, "Amen." They are scared.

It is interesting how well they work together in talking about labor when they are thinking in so many different ways. Some want detailed, factual information regarding anatomy and the like, others want to talk about fears, problems, and concerns relating to delivery, others want no part of it at all. Could these individual reactions be causing all the detours and branching off?

All of a sudden the group started on the subject of anesthesia. Mrs. Bark mentioned the use of "spinal block" and how wonderful it was. Another member said that she heard it could cause awful headaches and trouble. Someone else suggested that the use of spinal anesthesia was more perfected now and caused fewer aftereffects. Mrs. Dunn mentioned that her doctor used paraldehyde and she and another member had heard how awful it tasted. Another mentioned the use of ether and others, "shots." Another mentioned how wonderful pentothal was and hoped she could have that. During the discussion some didn't seem concerned about having so much anesthetic, another made brief reference to use of natural childbirth by some women, and one or two members laughingly said they wanted to be "knocked out" and not know anything that happened. Someone asked me to clarify this anesthesia business. If I remember correctly, I asked a question which led them to decide that many anesthetics were used and that a woman and her doctor could discuss this and decide what was best in her own case.

They still haven't packaged up this labor completely, but they've talked about many things of interest. Maybe they will give me another opportunity in another session to focus their attention to certain helpful facts I feel they should know.

One member in the group wanted to know how long it would take to discuss the baby. Several inferred that time was running out for them. Some might deliver before the classes ended. I told them that we could begin talking about the baby at any time when they were ready. Mrs. Bensen and others said they'd like to see a film on baby care and would rather do that than have a baby bath demonstration.

Now someone said, "How can we tell about chances of baby having blue or brown eyes. . . ." Others began to quickly think of other hereditary factors, defects, markings, and so on. Mrs. Roth was concerned because someone in her family had had harelip. She was afraid her baby would inherit this. Her doctor had given her some consolation. It was too late to get into any more areas of thought so I asked them if we could talk about these things later. The group suggested they might want to talk about these things regarding the baby that they were now thinking about for next week. Now I didn't feel it even necessary to remind them that we could talk about anything they desired next week. They know this.

We were at the end of the period and I realized we must stop somewhere. They had kept me mentally hopping today and I wasn't too sure what had happened or why at this point.

Meeting 4

Ten mothers were present today.

Even though the class was smaller then usual, we seemed to have one of our best meetings. Everybody was in fine spirits and all were so alert, "groupy," and interested today; in fact, I thought I would never get them to go home.

At the beginning of the class I reminded them that they had indicated they wanted to discuss hereditary factors today. I suggested that there were a few things about labor that we had not discussed and that they might or might not want to talk further about this at some time. I asked them what they would like to talk about today.

I don't recall actually who said what, but they began to throw out thoughts and reactions in general regarding labor. The things I had thought they didn't know or should talk about were things that the group did know and they brought up things I hadn't thought about as being of interest and concern. Mrs. Bensen said the whole business was "gruesome" and she certainly wanted to be knocked out. I asked if others shared this feeling. Many did. Mrs. Johnson said labor was such an embarrassing thing to have to go through. Feeling seemed to be unanimous on this. Mrs. Dunn was hoping "they" wouldn't tie her hands down during labor. She would feel so helpless with her hands tied because she says that when she hurts she likes to hold her forehead.

The talking eased into the discussion of pain. Mrs. May pointed out how differently people react to pain. She said she goes all to pieces at the time of pain and then is all right later. Her husband is like the "Rock of

Gibraltar" at times of crisis, but later reacts to strain. Many of the group recognized in individuals differences in capacity to take pain and then this led them to talk about needs for anesthesia. Some want to be "knocked out" and others wanted "just enough" to make delivery bearable for them. One pointed out that she actually had never suffered much pain and wondered if she could take it. Another said she is a naturally very nervous individual and she wants to be assured of enough anesthetic during delivery.

Mrs. Paul wanted to know how a woman could help in labor if she had enough anesthetic to relieve pain and make her unaware of everything. It was brought out that a woman could be made more comfortable but would not be given so much anesthetic that it would interfere with the delivery process. They discussed hearing some women say that they didn't remember a thing about delivery. It was brought out that some medications can create a feeling of amnesia.

During the previous discussion of needs for anesthetics it came out clearly several times that they understood the reasons why the woman can help during the second stage of labor by use of (voluntary) abdominal muscles. They also recognized the first stage as the time "to *try* to relax" when she couldn't help much. They apparently had read lots of books before these classes. Speaking of books, one member was laughing about her husband reading a book about labor and how petrified he had been since he read the part "telling what to do when the baby comes at home before the doctor can be reached." He is afraid he'll be caught in such a jam.

In talking about the delivery of the baby they mentioned the pressure on the rectum and realized why they would want to eat a light diet when labor begins, to maybe lessen discomforts that might be caused by too much waste material in intestinal tract.

Somehow they now got into a fascinating discussion of the baby. Mrs. George made some reference to how the baby would look. I asked how they expected a new baby to look and the reactions were certainly varied. Mrs. Bensen said she didn't want to see it until it was all fixed up because she knew it would be bloody, messy, and awful looking. Mrs. Arkin said it would be nice whatever it looked like (she was one who said labor could be satisfying to a woman). Another member said that the baby would have all that "old cheesy stuff on it." Another said she had seen new babies and it would make her ill if hers looked ugly and bad. Some talked about how different they all looked. Some have lots of hair, some have none, and so forth. They remarked that pictures of babies (for example, Gerbers' advertisements) always showed such pretty babies. Mrs. Carlson said she was afraid her husband and the families wouldn't like the baby if it was "homely" looking. They expressed all these feelings, but still their expressions on their faces seemed to tell me that they were prepared to accept and love this baby whatever it looked like.

In talking about the baby, someone mentioned the baby's head at birth and said that the bones of the head were not all closed together and stated that it took over a year for them to close completely. I asked if they had any thoughts about why these fontanels were not closed at birth. They were smart enough to relate this to the birth process and reasons why. Someone stated that the mother had to be careful with the baby's head until the fontanels closed.

In talking about the baby being born, they recognized what the baby has to face at birth as well as what they themselves have to face at delivery. Mrs. Bensen mentioned that the baby must not like being born and might be hurt at delivery after being so snug and comfortable for so long. I asked how they would imagine a baby could feel at birth. They said he had been warm, safe, and protected and now he has a completely new environment to which he must adjust. In mentioning adjustments, I asked what adjustments he would have to make to eating, elimination, and the like. They remembered that nourishment in uterus was through the placenta and now he would have to get food another way. They saw that all he would know to do would be to cry if hungry now. I pointed out (as they did not) that breathing, elimination, and other things would be accomplished differently now.

Next the group got interested in germs that the baby could be harmed by in the mother's body. One couldn't understand why, if a woman with a disease such as tuberculosis could have a baby without the disease, the doctors worry when a woman has measles when pregnant. Why wouldn't all diseases affect the baby? Mrs. Roth said that it was some of the virus diseases that harmed the baby. Mrs. George said she knew a woman who had a baby with a congenital heart defect and the baby died at three months. The baby's mother was told that it was caused by her having measles when she was pregnant. The group knew that the first trimester was the dangerous time for a woman to have measles. I asked if they had any thoughts as to why this was true. They knew that this period was when the baby was being formed and that there could be damage of formative structure and other things. It was evident that the group did not completely understand about what germs could or could not harm the baby in the uterus or why or why not. I explained why, as a rule, diseases of the pregnant woman would not affect the baby, but also the exceptions such as the virus that causes measles, which could penetrate to the baby. I tried to do this as briefly and as nontechnically as possible and I think they got the idea.

When the group was talking about labor and the muscular action of the uterus, someone remembered that Mrs. Bensen had said she might have to have a Caesarean section and asked her about this. Mrs. Bensen said that her doctor had said there was a possibility that she might need a Caesarean. I believe this came out in another class when weight gain was being discussed. Mrs. Bensen said she had been worried for fear she could not have other babies if she had to have a Caesarean. They related this to formation of scar tissues and the possible inability of the uterus to have usual elasticity in the area of scar tissue. One of the "positive thinkers" pointed out that Elizabeth Taylor had had several Caesarean sections and had come through satisfactorily. I then pointed out that the doctor would be able to advise a woman about pregnancies after a Caesarean.

This discussion led them to inquire about the ability of some of the pelvic bones to "give a little" when baby was being born. I explained this to them. Now they also are seeing the relation of pelvic structure and such to ease of delivery.

When talking about muscular action of uterus, they began to inquire as to how long it took the uterus to return to normal after delivery. I asked what they thought about this. Someone pointed out that it took about six weeks and they were able to see that the uterus had stretched tremendously and would need this long to return to normalcy.

In relation to muscles, they pursued the idea of the value of exercises to getting back muscle tone. One member said her sister took exercises after her first baby and her figure was nice and her stomach "nice and flat." After her second baby, she did not take exercises and now had a big stomach and her figure wasn't good. In relation to discussion of muscle tone and elasticity, there was some place where I asked if they could see any reasons why a woman who had had several children might sometimes deliver more quickly than a primipara. They saw that this might be possible and why.

I also remember that when they were discussing labor, someone asked how the body knows when the baby is ready to be born and why it usually is at just the right time. Someone said it was caused by some hormonal activity. I asked if there were other ideas. This led to thoughts about expansion of uterus, pressures, and so on. Now they wanted to know what the moon had to do with time of delivery. They laughed about this and said maybe it was one of the old wives' tales. They all had heard about this and many had figured out if the moon would be full or not when they were supposed to deliver. I pointed out that I didn't know of any scientific basis for people thinking that the moon had anything to do with delivery date.

At this point, one member brought out how the doctor figures the delivery date. They understood how this is approximated by the doctor but some wondered why they always have about two weeks variation in the expected date. One laughingly said she'd like to be told that she would deliver at "such and such a date on a definite time." I explained about ovulation and why the definite date would be impossible to determine.

We were running overtime, so I asked what they'd like to talk about next time. This is really getting to be a joke, because we all know that almost invariably we talk about something other than what we think we will talk about. Several women said they still would like to talk about heredity next time. They still want to talk about why a child will have certain color eyes, and one mentioned possibility of inherited height and other factors. (For example, "Will he be six feet like cousin Jim?") I'll have to refresh myself on Mendel's Law and all about the dominant and recessive traits.

I told the group farewell, but they wanted to stick around for a while. They gathered over in a corner. It occurred to me that the group discussion method has an advantage over the structured classes that I had not thought of. As a by-product it creates a "socializing" atmosphere that they never get in a structured atmosphere. They really get to know each other in the discussion group and begin to like and enjoy each other. The leader, too, gets to know the members as she never could in a role of teacher and lecturer.

As they chatted together, I naturally was "eavesdropping," as I busied myself getting things put away and straightened up. They talked about many things. They shared humorously with each other their difficulty in stooping down, tying shoes, and all such. This started them talking about how bad they knew they looked. One said her husband said she had not looked so pretty since her wedding and she said she told him she must have been a fright then at her wedding. Another said her husband said her complexion was so pretty now and they are all amazed that anyone could find them attractive now.

Two of the members began to tell about the possibility of their having twins and they are so excited and will be disappointed if they don't have twins. Another member was saying that she felt better than she ever had, since she got over her nausea early in pregnancy. They checked with Mrs. Bensen about her nausea now. They have taken Mrs. Bensen right into the circle from the start, even though she is only three months pregnant and they are all about "ready."

The group also discussed company coming after they get home from the hospital. They all don't want "people and family flocking in on them in droves, kissing and cooing over the baby, bringing germs. . . ."

As I left, a few were just enjoying a social time together and I was glad they felt free to stay and chat if this is what they wanted.

Meeting 5

Eleven mothers arrived today.

They were just full of complaints of stomachache, backache, heartburn, and all such. Everybody was happy today in spite of physical discomforts. It is so lovely outside today that it would be difficult to be unhappy. As I saw everything in bloom, I was reminded of what a member said last week when someone asked how the body knew when it was time for the baby to be born. She compared it with the unhurried wonder of nature as she said, "It's like a flower, it just blooms when it's ready and not before."

Several were early at class today and they sat around chatting. Mrs. White said she was sick last week, but she checked with Mrs. Bensen to learn what she had missed. They chatted about the cost of diaper service and several were interested to learn all about this service (how many diapers, delivery times, and so on) from Mrs. Dunn and others. They also talked about how time drags when one is so near to term. They also started comparing weight gain and they were amazed that Mrs. Arkin had gained only nine pounds and some had gained twenty to thirty pounds.

Some were interested in their problems of edema. Mrs. Roth's feet were swelling. This bothers her. Mrs. Walsh has had toxemia and was saying that she was on a low-salt diet and had to take "pills" to keep feet, ankles, and hands from swelling badly. She thinks she is taking Diuril. She had mentioned this problem earlier when we discussed diet needs in relation to weight. She had been put on a special diet and had lost twelve pounds.

The consensus was that there were a few things about heredity that they wanted cleared up in their minds. I suspected as much all the time, that they weren't so interested really in heredity as it related to color of baby's eyes or height, as they said, but rather their concern was with things that could be wrong with the baby as a result of heredity. In general, they were concerned with "will the baby be all right?" The discussion that followed confirmed my suspicion.

I asked what they really wanted to know about heredity or why they were concerned with this. Mrs. George said she was born with a rare circulatory condition and had had to have an operation as a child to help correct this. She had been told that even though her condition was a rare thing, it could crop up in another generation. She is concerned for fear her baby might have this. Mrs. Walsh said that about six people in her husband's family and her husband had some kind of inherited leg condition. All limp and have one leg shorter than the other. Also, harelip is in the family. "I'm scared to death my baby will have this trouble."

At this point my "positive thinkers" tried to give some measure of comfort. Several pointed out that doctors now check the babies carefully and can correct so many things that are wrong with a baby at birth. They mentioned how often babies with club feet and all such are put in casts or corrective appliances and are fixed up to be normal.

Mrs. May said her husband was of a very nervous nature (and all his family) and that she, too, was nervous. Could her baby inherit these nerves? She said one day her husband will be calm and the next day he may yell at the dog and be bothered by things that would not bother him otherwise. I asked the group what they thought about inheriting nerves. They recognized that one may inherit tendencies for things (some high strung, some placid, and so forth), but that because parents are nervous does not make it a definite fact that the child *has* to be nervous.

Another member said her mother had migraine headaches and sinus trouble. She said she was told that one could inherit tendencies for these conditions. Another mentioned a deaf and dumb couple who had a deaf and dumb child. Mrs. Bensen said she was cross-eyed as a child. Could this be inherited? I asked the group what things they thought could be inherited. One member had a fairly good concept of Mendel's Law and told the group what she knew. They recognized that one may inherit tendencies and not always the bad things. At this point I clarified points that seemed confusing about how we can inherit body structure, color of eyes, and the like.

Next, someone asked about the diseases that a baby can be born with. Another member said that syphilis could infect the baby before birth. I asked if they knew why their doctor took a blood test when he first saw them. They knew that this was a test for syphilis.

At this point, the group was germ conscious and one wanted to know if the mother had a cold, could the baby get it from nursing at the breast (from the milk). I asked the group where the infection was when a person had a cold. They saw that the germs were in the respiratory tract and not in the milk. I asked what a mother should think about if she has a cold and must nurse the baby. They suggested that wearing a mask and general cleanliness would help prevent infection. This led the group to think about effects of smoking, having cocktails, and other things, on the mother's milk and the baby. One member said her doctor said, "Go ahead and eat onions and what you want. It won't hurt." They questioned the mother taking laxatives, etc. One member said that moderation in smoking, etc., was the answer. After they finished, I summarized the current thinking on what does and does not have effects on mothers' milk.

They had led themselves right smack up to discussion of feeding the baby. I've forgotten who said what, but the group got to discussing breast feeding. One said that some books, and Dr. Spock was one mentioned, so highly recommended breast feeding that she would feel guilty if she didn't breast feed her baby. Others agreed, with feeling. They didn't think it fair to make them feel badly if they didn't breast feed. Some said, "we feel like a heel," "a dirty dog," and so on. I asked how they felt about breast feeding. Mrs. Bensen said she had seen women on buses and in public places nursing their babies and it was repulsive to her. Mrs. May said she just *couldn't* possibly breast feed a baby. The idea nauseated her. Mrs. Roth said she used to be an airline hostess and when she used to see mothers breast feeding their babies on planes, she would nearly die. Another said a dirty mother with a dirty baby nursing in public made her sick.

Mrs. White and Mrs. Walsh both said that they wanted to nurse their babies. They felt that it wasn't unpleasant and that it had advantages. I asked what were the advantages. The group pointed out that it was cheaper than making formula, it was easier, it was ready made, the right temperature, and so on. Another said she wouldn't have to get up all times of night to warm a bottle if she breast fed her baby. Someone said that sometimes a woman can't nurse her baby and no one should make her feel like a dog if she can't. She said sometimes a mother's milk doesn't agree with a baby. Another said the mother might have inverted nipples and couldn't nurse her baby; and other reasons were given. Someone pointed out that breast feeding was good for baby and mother. It helped the breast and helped the uterus contract and the organs to return to normal. Someone said, "I read that the organs will return to normal in six weeks, anyway." Another member pointed out that sometimes the baby may even have trouble getting adjusted to the proper formula (when it was pointed out that sometimes breast milk didn't agree with the baby). Mrs. Walsh said that she thought she should breast feed her baby for her own good because she would let her "diet slip and eat like crazy" if she didn't have to think about eating properly for baby's sake. Mrs. May said her doctor told her that it *used* to be thought that it was a woman's God-given duty to breast feed her baby and was a crime not to do so, but now it is recognized that a baby can be just as healthy if given a special formula and vitamins. Someone suggested that if they felt so strongly against breast feeding in public, they could have a bottle of formula for the baby when they had to be away from home with the baby at feeding time.

After they had discussed their feelings about breast feeding and bottle feeding and the pros and cons of each, I pointed out to them that they were saying this is an individual matter that they must decide for themselves and that they had given many reasons why it has to be an individual matter. It involved how they and their husbands felt about breast feeding, whether mother could or could not nurse baby, baby's adjustment to breast milk and/or formula, and so on.

I asked them what they thought were really the important things to think about in feeding a baby. One member of the class said that "good nourishment" was one thing to think about. I asked if they thought a baby could be well-nourished whether on breast or bottle. They said they saw no reason why not. I asked what else would they like to consider when feeding a baby. Someone said "T.L.C." (tender loving care) and another said that she could give the baby affection and comfort as well when bottle feeding as when breast feeding. I asked how this could be done. Someone pointed out that the important thing was to hold the baby when giving a bottle and he could get love and security the same as if he were breast fed. Another said you could convey your feelings by holding and cuddling the baby. Someone said that it would be easy and tempting to prop the bottle up for the baby. Another pointed out that it would be bad for the baby in many ways. One remembered seeing a baby struggling with a bottle and later it was discovered that the hole in the nipple was too little.

I remember that Mrs. Walsh said her husband didn't want her to breast feed the baby because she would be the closest to the baby then and he wanted to be close to the baby, too. I asked how they thought the new baby would feel about this feeding business. They remembered that last week they discussed the feelings and reactions of this newborn. One said, "If he is hungry, he'll just cry 'help me.'" They saw that feeding could mean comfort to him. One said that everything was new to the baby. His hunger and other things expressed by crying mean "help me," "satisfy me."

The feeding discussion led them right into asking why and how the baby should be "burped." I asked why they thought a baby should be burped. One member said that the new baby's stomach wasn't adjusted like an older person's and he could swallow lots of air and couldn't get it up easily, and this would cause him to spit up milk. She knew that the musculature of the new baby's G.I. tract is still weak. I discussed with the group "burping" during feeding and why. They wanted to know how to hold the baby to burp him. Some mentioned seeing the babies spit up all over the mother. At this point I got the doll and demonstrated burping positions and techniques. I was glad they led me into a demonstration. I have had very strong feelings that demonstrations at the *right time* not only are valuable, but need not interfere in *any* way with group thinking or discussion. Rather, I feel strongly that it reinforces and strengthens discussion.

They asked how to position the baby in the bed after a feeding. One member said it would be best to put the baby on its stomach after a feeding. I took the doll and placed it on its stomach and said, "What do you think about that?" Someone said, "Why, he might suffocate or strangle if he spit up if the mother wasn't there." Another suggested that the baby should be placed on his back after the feeding. Again I took the doll and placed it on its back and said, "How about that?" Immediately someone said that he might choke easily if he spit up in this position. The group decided that a side position would maybe be best for the newborn after a feeding. They discussed this and how to prop the baby with pillows, and so forth.

Somewhere in the discussion (earlier in the class), feeding schedules were mentioned. One member said her mother let her yell as a baby if she were hungry rather than get her off schedule and now it is known that rigid schedules are not good for the baby. Another said, "Babies aren't gluttons, they will tell you when they are hungry." The group members pointed out to each other that the baby will help determine his own schedule. In speaking of schedules, one said that some mothers won't even answer the telephone when feeding or bathing the baby. One suggested never rushing or hurrying. I asked them if they thought a mother should consider *herself* any in this matter of schedules. We decided that a mother needs to work things out for her own good as well as the baby's. One member said, "We need to get away occasionally."

At one time we discussed how long to let a baby nurse or take bottle. I asked what they thought about this. Someone said the baby would quit nursing when satisfied. (Maybe this led us to talk about burping.) I told them about usual nursing time and that baby could tire easily.

Mrs. Bensen is still worried about traveling with the baby (about eight or nine months from now!). She is concerned about formula, how the baby will sleep in the car, and the like. Some of the members gave her helpful suggestions about such conveniences as car beds and cribs.

All of a sudden, I discovered that we were running way overtime. I reminded them that we had better think about what to discuss next week. All want a baby bath demonstration and a discussion on handling a baby, in general. They felt we could bathe the baby and talk about positions and handling the baby, clothes, and other aspects of baby care all together. I agreed. They also suggested that they all bring one of the baby diapers they have and practice folding a diaper.

As usual, they rose to go, but gathered around to continue talking. They tried to hem me in to talk further—they wanted to talk about their breast changes (size, pigmentation, and all such) and edema that some were having. [They were even remembering what I said about sodium ($NaCl$) in salt.] They even wanted to talk about abdominal markings—stria—

and why some had these markings and some didn't. A couple of them wanted to know why they were having stomach cramp "low down" now. I said they were bringing up some interesting things and suggested they bring these up for discussion in class.

Meeting 6

Twelve expectant mothers came to class today.

They always greet each other as if it will be the last time together and for many, this is so true. They check their signs and symptoms together each time and are "all ready." They have as much fun before and after class as they do during class.

Before class they were chattering about many things. They got to talking about how their doctors treated them. Some said that their doctors ran them in and out like machines and didn't give them time to ask any questions or talk. One said her doctor would say, "Got any questions today?" but would be so busy she knew he wouldn't take time to answer them. Another said sometimes she'd have to wait two or three hours and then would have about five minutes with the doctor. One girl said she made a list of questions to take with her when she went to the doctor and it helped her remember what to ask. Another said she went to an obstetrical group of doctors and saw a different one every time, and that "doctors didn't do a thing for you anyway but weigh you and all such until you are about seven months pregnant," and that she told her doctor she was dissatisfied with the care and wanted to feel she was getting good care, attention, and opportunity to talk. Another said that her doctor was wonderful and that last week he talked with her for an hour and made her feel he was interested, even though she knew he was busy.

Before class they also checked delivery dates again with each other, and they asked the women who thought they might have twins about how things were going. One who thought she might have twins had found out she would not. She said she was disappointed at first, but now felt better about it. They were laughing about their sizes and several said they looked as if they might have triplets or more. Mrs. Walsh said she must be going to "have a cow." She also said she went to the hospital to visit recently, and went through the maternity ward and saw the delivery room and nursery. Some of the members who had been to a nursery recently were laughing about how ugly some of the babies were, but they were all cute. The before-class discussion could make a full report. These remarks were simply a small part of the talking that went on.

Before going to class today, I didn't know what to expect. I felt I had about run out of gas on what to do with the group and felt that maybe they were about out of interest. But how wrong I was. Today was unusual, but I don't know why. To me it was our best meeting. Instead of running out of interest, they are picking up momentum. Several wanted to know if we had to stop classes after eight times.

As we settled down for class, they looked over at the baby bath set up with eagerness and said, "Well, it looks like baby care today." At the beginning of class I reminded them that we didn't have much more time together and reviewed for them the topics and things they had mentioned earlier in classes and told them to be thinking about what they wanted to do in the last two classes. They considered things for discussion and several said they would still like to see the film on labor and delivery; quite a number said they didn't want to see this film. I asked what they would like to get or hope to get from a film that they didn't get from our discussions. They looked puzzled and said they really didn't know and maybe they didn't need to see a film. I told them that next week they could talk about whether they wanted to see this film or not. I told them that we were not committed to even have the baby bath today if they had other ideas. They all looked with eagerness at the baby bath preparation and wanted this demonstration today.

Before the demonstration I asked them what benefits to the baby a bath would give, and what did they hope they could accomplish when bathing the baby. They said it was good for the skin and kept it in good condition. Another said it should be a happy time for the baby and the mother. Other things were brought out and I suggested it was also an exercise time for baby and they picked this up and could see baby being handled and kicking around in water. When the member mentioned a bath being a "happy time," the group took off on an excellent discussion of parents' attitude in making a baby happy or otherwise. I asked if they had ever noticed differences in babies' actions or appearances which showed happiness or unhappiness and apathy. Many of them gave illustrations of their observations. One knew a baby whose mother really didn't want a baby and this baby looks so unhappy and never smiles or plays. The mother has never really accepted the baby and this reflects on the child. Another knows a mother who works and leaves her baby with a teen-ager and the baby should now be talking and doing things that he doesn't do. Others talked about children who don't talk because their parents don't take time to talk to them. They seemed so interested in the importance of doing things that would make for maximum emotional growth and happiness of the baby. They chatted on a while and then pulled themselves back to bathing the baby.

I pointed out to them that they might bathe a baby entirely differently from the way that I would demonstrate and that equipment, method, and the like, were not important if they considered a few basic things about the baby when bathing it. As I went through the demonstration, discussion and questions continued throughout and I invited their thoughts and suggestions as we went along. When we showed how to cleanse the baby's eyes, we talked about the eyedrops that are put in the baby's eyes. The group knew this was to protect the baby from any infection picked up in the birth process. This was discussed completely. When demonstration of cleaning the nose came up, they pointed out why "Q-Tips" and any such things could injure the nose. This discussion was pursued to completion and they even discussed why they should buy cotton in packages instead of cotton balls already prepared (less expensive).

During the demonstration they wanted to talk about special care of the cord. They talked about this from several angles, such as, "Does it hurt the baby?" "Will it hemorrhage if it is hit?" "When the cord is cut, will it hurt me or baby?" "Should we keep a dressing on cord until it is healed?" "Why do some navels stick out?" and all such. What they could not answer, I did. But I tried to let them always say what they thought first, and usually they knew the answers.

In discussing care of the genitals during the bath, they came up with lots of thoughts. They wanted to know all about when the baby boy would be circumcised, how they would care for the circumcision, whether it hurt or not, and all such. Also, at the beginning of the bath, they were very much interested in "cradle cap" and what to do about it and what caused it. Some members knew about this; I gave a few added suggestions.

They were interested in the bath and after it was over, decided that there was "really nothing to it," and suddenly seemed to be comfortable about it.

During the bath demonstration we also talked about handling the baby, position to hold him, and so forth. They saw and answered for themselves why support for head and back is necessary. They even knew that a baby has a fear of being dropped (and loud noises). In discussing positions of the baby in bed, I asked why his position should be changed occasionally. They recognized easily the different reasons why this was desirable.

After the bath demonstration, we chatted about other things in general that related to it, such as types of soap to use, how to cut costs of equipment (such as jars at home instead of buying fancy bath tray), and so on.

They had all brought a diaper to learn how to do all the different kinds of folds. They now were ready for this and were flapping them around. I had meant to get somebody to show me all the fancy folds before class time, so I could act learned and experienced, but had not had time to do this. I knew just one good way to fold a diaper and had done that many times, but I knew they would really have me behind the eight ball on anything else. But the group members themselves came to my rescue. Mrs. George started showing the group how to do a fancy triangular fold and they completely ignored me and started showing each other how and what to do. They didn't even ask me to show them a single fold. I sat there watching them and they'll never know that they taught me today! They discussed types of diapers, materials, and so forth. I did show them some different types of diapers, fillers, and such, after they had finished their practicing. They had said they were all so "green" on this matter of diapers and I had thought they didn't know all these things that they said were worrying them.

As the time was over, I tried to put an end to the discussion, but they just wouldn't stop talking. After fifteen minutes overtime, I started cleaning up. Finally they got out of their chairs but, as usual, grouped themselves together to visit some more. They say they don't want the classes to end and suggested they plan a "get together" after the babies come. They think this would be fun. They want to see each other again, and the babies, too.

The members talked together for thirty minutes while I cleaned up. Several were talking about stria, breast changes, and the like, and they were comparing differences. Some apparently have markings more than others, and one had no marking on abdomen at all. They talked about breathing difficulties and other discomforts. Some were having heartburn, nausea. Some were so uncomfortable that they had asked their doctors for pills to help them sleep. Some were talking about their weight gain. They talked together about their different food desires, problems, and needs. I also heard them discussing comfortable positions to assume in bed now.

They were kidding Mrs. Bensen about these late discomforts that she could look forward to later on. She is such a little thing and "not even showing," but she fits right in with the group. In fact, she actually is the one who vocally and by action seems to benefit and enjoy the classes the most. The group listens to her concerns with sympathy and understanding. They are willing to listen to each one and make each feel important and comfortable. As they continued to talk in the group comparing symptoms, one said she had been so well and had so little trouble that she hardly knew what they were talking about. They all thought this was wonderful and remarkable—"you lucky girl."

Some were talking about their recent visits to hospitals and about rules and regulations. Some have packed their bags to take to the hospital. They had decided in class that all should get things in order and all ready for this trip to be taken soon. They laughed about the interest people show when they now visit friends in the hospital. Several were planning to go by after class to visit friends in a hospital and know they will "shake the doctors and nurses up" when they go in; they hope they won't take them on to the maternity ward. (The group said that they wanted to talk about what to expect when they do go to the hospital for delivery. What do they do to you? What is the delivery room like? These and other things now are of interest and concern to them.)

Meeting 7

Twelve members showed up today.

As I watched them come in and heard their remarks, I wondered why on earth most of them even attempted to come. I almost wanted to say, "Let's call this all off and go home."

Mrs. Walk came in with a terrible cold and said she felt miserable. She is to deliver any time now. She tried to contact her doctor all day yesterday but he was busy with patients. She is concerned because she has heard it might be difficult to take an anesthetic with a bad cold and she wants something done in a hurry.

Mrs. Walsh came dragging in and said she felt awful. Even when sick she can be humorous, though. She looked around and said, "We are a dead bunch today." She didn't sleep well last night and told everybody she had "dropped down" since last week and showed everybody the proof.

Mrs. George came in drooping with her feet all swollen and said she would deliver before Monday, according to her doctor. She said her doctor had taken her completely off salt.

Mrs. Dunn said she was sick in bed all day yesterday and her feet are all swollen, too.

Mrs. May said she wasn't feeling well and looked it.

Mrs. Cass said she was so nervous and cried a lot recently.

As the group gathered in misery and dejection, Mrs. Bensen came tripping in like a little doll in a lovely sheath dress. She really looked as if she was in the wrong crowd today! She remarked that she probably would be the only one present next week. I told her we could have a private party together.

As I looked at them, I knew I had problems because I couldn't expect them to be alert, inquisitive, and as usual today. They looked at me as if to say, "Just give it to us today, we need help and don't want to talk too much." I knew I would have trouble getting them to come across. I reminded them that there were several things that had been mentioned as of interest that we had not discussed. We had not discussed formula preparation. They pointed out that each formula would be different and "just like a recipe" and they had all read up on how to sterilize equipment and felt like their pediatricians would tell them all they wanted to know about fixing formula and feeding the baby. This and other topics were mentioned and they really didn't seem terribly interested in anything at this point. For about ten minutes I struggled desperately trying to get them to hit on a topic of interest or on anything to perk them up. I hope I hid my concern from them. I had not had this problem before.

Finally I reminded them that they had expressed some interest in the things that would happen to them and be done to them when they went to the hospital. I began to get some response now and the talk eased along from that interest.

One member wanted to know where you stayed before you went into the delivery room and who was with you. Another wanted to know if all hospitals in their city let the husbands stay in the labor room with their wives. Different members named several hospitals where they knew this was possible and all seemed satisfied that their hospital would permit this. Some of them wanted their husbands with them, but some did not. Mrs. Cass said she wanted her husband to be there to see how bad it was and maybe he wouldn't want any more children. Mrs. May said her husband had been very concerned about her and every time she goes to the doctor he wants to know if she has asked the doctor if she will have a safe delivery. She wants her husband present when she is in labor. Mrs. Walsh, who obviously is devoted to her husband, said that she wanted him to be there because he doesn't seem too concerned over her discomforts and she wants him to see for himself.

As they were talking about this matter of husbands being in the labor room, they made other remarks about their husbands in general. Some had shown such excitement over their wives being pregnant and others had not been so expressive about the matter. Mrs. Bensen said her husband had called her long distance because he suspected she might be pregnant and he was so thrilled to find it true that "1500 sailors on his ship knew it before he hung up the phone." Mrs. May said her husband told everybody in his office that she was pregnant before she had told it. Some of them seemed to express disappointment that their husbands can't show interest and concern as much as others.

After talking about their husbands, they "got back into the labor room." We talked about the matter of preparation that they could expect. They knew that they would have to be shaved and that probably they would have an enema. I asked them if they knew why these things were done and they were able to understand reasons why and didn't seem to be bothered by the prospects of having these procedures done. They rather turned up their noses at the idea of the enema, but it didn't concern them.

They weren't worried about the rectal examinations that they probably will have but thought it would be an uncomfortable and undesirable thing. I asked if they knew why this was done. Mrs. Roth and others did a fine job of explaining reasons why, how it would be done, and showed understanding of anatomy by discussing closeness of rectum and vagina and how cervix could be felt through the rectum. The group also pointed out why a vaginal examination would be unwise as a rule.

They discussed some things about the delivery room. They knew that they would have sterile drapes. Some were concerned about possibility of having hands restrained. They think this would be terrible. One said a friend told her that when she was in the delivery room, her hands were restrained and "her nose itched so bad and no one would scratch it or even listen to her." I explained why sometime some slight restraint was necessary for safety reasons (to prevent contamination of sterile equipment, for example). They wanted to know how many would be in the delivery room, and what they would be doing. Now they wanted to talk a little more about anesthetics. They again discussed the kind they would get. They asked more questions about "spinal block," "demerol," "paraldehyde," "trilene," and so forth. There were a few things about the action and effects of drugs that they wanted cleared up.

In talking about "spinal block," someone mentioned knowing someone who had this and saw her baby being born by Caesarean and didn't like the experience of seeing all this at all. They remembered that Mrs. Bensen might have to have a Caesarean and asked her if she knew for sure yet. Mrs. Bensen said that she had a twenty-five percent chance of a normal delivery, but if she gained over ten pounds, she would definitely have to have a Caesarean operation. She has to watch her diet carefully. (With every class I understand more why diet was one of the first concerns of this group. Many of the mothers-to-be have given reasons why they were on special restrictions.)

They somehow got to talking about things that were happening to them now. Many have had "lightening" recently and say that they can breathe more comfortably, but it has brought on other discomforts, such as the need to empty the bladder more often. Some say they "hop up and down all night" and hesitate to go out anywhere for long in case they would need to go to the bathroom. Someone mentioned having increased vaginal discharge now and many perked up at this. It seems many are having this bothersome problem and some didn't realize this could be expected. They discussed irritation from this and how they handled the problem. One suggested wearing a pad and others just bathe with warm water frequently.

In speaking of "lightening" one of the girls who hasn't had this experience asked how you knew when you had dropped. Mrs. Walsh said, "It happened to me in about two minutes, ka-plunk!" Mrs. George said she didn't realize she had dropped until her doctor told her. Others said, "You'll know!" Someone asked exactly when this took place and it was explained that it usually happened from one month to two weeks before delivery. Another said, "If you have had a baby before, it drops sooner and quicker."

When they were talking about the delivery room, someone said she wondered how you really look after delivery. She said in the movies, the women always look so pretty and fixed up after the baby is born. Another said she knew she would look like a witch with her hair standing on end. All thought they would not look their best at that time.

When they were talking about their husbands, with affection but irritation, I asked how they thought the husbands were feeling about all this adjustment in their lives. They looked thoughful, but today everything is how *they* feel. They began to talk about their activities before marriage. Some said they thought it terrible if they stayed home a single night before marriage. Many of them said now they enjoyed staying home and don't want to run around much. Mrs. May said recently her husband suggested going out to dinner and she told him it was too expensive. She laughed and said he appreciated her being considerate and thrifty, when all the time she just didn't want to go out. Mrs. Walsh described her very active date life before marriage in such a funny way, but she said she wouldn't swap anything for her wonderful, happy married life. They fussed about their husbands and then expressed their satisfaction at marriage in a nice way.

At some time Mrs. Cass said she was so emotional recently and cried at any "ole" thing. Others chimed in with their feelings of "ups and downs." One said she would feel pretty good one day and hit a low the next. Several said they felt this way, too. Mrs. Cass revealed a concern of hers today that we had not known about. It seems her husband has been married before and has a child by the first marriage. Mrs. Cass said, "his" child is beautiful and she is so worried that "their" child won't be as pretty as this other child. She would be "sick if the baby is ugly."

In talking about how the babies will look, several are still afraid they will be ugly or not all right. Mrs. Bensen is still convinced hers will be cross-eyed. Mrs. Walsh said she wasn't worried at all. She said she couldn't imagine herself having anything but a pretty baby and she wasn't a bit concerned about it not being all right. This interests me because my guess is that she is one who could have some reasons for concern. She has told us about the long line of men on her husband's family who have this bone and joint trouble and harelip, plus the fact that she has constantly had trouble during pregnancy (such as toxemia).

Some have not selected a pediatrician for the baby and want to know how to go about this. One said she'd like to contact a pediatrician but doesn't know what to say to him because if she doesn't like him when she sees him, she doesn't want to feel committed to have him take care of the baby. The group shared their plans with each other.

At some place in the meeting, one member asked if she could be fitted for a diaphragm while in the hospital. Others told her that she would have to wait until her six-weeks' checkup, when her organs had returned to normal. They began to discuss these few weeks after delivery and asked how soon they would feel well enough to carry on all usual activities. Some recognized that they would need help around the house for a period of time after delivery. Others wanted to manage things themselves and felt that with husband's help they could do this. One said her husband was a good cook. They all are thinking about getting the baby home.

At one point they were discussing the active movements of the baby. One wanted to know if her tension could cause baby to move more. She said she knew there was no nervous connection with baby but she notices that he kicks more when she is tense. She also wanted to know about how easily the baby could be hurt by such things as licks on the abdomen. She had a friend who went to a chiropractor for an adjustment because her back hurt. She is pregnant and when the chiropractor was treating her, he crossed her legs over each other tightly and pulled on them. This friend is afraid it hurt the baby's head because her doctor said the head was down in her pelvis. Mrs. Walsh said she is always running into chairs and things and "whamming" her abdomen. Mrs. Cass said her mother has a fit if she sleeps or rests on her stomach and tells her it will hurt the baby. Another knew someone who was hit in the abdomen when in swimming. After all these stories, they reminded themselves of the protective bag of water, and other protection.

In talking about the baby moving and kicking around, two of the group said they "knew their babies moved at three and a half months but their doctors didn't believe it." One said the usual time for feeling the baby move was about four and a half to five months. Most of them say their babies are really "rambunctious" now. Mrs. May said she recently had an embarrassing experience. She was standing up and the baby kicked her hard "right in the bladder" and she soiled her clothes. The members looked sympathetic, as if to say, "The strangest things can happen now."

The group talked about things in a rather disjointed way today but, in a way, at the time it all seemed to relate. It seemed to be a time to kind of pick up loose ends. I thought it good that they came or talked at all today, considering their discomforts and miseries.

As time ended today, I reminded them that some had said they wanted to see a film on labor and delivery, and others had expressed a desire to see a film on baby care and I would like to know which they wanted to see. They want to see both!

Meeting 8

I was wondering how many of the group would still be "up and going" and able to come to class. Practically all of the members are either "due" or "overdue" for delivery. *Nine* came in today and with each grand entrance, there were expressions of surprise—because, "You were supposed to have delivered Monday!" "Don't tell me you haven't gone to the hospital yet?" . . . They all came in happy as larks. Last week they were feeling so physically "down" and today they looked so chipper, even though they had had another week of waiting and discomfort. I was amazed that they could look forward to a long session together at *this* time. They have had so much fun together and to my surprise even would like to continue classes! These members have not only had fun, but they have *worked* hard in learning. They have proved that a learning experience can be pleasant, but also that it is more meaningful when pleasant and "comfortable."

They really covered the waterfront today. There were *many, many,* little details and loose ends that they wanted to tie together. They really shared information and worked hard. They hit on dozens of topics and, as they talked, they made them relate.

As I listened to them chatter, I began to feel repaid for my overtime work, my fatigue, and so on. I heard such remarks as, "These classes must have helped me a lot because I'm not worried a bit any more about taking care of the baby or anything." Their remarks and even their looks told me that they were feeling more confident, adequate, and secure.

As they gathered today, they immediately missed Mrs. Dunn and asked where she was. I told them that she had delivered and had a baby girl. They were so delighted and thrilled.

Little Mrs. Bensen and all of her ninety pounds came tripping in wearing another lovely dress. She told the girls that she was designing and making her maternity dresses. The ready-made clothes are too small for her and furthermore she "refuses to wear dresses with a hole over the stomach like you can buy." She described her designs to the members and they were very interested. Those who have been wearing maternity clothes so long are threatening to "have a barnfire" and get rid of them as soon as possible. Someone suggested that "we may be sorry in about ten months if we burn them up." They were laughing at how horrible they thought they looked. Someone said she was uptown in a store and saw this tremendous creature and suddenly realized she was seeing herself in a mirror!

Some of these women really "worked their doctors over" today—again. They think it is awful that the doctors don't take enough time with them. Mrs. May told her doctor that she was dissatisfied with her care. Those going to the "obstetrical groups" feel that the care is very impersonal. This conversation was lengthy. I tried to make them feel a little differently by telling them, for example, that it doesn't take a well-trained doctor long to evaluate their condition. I think they really have confidence in their doctors, but are expressing their desire for a more personal recognition and more opportunity to talk things over with them.

They also spent more time talking about their weight gain and food problems. They were laughing about their food cravings. Mrs. Walsh and Mrs. May "just crave peanut butter now." One said she wanted to bring a peanut butter and jelly sandwich for lunch today and was afraid everybody would laugh. Mrs. Walsh craves "yogurt" sandwiches and the strangest stuff! Mrs. Arkin said she was "so tired of eating a well-balanced diet." They discussed their likes and dislikes and their displeasure at all their diet restructions, salt limitation, and so forth.

In discussing weight, they got to thinking of their figures after delivery. They knew that they would normally lose about fourteen pounds shortly after delivery and why (they referred to baby's weight, extra weight of uterus, amniotic fluid, blood volume, and the like). This led them to discuss exercises. Some are taking exercises now. I had given them an exercise booklet put out by the State Health Department. Most of their doctors had approved the use of these exercises. Some are planning to start exercises after delivery to get their figures back to normal. One said her doctor said any literature and information put out by the State Health Department was good.

At one time, someone wanted to know about blood pressure. One member said her doctor always takes her blood pressure and she has heard him call it out to the nurse to record. And each time it was "120 over something." She said the last time it was "135 over something," and the doctor didn't say anything to her about it. She wondered if it was all right. I tried to explain reasons for slight variations in blood pressure at times. I think she and the other women felt satisfied that their doctors would watch for any problems and take care of them.

Someone again brought up the question of "dropping" and discussed how it feels. From this, they discussed the beginning of contractions in labor. There were matters they wanted to clear up in their minds, such as, "how long pains would stay so many minutes apart." They talked about "counting pains" and the average length of time for each stage of labor and the variations for individuals. This also was a long discussion. I helped clarify anything that needed it, but usually someone knew the answers.

At some time they discussed further their breast changes and whether or not they would need larger brassieres when "the milk came in." They also brought up the fact that "some doctors give shots and pills to dry up the milk." Someone said it would make her "mad as fire if they gave her medicine to dry up her breast and she didn't know it." I told her this would possibly not happen in the hospital without her knowledge. They talked a while about this, which also led them to further express their feelings about breast feeding and how some are still made "to feel like dogs or heels if we don't want to breast feed our babies."

In talking about breast feeding and milk, someone asked if the baby got any protection from some diseases from mothers' milk. This led to a long discussion on immunity and immunizations. Questions came up as, "Doesn't the baby have a natural immunity for six months?" "I know a baby who was a few weeks old who had chicken pox." "Why was I given polio shots?" "My doctor didn't ask me anything, he just gave me polio shots." "Do I need four polio shots?" "Can we get shots at the Health Department?" "How often should adults be revaccinated?" "I had many revaccinations when going overseas with my husband and none 'took' and then I had one that did take, why was that?" They needed some help in this area of immunity and necessary immunizations for themselves and the babies. They were also interested and inquisitive about services of the Health Department. They wanted to know if a nurse could come help them with problems, such as care of baby, when they go home from the hospital. Again, I welcomed an opportunity to talk about nursing services of the Health Department. They also asked about services of the Visiting Nurse Association. I gave them this information.

As lunchtime arrived, they were still chatting like magpies and seemed to forget that we had to eat! (The group had decided to have lunch together since this was the last meeting.) After lunch, they settled back and had not once mentioned the films that they had requested me to have for them today. I asked if they did want to see the film on labor an delivery. Time was passing rapidly and I knew that if they wanted to see the film, I would have to show it soon because I could not stay with them all afternoon. I had already determined that we could see only one film. They said they did want to see the film, but Mrs. Walsh said she wanted to talk about babies' names first. She had not decided on a name for her baby and wanted some suggestions. I thought this would only take a few minutes. They started talking about names and they talked for ages about this topic as if it were the most important thing in the world. This led into birth certificates, school nicknames that would result from certain names, and all such. They had a hilarious time telling about the names of some children they knew.

At last we got around to the film, "Labor and Delivery." They seemed to enjoy it very much. By the discussion that followed, by the questions that were asked and the questions that were *not* asked, it was plain to me that they already were clear in their minds about the stages of labor and this whole business of labor and delivery. They did not seem concerned about the matter at all and did not appear fearful and apprehensive. In fact, today they seem very calm and relaxed about everything.

As the film was being shown, Mrs. Walsh was holding her abdomen. Some of the members noticed this and asked her if she was having pains. She said she was having some contractions "low down." Everyone was very interested and someone said we had seen the film and maybe *now* we would see the real thing. This was funny to Mrs. Walsh and she settled back with no idea of leaving to go home.

After the film they laughed about the expression of *mild* discomfort on the mother's face in the film when she was having contractions. They thought the whole thing looked *too* easy (and it really did). As the film showed the expectant mother struggling to get out of a chair, and so on, they said *that* looked real because getting up and down was now difficult for them.

Time was passing and I told them that we would not have time to see the film on "Growth and Development" of the baby. They were settled down for the rest of the day and I felt very sorry to have to bring our class to an end. I briefed for them what the film was all about and told them that there really wasn't much in the film that we had not talked about and that they didn't have in their literature which I had given them. I had given them some excellent literature on growth and development last week. We talked for a while about the baby's needs at each stage of development.

They weren't ready to go home, but all good things *must* come to an end. They all seemed so sorry not to be meeting again and began to wonder how they would know when each one had had her baby and how each could keep in touch. They discussed taking each other's telephone numbers. One member remembered that I had all the telephone numbers and as they all would call me to tell me when the baby was born, they wondered if I would let each one know about the other. They all promised to bring the babies to the Health Department to see me.

I hope it wasn't my imagination and just wishful thinking on my part, but as they left today, they seemed entirely unworried about labor and delivery. Rather, they seemed to be looking forward to the baby with happiness and confidence!

Record 2
DISCUSSION GROUP FOR PARENTS OF
ELEMENTARY SCHOOL AGE CHILDREN

Session 1

This group met under the auspices of the Parents Association of a public elementary school, one block from a housing project, in a deteriorating section of a large Eastern city. The meetings were held in the lunchroom.

The mothers represented a cross section of the population of the neighborhood: some were second generation Italian, some were Jewish, several were Negro, some seemed to have come from families who had lived in the area for many years and were not specifically identifiable.

At 9:55, with eleven members present, I started the meeting by asking the members to write their names on the large cards I had set at each place. I had printed mine and had it in front of me (last name only); someone said, "first or last names?" I suggested they could write both—these would probably be largely for my benefit in getting to know them since they obviously were acquainted with each other. There was some laughter and some remarks about all living in the project. I announced the meeting dates, remarking that we were fortunate in having the calendar clear of holidays so that we could meet regularly for the full eight weeks. I requested that members call me if they knew in advance that they could not attend a session, so we would not wait for them, and said they could leave a message for me with the school secretary.

I asked if all members present had been at the large Parents Association meeting when I had talked about how a discussion group proceeded; all nodded and I said that in that event I would not go over this again. I suggested we could start by going around the table asking each member to tell the ages of her children, a little about them, and what kinds of issues she would like the group to discuss.

Mrs. St., who was first, is a quiet, well-groomed woman a little older than the others. She said she didn't quite know how to start; she had two sons, age 10 and 15½, no special problems. She would like her boys to read more, they barely read outside their school work; she thinks it's important to broaden their interests. She would like them also to be more interested in their studies.

Mrs. K., a thin, tense woman, has a boy, 9½, and a girl of 5. "Like

Mrs. St., I would like him to do better in school. He doesn't apply himself as he should. I would also like to discuss discipline, what kind to use. When you beat him and he doesn't listen and you take away T.V. and he still does the same thing, what else can you do?" I asked if she could be a little more specific about "discipline," in relation to what kinds of things. Mrs. K. was eager to give her example. Last week her boy was due home at 4:30. He did not come home till after six. She hadn't known where to begin to look for him. When he finally came in and said he had been "just playing," first she had taken the strap to him, then taken away T.V. for some period (I forget how long). He did same thing again three days later! What should she do? I sensed the group getting restive; I said there was nothing more frightening to a mother than not knowing where a young child was. The group relaxed; there were murmurs of sympathy, Mrs. K.'s eyes reddened, someone at the other end of the table said her child had done this to her once, too; Mrs. K., more quietly, said he was a "handful." I said we might want to talk about situations like this when children were growing up to want to be more on their own. There were many nods, and we passed on to Mrs. W., a quiet, rather tight-lipped mother who has two girls, 9½ and 5½. She was interested in discussing homework, study habits, how you got a child into the right routine.

Mrs. E. is neat and rather quiet, her sentence phrasing giving the impression of schoolteacher precision. Her major concern was that of fighting between the two boys, ages 11 and 7½. (That got a rise from the group, "oh yes, that," "mine, too," "I forgot to even mention it, I take it so much for granted.") There is a little girl, age 2½, also, but the boys give her the greatest concern. Her older boy has some hesitancy in speech, for which he attended a Speech Clinic for one or two years. She was told there that she had to handle him differently, "take some of the pressure off," and she has been trying. (There was a big "but" in her voice.) He no longer attends the clinic, because he doesn't really stutter, and they felt further treatment was unnecessary.

Mrs. B. says of herself, "I'm on the point of getting hysterical so much of the time, it isn't funny." (She does give the impression of being under severe tension.) Her voice got tight and chokey as she talked about the fighting and jealousy between her two older boys, ages 15 and 10. "And now it's starting with the baby—what's the 10-year-old got to be jealous of in him (age 2)? He makes a fuss over him, wants to hold him, and then I find him taking secret pinches." (At some point later in the discussion Mrs. B. prescribed sedatives for all mothers.)

Mrs. P., a quiet, sweet-faced young woman, speaks diffidently. Her only child, a girl, age 9, is "bossy," won't listen and mind as mother feels she should. She's afraid daughter is getting spoiled and selfish. Relations between them are getting more strained; she wants to know more about handling girls that age.

Mrs. L., friendly, outgoing, speaks with humor of the "fights" between the girl, 8½, and the boy, 12½, and she wants discussion of this. But she is also concerned because her daughter clings so much to her, "always wants to be with me, doing things with me. I want her to get out more on her own."

Mrs. Kr., a pleasant-faced, thoughtful woman, feels she may be too strict with her boy, 12½, and girl, 10. She has no fighting or discipline problem, but her children are pointing out to her more and more frequently that other children are permitted to do many more things than they are. How to keep her own standards in her home when she and the children are aware that she does do things differently from many other parents in the project.

Mrs. F. was very quiet and "tight" throughout the session. She made her introduction extremely brief, "squabbling between the children, boy, 11, boy, 7." Her older son, like Mrs. E.'s, stammers. She took him to speech clinic, withdrew him after a short time since she saw it wasn't helping. She knew the problem was at home, that she had to "handle him more carefully."

Mrs. D. is president of this P.A. When her turn came, I recognized that she had not formally registered for the group by saying lightly, "Are you with us, Mrs. D.?" She laughed and said she had thought she was coming as an observer this morning but she was already feeling so involved that she was going to come every week and be a member. She has a girl of 10 and a girl of 6. There is squabbling between them, especially when their own friends are in. She and her husband differ on handling the children (this drew many nods and some comments about it being a good topic to discuss). Mr. D. works at night, sleeps during the day—there is a problem because she feels it important for the children to be able to have friends in after 3 o'clock; she doesn't like to keep hushing them. "I was a lonely child myself, and I want my children to have their friends," she commented with considerable feeling.

Mrs. S., a warm, likeable woman who seems to underestimate herself, has a boy, 12, and a boy, 8. The younger is a "very stubborn child," always has baffled her because of his intense desire to do things his own way. How to give him this sense of independence he needs so much and still control him is the way she phrased her chief concern at home.

Mrs. Eb. has a taut, white face and a somewhat distraught look about her. She came in very late, in time only to hear Mrs. D. and Mrs. S. I explained what we had been doing. Mrs. Eb. has a girl, 8, boys of 12 and 15. Her daughter is the one who "starts everything in the house; keeps us all upset. Whatever she has, she never has enough, always claims the boys get everything."

There was laughter as I said we had enough topics to talk about for months. I went briefly over the areas of common concern—tension between children in the home; when parents differ on handling children; differences between families on what children are permitted or not permitted; involving children more in their schoolwork and out-of-school cultural interests; discipline and where, when, and how parental authority comes in; the older child's growing independence. Asked where they would like to start, Mrs. B. said the question of discipline and parental authority seemed most immediate; several nodded vehemently. I checked for other preferences; Mrs. L. said, "it doesn't really matter which one we start on, they're all interesting." All agreed.

Mrs. B. began to talk about the racket in her house with the three boys and her struggles to control this. There was general discussion of pros and cons of cutting off T.V. as a means of control, how to punish one child without depriving another who "was entitled to listen." As I listened, I got the impression that many were struggling with the reality of limited space and tension arising from lack of privacy and much-needed quiet. When I recognized this aloud, even the two quiet members joined in the airing of pressures of small apartment living—no place for mother to get away to sit down or lie down quietly for a few minutes, children sharing small bedrooms, no place for their possessions, lack of privacy for children to have own friends without sibling interruption, two husbands who work at night, sleep during the day, and so forth. Mrs. B. took out her knitting and began to relax.

I brought them back to the topic, suggested they tell about specific situations that called for parental action. Mrs. S. and Mrs. K. contributed two parallel situations involving direct defiance of mother's wishes about wearing clothing for school, each boy refusing to go to school in trousers selected by mother. Again the discussion became very lively as Mrs. D. contributed her efforts to give her daughter leeway in choice of clothing, yet maintain control of standards and budget. Mrs. Kr. agreed that children learned by being given choices, even learned from the mistakes they made in selecting thin footwear, as her daughter had. Mrs. K. was pleasantly surprised to find a lot of support in the group to her "confessing" that she had finally let her son choose another, equally appropriate pair of trousers. Mrs. L. said she had "learned the hard way" not to make a big issue of small issues like clothing choices. It saved much tension in the morning if, when her daughter said belligerently, "I won't wear *that* dress," she said indifferently, "there are two others in the closet," and if it wasn't so clean, only she herself knew. Mrs. B. brought in the

matter of budget and difficulties of letting children choose clothes fashion-
able right now, and "then they hang in the closet," hardly worn. Some
considered this an investment, suggested buying cheaper clothing for
growing children, as Mrs. B. had mentioned a $15 pair of pants. I brought
in the meaning of clothing to people, suggesting that each of us had a
dress "hanging in the closet," that had represented something to us on
purchase. The discussion took a more thoughtful turn as child's desires to
"be like the others" began to seem more a sign of a new step in growing
up and establishing an identity for himself different from how mother sees
him. When I said something about how children see situations differently
from the way adults do, Mrs. K. said, "I just thought of something. The
time my boy stayed out so late, he really didn't feel he was doing anything
wrong, he was so busy playing he didn't realize the time."

Mrs. Eb. was still concerned about the effect on youngsters of permitting choices that required the outlay of money. Didn't parents run the
danger of spoiling children by always giving what they wanted? A discussion followed, sparked by Mrs. D., as to what extent children should
be made aware of family finances. Mrs. B. and Mrs. E. talked about their
feeling guilty when they couldn't meet a request from their children for
material things. Mrs. St. came in with some relevant remarks about how
she had helped her son to get the sweater he wanted, using his own
money, and showing how to shop so that he didn't spend it all. Mrs. D.
again came back, with considerable emotion, about giving choices within
the reality of budget, relating this to her childhood and her mother giving
her a choice of one pair of outsize shoes purchased with a precious ration
coupon during the war. This led to discussion of how each one's childhood colored feelings about "giving" to his children. Mrs. E. and Mrs. B.
felt they wanted to be able to give because they themselves had had
economic hardship as children. Mrs. Kr. and Mrs. L., both of whom had
been in more favorable circumstances, felt it hadn't spoiled them, but
they didn't find it so hard to say "no," or "we can't afford it." Mrs. Kr.
said it was fine to give, within reason, but also to expect something from
children in the way of chores, assumption of responsibility, and the like.
Mrs. D., again with considerable emotion, said she wanted her children
to have a childhood with fun and friends; they would get the hardships
as they grew older. Mrs. P., silent through most of this, obviously em-
pathized, as I gathered from her nodding.

I summed up how we had started with taking action to control children,
and saw how many different things played into this, physical circumstances that provoked conflict and tension, differences between parents'
and the child's point of view on a given situation, examination of the situation and issue to see whether parents really needed to take a firm stand.

On the issue of clothing and choices this morning, there was the sense that fairly wide latitude might be given, but weren't there other issues where limits might have to be firmer and narrower? We could talk about these next time, if they cared to.

"This was so interesting," "We really got started right away," "We'll want eighteen sessions instead of eight," were typical comments made as the group broke up.

Sessions 2 and 3

[Three new members came to the second meeting.]

The leader gave a brief summary of the concerns that had been brought up at the first meeting, asked the new mothers to introduce themselves and to mention any other matters they would like added. They took their place easily in the discussion, which continued on the issue of children's choices about clothes. With many of the mothers participating, the group moved on to experiences in which mothers and fathers were not in agreement about the handling of situations, the need for "consistency," on the one hand, and the value for children of knowing that parents do not always agree, on the other.

This general area was carried on into the third session, with many examples of tension and antagonism between children in the family and parental difficulties in coping with this. There was more interaction between the members as they listened to one another and agreed or disagreed about the handling of specific situations, and as they came closer to the underlying concern of how they—as individuals—could help their individual children take their proper place in the family.]

Session 4

PRESENT: D., St., B., W., Kr., K., F., T., C., Wa., N.

ABSENT: L. (at Book Fair in school), P., S., (illness at home), E., Eb.

I started the session by going over some of the specific material that had come out of the first meeting and pointed this toward some of the typical developmental reactions of children in this age group. For example, I noted how many parents had mentioned increasing "independence," with regard to choices in clothing, shopping, and so on. I related this to child's increasing awareness of his own individuality as a person in a school group and peer group as well as a member of his family. I said, "They seem to be saying, 'look, Mom, I'm not the little boy (girl) I used to be; see me in a different way,'" using the specifics they had given about boys wanting to choose their own pants for school, and the like. Also, their noting how children were insisting on their "rights" and "fairness" from parents. I generalized from Mrs. Wa.'s specific and typical experience with her son in the matter of the T.V. program he had missed because he had acceded to her request that he sit with sister a little while at bedtime and so missed his T.V. program. I related this to a child's concept of time, and how they still need help to understand how many activities can be fitted into sixty minutes—how children try to fit too much into a given time, not realizing they need time, for instance, for transitions and reorganization of materials. Back to the home situation, I pointed out how a child this age still wants to please parents (sit with sister to please mother), but wants his own needs satisfied, and needs adult help to plan this. I pointed out how they had said in many connections, "but they're still children," how this might relate to their own discomfort at using "long-range punishments," and how, when they removed this after the heat of the moment, they were really showing that they saw how much children live in the present. This summary took about ten minutes, and from the rapt faces, comments, and nodding reactions, I felt that some of what the group had been talking about in different areas was beginning to make sense, in a new way.

They talked a few minutes about how parents themselves forgot the next week what they were still banning T.V. for, how much less sense it made to kids. Mrs. B. quoted a newspaper article about how juvenile delinquents had told a research group that what they had wanted from parents was, "Don't let us give in to our impulses, don't let us get away with everything and give us everything we want—also, let us make up for the things we did wrong, punish us and let us make retribution." I asked if the point made in the article had some connection with parental control as we had been discussing it in regard to the behavior of the children in this group.

Mrs. B. had an example: Her 10-year-old had gone through his older brother's things, found some pictures of seminudes, taken them to school and showed them around among his friends. Another mother had called her—"she wasn't too disturbed, she's the kind who understands kids"—and Mrs. B. had taken this up with her child. "What should I have done?" she asked the group. I asked Mrs. B. to tell us what bothered her most about the situation before we got into the handling of it. She wasn't quite sure—first it was the fact that he had taken something from his older brother's things, despite her repeated rules that the boys both had the right of privacy to their possessions; but she was equally disturbed because she thought the 10-year-old had taken the pictures to show around to get attention from age mates: he didn't get along well with other children his age because he "lacked confidence in himself." The implication was that this was a facet of his being a "problem child," his way of getting peer attention. I asked the group if any saw this situation as something that had implications for other parents. Many agreed the issue of children taking things from siblings and from parents without permission, "borrowing clothes," "going through siblings' toys and drawers," and the like, was of general concern. Mrs. D. saw the issue of sex curiosity in this situation—told how her daughter and friends retired giggling to the bedroom on occasion to "talk about pictures or articles they saw in the papers," saw this as normal curiosity about sex. Mrs. B. responded, "Oh, no—he's too young to be curious about sex"; others disagreed—this was an age of normal curiosity. Mrs. C. saw three things of interest in the situation that Mrs. B. had told about—how one child wanted to be as old as, have things, do things like the others in the family—now she agreed with Mrs. B. that the important thing in this situation was J.'s bid for attention because he "lacked confidence in himself," so did her older daughter, with specifics of clinging to her. Finally, the issue of taking things, which she saw as another facet of a child's lack of confidence in herself, "like my daughter used to want to wear my gloves, my jewelry, and such, till I got her out of the habit."

At this point I summarized the issues before the group growing out of Mrs. B.'s comments, asked which one they wanted to start on. Mrs. D., Mrs. F., Mrs. B., Mrs. N., all chimed in that the issue was building self-confidence in their children. Mrs. C. was strong for this discussion, too. I asked if they would say how they saw this, what were the children doing that made them feel the individual child had a "lack of self-confidence." During the recounting of incident that followed, Mrs. B. tried to get the group back to "her problem child;" Mrs. D. pulled it back to the general topic of how children showed confidence or lack of confidence in themselves, saying, "I think lots of kids this age aren't as sure of themselves as they try to make us believe by the way they carry on at home." Mrs. C. "has a problem" with her older daughter, D., who has no friends, clings to mother, is afraid other children don't like her. At one point in the discussion, Mrs. C. said, "The younger one isn't like this, and I think it's because I gave her more confidence in herself when she was little because I wasn't so insistent on having her do things *my* way. With D., I was always making her wear what I wanted her to, act the way I wanted her to in company, play with the kids I wanted her to. With the little one, I wasn't so strict or so anxious, and she's much better able to get around and take care of herself." Mrs. D. underscored this spontaneously by referring to her own childhood, mother dominated; her own shyness, longing to be "like the other kids," but, in a way, really different. "I felt different, and I was. I wasn't as popular as my sisters, but then, I wanted to read more and do different things from the rest." Mrs. T. said, in reaction to this, that she thought one symptom of lack of self-confidence was the child's insistence on wearing what the group did. Several jumped in and said, "but this is normal," "it doesn't show lack of self-confidence."

I slowed things down by inviting more discussion of this point, Mrs. F. and Mrs. Kr. both related incidents, on opposite sides of the issue. Mrs. St. at this point said that she was confused: "Are we saying children have confidence when they're *like* others their age, or just what is *self*-confidence?" Mrs. B. and Mrs. C. concurred that self-confidence was a feeling that came from inside, that made the child "act happy," and feel happy, but both equated it with sociability and active membership in a peer group at this age. Mrs. D. pointed out that both also had said earlier that each had a child who felt inferior to a sibling, as she herself had as a child. Mrs. B. glared, and withdrew from the discussion. Mrs. C. felt Mrs. D. had hit the nail on the head, recounted her attempts to build her older daughter's confidence by giving praise, approval, recognition, and so forth. Others chimed in with their attempts to "give more" to the child who was feeling inferior.

Since I felt this was bogging down in a welter of guilt, I took the discussion back to Mrs. St.'s point about what were parental expectations of what a child "should be like," "at this age." At this point I referred to a topic that had been used at a parent membership meeting, "My Dream Child, and What I Have." It brought a laugh and some interchange that moved the discussion on to an examination of the stereotype of the happy, self-confident child, with Mrs. St. enlarging on her point that popular, peer-group leaders weren't always necessarily happy, or so sure of themselves. Mrs. C. felt she had been "pushing" D. toward friendships. "I myself like to be alone during the day, and don't feel sociable till the evening." Mrs. K. came through with the statement, "When you look at it, this isn't an age when they want it all to come from us, anyway . . . ," and told about how her child began to get more confidence in himself when the school made him a street-corner guard, and the difference it made in his feeling about himself. Mrs. W. described how she had helped her daughter gain a feeling of status by quietly reminding the teacher that her child had never "held the flag in assembly," and the teacher's good response to this, and the positive effect on her child.

Mrs. St. raised the question, "How does a parent know where a child is really unhappy, or his lack of confidence is a passing thing, or a phase of his growing up." Mrs. D. countered by saying, "If it lasts more than a year or two, and nothing you seem to do helps." Others agreed a prolonged pattern was significant.

I said we could go on with the discussion next time, if they wanted to, and perhaps talk more about ways of helping a child grow in self-confidence and what signs might show that it was growing from within.

Mrs. B. came up at the end of the meeting to tell about how J. has a status in the family as the "car-buying consultant." Because he doesn't play out much with boys his age, and he is interested in cars, he studies car models, car prices, lists, and dealers and is consulted by aunts and uncles, half in jest and half in earnest, when a trade-in is in process.

Sessions 5 and 6

[The group went back to the question of fighting among brothers and sisters and talked in more detail about what their children were doing. There began to emerge from the back-and-forth a sense of the "normal jealousy" of children and their competitiveness for their parents' love and attention (and their resentment and rivalry toward the parents of the opposite sex); and the mothers began to talk more freely about their children—different children—and the difficulties they and their husbands had in meeting their children's varying needs at different ages and stages.

At one point] Mrs. B. came in with a long and involved story of a Sunday night experience in her home—this time with J. and brother and father involved. Though the initial point of take-off was father's role, it got lost in her guilt reactions to J. Mrs. St., sitting next to her, challenged her handling of J.—there was a beginning one-to-one interchange between them. I stepped in and asked if Mrs. B. would say what she felt was the major point for her in the incident. With considerable feeling she said, "I've suddenly realized J. is the scapegoat in our family—we really make no place for that child. I realized I punished him Sunday night for no real reason—he hadn't done anything so wrong, except upset his brother by moving books off of what was really his own desk." Murmurs of support and sympathy from the group and agreement with her that there had really been no punishable offense.

Session 7

PRESENT: B., S., P., Eb., T., Wa.

At 10 A.M. Mrs. S., B., T., and P. were present, and Mrs. S. was looking through a listing of pamphlets I had brought at her request. *Facts of Life for Children,* which she had borrowed, was praised by her and she expressed hope that this topic could be discussed. Mrs. T. was immediately interested, and so was Mrs. P. Mrs. S. said maybe we should wait for a "bigger meeting," there was a little discussion of the pros and cons of holding this topic in abeyance until next time. It was clearly the wish of the group to get into the topic of sex, but also there was typical reluctance about this. I recognized this aloud, and Mrs. S., with a sigh of relief, said "Well, let's start today and the others can catch up."

Mrs. T. began to talk rapidly about how she was "old-fashioned" and was not going to tell her 9-year-old daughter about menstruation for several years. She was not going to give her child information and then have the neighbors come back at her and ask her why she was telling her child the facts of life so early. Mrs. S. and Mrs. B. immediately began to react to this—Mrs. S. saying, "Nine is not too early," Mrs. B. reacting to "the neighbors." I asked them to hold this for a minute while Mrs. T. told us whether her daughter had asked questions and what they were. Mrs. T. said her daughter had asked about pubic hair, her friends were beginning to show signs of this; Mrs. T. had told her, "Don't rush things, you've got a long time before this happens to you." Then she said she herself had been completely unprepared for menstruation, which started with her at 14— how she had called her mother, frightened, and asked if there were bedbugs in bed she had squashed that caused the stain. Mrs. S. asked, didn't she want her daughter better prepared so there would not be the shock. Mrs. T. said "Yes, but I figure I have five years yet—it's a messy thing— I don't want to scare the child now—she's a baby yet."

There was an interchange of personal experiences on when and how menstruation had started with them as girls: none had been prepared by mothers, Mrs. B. gave verbatim account of her experience and misinformation she had from friends—stressing her feeling that preparation and honest answers to children was a responsibility parents had now. She also gave her point of view about "neighbors": "I would resent any parent coming to me to tell me what I should tell my kid!"

I asked for other experiences mothers were having with daughters now. Mrs. P. really talked today—she had given a pamphlet on menstruation to her 9-year-old girl when the girl had said her friends were talking about this. Then she had discussed pamphlet with her daughter, felt the child had taken this without upset, gave the group the sense that she had felt good about her handling of this. Now she had another pamphlet ready on "the birds and the bees" for further questions about conception. Mrs. T. was deeply interested that child had not been frightened about menstruation. Mrs. Eb.'s girl is 8, has not asked questions about menstruation, had noticed pregnant women, knows babies are growing inside, but Mrs. Eb. has not discussed this with her further. Mrs. Eb. was holding a Health Department pamphlet she had borrowed last time; she said she had left it around the house and the two boys had read it—had not discussed this with her—they had talked with their father on this topic, when they were younger. She felt boys should talk to their fathers. I asked for reaction to this.

Mrs. S. said her oldest had asked few questions in his growing up, she felt that he had discussed many things with a cousin slightly older, and that the two boys had some solid information between them. However, on occasion he did ask her or his father (it didn't seem to matter to him which one) for clarification on some point. For example, a few weeks ago he had asked her if the word for seminal discharge was "scum," and she had told him the correct word was sperm. Mrs. S. went into a description of how the boy had called her into the bathroom while he was bathing to ask her this, adding she sometimes wondered if he was too free about exhibiting himself—when guests are in the house he comes in in his shorts, or will walk through a room half undressed. Mrs. T. reacted to this. She did not believe in parents walking around half dressed in front of children or children parading around undressed, especially after they were "growing up." Described how she made her husband, from the time children were babies, at least keep his pajama pants and bathrobe on. She knew she was "old fashioned" but didn't approve of nudity. Mrs. B. said it depended on the household; in her household they were "free," and boys were used to seeing her walk around in bra and slip—it was their custom, the boys never reacted to this—her husband was informal too. Mrs. S. said her husband liked to walk around in shorts too, maybe that's why older son did this without concern; however, she had noticed just recently that when her boy passed the bedroom door when she was changing, he had given a "wolf whistle," and it made her wonder. I asked what it made her wonder. Hesitantly, she brought out that maybe he was at the age now where he "got aroused." Mrs. Wa. agreed there was something in this —her 10-year-old reacted to a T.V. program featuring a girl in a low-cut gown, and he was chanting "lower, lower." When she asked him about this, he said that his friends had told him that's what he was supposed to say. She wasn't sure but that maybe he was feeling something too, but she didn't want to make too much of an issue of this.

Mrs. P. brought up her daughter's recent self-consciousness at going to the doctor and undressing for a physical exam. She herself had always been self-conscious, even with doctors, and she was trying to explain to the child that the doctor was not going to hurt her, that he was different because he was a doctor. Mrs. T. said she had decided to change doctors recently because the pediatrician who had taken care of her daughter since birth had recently begun to make remarks about "hasn't she begun to change yet," jokingly tickling the girl's breasts, poking at her genitals, and the like. Again, Mrs. T. said maybe she was old-fashioned but she didn't like this. Mrs. E. said "Isn't that unprofessional of the doctor?" All agreed that "even if he didn't mean anything by it," they felt it wasn't good for the child. Mrs. P. said their doctor was quite objective and had never joked or teased, but still it was a problem for her daughter to undress in his office. I underscored their sensitivity to children's feelings about their bodies, the growing self-consciousness of preadolescent youngsters—that it was a time when parents would not want to add to stimulation or "arousal" (Mrs. S's word); some of Mrs. T's "old-fashioned" methods really gave protection to children who might have enough trouble handling such stimuli as T.V. programs, newspaper reports, magazine pictures.

I asked if Mrs. P. felt daughter would feel better about woman doctor. The group said they knew grown women who preferred women doctors, especially gynecologists.

The discussion turned to words and concepts children got from newspapers that put demands on parents such as explaining "rape," "homosexual," "unwed mother." Time was running out. I suggested we pick up here next time. Members asked me to bring other pamphlets next week.

Session 8

[At the last session, with seven mothers present, the group continued the discussion of the last meeting, one or two starting hesitantly but gradually becoming more involved as they got caught up in the subject. They mentioned their children's increasing sex awareness in the home and outside and the children's growing wish for privacy. At the same time, the members felt that too much emphasis on privacy on their own part might "make a big deal" of the matter and might be just as stimulating to the children as too much bodily exposure. The meeting went on as follows:]

Mrs. T. again came in with her question about, "Why did you have to *explain* about menstruation to a 9-year-old?" and the group got off into this topic. Despite others in the group agreeing that it was important to prepare a girl for menstruation and Mrs. Kr. saying how she had done this with her daughter without more than an interested, accepting reaction on the child's part, Mrs. T. kept insisting "It will frighten a child." When I asked how she anticipated this, what reaction did she feel a girl would have—she wasn't sure. "It's so messy, and to talk about blood and bleeding," she said with a shudder, "she'll get scared." Others, including Mrs. F., chimed in with, "Wouldn't she be more scared if she didn't understand this, like we were when our mothers told us nothing?" Again, there was an exchange of childhood experiences.

During this interchange, I got the impression from listening to Mrs. T. that at least one of the reasons for her reluctance to "tell her daughter" was that she herself was not clear on the physiology of menstruation. To meet this, I made a summary at this point of what they had been saying about preparing a child for menstruation—including in it a question to the effect, "Would a little 9-year-old necessarily be scared if she were told how an egg forms in the body?"—a simple step-by-step explanation of the menstrual cycle as one would gear it to a child. From the intensity with which Mrs. T. watched my face as I was talking, I felt I had hit "pay dirt" with some of her anxiety.

From here, Mrs. Eb. raised the question of preparing boys for their body changes—there was some discussion about this—some expression that fathers be prepared to do this for boys. Two women said, "Oh, my husband is less prepared than I am to talk about sex to a child."

Time was drawing to a close. I expressed regret that we could not have more time with this topic. I distributed booklets, took some additional orders for *Facts of Life*, which I would leave with the school secretary. The group broke up in final goodbyes, expressions of regret at parting, and the members were still talking as they went out the door.

Appendix IV
Sample Schedules of Training Institutes

1. Training for Nurses in Leadership of Expectant Parent Groups (1960)
2. Training for Nurses in Supervision of Leadership of Expectant Parent Groups (1961)
3. Training of Social Workers for Leadership of Discussion Groups for Parents of Handicapped Children (1960–61)
4. Training for Family Caseworkers in Parent Group Education Leadership (1963–1964)

1. TRAINING PROGRAM FOR NURSES IN LEADERSHIP OF EXPECTANT PARENT GROUPS
Conducted by
The Child Study Association of America
under the Joint Sponsorship of
The New York State Department of Health
and
The Children's Bureau, United States Department
of Health, Education and Welfare
1960

INITIAL THREE-WEEK INSTITUTE
given at CSAA headquarters
February 23–March 11, 1960.

The nurses met from 8:30 or 9:00 A.M. to 4 or 5 P.M. each day. The program consisted of theoretical sessions conducted by "guest faculty," staff presentations, seminar discussions, written records and taped recordings, and individual conferences with their CSAA staff consultants.

The following pages indicate the scope and variety of material that was presented and discussed. Although of necessity the various parts are described separately, they form an integrated whole.

THEORETICAL SESSIONS

A. Psychological, Emotional, and Social Aspects of Pregnancy, Birth, Care of the New Baby and Growth of the Family

Feb. 23 2–4 p.m.	Newer Concepts of Obstetrical Care Justin T. Callahan, M.D., obstetrician and gynecologist
Feb. 24 2–4 p.m.	Psychological and Emotional Aspects of Pregnancy—as seen in Obstetrical Practice Norman Pleshette, M.D., obstetrician
Feb. 25 2–4 p.m.	Psychological and Emotional Aspects of Pregnancy—as seen in Psychiatric Research Benjamin B. Brussel, M.D., psychiatrist
Feb. 29 2–4 p.m.	Pregnancy—A Period of Psychological and Emotional Growth Edward Mann, M.D., obstetrician

Mar. 1, 2, 3,
and 4
8:30–
  9:30 a.m.
	Special Areas of Interest to Expectant Parents
	    Aline B. Auerbach, Child Study Association of America

Mar. 1
2–4 p.m.
	The "Crisis" of Homecoming
	    Wanda Robertson LeRoy, R.N., Consultant in Expectant
	    Parent Education

Mar. 2 2–4 p.m.	The Child's First Year Milton J. E. Senn, M.D., pediatrician and psychiatrist
Mar. 3 2–4 p.m.	Parent-Child Interaction in Early Infancy Barbara M. Korsch, M.D., pediatrician
Mar. 4 12:30–2 p.m.	The Growing Child: Parental Responses to Stages of Growth Peter B. Neubauer, M.D., psychiatrist, psychoanalyst
Mar. 7 1–2:30 p.m.	Growth into Adulthood Gerard Fountain, M.D., psychiatrist, psychoanalyst
Mar. 9 2–4 p.m.	Variations in Cultural Attitudes Toward Parent-Child Relations Charles Lawrence, Ph.D., sociologist-anthropologist
Mar. 10 2–4 p.m.	Community Resources for Counseling and other Services to Parents; Indications for and Methods of Referral A. D. Buchmueller, Child Study Association of America

Note: This program was predicated on the knowledge that the nurses who are in this program have a thorough background of medical-nursing knowledge. The material presented in these presentations reviewed and explored the psychological and social aspects of expectant parents' needs and reactions.

B. Philosophy and Method of Group Education for Expectant Parents

Feb. 25
8:30–
  9:30 a.m.
	Establishing the Group Atmosphere
	    Aline B. Auerbach, Child Study Association of America

Feb. 26   Group Education for Expectant Parents: Philosophy and Goals
12:30–2 P.M.   Peter B. Neubauer, M.D., psychiatrist, psychoanalyst
Feb. 29   The Role of the Leader
9–10:15 A.M.   Aline B. Auerbach, Child Study Association of America
Mar. 3   The Use of Demonstrations
4–5 P.M.   Ruth Marvin, R.N., Child Study Association of America
Mar. 4   Developing the Content of Group Discussion
10:30–   Salvatore Ambrosino, Ed.D., Child Study Association of
11:30 A.M.   America
Mar. 10   The Meaning and Use of Group Interaction
9–10:30 A.M.   Aline B. Auerbach, Child Study Association of America

Other aspects of techniques in group education were discussed in seminars in relation to these presentations, observations of groups of parents of young children at CSAA headquarters, observations of several types of group activities at New York Hospital, the showing of the film "From Generation to Generation" at the Maternity Center Association, and the written report of a continuous series of expectant parent group meetings.

✿   ✿   ✿   ✿   ✿

Following this institute, the nurse-leaders conduct two expectant parent groups in their own communities with supervision and consultation from Child Study Association training staff. They return for a one to two week institute in September, and then conduct two more groups, again with consultation from Child Study Association staff.

This training program is organized and conducted by The Department of Parent Group Education, Child Study Association of America.

2. A TRAINING PROGRAM FOR NURSES IN SUPERVISION OF LEADERSHIP OF EXPECTANT PARENT GROUPS

Conducted by
The Child Study Association of America
under the Joint Sponsorship of
The New York State Department of Health
and
The Children's Bureau, United States Department
of Health, Education and Welfare
1961

TWO WEEK INSTITUTE
given at CSAA Headquarters

January 30–February 10, 1961
in connection with
Second Year of Leadership Training Program

This part of the program (identified in the project outline as "Step II") provides training in supervision of leadership of expectant parent groups to a number of nurses who participated in the 1960 Program of Training held at CSAA. They gain experience in this type of supervision by supervising nurses from their own areas who are participating in the 1961 Training Program in their leadership of the expectant parent groups which serve as the new nurses' field work in their total program of training. The supervisors-in-training, in turn, work with CSAA staff through weekly correspondence and a field visit.

These nurses, who are preparing for supervision of expectant parent group leadership, attend sessions from 9:00 A.M. to 4:00 P.M. each day. Their program consists of theoretical presentations, observations of expectant parent groups, seminar discussions, study of problems of supervision raised by written records of expectant parent group meetings, and individual conferences.

This institute is coordinated with the basic 1961 Institute, and provides the opportunity for both groups of nurses to meet together in a number of theoretical and seminar sessions. (In these seminars, this group of nurses will participate as observers only.) The designation "planned seminar" is given to those sessions devoted to the presentation and discussion of particular problems raised by the participants.

Planned Seminars on Important Aspects of Supervision

Jan. 30 2:45–4:00 P.M.	Principles of Supervision of Expectant Parent Group Leadership
Feb. 1 2:45–4:00 P.M.	The Meaning of This Type of Supervision to the Nurse-Leader
Feb. 3 1:00–2:45 P.M.	The Supervisor's View of Her Supervisory Role
Feb. 6 2:45–4:00 P.M.	Individual Problems in Supervision: Resistance and Anxiety in the Nurse-Leaders
Feb. 7 1:00–2:30 P.M.	Individual Problems in Supervision: Personality Problems of the Nurse-Leaders.
Feb. 8 10:45–12 M.	Meeting the Educational Needs of the Nurse-Leaders.
Feb. 9 1:00–2:30 P.M.	Supervision in Relation to Individual Patterns of Learning.

This training program is organized and conducted by The Department of Parent Group Education, Child Study Association of America.

3. DEMONSTRATION PROJECT IN
TRAINING OF
SOCIAL WORKERS FOR
LEADERSHIP OF DISCUSSION GROUPS
FOR PARENTS OF HANDICAPPED CHILDREN
1960–1961

The program will be conducted at CSAA Headquarters every Wednesday as indicated below, from 1:15 to 4:30 P.M.

A.   Parental Concerns about Their Handicapped Children: Their Meaning for Parent Group Education (15 sessions).

Oct. 5, 1960
2:00–3:30 P.M.
Parent Group Education for Parents of Handicapped Children: Philosophy and Values
Peter B. Neubauer, M.D., psychiatrist, psychoanalyst

Oct. 12, 1960
1:15–2:45 P.M.
Medical Aspects of Rehabilitation: Parental Concerns as Seen by the Physician
Howard A. Rusk, M.D., professor of physical medicine and rehabilitation

Oct. 19, 1960
1:15–2:45 P.M.
Child Development and Parental Concerns (Critical Aspects of Normal Growth and Variations Due to Handicapping): The Antepartal Period and the Child's Early Months
Aline B. Auerbach, Child Study Association of America

Oct. 26, 1960
1:15–2:45 P.M.
Psychiatric Considerations Underlying Parental Concerns for their Handicapped Children
George E. Gardner, M.D., psychiatrist

Nov. 2, 1960
1:15–2:45 P.M.
Child Development and Parental Concerns: The Child from Two to Five
Barbara M. Korsch, M.D., pediatrician

Nov. 9, 1960
3:00–4:30 P.M.
Child Development and Parental Concerns: The Child from Five to Nine
Albert J. Solnit, M.D., pediatrician, psychiatrist

Nov. 16, 1960
1:15–2:45 P.M.
Child Development and Parental Concerns: The Child from Ten to Thirteen
Marjorie Harley, Ph.D., child psychoanalyst

Nov. 23, 1960
1:15–2:45 P.M.
The Effect of Disease on Growth and Development
Isabelle Valadian, M.D., pediatrician

Nov. 30, 1960
3:00–4:30 P.M.
Child Development and Parental Concerns: Adolescence
Isadore Bernstein, M.D., psychiatrist, psychoanalyst

Dec. 7, 1960
1:15–2:45 P.M.
Children's Perception of Other Children and Themselves
Stephen A. Richardson, Ph.D., sociologist

Dec. 14, 1960
1:15–2:45 P.M.
Parental Attitudes and Expectations for the Handicapped Child
Ernest K. Koller, sociologist

Jan. 4, 1961   The Effect of Having a Handicapped Child on Intrafamily
3:00–4:30 p.m.   Relations
        Samuel Ritvo, M.D., psychiatrist, psychoanalyst

Jan. 11, 1961   Problems of Education of Handicapped Children as they
1:15–2:45 p.m.   Have Impact on Parents
        Richard M. Lubell, educator

Jan. 18, 1961   Special Implications of Discipline
1:15–2:45 p.m.   Salvatore Ambrosino, Ed.D., Child Study Association of
        America

Jan. 25, 1961   Variations in Cultural Attitudes Toward Handicapping and
1:15–2:45 p.m.   Having a Handicapped Child
        Bernard Kutner, Ph.D., sociologist

B. Seminars on Techniques of Leadership in Parent Group Education

Seminars will provide the opportunity for participants to discuss the techniques of leadership in parent group education, the relation of this approach to their previous work, their observations of parent group sessions, and aspects of organization of groups in various settings.

The hour-and-a-half seminars will be in the form of both teaching seminars and open seminars as outlined below. The teaching seminars will deal with various aspects of group skills. These teaching seminars will alternate with open seminars focused on the interests and needs of the leaders-in-training, as these needs and interests develop during the program. They will be conducted by members of the Child Study Association training staff.

Oct. 5, 1960   Practical Applications of the Theory of Parent Group
        Education

Oct. 12, 1960   Establishing the Group Atmosphere: Aspects of Recruitment
        and Interpretation

Oct. 26, 1960   Open Seminar

Nov. 2, 1960   Developing Content

Nov. 9, 1960   Open Seminar

Nov. 16, 1960   The Role of the Leader

Nov. 23, 1960   Open Seminar

Nov. 30, 1960   Group Interaction throughout a Series of Meetings

Dec. 7, 1960   Open Seminar

Dec. 14, 1960   The Handling of Individual Parental Concerns in the Group
        Setting

Jan. 4, 1961   Open Seminar

Jan. 11, 1961   Open Seminar

Jan. 18, 1961   Open Seminar

Jan. 25, 1961   Open Seminar

C. Observation

Observations of parent groups at CSAA headquarters will be individually scheduled. They will all take place on Tuesday and Wednesday mornings. Discussion of observations with CSAA leaders will be held for 45 minutes immediately following meetings observed.

D. Field Work in Group Practice

Around the end of October or early November, each participant will begin to conduct a parent group in his own setting with consultation from a member of the Child Study Association training staff. Each practice group will meet for from ten to twelve weekly sessions. Each session will be summarized in weekly written reports. Each group will be observed at least twice by the CSAA staff consultant, and individual conferences will be scheduled periodically. It is expected that each participant will conduct two such field work groups before the end of May, 1961.

During the springs months of February, March, April and May, the Group Seminar will meet for two-hour sessions on alternate Wednesday afternoons. Occasional presentations on special topics will be added, to meet the needs of the training group.

This training program is organized and conducted by The Department of Parent Group Education, Child Study Association of America.

4. TRAINING PROGRAM FOR FAMILY CASEWORKERS IN PARENT GROUP EDUCATION LEADERSHIP *

Conducted by
Child Study Association of America
under the Joint Sponsorship of
Family Service Association of America
and
Child Study Association of America
1963–1964

The Family Service Association of America and the Child Study Association of America, two voluntary national organizations with headquarters in New York City, are jointly sponsoring this exploratory project in parent group education. The project will consist of two phases. The

* This project is supported by National Institute of Mental Health Grant Number MH 684-A1.

first phase will be a program of training for leadership of parent discussion groups, conducted by the Child Study Association of America for caseworkers on the staffs of selected member agencies of the Family Service Association of America within a 1000-mile radius of New York City. The second phase will consist of the conducting of multiple series of parent education groups under the auspices of their local Family Service Agencies, who will be required to offer some groups to individuals in the community not previously served by the agencies through parent group education methods.

The long-term goal of this joint effort, of which this program is the first step, is to extend the quantity and improve the quality of group educational programs for parents offered by Family Service Agencies, in the interest of sustaining and strengthening the mental and emotional health of parents and children. It is hoped that through this project, Family Service Agencies will be stimulated to initiate, extend, and improve the quality and number of group educational programs for parents.

As a part of this project, a series of evaluative studies will be undertaken. These will include an exploration of the situations encountered when family agencies undertake to extend, increase, improve, or initiate parent group education programs as part of their services. There will also be an exploration of the kinds of parents availing themselves of group education programs and their responses to this type of service, and an exploration of the curriculum of the training program and the relationship of the training experience to the ability of the social workers to act as parent group leaders.

The training program is divided into four parts. An initial three-week institute beginning October 14, 1963, will cover the philosophy, method, and technique of parent group education through presentations, seminars, observations of parent groups, and a review of current concepts of child development and family relations. Since family caseworkers have a wide knowledge of child growth and development and family relationships, these areas will be reviewed from the point of view of the use of this material in parent group education. Sessions on content and methodology will be closely integrated, since it is felt that the methodology must be developed in relation to the special nature of parental needs and concerns.

After the initial three-week institute, the social workers will return to their communities to lead two series of parent group meetings with supervision from a member of the training staff of the Child Study Association of America carried on through the mails and one field visit. During this field visit, the Child Study Association of America staff consultant will observe group sessions and will discuss with the leader specific problems of leadership. Time will also be allotted to meeting with the administrative personnel of the Family Agency to discuss any aspects of the overall program.

Following this field work period, the social workers will return to Child Study Association of America headquarters for a one-week follow-up institute, beginning March 16, 1964. At this institute the workers will review their experiences in parent group education leadership and will discuss those aspects of their leadership that need further exploration in order to help them consolidate their group skills. Following this, the workers will again return to their communities to lead two additional series of parent group meetings under the same arrangements as during the first field work period.

The following year a similar program will be carried on with representatives of another group of Family Service Agencies. It is estimated that at the end of this two year project, some 36 social workers from some 36 different agencies will have been involved in this training program in parent group education leadership. It is also estimated that over the two year period, approximately 1,400 to 2,800 parents will have been reached through this project, many of whom will not have been previously involved in parent group education programs.

INITIAL THREE WEEK INSTITUTE
given at CSAA headquarters
October 14–November 1, 1963

Sessions are held from 9:00 A.M. to 4:30 P.M. each day. The program consists of theoretical sessions conducted by guest faculty, staff presentations, seminars, discussions, study of written records of parent group meetings, observations of ongoing parent groups, and individual conferences.

THEORETICAL PRESENTATIONS

**A. Concepts of Child Development and Family Relations:
Their Meaning for Parent Education**

October 14	What is Involved in Parent-Child Relationships
12:30–2:00 P.M.	Peter B. Neubauer, M.D., psychiatrist, psychoanalyst
October 17	Preparing for a Family and Meeting the Child's Needs During the First Year
	Milton J. E. Senn, M.D., pediatrician, psychiatrist
October 18	The Child from One to Three
10:30–12:00 noon	Margaret M. Lawrence, M.D., psychiatrist, psychoanalyst

October 21	The Child from Three to Five
1:00–2:30 P.M.	Eleanor Blumgart, nursery school director
October 22	The Child from Five to Twelve
1:00–2:30 P.M.	Gerard Fountain, M.D., psychiatrist, psychoanalyst
October 24	Early Adolescence, Adolescence and Growth into Adult-
9:00–10:30 A.M.	hood
	Earl Saxe, M.D., psychiatrist, psychoanalyst
October 25	Parental Concerns in Understanding and Guiding Chil-
3:00–4:30 P.M.	dren's Developing Sexual Interests Throughout Childhood and Youth
	Marianne Kris, M.D., psychiatrist, psychoanalyst
October 28	Concepts of Growth
2:30–4:00 P.M.	Marthe Gassmann, M.D., psychiatrist
October 29	Helping Parents to Understand and Guide Their Children's
9:00–10:30 A.M.	Social Needs
	Rena Schulman, psychiatric social worker
October 30	Helping Parents Understand and Guide Their Children's
2:30–4:00 P.M.	Formal Educational Needs
	Lawrence Brody, M.A., educator
November 1	Cultural Variations in Patterns of Child Rearing
9:00–12:30 A.M.	Solon T. Kimball, Ph.D., anthropologist

B. Philosophy, Methods and Techniques of Parent Group Education

October 14	Opening Session
9:45–10:15 A.M.	A. D. Buchmueller, M.S.W., Child Study Association of America
	Clark W. Blackburn, M.S.W., Family Service Association of America

Subsequent hour-and-a-half sessions to be given by members of the Child Study Association training staff.

October 14	Parent Group Education: Philosophy, Principles and Goals
October 15	Planning for Groups
October 15	Establishing the Group Atmosphere and First Meetings
October 16	The Role of the Leader
October 18	Developing the Content
October 21	Group Interaction: Its Meaning for Learning
October 22	The Meaning of Individual Behavior in the Group
October 25	The Use of Casework and Social Group Work Concepts in Parent Group Education
October 29	The Use of Resource Material and Other Techniques in Continuous Parent Groups
October 31	Single Meetings: Values and Limitations

C. Seminar

Seminar sessions will provide the opportunity for participants to discuss the philosophy, goals, methods, and techniques of leadership in parent group education and concepts of child development and family relations as these are used in parent discussion groups. These seminars will focus on the interests and needs of the leaders in training, as these needs and interests develop during the program. Here the social workers will relate the material covered in this program to their previous knowledge and experience, and to their future functioning as parent group education leaders. Seminars will be under the leadership of the Child Study Association of America training staff.

D. Observations

Observations of three parent discussion groups will give the institute participants the opportunity to see the application of the theoretical framework of parent group education to the live material brought out in parent group sessions. They will also alert the leaders to the feeling-tones of group discussion and group interplay. The observations of parent groups will be held on Wednesday mornings at Child Study Association of America headquarters and will be individually scheduled. A 45 minute discussion period will be held with individual group leaders immediately following the meetings observed. These observations will also be discussed in seminar.

E. Case Record

The record of a continuous series of eight meetings for parents of children in the first three grades of an elementary school will be discussed in detail. This group was conducted by a leader who had participated in a program of training for leadership in parent group education given by the Child Study Association of America. The record is the leader's own narrative account of the meetings and has been selected for teaching purposes. The names and places in the record have been disguised to protect the identity of the group members. This material is confidential and is to be returned at the end of the three week institute.

F. Field Work

All leaders-in-training are expected to conduct four groups during the year of training, with two to be held in the first field work period between November, 1963, and the end of February, 1964. At least one of these groups should be recruited from parents not previously served by the Family Agency in group education programs. The enrollment in each of these groups should be preferably between twelve and fifteen members. Groups will meet once a week for ten weeks.

Supervision of the leadership of these groups will be provided by members of the training staff of the Child Study Association of America. Supervision will be carried on through weekly correspondence based on the leader's narrative record of each group meeting and through one field visit in which the Child Study Association of America staff consultant will observe group meetings and discuss with the leader aspects of his performance in the leadership role. While on the field visit, the Child Study Association of America consultant will also meet with administrative personnel and others integrally related to the project, as appears indicated.

This same plan will be followed during the second field work period, with two more practice groups to be held between April 1st and June 15th, 1964.

G.   Research

As part of this project, the social workers in training for leadership of parent discussion groups will be asked to serve as subjects in that part of the research concerned with the relation of the training program to their group leadership role performance. They will also be asked to administer selected questionnaires to the parents in their field work groups. All questionnaires submitted will be held in strictest confidence and analyzed only by the Director of the Research Project. This aspect of the training program and the social workers' part in it will be explained and handled by the Director of Research.

✻   ✻   ✻   ✻   ✻

This project is sponsored jointly by the Family Service Association of America and the Child Study Association of America. Representatives of the two agencies who participated in the planning and organization for the project were:

Child Study Association of America
  Alfred D. Buchmueller, M.S.W., Executive Director
  Aline B. Auerbach, Assistant Director
  Oscar Rabinowitz, M.S.S.S.
Family Service Association of America
  Clark W. Blackburn, M.S.W., General Director
  Dorothy Fahs Beck, Ph.D.
  Aaron Rosenblatt, M.S.W.
  Elinor P. Zaki, M.S.W.

This training program is conducted by the Department of Parent Group Education, Child Study Association of America, under the general direction of Aline B. Auerbach, Assistant Director.

Appendix V
Recommended Readings

1. METHODOLOGY OF GROUP EDUCATION

Association for Supervision and Curriculum Development, *Learning and Mental Health in the School*, National Education Association, 1966.

Association for Supervision and Curriculum Development, *Perceiving, Behaving, Becoming*, National Education Association, 1962.

Auerbach, Aline B., *Trends and Techniques in Parent Education: A Critical Review*, Child Study Association of America, 1961.

Brim, Orville G., Jr., *Education for Child Rearing*, Russell Sage, 1959; Free Press, paper with new introduction, 1965.

Cantor, Nathaniel, *Learning Through Discussion*, Human Relations for Industry, 1951.

Cantor, Nathaniel, *The Teaching-Learning Process*, Holt, Rinehart, and Winston, 1953.

Caplan, Gerald, *An Approach to Community Mental Health*, Grune and Stratton, 1961.

Durkin, Helen, *The Group in Depth*, International Universities Press, 1965.

Hare, A. Paul, Edgar F. Borgatta, and Robert F. Bales, eds., *Small Groups: Studies in Social Interaction*, Knopf, rev. ed., 1965.

Klein, Wilma H., Eda J. LeShan, Sylvan S. Furman, *Promoting Mental Health of Older People Through Group Methods*, Mental Health Materials Center, 1966.

Konopka, Gisela, *Social Group Work: A Helping Process*, Prentice-Hall, 1963.

Lifton, Walter M., *Working With Groups: Group Process and Individual Growth*, John Wiley, 2nd ed., 1966.

Lippitt, Ronald, and others, *The Dynamics of Planned Change*, Harcourt, Brace, and World, 1958.

Parad, Howard J., ed., *Crisis Intervention*, Family Service Association of America, 1965.

Rabinow, Mildred, and Oscar Rabinowitz, "The Use of Casework Concepts in Parent Group Education," in *Casework Papers*, Family Service Association of America, 1961.

Slavson, S. R., *Child-Centered Group Guidance of Parents*, International Universities Press, 1958.

2. CHILD DEVELOPMENT AND FAMILY LIFE

Ackerman, Nathan W., *The Psychodynamics of Family Life*, Basic Books, 1958.

Arnstein, Helene S., *What To Tell Your Child*, Pocket Books, 1962.

Blair, Arthur Witt, and William H. Burton, *Growth and Development of the Pre-Adolescent*, Appleton-Century-Crofts, 1951.

Blos, Peter, *On Adolescence: A Psychoanalytic Interpretation*, Free Press, 1962.

Bowlby, John, *Maternal Care and Mental Health;* Ainsworth, Mary D., and others, *Deprivation of Maternal Care* (two volumes in one), Schocken Books, 1966.

Cervantes, Lucius F., *The Dropout: Causes and Cures*, University of Michigan, 1965.

Clark, Kenneth B., *Dark Ghetto: Dilemmas of Social Power*, Harper and Row, 1965.

Erikson, Erik H., *Childhood and Society*, rev. ed., Norton, 1963.

Erikson, Erik H., *Identity and the Life Cycle*, Psychological Issues, Vol. 1, No. 1, International Universities Press.

Erikson, Erik H., *Youth: Change and Challenge*, Basic Books, 1963; *The Challenge of Youth*, paper, Anchor Books, 1965.

Ferman, Louis A., and others, eds., *Poverty in America: A Book of Readings*, University of Michigan, 1965.

Fraiberg, Selma, *The Magic Years*, Scribner, 1959.

Frank, Josette, *Your Child's Reading Today*, Doubleday, rev. ed., 1960.

Frank, Mary, and Lawrence K. Frank, *How to Help Your Child in School*, New American Library, 1954.

Gans, Roma, *Common Sense in Teaching Reading: A Practical Guide*, Bobbs-Merrill, 1963.

Gruenberg, Sidonie M., ed., *The Encyclopedia of Child Care and Guidance*, Doubleday, rev. ed., 1967.

Gruenberg, Sidonie M., *The Parents' Guide to Everyday Problems of Boys and Girls*, Random House, 1958.

Hoffman, Martin L., Lois Wladis Hoffman, eds., *Review of Child Development Research*, Russell Sage, Vol. 1, 1964, Vol. 2, 1966.

Johnson, Ronald C., and G. R. Medinnus, *Child Psychology: Behavior and Development*, John Wiley, 1965.

Kessler, J. W., *Psychopathology of Childhood*, Prentice-Hall, 1966.

Maier, H. W., *Three Theories of Child Development*, Harper and Row, 1966.

McKinley, Donald G., *Social Class and Family Life*, Free Press, 1964.

Medinnus, Gene R., ed., *Readings in the Psychology of Parent-Child Relations*, John Wiley, 1967.

Murphy, Lois, and others, *The Widening World of Childhood*, Basic Books, 1962.

Raymond, Louise, *Adoption and After*, Harper and Row, 1955.

Riessman, Frank, and others, eds., *Mental Health of the Poor: New Treatment Approaches for Low Income People*, Free Press, 1964.

Rose, Arnold M., and Caroline B. Rose, eds., *Minority Problems: A Textbook of Readings in Intergroup Relations*, Harper and Row, 1965.

Spock, Benjamin, *Baby and Child Care*, Pocket Books, rev. ed., 1968.

Spock, Benjamin, *Problems of Parents*, Houghton Mifflin, 1962.

Stone, L. Joseph, and Joseph Church, *Childhood and Adolescence: A Psychology of the Growing Person,* Random House, 1957.

Thomson, Helen, *The Successful Stepparent,* Harper and Row, 1966.

Torrance, E. Paul, and Robert D. Strom, eds., *Mental Health and Achievement: Increasing Potential and Reducing School Dropouts,* John Wiley, 1965.

Young, Leontine R., *Out of Wedlock,* McGraw-Hill, 1954.

PAMPHLETS ON CHILD DEVELOPMENT AND FAMILY LIFE
Published by the Child Study Association of America

Auerbach, Aline B., and Katherine M. Wolf, *As Your Child Grows: The First Eighteen Months.*

Child Study Association of America, *What To Tell Your Children About Sex.*

Book Review Committee of Child Study Association of America, *Recommended Reading About Children and Family Life.*

Book Review Committee of Child Study Association of America, *Recommended Reading on Sex Education.*

Mayer, Greta, and Mary Hoover, *When Children Need Special Help With Emotional Problems.*

Redl, Fritz, *Pre-Adolescents: What Makes Them Tick?*

Wolf, Anna W. M., *Helping Your Child to Understand Death.*

(For a complete catalog of publications, write CSAA, 9 East 89th Street, New York, N.Y., 10028.)

3. PREPARATION FOR PARENTHOOD—THE PRENATAL PERIOD

Auerbach, Aline B., and Helene S. Arnstein, *Pregnancy and You,* Child Study Association, 1962 (pamphlet).

Buxton, C. Lee, *A Study of Psychophysical Methods of Relief of Childbirth Pain,* Saunders, 1962.

Goodrich, Frederick W., *Preparing for Childbirth: A Manual for Expectant Parents,* Prentice-Hall, 1966.

Guttmacher, Alan F., and others, *Planning Your Family,* Macmillan, 1964.

Schaefer, George, and Milton L. Zisowitz, *The Expectant Father,* Simon and Schuster, 1964.

Maternity Center Association, *A Baby Is Born,* Maternity Center Association, rev. ed., 1964.

4. THE IMPACT OF THE PHYSICALLY AND EMOTIONALLY DISABLED CHILD ON THE FAMILY

Levinson, Abraham, *The Mentally Retarded Child,* John Day, rev. ed., 1965.

Ross, Alan, *The Exceptional Child in the Family,* Grune and Stratton, 1964.

Spock, Benjamin, and M. O. Lerrigo, *Caring For Your Disabled Child,* Macmillan, 1965; also paper, Collier.

Wright, Beatrice A., *Physical Disability—A Psychological Approach,* Harper and Row, 1960.

Index

J